W9-BXT-530

THE HISTORY OF AMERICAN SAILING SHIPS

THE HISTORY OF
AMERICAN
SAILING SHIPS

BY

HOWARD I. CHAPELLE

With drawings by the author and
George C. Wales and Henry Rusk

BONANZA BOOKS • NEW YORK

Designed by Robert Josephy

To A. Z. C.

CONTENTS

CONTENTS

LIST OF ILLUSTRATIONS

LIST OF ILLUSTRATIONS

LIST OF ILLUSTRATIONS

LIST OF ILLUSTRATIONS

xii

LIST OF ILLUSTRATIONS

LIST OF ILLUSTRATIONS

AUTHORITIES AND ACKNOWLEDGMENTS

In addition to the sources mentioned in the footnotes throughout the text, the following books have been consulted:

"Forests and Sea Power," Robert Greenhalgh Albion, Ph.D. Harvard University Press, Cambridge, 1926

"Maritime History of Massachusetts," Samuel Eliot Morison, Houghton Mifflin Company, Boston and New York, 1921

"Early History of the U.S. Revenue Marine," Captain H. D. Smith, U.S.R.C.S. (edited by Elliot Snow), Naval Historical Foundation, 1932.

"Catalogue of the Watercraft Collection in the United States National Museum," Carl W. Mitman, Government Printing Office, 1923.

As far as was possible, original sources were consulted, the manuscript collections in the Essex Institute, Salem, Massachusetts; Massachusetts Historical Society, Boston, Massachusetts; Library of Congress; Massachusetts State Archives; New York and Boston Public Libraries; Navy Library; Admiralty Library; and those in many private hands have been of great assistance. Collections of log-books, shipyard day-books, and similar manuscripts in the Navy Library have furnished much valuable information, though the task of inspecting these is by no means complete.

In a study of naval architecture, models and plans are of the utmost importance. Collections of half-models in the Peabody Marine Museum, Salem, Massachusetts; United States National Museum; New York Yacht Club, those of members of the Marine Society of Mystic, Connecticut and also collections in private hands have been made accessible to the author, for which he is most grateful. Plans have been obtained, to the number of about 1200, from half-models in the collections mentioned, as well as from the British Admiralty, Bureau of Construction and Repair, U.S.N.; Bureau of Construction and Repair, U.S.C.G.; Mr. Lewis Story, Mr. Wil-

AUTHORITIES AND ACKNOWLEDGMENTS

liam Muir, Massachusetts Institute of Technology, Mr. C. R. Sawyer, Mrs. Henry Rodman Booth, Mrs. Lewis W. Le Duke, Jr., Mr. Clarkson A. Cranmer, Mr. Bryant K. Rogers, Mr. Mark Hennessy, Mr. Alfred W. Paine, Mr. Lincoln Colcord, Mr. J. P. Shaw, the Peabody Marine Museum, Mr. L. Francis Herreshoff, Mr. Carl C. Cutler, Mr. M. V. Brewington and others. The kindness of institutions and individuals in permitting plans to be copied, and the courtesies extended in the Navy Department, Coast Guard, and Admiralty, have been of great assistance in this study of the American sailing vessels. Particular credit is due Mr. H. Richardson, the Admiralty Curator, and to Mr. C. Knight, the former Curator, for the patience and labor they expended in complying with the author's many requests for information. The courtesies extended the author by the Lords Commissioners of the Admiralty are gratefully acknowledged. The assistance of Constructor F. A. Hunnewell, U.S.C.G. in obtaining plans of cutters and historical information must also be acknowledged.

The author wishes to express his obligation to Captain Stephen C. Rowan, U.S.N., Captain D. W. Knox, U.S.N. (retired), the staff of the Navy Library and of the U.S. National Museum, Mr. George H. Stegmann, Mr. D. Foster Taylor, Mr. Ralph J. Robinson, Mr. Dudley C. Lunt, Mr. Chas. H. Taylor, Mr. James E. Hancock, Mr. R. C. Anderson, Mr. William H. Fisher, Captain Charleton L. Smith, Mr. A. D. Wills, Mr. W. P. Stephens, Professor S. E. Morison, Mr. Basil Lubbock, Mr. Kenneth Roberts, the Fort Ticonderoga Museum and Mr. S. H. P. Pell, Mr. Robert E. Farlow, Mr. L. A. Jenkins, Yachting Publishing Company, Mr. Herbert L. Stone, and Rudder Publishing Company for generous assistance; also Mr. O. G. Ellis, Jr., and Mr. Edward S. Clark.

The assistance of Mr. George C. Wales and Mr. Henry Rusk, in the matter of illustrations, has been of immeasurable value; as must be obvious by even casual inspection of these pages. Mr. Wales requires no introduction to lovers of ships; his workmanship, as expressed in his fine marine etchings and water colors, is known to all. The primary requirement of marine research is to enable the reproduction of ships of the past. Plans are

AUTHORITIES AND ACKNOWLEDGMENTS

of great importance in work of this kind, but perspective drawings clarify many obscure details that otherwise would remain in doubt. Drawn from the plans, the perspective drawings are accurate portraits of the original ship. The understanding and sympathy of Mr. Wales' treatment of perspective views of ships adds much to the inherent value of these drawings. The value of Mr. Rusk's pen-and-ink sketches is also obvious. The author has been particularly fortunate in obtaining the work of so enthusiastic a ship-lover, who combines an intense interest in ships with the artistic skill to portray them, as Mr. Henry Rusk. The author cannot express his gratitude to these two gentlemen for the encouragement and assistance that they have so generously given.

Howard Irving Chapelle

Quincy, Massachusetts

THE HISTORY OF AMERICAN SAILING SHIPS

INTRODUCTION

THE affection which most men lavish on but two of their inanimate possessions, sailing ships and weapons, is a prominent characteristic of human nature. In developing or obtaining either for their particular use, men of all periods have spent unlimited time and effort, as well as immense sums of money. Once in hand, these objects are treated with meticulous care and loving attention amounting to veneration. The comparisons that are naturally made by the owners of either the sailing ship or the weapon lead to improvement in design, detail and ornamentation, in order that the proud possessor may feel that his is the best to be had.

The fisherman's schooner and the backwoodsman's rifle share like importance in the opinion of their owners; both are commonly cherished beyond all other goods. This is understandable, for on the schooner or the rifle the life of the owner may depend. More than this, it requires great skill to use each of them to the utmost advantage and this necessitates both study and practice. As a result, the owner of either acquires respect and appreciation for the qualities and possibilities of his property. This may explain why sailors rarely have the same feeling toward power or steamships that they have toward sailing craft. Certainly this accounts for the lack of sentiment most men seem to feel toward their other possessions, such as automobiles, furniture or even houses.

The importance of the sailing ship or the rifle in the story of the national development of the United States cannot be overlooked. Without the sailing ship the early colonists could not have existed, nor could their successors have achieved independence and national distinction. If the famed "long-rifle" in the hands of Kentucky backwoodsmen pointed the way to the conquest of the West, the sailing ship in the hands of men of the coast towns was no less important in the financial and national security that made the conquest a fact.

The story of the evolution of the American sailing ship is interesting

1

from many points of view. The romantic and tragic adventures of ships and men have long interested a great portion of the reading public. Stories of captains, crews and ships offer much in the way of interest, but the difficulties and troubles of the men who designed the ships and on whose shoulders rested the responsibility for their speed and seaworthiness are equally interesting. Histories of certain ships and ship-types have been written, but these usually glorify their subjects in importance. There would be no serious objection to this, perhaps, were it not for the fact that this glorification has invariably been at the expense of worthier ships and types. To quote but two examples, the *Constitution* and *Flying Cloud* have been made to appear the most important and best ships of their periods, and their designers have been made to appear as supermen. This is quite unwarranted, and the false picture should be corrected. In addition, the passage of time has developed many ideas and claims, relating to the "invention" of this or that type or rig, that have no historical foundation. Popular beliefs concerning the development, and influences thereon, of the American sailing ships are too often mere fables when the facts are learned.

An account of the evolution of the American sailing ships has many possibilities; it is an opportunity to reproduce a little of the beauty of the rakish or stately ships of the past, to identify their designers and to discover, as well as appreciate, individual designers who were important for one reason or another. Then, too, there is the possibility of obtaining the real facts as to "inventions" and "influences." Also, it is possible to arrive at certain conclusions as to the comparative importance of certain types, ships and builders or designers.

Greatest of all possibilities, however, is that of learning to appreciate the intellect and ability of past generations. It is perfectly natural for each successive generation to look upon itself as far better equipped mentally than the ones before. If, however, one may judge by a comparison of naval architecture of the past with that of today as represented by modern sailing craft, there is little to support this self-admiration.

INTRODUCTION

In order thoroughly to understand history it is necessary to realize the fact that men of earlier years had the same abilities and powers of reason and intellect that can be found in similar stations of life today. If the American of colonial days did not have the accumulated knowledge and the ease of obtaining information that is possible today, he most certainly had the same amount of curiosity and power of observation as the present generation. The stress and difficulties under which the colonial and his immediate successors existed made for great independence of mind, common sense and self-reliance. Ingenuity, courage and business acumen were even more necessary in earlier times than today. Once this point of view is understood, history becomes more than a mere tale of the past. Hence, if we find Americans of a certain period sailing ships that would appear strange to modern yachtsmen, we may be assured that it is not evidence of their stupidity, prejudice or lack of initiative but rather their intelligent adaption of material and knowledge to meet the requirements of the time and usage.

If these possibilities are kept in mind, there should be much interest in a study of the development of American sailing craft.

Chapter One THE COLONIAL PERIOD

"ON your decision depend the lives and property of men." This is the real responsibility of the men who design and build ships. The price of errors in judgment, ignorance, stupidity or dishonesty on the part of these men is revealed by the terse comments in the shipping news. "Lost at sea with all hands." "Taken or destroyed by the enemy." "Wrecked, ship and cargo a total loss." Every naval architect and shipbuilder worth his salt, from ancient to modern times, realizes that this is the judgment of a court from which there is no appeal. No excuses will serve the craftsman if loss results from his acts.

This is one of the reasons for the conservative attitude of men who were responsible for the development of the sailing ship in the United States. There were other considerations, however, for ships must be built to serve certain purposes which may make it necessary for the designer and builder to take chances on loss. It is in ships of this kind that the judgment and technical skill of the craftsman becomes evident. And it is to this judgment and skill that the distinction of American shipbuilders in the days of wooden ships and sail may be traced.

Though the real evolution of American sailing ship types cannot be traced earlier than the period of the American Revolution, the foundation for it was laid in colonial times. Conditions on land and sea were then of such nature that certain trends of design were started. From these came fast and striking ships of various types, rigs and classes designed to meet stringent requirements of trade and warfare. So well were the specifications met, in certain types and rigs in particular, that the American shipwright achieved more than national distinction. The ability he displayed in developing models to meet peculiarities in trade or employment must be the theme of any account of his work. If it is really possible to pick out a single important factor in the evolution of the American sailing ship it is the untiring search for speed. On this factor rested the

4

safety of crew and cargo during the early days of the Republic. It must be understood, however, that speed could not be had at the expense of seaworthiness or the requirements of trade. In short, certain proportions of speed, capacity and seaworthiness must be combined for a given trade to meet the specifications of time and man.

There are no accounts of the use of sailing craft by the Indians in the records of the first English or Dutch settlers of North America and so it may be presumed that the Indians were wholly unacquainted with the art of sailing. Some writers have stated that the early Spanish explorers found a species of sailing raft now called "Jangadas" in use among savages of certain portions of South America. The truth of this cannot be verified as no record of it has yet been found in the reports of these Spaniards.

Naturally, the first sailing craft built by colonists in America were makeshift vessels and not models that had any influence on later types. It is obvious that these early vessels would be from European models, which the settlers had seen and used at home. They are of importance in our story only so far as they indicate the beginning of American shipbuilding and the localities of its origin.

If we were to leave our homes and voyage to a bleak and inhospitable shore to establish new settlements, depending upon our own resources and knowledge to eke out a livelihood, we can imagine the hardships we would undergo. Contemporary records of any of the English settlements make it plain that this was the common case then. Few men were fitted either by training or temperament for a pioneering life, with the result that many unnecessary difficulties beset those living in the colonies. One was the inability of the colonists to obtain boats or ships. In spite of the plain necessity of settling on the coast, it is apparent that none of the promoters of the early settlements had enough gumption to plan for this condition by at once sending men capable of building boats. The Dutch settlement of New Amsterdam seems to have been much better planned in this respect, perhaps because more of the settlers were from maritime localities of the mother country. In the case of the Spaniards a great deal of information is lacking at present, but because all of their colonies were in a mild and friendly climate, any shortcomings in water-transportation were of less importance in their history.

So far as is known, the first sailing vessel of any size to be built in America by English settlers was the thirty-ton *Virginia* constructed at the mouth of the Kennebec River in Maine. In 1607 some settlers had tried to start a fishing station on Stage Island, near the mouth of the river, but a very severe winter discouraged them. Homesick and disillusioned, they built this little vessel the next spring in order to get home. She seems to have been a two-master of some sort, about fifty or sixty feet long. In later years the *Virginia* made a number of voyages to America, but her end is not recorded.

The next to build a sailing vessel in what is now the United States were the Dutch of New Amsterdam. In 1614 they lost by fire one of their small ships named *Tiger*, which they had brought with them from Holland. As it was quite necessary to replace her, Adrian Blok built a "jacht" named the *Onrust* in 1615–16. She was about sixteen tons burden and 38 feet long on the keel, about 44 feet 6 inches on deck and 11 feet beam; she was probably sloop rigged and fitted with lee-boards. Nothing definite is known about her appearance, but it is likely that she was a small, and less decorated copy of the standard Dutch "Statenjacht" of the seventeenth century. Blok used her to explore Long Island Sound and the shores of what is now Connecticut and Rhode Island; she then went south from New Amsterdam to investigate the shores of Delaware Bay. Later she was sailed to Holland with a cargo of furs.

In 1631, the English colonists of Massachusetts Bay built the next vessel, the *Blessings of the Bay*, on the Mystic River. She was built by the order of the governor, Winthrop, and seems to have been a "government ship." A strong vessel being desired, it is said she was built wholly of locust wood. Intended for trade along the coast and communication with the Dutch at New Amsterdam, she was what would then have been a sizeable vessel, her tonnage given as thirty tons. She does not seem to have had a long career, disappearing from the records very quickly after her launch. She may have been the vessel sent out by Winthrop and others to Virginia loaded with furs and fish in 1633 which was lost on the voyage. In appearance and dimensions she may have been similar to the Pilgrim ship *Sparrow-Hawk* which brought forty passengers to the Plymouth Colony in 1626 and was wrecked on Cape Cod. In the latter part of the nineteenth century her wreckage was discovered and placed in Pilgrim Hall in Plymouth, Massachusetts. Dennison Lawlor, then a famous Boston naval architect, measured up the portions of the hull that were preserved and restored her lines as far as was possible. From this a model was made for the Watercraft Collection of the United States National Museum in Washington, D. C. Except for the lower portion of the hull, these "restorations" are open to doubt as to their accuracy. The *Sparrow-Hawk* seems to have been a ketch, but whether the *Blessings of the Bay* was so rigged is not known.

After 1634 there were occasional vessels of moderate size laid down in the various settlements, but it was not until about 1640 that any ships of comparatively large dimensions were built. At about this time the West Indian trade began to interest the New England colonists and large ships suitable for the lengthy voyages to the islands and home were in demand. A ship of approximately four-hundred tons burden was as large as was then required for the business, this ship being in the neighborhood of ninety to a hundred feet in length and twenty to twenty-six feet in breadth. It might also be added that ships of this size were large for merchantmen of this period.

Most authorities place the beginning of American shipbuilding as an industry in the period between 1641 and 1650 owing to the increase in shipping that resulted from the West Indian trade. The existing records show no year, however, from 1640 to 1700, in which more than sixty vessels were built in all of the colonies together. One of the serious problems of the English colonies in developing their shipping was the competition of the Dutch in both oversea and coasting trades. The English

Navigation Act of 1651 put a stop to Dutch intrusion into these trades, thus improving the condition of the colonial merchants and, therefore, colonial shipbuilders.

If we were to build a wooden vessel ourselves, our common sense would tell us to choose a place where materials could be obtained easily and cheaply, and where we could get the necessary help. It was the application of this logic which decided the localities where shipbuilding was to flourish. Timber was rarely a problem, though not all settlements had the combined advantages of deep water and suitable timber for the construction of large craft. The greatest difficulty seems to have been to find skilled labor, but by importing English shipwrights and training apprentices this problem was gradually overcome. Once a settlement started shipbuilding, shipwrights were attracted and made their homes there. Hence, it is found that places where this industry started because of advantageous natural conditions will continue to devote itself to this business long after timber, or even natural deep water, has disappeared. Colonial shipbuilding was often a part-time job, particularly the construction of fishing and other small craft. These were not uncommonly laid down in the fall, some distance from the water, and when completed during the winter months were hauled by oxen over the snow to the water's edge. Some surprisingly large vessels were built this way.

Because of the natural advantages, a good deal of colonial shipbuilding started at the mouths of rivers; the Merrimac, the Mystic, the Charles, the Connecticut and the Hudson all had shipyards on their shores. The deep bays, harbors and coves also offered advantages for shipbuilders, and Scituate, Ipswich, Beverly, Salem, Charlestown, Boston, and Weymouth in Massachusetts, Newport in Rhode Island, and New London and New Haven in Connecticut built ships very early in their existence. It has been the fashion to dismiss shipbuilding south of New York as unimportant and undeveloped in colonial days. This was probably due to a lack of records as compared to New England. But the conclusion is ridiculous. Virginia and Pennsylvania, as well as Maryland, had well developed shipbuilding industries by 1700. Though Pennsylvania and Maryland were not permanently settled by the English until some years after New England, there is a good deal of evidence showing that they began to build ships very early. Virginia-built ships are mentioned in colonial records during the years that New England was rising to prominence in the production of ships. If the southern vessels were not so numerous or were not built so early as those of New England, it can be said that they developed in design so rapidly as to outstrip their competitors in reputation by the time of the American Revolution.

The methods employed in American shipbuilding in early days were naturally crude. All planking was sawn by hand, of course, and all heavy stuff was shaped and fitted by use of adze, broadaxe and plane. Sawing plank was a laborious process. A pit was dug and a staging set up across it, the log was levered out on the staging and sawn by the use of a long two-man handsaw, similar to the modern timberman's cross-cut saw. One man stood on the staging, astraddle the log and facing opposite to the direction of the saw-cut. The man in the pit faced the direction of the saw-cut, to avoid sawdust, and by alternately pulling on the saw the men could rip a log into plank. The work was slow and required so much skill that the "sawyer" became a recognized trade. A "gang" usually consisted of the sawyer and his helper, with a third man whose job it was to shift the log at intervals, so that the saw would clear the staging or to start a new cut.

Even with cheap labor, the cost of converting timber was great. Because of this and the general shortage of money, little timber stock was kept on hand by the shipbuilder, with the result that it was commonly necessary to use a good deal of green lumber in a ship. There has long been a smug assumption on the part of American writers that ships built in this country were always noted for the excellence of their construction and workmanship as well as for their durability. It is a sad fact that this has never been wholly true, for American ships in any period exhibited but few examples, comparatively, that were on a par in this respect with English or French-built ships. In the years before the Revolution, the chief advantage of American ships over those built abroad was the cheapness with which they could be produced, in competition with foreign shipbuilders. After the Revolution, however, the American-built ships also had the advantage in model, and in occasional examples they were nearly as well built and as durable. The excellent models on which they were built then were mainly responsible for the later fame of American-built ships and not their construction or durability. This matter will receive more attention later.

The uncertainty of employment in colonial times prevented the American shipbuilder from gaining the proper training and experience to build ships of comparatively large size. However, from 1650 to the time of the Revolution, a large number of ships were built in America for foreign owners, most of which were small traders. A great number were built for the accounts of West Indian merchants, others were for English owners, and many of both were laid down by their builders in a dull season on speculation. Vessels built on "spec." were usually sent out with a cargo by the builder and offered for sale on arrival at their destination. Most of the settlements engaged in this building did not launch more than a vessel a year; in fact, the majority did not lay down a ship oftener than every third year. Nevertheless, there was a steady increase in colonial production, so that in spite of the apparently unimpressive yearly output of American ships, English merchants and politicians felt alarm as early as 1670. It is difficult to compare the production of colonial ships with that of the mother country, however, until records probably in existence come to light.

It is not difficult to obtain general information on the rise of shipbuilding in the American colonies before the Revolution, but to find detailed information on the ships themselves is quite a different story. The general classifications of type and rig that were popular with the colonists are easily listed, as they are given in the records and elsewhere. But some allowance must be made for the ignorance of the recorder, for the listing of a single vessel as a "bark," "ship" and "brigantine" in a single paper is not at all uncommon. Generally speaking, there are seven classifications in colonial records. Ships, sloops, pinks, brigantines, shallops, ketches and barks are all noted in these records up until about 1717 when "schooners" are listed. It is impossible to understand clearly from American sources alone what these names indicated. It is safe to assume, however, that the

HOY RIG, 1760   ENGLISH CUTTER, 1760

American types in these records corresponded in design and appearance with their counterparts in England.

The records agree in indicating that the bulk of colonial craft were small. The largest proportion of vessels in the lists are sloops, from twenty-five to seventy tons burden. The sloop rig of those days was a fore-and-after; one mast, carrying a gaff mainsail, two to three headsails, and square topsail and "course" (square lower sail). Next in popularity were the brigantines, from thirty to one-hundred-and-fifty tons. Just what the rig of the brigantine was at this time is open to argument. It is apparent that they were not only rigged as brigantines, square sails on the fore mast, fore-and-aft on the main, but also as brigs; perhaps as schooners before a distinction was made in the last rig. The application of the name "brigantine" to rigs of vessels has varied a good deal. In the

Royal Navy brigantines differed from brigs only in having more hoist to the main gaff sail. This was true until about 1812, if not later. Illustrations of brigantines of before 1720 show a two-masted vessel, square-

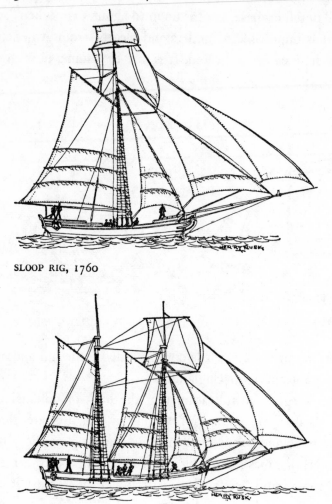

SLOOP RIG, 1760

SCHOONER RIG, 1760

rigged on the foremast, fore-and-aft on the main, but with a square topsail also. After 1720, the main square topsail was omitted in most brigantines. In speculating on the relation of the brigantine to the schooner, it can be pointed out that in either case the only difference between them

12

would be the substitution of a triangular main staysail in the brigantine for the schooner's gaff foresail, there being schooners with and without main topsails combined with fore topsails. The childish fable of the "invention" of the schooner in Gloucester, Massachusetts, has been completely exposed by the discovery of illustrations of the rig far earlier in date than that given in the story. These early schooners, if they may be called that, appear to have been fore-and-aft rigged only, but as the illustrations are of small vessels, it may be possible that in large vessels the rig approached the brigantine's in design, and was referred to by the same name.

KETCH RIG, 1760

Ketches were used a good deal in the offshore fishery until about 1700, when they lost popularity. A few were built afterwards, but the rig never regained its early widespread favor. It has been claimed that the colonial fishing ketches were rigged the same as the "bomb-ketch" of the European navies. A model of a ketch in the Watercraft Collection of the United States National Museum purporting to be one of these fishermen may have prompted the idea. Since colonial records show the ketches then in use ranging all the way from eighty tons down to twenty, it becomes evident that such a complicated rig as that of the naval bomb-ketch must have been considerably modified. The naval ketch was a two-masted square-rigged vessel, fitted with a main mast nearly amidships on which there was a course and square topsail and topgallant; after about 1720 there was a gaff sail as well. In a ketch this was called a "wingsail."

FRIGATE, 1760

On the mizzen mast there were the same square sails as on a ship's mizzen, and also a spanker. The general appearance of this rig was that of a ship with her foremast out.

It seems logical to believe that this rig would be unpractical in a small fishing ketch. Probably the colonial ketch did not have her main mast as far aft as the naval type, and had only a square course and topsail on it. Toward the beginning of the eighteenth century, the colonial ketch may have had a gaff wingsail as well. On a mizzen mast stepped near the stern a fore-and-aft sail was carried, lateen, sprit or gaff sail, according to date.

It is very likely that the large trading ketches built after 1700 were rigged more like the bomb-ketch.

Pinks were not anything like the later fishing "pinkies" except in having a sharp stern and false overhang of a similar design. They were about the same size as the colonial ketch and, as a rule, were also offshore fishermen. No particular rig distinguished the type, as in the later "pinky," and so pinks are noted as being rigged as ships, brigantines and ketches. They appear to have been a rather favored type in the fishery.

Shallops were a nondescript class of small boat, open or half-decked, ranging from an ordinary ship's boat to a decked two-master something like the later "Chebacco Boat" out of Gloucester and Essex. Some of these boats were used in the shore fisheries and others were farm or household boats.

Barks were square-sterned carriers, usually flush-decked, and like the pinks had no special rig. The name was not then applied to a rig, but was a shipbuilder's name for a hull type. The name is very loosely applied in colonial records, and is often used in place of "ship" or "vessel." Most of the colonial barks seem to have been brigantines, though some were rigged as ships or ketches.

Ships in colonial records, where tonnage is given, seem very small. They were three-masted vessels, of course, square-rigged on all three masts, with a spanker on the mizzen as well. The ship, in America, seems to have carried the lateen yard for the spanker until about 1740. After that the gaff sail replaced the old yard in all but large ships. By the time of the American Revolution the lateen was rarely seen as a spanker, or, as it was sometimes called, the "driversail."

Before leaving these rigs it is worthwhile to mention the brig and snow. These gradually came into use in American vessels during the early part of the eighteenth century. They were two-masted vessels square-rigged on both masts. The brig set a gaff spanker on her main mast, schooner-fashion. Above this were the usual square sails. Because of the interference of the gaff-jaws it was difficult to set a square mainsail, and so in a brig this was omitted. A snow set her spanker on a "trysail mast," set on deck, a foot or so abaft the main mast, and secured aloft to the trestletrees of that mast. This enabled the snow to set a square main course and was the only difference in the two rigs. So narrow a definition could not last long; hence the word "snow" went out of use, though all men-of-war brigs after 1800, in the United States Navy at least, were really snows

BRIG RIG, 1760

for they all had trysail masts. Later many full rigged ships adopted this spar on all masts; it was then called a "spencer mast."

As we have said, it may be safely assumed that the colonial craft of the seventeenth and early eighteenth centuries were little different from similar rigs and types used in the mother country. This is logical, for none of the trades, not even the fisheries, gave constant employment, and so vessels were not built to meet the requirements of any special trade. Small craft were used as fishermen, farm-produce carriers and coasting traders, as the demands of the moment dictated. The large vessels were employed in any trade or business that had possibilities of a profit, from fishing to trans-Atlantic voyages. Models and types developed at home, in England, would serve the colonists; therefore we find so few distinct colonial types listed in the records. Altogether, such conditions had little tendency to produce new rigs or types. It was not until the rise of the smuggling trades during the middle of the eighteenth century that a condition arose making a new and distinct type or hull model necessary.

Description alone is quite insufficient to give a picture of what colonial vessels were like in appearance and design. Obviously paintings or plans are required. Paintings exist, either in rare ship portraits or in pictures of

SNOW RIG

harbors and towns. Plans are of far greater assistance and a few can be found. Contrary to common belief, plans were then in use, in fact, for a good many years prior to the first English settlements in America, shipbuilders had used plans or, as they were then called, "draughts."

The evolution of the designing methods now used in naval architecture began as early as Elizabethan times, if not earlier. Crude drawings are in existence that show the slow development of "draughts" during the seventeenth century; by the beginning of the eighteenth, well-drawn plans could be made. The British Admiralty, by a regulation passed about 1650, ruled that plans of all naval ships should be preserved in their records, but it was not until twenty-five years later that the draughts were actually kept. To supplement the plans, framed and detailed scale-models were also used, in the design of large and important ships, and a few English and French models of this class are still in existence. But the immensely valuable Collection of Draughts belonging to the British Admiralty is the best source to which we can turn for information on early sailing ship design. Obviously, this collection will be composed of men-

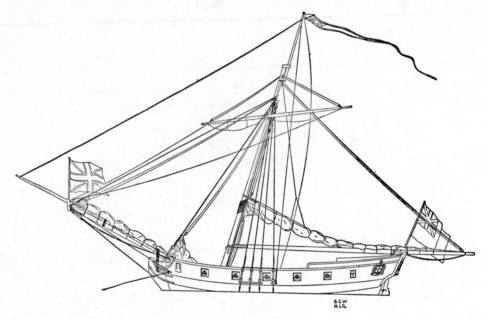

SLOOP OFF BOSTON LIGHT, 1720. (*After Burgis's drawing*)

of-war and vessels of naval character. Fortunately, the Admiralty not only retained the plans of newly designed craft, but often had plans made from completed ships obtained by purchase or capture. As a result, a few plans of American ships made prior to the Revolution can be found. Furthermore, the relation between the designs of the smaller men-of-war and merchant craft was very close in those days. The naval craft were often more ornate and of faster models, but there was much similarity otherwise, for merchant craft were built to carry guns and to run when necessary. This similarity can be inferred by the numerous cases in which merchant craft were converted to regular armed cruisers. For example, the *Alfred, Providence, Columbus* and *Cabot* of the American colonial navy and the British convoy-guards such as *Shark* or *Cupid* of the same period were converted vessels. The similarity was much stronger, however, before the Revolution than afterwards, although the employment of merchant vessels of certain types as men-of-war continued throughout the sailing ship era.

As pointed out earlier, the bulk of colonial ships were sloops. It would be too much to expect to find a plan of one of these sloops in the Admiralty Collection of Draughts. It is possible to illustrate the type fairly accurately, however, by the use of a man-of-war sloop of the proper date. Figure 1, showing one of the latter, represents the lines of the *Ferrett* of 1711. The *Ferrett* was larger than the general run of colonial sloops, without question, and was also built on a sharper model than many. She is so much like the sloop shown in the well-known painting of Boston Light of 1720, however, even to the number of gunports and position of the mast in relation to them, that she may be taken as typical in most respects.

The appearance of plans may frighten those who do not understand them. The explanation of the meaning of each line that is shown is necessarily somewhat involved, but no more so than rules for Contract Bridge or Income Tax Blanks. Reference to the plan of the *Ferrett* will make the description understandable. There are three elevations, or views, of the hull in a draught: the profile or "sheer" plan which shows the broadside view; the "body" plan which shows the shape of the various sections taken across the ship to show its form; and the "half-breadth" plan which shows a view of the hull from above, indicating the shape of the rail plan, deck and sections taken at various levels parallel to the keel or the load waterline.

The sheer plan shows the profile in detail, the shape of the stem, the

19

location of gun-ports, mouldings, carvings, masts, decks, rake and profile of the stern and rudder, as well as the general appearance of the vessel when seen from alongside.

The body plan shows the shapes of the "control" frames or "moulds" that fix the shape of all intermediate frames when the builder sets them up on the keel. In addition it may indicate the shape of the transom or stern, and in a general way, shows the appearance of the hull viewed from astern on one side of the body plan, and from forward of the bow on the other.

The half-breadth plan, as already explained, shows the outline of the rail, deck, load and other waterlines when viewed from above the vessel. These plans are not pictures, for they show the actual scale dimensions of each part that is drawn, and are not in perspective as would be the case in a picture or photograph of the hull.

To grasp the detail of design represented by the various curved lines it is necessary to imagine that we have a solid block of wood in the shape of the hull of the *Ferrett*, and a saw. Cutting it lengthwise along the centerline, we have two half-models. Taking one of these, we lay it over the sheer plan so that the newly cut face is flat on the drawing and so that its outline corresponds with the profile. Now the similarity between the sheer plan and the model in profile can be seen.

Referring to the other views, it will be seen that there are straight lines parallel to the centerline on each elevation. These indicate the position of the "buttock lines," which are represented on the sheer plan by sweeping curves running the full length of the hull and reaching above and below the waterlines. In the example, there are three of these. If we cut our half-model to correspond with the straight lines in the body and half-breadth plans just mentioned, the outlines of each slab so formed would correspond with its equivalent on the sheer plan (unless the draftsman has fallen down on his job). Gluing the slabs together again, we can verify the other views or plans.

In looking at the sheer plan, it will be noticed that the "load waterline,"

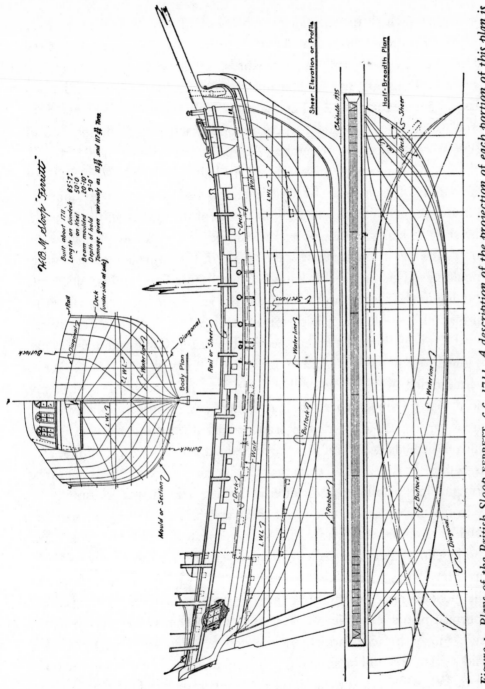
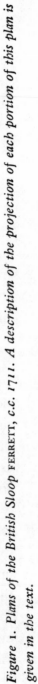

H.M. Sloop "Ferrett"

Built about 1711.
Length on Gundeck   65'·7"
        on Keel   50'·0"
Beam moulded   20'·10"
Depth of hold   9'·0"
Tonnage given variously as 103⅔ and 117 49/94 Tons

Buttock
Rail
Deck (under-side at side)
Diagonal
Buttock
L·W·L
Water-line
L·W·L
Body Plan
Diagonal
Rail or "Sheer"
Buttock
Mould or Section

Rail
Deck
Wale
Deck
Scuppers
Water-line
Buttock
Wale
Deck
Buttock
Rabbet
LWL
Sheer Elevation or Profile
Chapelle 1935

Deck
Sheer
LWL
Half-Breadth Plan
Water-line
Buttock
Diagonal

21

Figure 1. Plans of the British Sloop FERRETT, *c.c. 1711. A description of the projection of each portion of this plan is given in the text.*

or depth at which the ship swims when loaded, is indicated by a heavy line sloping downward from the stern to the bow. This shows that the ship "trims by the stern"; in other words, she draws more water aft than forward. There are also straight lines paralleling the keel, and a dot and dash line indicating the level of the main deck, shown in this view. Suppose we cut the half-model to correspond exactly with the location of these various lines, and at right angles to the back of the model as well. Now, if we lay each of these slabs on the half-breadth plan, we find that the outline of each successive slab corresponds exactly with its counterpart on the plan, which will account for six of the curves on the example, the seventh being the curve of the outline of the rail in plan view. In most cases this curve is taken at the height of the underside of the railcap mouldings. This line is also known as the "sheer line" and is, of course, the line in the sheer plan to represent the amount of fore and aft curve in the rail line. Hence, it is customary to speak of the amount of sweep on the top of the rail as the "sheer" of a vessel. Once again the model is glued together and we can investigate the body plan.

In looking over the reassembled model, turn it end on. It will be noticed that the lines, where we cut earlier, correspond in appearance to the waterlines as represented by straight lines at right angles to the centerline on the body plan, and that the deck, load waterline and rail line show as curves. It will also be seen that the buttock lines cut first appear as straight lines parallel to the centerline, when held in this position.

In the sheer plan of the *Ferrett* there are thirteen stations, or sections, which are represented by straight lines, vertical to the keel (which is also the baseline). It is also seen that these stations are shown on the half-breadth plan as straight lines perpendicular to the centerline. If we cut the model as indicated by these lines, in the case of the *Ferrett*, we have fourteen pieces. One piece is very thin and is the widest section of the hull, and both faces formed by the new sawcuts are alike; this is the mid-section and will be shown on both sides of the centerline in the body plan. When we lay this piece on the body plan, we find that the outlines of both faces correspond with the curve representing this section in the plan. In some vessels the mid-section is taken as a single station on the sheer plan, but the body plan represents the shape of it in the same way. Each of the pieces can be checked against their corresponding sections in the body plan in the same way. Finally, the outline of the transom can also be compared. The heights of the rail in the sections in the body plan are the same as those in the sheer plan, it can be seen.

The remaining curves are the diagonals, which are shown superimposed over the curves of the half-breadth plan, but curved in the opposite direction. On the body plan, there can be seen four straight lines meeting the centerline at varying angles. The four dot-and-dash curves superimposed over the half-breadth plan are outlines of slabs obtained by cutting the model along the lines in the body plan just referred to.

In the sheer plan there is a double line extending along the keel and up the bow and stern. This is the double seam formed by the junction of the inside and outside of the planking with these members of the hull. If a double line is shown, as in the *Ferrett*, the lines are to the inside of the planking and show the shape of the hull to the outside of the frames only. A single line indicates the hull is drawn to the outside of the planking and that the builder will have to deduct the thickness of the plank to obtain the true shape of the frames.

The drawing of the *Ferrett* has been marked so as to help in making these descriptions clear. The "wales" are also marked; these were made of a belt of plank thicker than the bottom or rest of the side, running the length of the vessel to strengthen the hull. Just forward of the foremost gun-port a pad of plank is shown above the wale; this prevented the anchor from damaging the topsides when being hoisted aboard.

The use of oars or, properly, "sweeps" was common in vessels during colonial days and well into the nineteenth century, even in craft as large as frigates and other full-rigged ships. In the *Ferrett* may be seen the sweep ports located between the gun-ports in her side. Sweeps were used to move the vessel in calms and to swing her so that her guns would bear when in action in light weather. Amidships there was a long "channel" or shelf, so to speak, which extended out from the sides below the gunports sufficiently to enable the lanyards, used to tighten up the shrouds, to clear the rail by six to twelve inches.

The armament of colonial vessels was an important item in their equip-

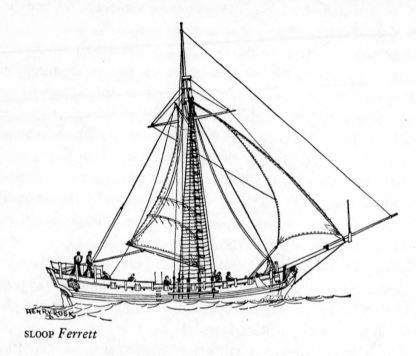

SLOOP *Ferrett*

ment. The constant wars and disturbances of the seventeenth and eighteenth centuries made it necessary to design all merchantmen of any but the smallest size to carry a practical armament. The mounting of guns through ports in the sides was in use throughout the whole period of the American sailing ship till about 1850. This practice is too well known to require lengthy discussion here. Wheeled carriages were used, very similar to the ones that can be seen in the main battery of the restored *Constitution*. The guns of colonial ships were much smaller, however, three- and six-pounders being the popular calibers before the Revolution.

On the plan of the *Ferrett* upright timbers can be seen between the gun-ports and on the quarterdeck; these are "swivel stocks." These timbers were usually bolted to the outside of the hull and were fitted with an iron cap and socket to take an iron fork shaped somewhat like a common oarlock. This fork was a part of a special class of firearms, generally classified as "swivels." These guns varied considerably in caliber and design. One very popular type was a miniature cannon, some three feet in length, with a bore of about an inch and a half diameter. It had a wooden handle, about the shape of a shortened baseball bat, attached to its breech by being driven onto an iron prong and banded, in much the same manner as the handles of old farm rakes used to be attached. When fired, the gun was trained with this handle. The same stock was used for a very long and heavy musket firing a large ball; this was called a "wall-piece" or, more commonly in American accounts, a "buccaneering-piece." Still another gun mounted this way was a heavy "blunderbuss," a bell-mouthed weapon usually associated with the Puritans and Thanksgiving Day. The blunderbuss fired loose shot in the manner of the modern shotgun. At about the time of the Revolution still another type is mentioned, the "howitzer," which was a short cannon mounted in the same general way as the swivels, but with the stock inside the bulwarks. The howitzer seems to have been of larger bore than any of the swivels, and was really a forerunner of the later carronade.

Below the main deck of the *Ferrett* there were two short decks or "platforms," the forward for the accommodation of the galley fireplace, and in merchant vessels, the crew. Abaft this, in merchantmen, was the cargo hold, but in men-of-war this space had a portable deck for the accommodation of the large crews that were required in that class of ship. Aft was the "great cabbin" and after "platform," forming staterooms or "bedplaces" for the officers.

The clear sweep of the spacious main deck was broken by a ladderway, or companionway on one side, and a galley hatch on the other, over the forward platform. In merchant craft there would be a hand-spike

25

windlass athwartships, right up in the bows. In either men-of-war or merchant ships there was a bitt at the heel of the massive bowsprit, and a riding bitt at the foot of the mainmast. Abaft the mast, one or two boats were placed in a cradle athwartships, if room permitted. If more than one boat was carried, they were nested one within the other. A large hatch over the hold and a ladderway and sometimes a skylight over the after platform completed the list of deck openings. Two pumps with wooden barrels came up through the main deck and after platform, from each side of the keel, probably just opposite the aftermost gun-port. On the *Ferrett* a centerline for a deck fitting was indicated on the sheer plan at main deck level underneath the second gun-port from the stern; this was undoubtedly the center of the capstan. In the stern there was a short raised quarterdeck, formed by the roof of the "great cabbin." The entrance to the cabin was through a doorway in the bulkhead at the fore end of the quarterdeck, opening on the main deck, and covered by a domed hatch. The floor of the "great cabbin" was sunk below the level of the main deck so that the quarterdeck would not be excessively high. The sloop was steered by a long tiller on the quarterdeck. In the *Ferrett* the quarterdeck was probably fitted with iron stanchions as shown in the plan, but most colonial sloops had an open wooden rail on this deck, for iron was too expensive for this purpose.

At the stem there was usually a figurehead, or if this was too expensive, there was either a simple carved billet, or the whole cutwater knee and head rails were omitted altogether. The *Ferrett's* figurehead was omitted on the original plan, but it was probably a lion. Incidentally, the idea that the figurehead had a definite relation to the name of the vessel is untrustworthy, not only in the British Navy, but also in early American vessels. For instance, the Massachusett's brig *Hazard* of Revolutionary War fame had a figurehead of Minerva, and the American frigate *Hancock*, after her capture by the British, retained the full-length figure of Mr. Hancock on her cutwater but was renamed *Iris*, a doubtful compliment to that patriot.

The rigs of sloops like the *Ferrett* were fairly well standardized by 1700. No dimensions for *Ferrett's* spars are available, but the general proportions as taken from contemporary American paintings are as follows: length of main mast, deck to cap, was equal to the length of the hull on deck; the main boom was the same length; the main gaff was from one-third to three-sevenths the length of the boom; the length of the topmast was roughly one-third the main boom, the main mast head or "doubling" being one-fourth of the whole length of the topmast; the square yard, used to spread the square topsail foot, was about the same length as the topmast, or perhaps twice the beam of the hull; the length of the bowsprit outside the rabbet of the stem was equal to approximately half the main-boom; the jib boom projected a distance out from the cap of the bowsprit about equal to two-thirds the outboard length of the latter. Aloft, on the topmast, there was a topsail yard whose length was equal to the beam of the hull.

The sails are indicated by the spars; a gaff mainsail, a squaresail, or course and topsail, and a fore staysail, jib and jib topsail made up their suits. Small vessels omitted some or all of the squaresails and part of the head sails. Some sloops set topgallant sails above the topsail during the eighteenth century. The gaff mainsail was always loose-footed. The gaff was always lowered to furl the sail, the so-called "standing-gaff" that remained aloft was never popular in America.

We have spent more time in talking about the *Ferrett* than her importance to our subject warrants, but the description of her details will apply to other and later craft. Before leaving her, however, there is one more thing that must be mentioned. Plans of ships, particularly sailing ships, that are complete in every detail are extremely rare. The reasons for this were many, the most important being that at certain periods many details were so standardized that it was considered a waste of time for the draftsmen to show them, while others, such as carvings, were best left to the specialist who furnished them. As a result, Admiralty and other plans do not always show much detail, particularly in new designs.

27

In plans "taken-off," or made from measurements of a completed vessel, more detail, particularly of the carving and deck fittings, can be found. It is not at all uncommon to find the figurehead omitted from a plan. As this piece of carving was often unshipped, it may indicate that it was lost or was to be changed when not shown in a "take-off," or that its design was to be a standard one or was undecided in a new draught. In the case of the *Ferrett* the figurehead was omitted from the original plan in the Admiralty files, as was stated earlier. Also, unfortunately, the shape of her transom, quarter windows and galleries, quarterdeck details and railing were also left open to doubt, and so these were "restored" from other draughts of ships of the same approximate size and date in which these details were shown. Apparently the plan was an unfinished office copy. Other plans in a similar state of incompleteness are to be found. Since there might have been some variation in these restored details, they are not wholly accurate as applied to this sloop, but they are at least typical. The buttock lines were also added, these not being in use so early.

For an example of a two-masted rig of early date we must again turn to an English-built man-of-war. This is the *Swift*, a brigantine or snow, built in 1721. She was called a "sloop," as will be noticed in Figure 2. It is this kind of thing that makes naval records so exasperatingly vague as to ship descriptions. A naval "sloop" could be a vessel of almost any rig as long as she carried her guns on a single deck. She could also be a "sloop" if she were commanded by an officer one grade below a captain in rank. Hence the word "sloop" as applied to naval craft is more descriptive of rank and battery than of rig. It is usual, however, to refer to these vessels as "brig-sloops" or "ship-sloops" as required.

The *Swift* is only of importance in our account insofar as she indicates the condition of naval architecture at the time of her build. Here is no high-sterned and cumbersome ark, but rather a workmanlike and intelligently designed carrier. The degree of knowledge incorporated in this design is remarkable in the light of recent developments in naval architecture. The peculiar shape of the mid-section of the *Swift* should be

View of an old Maryland shipyard owned by Richard Spencer, from a painting on a wood panel originally over the fireplace in the reception room of "Spencer Hall." The artist is unknown, and the date of the work is conjecture except that it was prior to the Revolution

(Courtesy of the Maryland Historical Society)

American Attack on Tripoli　　　　　　　　　(*Courtesy United States Naval Academy*)
Showing VIXEN, ENTERPRISE, SYREN, ARGUS, CONSTITUTION, NAUTILUS

Battle on Lake Champlain. September 11, 1814　　　　(*Courtesy S. H. P. Pell, Esq.*)

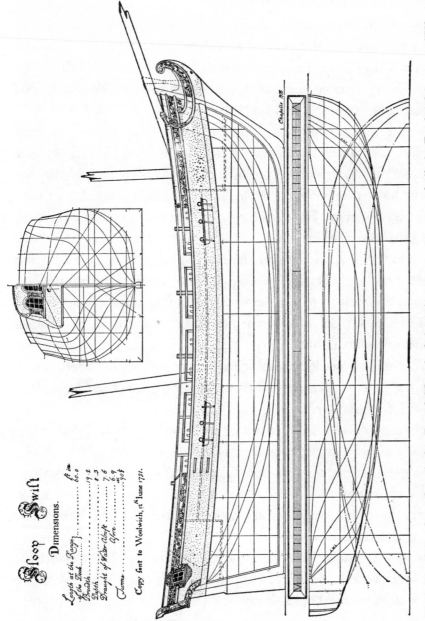
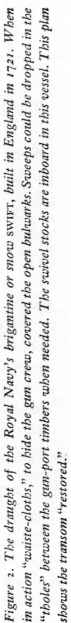

Sloop Swift

Dimensions.

Length at the Range
of the Deck .... ft. in. 60. 0
Breadth 19. 2
Depth 8. 3
Draught of Water Abaft .. 7. 6
Afore 6. 9
Burthen .... 90⁴⁄₉

Copy sent to Woolwich, 12ᵗʰ June 1721.

Figure 2. The draught of the Royal Navy's brigantine or snow SWIFT, built in England in 1721. When in action "waiste-cloths," to hide the gun crew, covered the open bulwarks. Sweeps could be dropped in the "tholes" between the gun-port timbers when needed. The swivel stocks are inboard in this vessel. This plan shows the transom "restored."

29

noticed. It might be described as the ordinary mid-section of a flat-floored cargo vessel with the bilges cut off at about forty-five degrees. It will also be seen that the underwater sections of this little vessel have certain portions of their curves nearly parallel to the two straight portions of the mid-section. From 1721 to 1921 is a two-hundred-year period. About 1921, a naval architect in Germany carried out an extensive experiment in the "test-tank" to find a hull form that could be propelled at suitable speed with the minimum of power; in other words, one that showed small resistance. As a result he developed a hull form whose mid-section was a rectangle with its lower corners cut off at forty-five degrees and the sections in the body plan showing parallelism to the forty-five degree portion of the mid-section. This hull form was patented under the name of "Maier-form," after its inventor, and a number of steamers have been built on its principles. Analysis of the two hull designs is an interesting commentary on the "advance" in knowledge in naval architecture. The French used this hull form very extensively during the seventeenth and eighteenth centuries, but whether or not they deserve the credit for its development remains an unanswered question. Since the British and other shipbuilding nations used it more or less during the same period, it can hardly be called a strictly French element of design either during American colonial days or later.

These vessels, though not American in design, serve to indicate the development of naval architecture in the early eighteenth century. There can be no question but that the principles of hull design shown in these examples were known to American builders, and, as the requirements of their trades demanded, they would use these features in their own ships.

The evolution of American sailing ship models during the early eighteenth century was slow. The wars and troubles at sea that would later have put a premium on speed had little influence so long as the Americans could depend upon the British Navy and its convoy system for protection. This was the case in the overseas trade employing large ships. And we, therefore, find the colonial vessels of this class plying out of the more important centers of overseas trade as Boston, Philadelphia and New York, differing but little from those of their British brethren.

The period was not one of prosperity for the colonies as a whole, however, and from various causes a large illegal trade grew up. A flourishing business developed of smuggling goods into the Spanish settlements of the West Indies and of return cargoes into the colonies. New England and the other colonies were engaged in this business, but the part New England played has been greatly exaggerated in history, doubtless because of the importance of some of her citizens who were in the trade. Because of their proximity to the West Indies, their lack of large and prosperous towns and their distance from Europe in relation to Boston and New York, the southern colonies, such as Virginia and Maryland, directed their attention toward illegal trade to a far greater extent than other places.

It was obvious that vessels engaged in illicit trade could not depend upon the British Navy for protection; in fact these vessels would be legal prizes of the naval ships if caught. Smuggled goods are commonly handled in comparatively small cargoes, and small vessels are more easily handled in the small smuggling ports and are likewise more easily hidden than large craft. A pertinent illustration of the application of these requirements is the "bootlegger," "bootie" or "liquor-runner" of the late Prohibition Era. It is not surprising, therefore, to find the southern shipbuilders developing a type of sailing vessel suitable in size, speed and handling qualities for the business, long before similar craft were built elsewhere.

It is quite impossible to establish an exact date for the beginning of the development of the fast southern model that later won renown as the "Baltimore Clipper." It must have been somewhere in the neighborhood of 1730, for mention of sharp schooners built in the south appear in records and newspapers soon afterwards. The first reference, that is at hand, to vessels of this class in contemporary newspapers is dated in November, 1746. The first of these sharp and fast vessels were probably sloops, but the schooner rig was adopted very quickly. The schooner rig, being weatherly and capable of handling by a smaller crew than the sloop, was particularly suitable for a fast vessel. Furthermore, the schooner rig could be used in a longer and narrower vessel than a sloop It was found by experiment that if two vessels of the same capacity, or displacement, were built, the longer was the faster of the two. Then, too, the narrow waters in which smugglers usually operated made the fore-and-aft rig a prime requisite.

It is very unfortunate that but one plan of a clipper schooner of the pre-Revolutionary type has yet been found. There are, however, a few plans of American merchant schooners of a date prior to the Revolution in the Admiralty Collection. Before introducing these, it might be well to speak of American-built men-of-war in the British Navy before the Revolution. The first of these was a "4th Rate" named the *Falkland* built at Portsmouth, New Hampshire, in 1690. This vessel was followed by others, among them one named the *Bedford*. The last ship of large size was the *Boston*, also built at Portsmouth and launched in 1749. An earlier *Boston* had been built at Boston in 1745. In American accounts this 1749 vessel is always called the *America;* if she were launched with the latter name it was changed on her arrival in England. This *Boston* was a forty-four gun ship with her battery on two decks and was somewhat similar to the later *Serapis* taken by John Paul Jones in 1779. No plans of these ships are at hand, but there is very little likelihood that any of them were designed in America.

In speaking of these vessels we should mention the period of change from the early "spritsail topmast" and the lateen yard on the mizzen to the jib boom and spanker gaff. It is impossible, of course, to set an exact date for this, for the change was very gradual. The small vessels adopted the jib boom and gaff as early as 1700, if not before. The large ships were slowly accepting these improvements during the first thirty or forty years of the century, but the lateen mizzen yard could be occasionally seen in ships-of-the-line until 1806. However, the lateen yard was rare in American ships after 1760.

After 1749, few vessels were built in America for the British government. On the Great Lakes, two sloops, the *Ontario* and the *Oswego*, a couple of small schooners, and a snow or two were built between 1755 and the Revolution. On the seaboard a few small schooners were launched, among them the *Earl of Egmont* and the *Sir Edward Hawke*, laid down in New York in 1768. All of these vessels are supposed to have been designed by the Admiralty surveyors, or constructors, of the time, or were purchased on the stocks.

The British government, however, found it desirable to increase the naval and revenue forces on the American coast about 1768, so they purchased a number of schooners. Between 1764 and 1775, the British Navy owned about twenty vessels of this class, of which fourteen are known to have been built and purchased in America; among them two that played some part in history, the *Gaspee* and *Halifax*.

The plans of the *Halifax*, or rather the *Hallifax* as spelled on the original draught, are shown in Figures 3 and 4. This little schooner was very active in the vicinity of Boston during the early days of the Revolution. She was one of the schooner-transports that was used to land the British troops at Boston in 1775. Her fame, if so it may be called, rests in the part she played in the burning of Falmouth, now Portland, Maine, in 1776.

It seems that certain of the New England coast towns had made themselves conspicuous by active opposition to the Crown, and the British naval commander at Boston felt that their insolence should be punished. This officer, Vice-Admiral Graves, directed the fitting out of a small squadron, composed of the *Hallifax*, the armed ship *Canceaux*, and the armed sloop *Spitfire*, all carrying 6 guns. These he placed under the command of Lieutenant Henry Mowatt, with orders to "operate against certain enumerated towns." Before sailing on his mission, Mowatt was also given the armed transport *Symmetry* of 18 light guns.

One of the towns against which he had orders to act was Falmouth. Arriving on October 17th, 1776, he sent an officer ashore with the de-

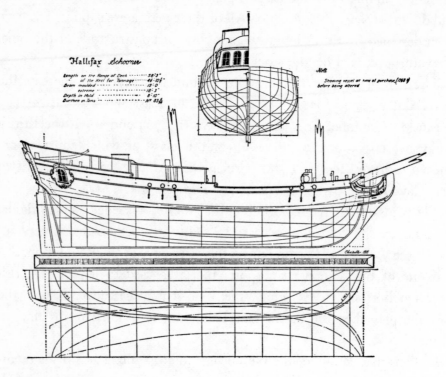

Figure 3. The lines and outboard profile of an American-built commercial schooner of about 1765, HALLIFAX. *The plan shows a small and rather slow carrier. Note the fullness of the waterlines and buttocks at bow and stern. Figurehead not shown in original draught.*

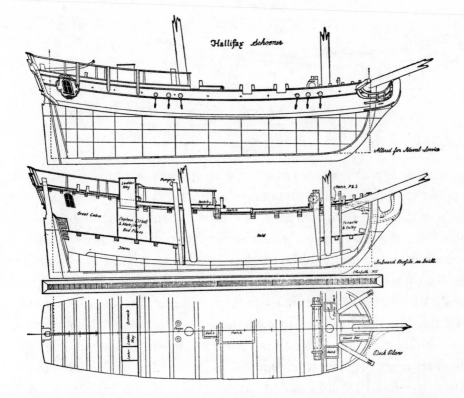

Figure 4. HALLIFAX, *upper portion shows the outboard profile of this schooner as altered for the Royal Navy. The lower portion shows the inboard details of the schooner before the alterations were made in her rails. Note the method of fitting the hawse-holes below deck level, an item of construction rarely seen in the period in which this schooner was built.*

35

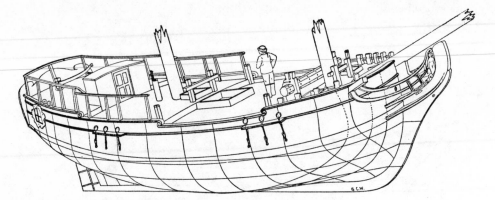

Hallifax SCHOONER

mand that the townsmen remove themselves, their families and goods
out of the village within two hours as he intended to carry out his orders
to burn the place. To appreciate the situation fully, it must be remembered that the season of the year was so advanced that if these intentions
were carried out it would be too late for the inhabitants to obtain new
homes without great privation. It may also be doubted whether Mowatt
really had the orders he claimed to have, not only because of his actions
but also, according to British naval historians, because "his instructions
were tempered with moderation." At any rate, the townsmen sent off a
deputation to beg that the reputed order should not be carried out.
Mowatt refused to promise but proposed that if the settlement would
surrender all its firearms, including four small pieces of artillery, and all
ammunition, as well as turn over four hostages, he would refer the matter to his superior at Boston. After some deliberation, the townsmen re-
jected the proposition as too uncertain in results compared to the loss of
the protection of their firearms in a wilderness. Mowatt therefore burned
the village the morning of the next day. Great suffering resulted, but of
more importance, the whole coast was aroused against the British. Realiz-
ing the unfortunate results of his action, Mowatt at once returned to
Boston without attempting more. American and British historians have
disagreed over the morality and need of destroying this town, but the

lack of common sense that the act exhibited needs no defense. The possibility that Mowatt exceeded his instructions is strengthened by the fact that his promotion was withheld for a time afterwards.

There were two vessels in the Royal Navy named *Hallifax* between 1768 and 1776, the schooner of the Falmouth affair and another vessel on Lake Champlain. The *Hallifax* which played the part in the burning of Falmouth was purchased in 1768 in New England, but her previous

Hallifax SCHOONER

history is unknown. Figure 3 shows the lines of the vessel as she was originally, and Figure 4 shows not only her original deck plan and inboard profile, but also her outboard profile as a naval vessel. Her figurehead was not recorded; in view of the mermaid on her head rails, it may be that she had Neptune for the central figure. The lion rampant, though, was the most common figurehead in the British Navy at the time of the *Hallifax*. In spite of the small size of this schooner she probably carried square topsails on both fore and main masts.

Another example of a schooner of this class, the *Chaleur*, is shown in Figures 5, 6 and 7. This is a somewhat larger vessel than the *Hallifax* and

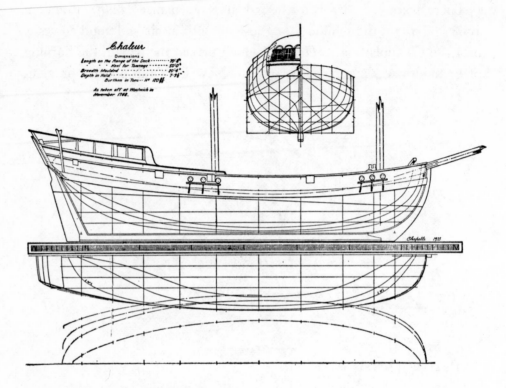

Figure 5. CHALEUR, *a schooner of about 1764. An excellent example of a popular type in pre-Revolutionary days. She was probably a fast sailer in moderate weather, but poor to windward in heavy going. The dot and dash line running from bow to stern and crossing the top of the wale on the sheer elevation is the line of "greatest breadths" in each section, and is a fairing line that does not enter into the construction.*

38

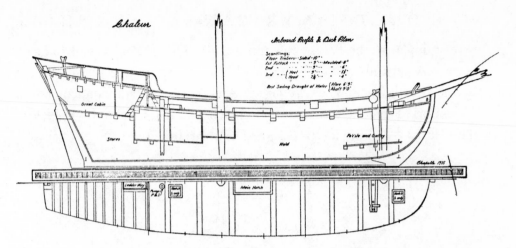

Figure 6. CHALEUR. *The inboard details and deck arrangement.*

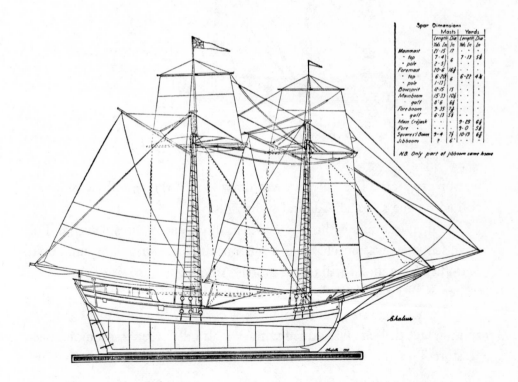

Figure 7. CHALEUR—*Sail plan.*

39

is very similar to the *Baltick* [1] in appearance. The *Chaleur* is said to have been an American-built schooner that had been captured from the French by the British frigate *Favorite* on the American coast and condemned at New York. Here she was finally purchased, in 1764, for the Royal Navy. The *Chaleur* was obviously designed as a cargo vessel, not as a man-of-

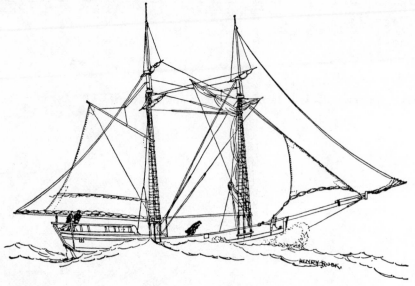

Chaleur

war or privateer. The sail plan was drawn from the spar dimensions recorded on the original Admiralty draught.

The final example is the tiny *Sultana*, shown in Figures 8 and 9. This small schooner was purchased in 1768, but the place of build is unknown. An official statement makes it "North America"; a private letter refers to her as "English-built." The interesting features of her design, however, are her small size, her sharp lines, as compared to the other examples, and the fact that she was armed with swivels only. Her transom has been "restored" in the drawing as it was omitted in the Admiralty draught.

[1] A picture of the *Baltick* is in the Peabody Marine Museum at Salem, Massachusetts; reproductions have been published. ("The Fore-and-Aft Rig in America" by E. P. Morris, New Haven, 1927; page 176.)

The *Sultana* gives an idea of the small size of some seagoing traders in colonial times.

All these examples of early schooners show the full-lined type. This class of schooner was purchased by the Royal Navy for transport service, hence the number of plans available in the Admiralty files. So far but one

Sultana, SCHOONER, 1768

plan of a sharp pre-Revolutionary American schooner has been found; but this example is enough to prove the existence of that type in colonial times. This individual will receive attention when the development of the "Baltimore Clippers" is discussed later on.

Though the information that is now available on American designed and built sailing craft of the colonial period is insufficient to permit of more than general conclusions, it seems apparent that the first distinctive type was the schooner. Developing gradually during the eighteenth century, by the time of the Revolution the schooner was in such general use as to be the most numerous of all classes of carrier. Because of the

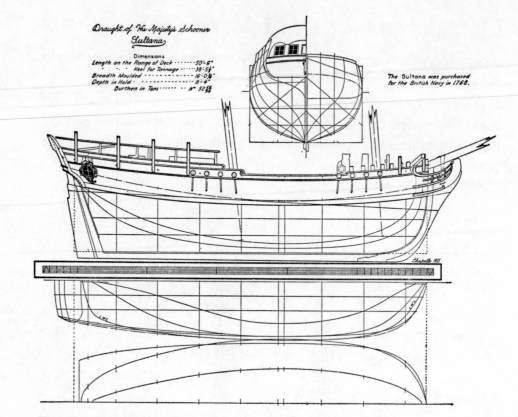

Draught of His Majesty's Schooner
Sultana

Dimensions
Length on the Range of Deck ······ 50'-6"
        Keel for Tonnage ······ 38'-5½"
Breadth Moulded ·············· 16'-0¼"
Depth in Hold ················ 8'-4"
Burthen in Tons ··········· Nº 52 56/94

The Sultana was purchased
for the British Navy in 1768.

Figure 8. Lines of the British schooner SULTANA.

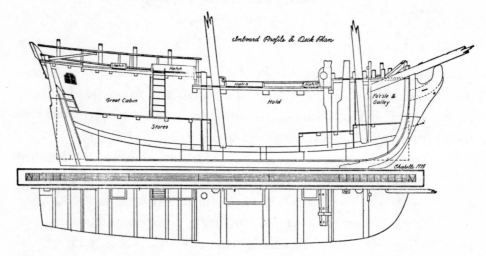

Inboard Profile & Deck Plan

Great Cabin   Hold   Fo'c'sle &
                                   Galley

Stores

Figure 9. Inboard details and deck plan of SULTANA.

42

trade conditions that have been mentioned, the evolution of the colonial schooner in the direction of the later highly perfected schooner models was very slow until the war extensively altered requirements.

At the beginning of the Revolution, then, we find the bulk of colonial shipping made up of small and slow-sailing carriers rigged as ships, brigs, brigantines, snows, sloops and schooners, of no special features of design that set them apart from similar craft in England. In addition to these, however, there were the smugglers and illegal traders, a rather numerous class made up of small and fast fore-and-afters, mostly schooner rigged. None of this class was of sufficient size, however, to be useful in war.

While certain localities had developed the fast-sailing vessel to a greater extent than others, the features that were required to produce a vessel of this type were known in nearly all the shipbuilding sections. This is evident from the widespread building of vessels designed for speed that began with the Revolution, as well as the extensive building of small smuggling craft in the earlier years in settlements all the way from Massachusetts to the Carolinas.

THE most severe test of skill in the design of wooden sailing ships was the production of men-of-war. When a yachtsman looks at the plans of one of these old vessels he instinctively compares her lines to those of a large sailing yacht or of a clipper-ship, to the disadvantage of the man-of-war. The full round bow, high freeboard and massive bulwarks, heavy displacement and rather cumbersome appearance of the man-of-war will usually impress him with the apparent ignorance of her designer. It is safe to say, however, that the modern yacht-designer would find it difficult to improve on the design of old war vessels if he had to meet the same requirements of armament, fighting tactics and construction. This opinion may seem rather far-fetched at first glance, but a consideration of the necessary qualities of a wooden sailing man-of-war will show, to the yachtsman at least, the difficult problem of her design.

Any yachtsman who has ever carried a heavy dinghy on deck in a small sailing yacht will appreciate the effects of a heavy deck load on sailing, stability and hull construction. A walk around almost any boat yard cannot fail to impress one with the difficulty of building long wooden hulls that will not change shape longitudinally; yachts with "hogged" sheers (drooping ends) can be seen all along the coast. In a wooden sailing man-of-war these two problems had to be overcome, because of the nature of her armament; therein was found the chief problem in her design.

The guns in use during the period of sail were muzzle-loaders with a low rate of fire. The size and weight of shot these guns could handle was limited by the fact that they must be loaded manually, and problems in their manufacture made them heavy, inaccurate and having only a short range of fire. The only way the designer could insure sufficient "hitting power" was to crowd as many guns into a ship as space would permit; this meant arranging the guns in rows along the sides. As it was practically impossible to fire ahead or astern with this type of battery it was necessary to allow for more guns in the extreme bow and stern; these were the "chase" guns. Muzzle-loading cannon required large gun-crews and still more men would be needed to work the ship when she was in action. This called for enormous crews when compared to the number of men needed in a merchant vessel of the same size. Stowage of provisions, ammunition, water, ship's stores and the berthing of the large crew offered difficult problems. Obviously, the guns had to be on deck, and ought to be as high above waterline as was practical in order to fight the battery in rough water. The long rows of guns, extending the whole length of the ship, prevented the use of extensive deck structures, and everything not needed in action must stow below the gun-deck.

A wooden hull was elastic; the larger she became, particularly in length, the harder it was to obtain sufficient longitudinal strength to prevent hogging and resultant straining. The lack of displacement at the bow and stern brought about by the sharp ends of the ship gave no support to the weight of structure or guns in these portions of the hull other than what could be obtained through the construction of the frame. Weights placed high above the water had a tendency to distort the hull, as the vessel rolled, causing further weakness. To overcome these tendencies it was necessary to use very heavy and massive construction in the hull which was reinforced by interior bracing as ships grew longer, all of which reduced capacity and added weight to the hull. The weight of guns, hull, ammunition, gear, spars, sails, stores, water and crew was enormous and a heavy displacement became necessary as a result.

To bear the weight of the chase guns and the end guns of the broadside batteries it was necessary to fill out the bow and stern, thereby obtaining support through displacement for those portions of the hull, since the wooden structure alone was found to be insufficient. This was particularly the case in the large men-of-war. But it was quickly discovered that full ends on a ship made her slow, and speed had obvious advantages in action. On the other hand, too sharp bows and sterns permitted the ship to hog and strain, and it might even prevent her carrying her battery well. This left the designer facing the task of finding the happy medium, if he could.

The heavy displacement and the necessarily rather full ends required a great spread of sail if the ship was to have any claim to speed. Since speed was essential to a naval vessel, that she might escape or overtake her enemies or manoeuver quickly in action, she was given a tremendous rig and sail area. The problem of getting such a rig to stand, with only elastic hemp standing rigging, will be appreciated by every yachtsman.

Naturally, there was a demand for larger and longer ships as time went on. Experiments soon showed that there was a limit to beam and depth, without a proportionate increase in length. Too wide a hull produced a slow ship and one that was hard on her gear; too narrow a hull produced an unsteady gun platform and a ship that could not carry sail. Too deep a vessel could not use the shoal harbors or approach the coasts without great danger, which limited her usefulness. Too shoal a hull made a leewardly ship that could not beat to windward or hold her station in a squadron. Hence there was a marked tendency to build high-sided ships to obtain more than one deck and so more than one row of guns. It was soon found, however, that such design did not produce a fast ship; as a result experiments in construction methods that would enable long ships to be built became popular. It took naval architects generations to solve the problems that arose in building ships of great length; in fact, it was not until the introduction of iron strapping and knees that exceedingly long wooden ships became possible.

There were still other, though minor, problems to be considered. Since actions must be fought at close range, by reason of the limitations of ships' batteries, some protection to the men working on deck was necessary. As a result high, strong bulwarks were used. These bulwarks had to be sturdy enough to withstand the recoil of the batteries and so thick that small-arm fire would not penetrate them. However, in small ships, such bulwarks were a danger, because of the water they might hold on deck when a sea had been shipped, and so in these craft there was often compromise in their use. The hull construction had to be of such nature that shot holes could be quickly and easily plugged; the bottom of the vessel should be built so that it would not leak badly if a plank or butt gave way. Most of these matters, of course, led to further increases in weight in construction.

The important qualities of weatherliness, seaworthiness and good steering were matters of hull design, apart from the requirements laid down by armament, speed and construction. Because of the importance of having the weather-gage in an action under sail, weatherliness in a naval vessel was a prime asset. The weatherliness of a vessel, that is, her ability to work to windward and to go where she was pointed without undue amount of leeway or side drift is fixed by the type and design of the rig (fore-and-aft rigs being more weatherly than square-rigs) and by the shape and area of the underwater profile of the hull. There are other technical factors, but these are the important ones. Weatherliness has no automatic relation to speed through the water; in other words, a slow ship might be more weatherly than a fast one.

Size has an important bearing on speed, but weatherliness can be had regardless of dimensions. The use of the square-rig in large sea-going vessels, in spite of its being less weatherly than the fore-and-aft rig, was made necessary by structural and tactical considerations. No rig of the fore-and-aft variety could be made to stand if it contained the same area of sail as the square-rig, and a tremendous sail area was indispensable in men-of-war. Furthermore, the fore-and-aft rig has certain drawbacks as a seagoing rig, when the sail area is large, in the difficulties of handling and reducing sail in bad weather. From the tactical point of view, the square-rig was better, for with it a vessel could be stopped dead on her course and even backed if necessary, without swinging her head or requiring much time. These manoeuvers had obvious value in a naval action under sail and were quite impossible with a fore-and-after. This is the important reason why no vessels designed for regular naval service were without square-sails, even if otherwise fore-and-aft rigged, and why all important fighting ships were square-riggers. The modified fore-and-aft rig (with square-sails in addition) was relegated to small craft which might need it in escaping from larger and faster but therefore less weatherly men-of-war. A vessel that will work out to windward may well outsail a faster, though less weatherly, ship because she can sail the shortest distance in reaching a position dead to windward.

The importance of seaworthiness and of good steering is obvious, the naval vessel required these features just as much as any other class of seagoing ship. Seaworthiness and safety went hand in hand; in most cases the requirements of a man-of-war, such as weatherliness and strength, made for seaworthiness, the occasional exception being the use of too large a rig and overloading in the small naval craft. Good steering is obtained by the proper balance of hull and rig and is not particularly hard to get in a design. If the naval vessel steered badly when new, it was usually possible to improve her by alterations in the positions of the masts or in the lengths of the spars and recutting the sails.

It is quite plain that all the good qualities of a man-of-war could never be incorporated, to the ultimate degree, in a single ship. Therefore, good design in naval architecture is the art of making the best compromises of opposing factors with a view to the use for which the ship is intended. Hence, naval ships that were of the most powerful type did not have the speed of the scouting vessels and so did not have to make the same sacrifices in fighting efficiency. The same old rules of class distinction that were then in force are to be seen now in modern navies, where battle-ships are slower, but more efficient fighting machines than the cruisers.

No study of American sailing ships can be complete without reference to speed. Speed is a comparative quality. On what grounds shall the comparison be made? Marine historians and writers have either accepted the comparative time two vessels have taken to cover some given distance, or have taken the passing of one ship by another in an informal brush as proof of comparative speed. From such reasoning attempts have been made to draw conclusions as to the comparative speed, not only of two contemporary ships, but also of ships of widely varying periods. There is, too, the method of comparing the highest recorded speed of each ship.

DESIGN OF A SHIP FOR LAKE CHAMPLAIN, 1777.

In each case it will be seen that the vessels are compared boat for boat, without allowance for difference in size. The unfairness of this is obvious; one should as well expect a Star Boat to outsail the big racing sloop *Yankee* around a fifteen-mile course as to expect a schooner to beat a clipper ship, or any small vessel to beat a big one, for that matter. It is an axiom in naval architecture that "other things being equal, the longest (or largest) ship is the fastest."

It was the realization of this rule that led to the use of "time allowances" in the racing of yachts of varying dimensions. Handicapping of this type is often unsatisfactory, and so class racing developed. If dissatisfaction existed with racing yachts, boat for boat, around a carefully measured course, what can be said about the comparison of the speed of ships

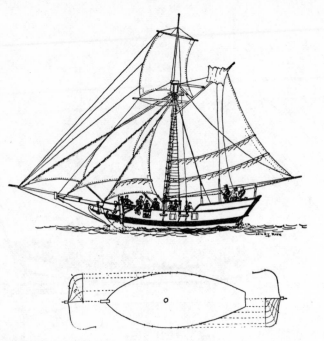

SLOOP FOR LAKE CHAMPLAIN 1777–80. SKETCH OF A PROPOSED AMERICAN VESSEL (NOT BUILT) DRAWN FROM A ROUGH CONTEMPORARY PLAN, DIMENSIONS UNKNOWN.

without regard to size? The method used by naval architects to place a value on a design in regard to speed is a simple one, though its accuracy depends upon the reliability of the information on which it is based. The speed of a vessel is expressed by a numerical factor, found by dividing the highest recorded rate of speed by the square-root of the waterline length. The vessel with the largest factor is the fastest design and is, therefore, the best design from the standpoint of speed as viewed by a naval architect. Here is a practical example: the schooner yacht *Sappho* built in 1867 ran 316 miles in 24 hours, her best rate of speed by the log being 16 knots. This run was made at sea in 1869 while crossing the Atlantic. The clipper ship *James Baines*, built by Mackay in 1854, made a 24-hour run of 423 miles in 1855, during which she went 21 knots by the log. She was 240 feet long on the waterline while *Sappho* was 121 feet. Which vessel has the better hull form for speed, or to put it differently, which is the faster design? By all usual comparisons, maximum recorded speed or the best 24-hour run, the *Baines* is the faster ship and, therefore, the faster design. But see what happens when length is taken into consideration. The square-root of the *Sappho's* waterline length is 11.000; dividing 16 by this we get the factor 1.455. The square-root of the *Baines'* waterline is 15.492; dividing 21 by this we get 1.355. Now, then, *Sappho* has a "speed-length ratio," as it is called, of 1.455 against the *Baines'* 1.355; the *Sappho* having the larger factor must be accepted as the faster hull design of the two. In short, foot for foot of waterline length she is a faster vessel. If the speed-length ratio of any vessel exceeds 1.250, it may be safely concluded she is a very fast vessel. It will be on this basis of comparison that the subject of speed will be discussed, hereafter. It will be observed that the highest speed of a sailing vessel is reached when the wind is about abeam or on the quarter.

Before entering into a discussion of the American naval ships, it is necessary to describe the various types of ships used for naval purposes. These descriptions apply only within the period of the American sailing men-of-war, 1775 to 1850. Sailing men-of-war were divided into classes in accordance with the number of their guns, arrangement of battery, rank of commander and, to some extent, the size and rig of the ship.

The first and largest type was the battleship, known as the "ship-of-the-line" or, for the sake of brevity, "liner." This class included ships carrying from 70 to 140 guns on two or more completely armed decks, with armed forecastle and quarterdeck in the smaller and earlier ships. At the time of the American Revolution, some navies classed ships carrying as few as 60 guns as of the "line," but these ships were dropped from this rating in nearly all navies during the last part of the eighteenth century. The American Navy had no ships-of-the-line in service until after the War of 1812, and even then never had very many ships of this type.

In some navies there were vessels carrying from 44 to 64 guns which were classed merely as "ships," with the number of guns prefixed. The "64-gun ship" of the British Navy was an example, but no vessels so rated were ever carried on the American Navy list.

The "frigate" was the next largest class; these vessels always formed the most important part of the American sailing Navy. From the beginning of the American Revolution to 1813 the frigate was usually a vessel officially carrying from 24 to 44 guns on a single flush gun-deck, and on both forecastle and quarterdeck, which were connected by gangways along the side during most of the period. Before 1785, most frigates seem to have been without gangways. As will be shown, the Americans were among the first to place guns on the gangways. After the War of 1812, the gangways and both forecastle and quarterdeck were armed, giving the ship the appearance of having two complete, armed decks; these were called "double-banked frigates." The popular classes of frigates in the American service were the 28, 32, 36, 38 and 44-gun vessels.

The ships carrying less than 24 and more than 18 guns on the gun-deck and armed quarterdeck were called "post-ships" in the British Navy; they were the lowest rate that a captain could command. Ships of less than 28 guns, in the French Navy, were classed as "corvettes"; some were flush-decked and some had armed quarterdecks. In service, some of the vessels of these classes were actually armed as frigates; the only vessel in the American Navy that might fall into this class was the *Cyane* taken from the British during the War of 1812, but all American vessels of 22 guns or less were called "sloops" if ship-rigged.

"Sloops" were a class of vessel armed on a single deck and sometimes on the quarterdeck, carrying less than 18 guns in the British Navy, and rigged as ships, barques, brigs, brigantines and snows. At certain times, the British Navy had schooner and cutter-rigged "sloops." In the American Navy the term "sloop" was usually applied only to the ship-rigged vessels of less than 24 guns. In the Revolution and in the quasi-war with France a few quarterdecked ship-sloops were built.

In the American Navy, armed vessels of the brig or brigantine rigs were called "brigs"; the British usually referred to vessels of this class as "brig-

DRAWING OF A SCHOONER PROPOSED TO BE BUILT ON LAKE CHAMPLAIN DURING THE REVOLUTION, RE-CONSTRUCTED FROM THE ORIGINAL IN THE POSSESSION OF MR. S. H. P. PELL.

sloops" or, if small, as "gun-brigs." All other vessels were classed according to rig as "schooner," "cutter," "sloop," etc. Small craft of one to four guns were usually classed as "gunboats" and this class included boats rigged as sloops, schooners, cutters, one-masted lateeners, two-masted lateeners (called "settee-rig") and lug-rigged vessels.

During the American Revolution and from 1794 until 1815 the Americans used vessels called "galleys." As might be expected, these craft were all fitted for rowing and were rigged as one- or two-masted lateeners, cutters, sloops and schooners. They ranged in size from 40 to 75 feet on deck and carried from one to twelve guns. The American galley, however, rarely showed a greater number of oars or sweeps than a schooner, sloop or cutter not so classed. In fact, the distinguishing feature of these galleys was often nothing more than light draft, though all of them showed sweeps.

Another class of vessel in use during the Revolution was the "gondola." This was a flat-bottomed and double-ended vessel, 40 to 60 feet long, cutter-, sloop- or hoy-rigged. The type was used a great deal on Lake Champlain. The British re-rigged one of these vessels, taken from the Americans, as a bomb-ketch. The gondola, as a rule, had neither deadrise nor rocker in her bottom and sometimes had flat sides in sections; at other times the sides had a little curvature. The gondolas all had deep bulwarks and gun-ports.

"Radeaux" were also used for harbor defense in the Revolution by both belligerent parties; they were merely square-ended "scows" or punts fitted with deep bulwarks, sweeps, gun-ports, and rigged as a schooner, cutter, brig, ketch or even ship. They ranged from 40 to 95 feet long. Though poor sailers to windward, they were by no means slow on other points of sailing. The British used a large ketch-rigged radeau on Lake Champlain against Arnold's squadron.

Many open boats, fitted with sails as auxiliaries to their oars, were employed in naval service alongshore and on the lakes. These included large round-bottomed whale-boats and square-sterned "barges." This class of boat carried one or two guns and had weather-cloths all around to mask the crew from small-arm fire when in action. "Bateaux" were similar but flat-bottomed and mostly sharp at both ends. These latter craft were found on rivers, bays, and lakes; they were very popular on Lake Champlain. The term "bateau" was also loosely applied to any rowboat. Some of the whale-boats, barges, and bateaux were large; 60-foot boats being not uncommon. All of these small-boat types used sails with fair winds, usually a single lateen sail, though some were equipped with two leg-of-mutton sails.

The employment in America of the radeau, gondola, and bateau as naval craft ceased at the end of the Revolution. The galley and barge

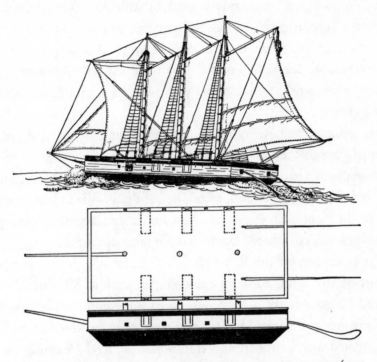

AMERICAN RADEAU, 1776–7. PROPOSED FOR LAKE CHAMPLAIN (NOT BUILT). DRAWN FROM A CONTEMPORARY PLAN, DIMENSIONS UNKNOWN. RIG NOT SHOWN ON ORIGINAL DRAWING.

survived until about 1825 as these types were found useful in West Indian service. All of these small war-time craft, however, were of little use in times of peace and were generally disposed of with the ending of hostilities.

The "fire-ship" was another class that receives occasional mention in American records. This was usually an old coaster, or other merchant craft, filled with combustibles and sent out to grapple enemy ships, and then set afire. The British, however, actually built special ships for this purpose, regular ship-sloops in appearance. These vessels were employed as sloops-of-war until they became old and weak; they were then used as fire-ships if the necessity arose. No vessels of this type were built by the Americans, though fire-ships were used a few times in the Revolution.

The "bomb-ketch" was rarely used by the Americans, though the Navy had a few brig-rigged vessels, carrying mortars, in service in the nineteenth century. One or two ketches were also employed. Bomb-vessels were only used for bombarding fortifications and were of little value for other work; hence they were purchased and fitted out when the need arose.

At the time of the Revolution most ships actually carried the same number of guns as they officially rated. The British Navy first employed the carronade in 1779, and the practice of not counting these cannon as "guns" led to much confusion, as can be seen later. The changes of gun-design in the American Navy can best be followed as the development of the ships is traced; this too can be left for later discussion.

At the beginning of the Revolution, of course, the Americans had no war craft of any kind. Some of the colonies, such as Virginia, Pennsylvania and Massachusetts, at first purchased small commercial vessels and fitted them out as cruisers. These craft were only suitable for attacks on weakly armed merchantmen and transports. General Washington chartered some small schooners for the same purpose; these are often referred to as the first ships of the American Navy. However, they cannot be classed as men-of-war in the sense that they could oppose the regular naval craft of the enemy. One fact that cannot be overlooked when inspecting the naval papers of this time is the complete lack of large, fast ships suitable for naval or privateering service. The merchantmen that were first employed for these services were almost complete failures. This led to the early construction of both men-of-war and privateers, designed with special regard to the conditions of their work.

By December, 1775, the Americans realized that they were facing a long-drawn-out war and one that must be prosecuted vigorously. No suitable ships being available for naval service, they ordered, on the 13th of that month, the building of thirteen sail, five to carry 32, five to carry 28 and three to carry 24 guns. These were followed, as the war went on, by three more frigates and three quarterdecked ship-sloops. In addition, a few frigate-built vessels and men-of-war were obtained abroad. The states also built men-of-war. Of the first thirteen seagoing ships of the Continental Navy that were built or designed as men-of-war, the 32-gun *Washington* was laid down at Philadelphia but was burned by a British expedition before she was complete. The *Raleigh* laid down March 21, 1776, at Portsmouth, New Hampshire, by John Langdon and James K. Hackett was a 32-gun frigate and was launched 60 days later on May 21st. The *Raleigh* was taken by two British ships, off the Penobscot on September 27, 1778, after being chased ashore. She was afterwards hauled off and purchased into the British Navy. The *Hancock*, 32 guns, built at Newburyport, will be described in detail further along. The 32-gun *Randolph* was built by Wharton and Humphreys at Philadelphia and was blown up in action with the British 64-gun ship *Yarmouth*, March 7, 1778. The *Warren*, 32 guns, was built by Sylvester Bowers at Providence, Rhode Island. To prevent capture she was destroyed in the Penobscot by her commander on August 14, 1779.

The 28-gun ship *Virginia* was built by a Mr. Wells at North Point, near Baltimore, Maryland. She ran aground and was captured by the British ships *Emerald* and *Conqueror* in 1778. Afterwards she was carried on the British Navy list as a 32-gun frigate of the same name. The 28-gun *Trumbull* was built at Chatham, Connecticut, and was captured off the Delaware by H.B.M. ships *Iris* (ex-*Hancock*) and *General Monk* (ex-*General Washington*, privateer) in 1778. She was taken into the British Navy as the *Tobago* and because of poor construction was reduced to 20 guns. The *Effingham*, 28 guns, was built at Philadelphia and burned by the Americans in 1778 to prevent her falling into the hands of the British. The *Congress*, of the same rate, was built at Poughkeepsie, New York, by Lawrence and Tudor; she was burned by her crew in the Hudson River, in 1777, to prevent capture. The 28-gun *Providence*, another ship built by Sylvester Bowers at Providence, was captured by the British at the fall of Charleston, South Carolina, May 12, 1780, and was purchased into the Royal Navy as a 32-gun frigate of the same name.

The 24-gun frigate *Boston* was built at Newburyport, Massachusetts, by Jonathan Greenleaf and Stephen & Ralph Cross. She too fell into British hands at Charleston and was taken into their navy as the *Charlestown*, 20 guns. The *Delaware* of the same rate was built at Philadelphia. She went ashore in the Delaware River and was captured. When the British got her off they added her to their navy as a 28-gun frigate of the same name. The 24-gun frigate *Montgomery* was built by Lawrence and Tudor at Poughkeepsie and, like the *Congress* built by the same firm, was destroyed in the Hudson River to prevent capture, probably at the same time.

All thirteen vessels were laid down at about the same time and those that were launched were in the water early in 1777. It will be noticed that these ships were built at widely separated points; this was due to the difficulty of obtaining enough skilled men and suitable materials in any one community for more than one or two ships. So few of the thirteen ships got to sea that it was necessary to lay down the other frigates and the ship-sloops during the same year.

The later frigates, three ships, were all apparently of 32 guns; the three ship-sloops were designed to carry 18 guns. The largest of the three new frigates was the experimental galley-frigate, *Confederacy*, built by Jedidiah Willets at Norwich, Connecticut, and launched in 1778. She was rated as a 32-gun ship though large enough to carry 36 with ease. She was largely employed as a packet by the Continental Congress until her capture by the British ships *Orpheus* and *Roebuck* off the Virginia Capes in 1781. She was afterwards carried on the list of the British Navy as the 36-gun frigate *Confederate*. Another of these frigates was the *Alliance*, designed and built by William Hackett at Salisbury Point on the Merrimac River. William Hackett was the best-known ship designer of the period, and one of the greatest American naval architects of the sailing ship era. He was born in Salisbury, Massachusetts, May 1, 1739, the son of William and Elizabeth Hackett. His father and an uncle, John, were shipbuilders, and William Hackett was so interested in ships that at the early age of 12 he was given permission to leave school to work in the shipyard. At the death of his father, before the Revolution, young William succeeded to the partnership with his uncle. The partners launched the *Alliance* in 1777; this ship was the only American-built frigate left in the Continental service at the end of the Revolution. She was sold out of service at Philadelphia on June 3rd, 1785, and was then employed for a time as an East-Indiaman; finally she was wrecked at the mouth of the Delaware River. The third frigate was built at Middletown, Connecticut; she was laid down in 1780 and launched in July, 1783, as the *Bourbon*. In September of the same year she was ordered to be sold, apparently incomplete. The *Bourbon* never received her armament and it is not known for certain whether she was designed to carry 28 or 32 guns.

Of the three ship-sloops, the *Ranger* was the most famous; she was built at Portsmouth, New Hampshire, in 1777. William Hackett seems to have been her designer, and his cousin, James K. Hackett of Portsmouth, the builder. The *Ranger* was another American ship that fell into British hands at Charleston, South Carolina, in 1780. She was taken into the British Navy as the *Halifax*. When first built, the *Ranger* was very much over-hatted (over-canvassed), having the spars of a larger vessel. The *Saratoga*, of the same rate, was built at Philadelphia in '77 and was lost at sea with all hands in 1780. The third of the class was the rather mysterious *General Gates*, of which little is known save that she was launched in 1777 and sold the next year.

The Continental Congress also resorted to the purchase or charter of ships abroad. They obtained the 28-gun frigate *Queen of France* in this manner in 1777. She was a French-built ship, as indicated by her name, and was sunk at Charleston in 1780, to avoid the fate of the *Ranger*, *Boston* and *Providence*. Another ship from abroad was the 32-gun frigate *Deane*, built at Nantes, France, in '77. In '82 she was renamed *Hague;* with the *Alliance* she shared the distinction of being one of the two frigates left to the Americans at the end of the Revolution. The only other vessels of much importance that were procured in Europe were the old French Indiaman *Duc de Duras*, the *Duc de Lauzon, Pallas*, and *Ariel*. The *Duc de Duras*, which under the name *Bon Homme Richard* should need no introduction to Americans, was purchased in 1779 and sank September 23, 1779, after her famous action with the *Serapis*. The *Duc de Lauzon* was purchased or chartered in 1782 and disposed of the next year, while the *Ariel*, a 20-gun ship, was borrowed from the French government in 1779 and returned later in that year, as was the *Pallas*, a 30-gun merchant ship.

Besides the two frigates, the *Alliance* and the *Hague*, left in the American service at the end of the war, there was a 24-gun "armed-ship," the *General Washington*. This ship had been built as a privateer and was, for this date and purpose, a large ship. After her capture by the British she was taken into their service as the *General Monk*. On April 8, 1782, she was retaken by the Pennsylvania State cruiser *Hyder Alley* off Cape May, New Jersey, and then bought into the Continental service where she remained until sold in 1784. Another ship that deserves mention is the *America*, ship-of-the-line. She was designed by William Hackett and was laid down at Portsmouth, New Hampshire, in May, 1777. Launched November 5, 1782, she was never fitted out as an American man-of-war, having been presented to France in September of that year. She is often confused with the French *America* captured by the British in the engagement of "the Glorious 1st of June" in 1794. The American-built ship was broken up in France about 1786.

In addition to these large vessels, the Continental Congress built a few small craft, such as the packet-ketch *Mercury* built at Plymouth, Massachusetts, toward the end of the war. In all, the Continental Navy was made up of about 53 purchased or chartered vessels, excluding those already itemized and the squadron on Lake Champlain. Some of these may have been armed vessels borrowed from the states; four were prizes taken from the British (of which one was a man-of-war brig) and four or five were purchased in France. This fleet of converted craft ranged from 24- and 20-gun ships down to 6-gun sloops and schooners, few of which accomplished much as men-of-war.

The state navies were usually made up of purchased and converted merchant craft, or of galleys and radeaux for harbor defense. There were a few large state-owned ships, however, which should be mentioned. Massachusetts possessed a 26-gun frigate named the *Protector* which was built in 1779. She was captured May 5, 1781, by H.B.M. ships *Roebuck* and *Media* and taken into the British Navy as the *Hussar*. The state of South Carolina bought a very large and powerful ship-of-war abroad, the French-designed and Dutch-built *Indien*. She was renamed the *South Carolina* but was captured by the British before she accomplished much. Another large ship of this class was the Connecticut state-ship *Oliver Cromwell* which was also captured by the British. In addition to these ships, the states had a few brigs and brigantines that were built entirely for war service, but they accomplished nothing of importance beyond annoying enemy commerce.

It would be fascinating to trace the history of all of the vessels that have been mentioned, but that is outside the field of this discussion. The history of the American Navy, based on modern methods of research and criticism, has yet to be written. The incomplete information in the hands of naval historians has led to grave errors that reflect on the Navy. A mere account of actions and personalities, without regard to naval policy and material, is insufficient.

It is now time to return to a discussion of ships in detail. It has often been said that no one had any experience in the design and construction of men-of-war in this country when the Revolution began. The last ship

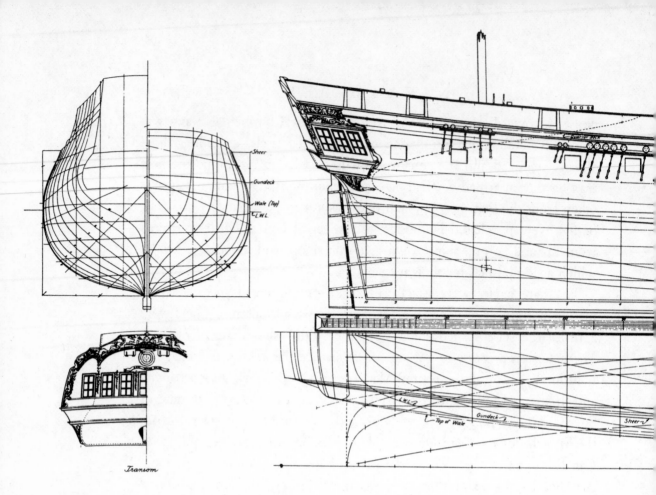

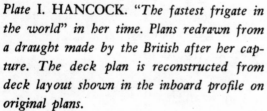

Transom

Plate I. HANCOCK. "*The fastest frigate in the world*" *in her time. Plans redrawn from a draught made by the British after her capture. The deck plan is reconstructed from deck layout shown in the inboard profile on original plans.*

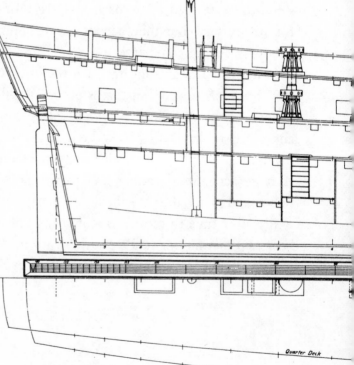

Continental Frigate
"Hancock"

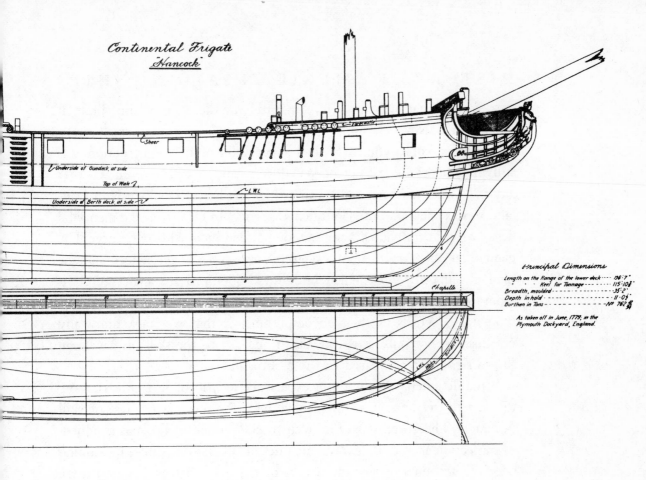

Sheer

Underside of Gundeck, at side

Top of Wale

LWL

Underside of Berth deck, at side

Chapelle

Principal Dimensions

Length on the Range of the lower deck ---- 136·7
Keel for Tonnage ---- 115·10¼
Breadth, moulded ---- 35·2
Depth in hold ---- 11·0¼
Burthen in Tons ---- N° 762 35/94

As taken off in June, 1779, in the
Plymouth Dockyard, England.

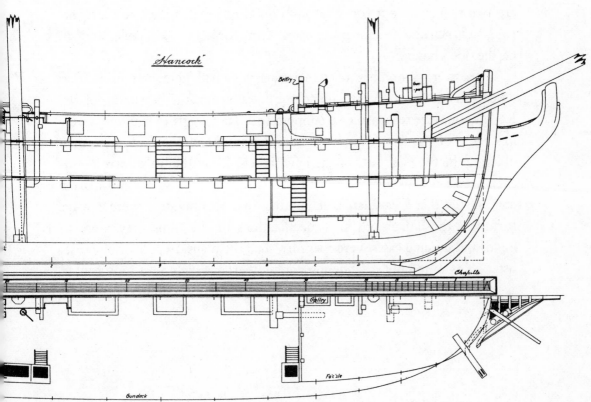

"Hancock"

Belfry

Gun port

Chapelle

Galley

Fo'c'sle

Gundeck

of this class that was built in America was the 44-gun ship built at Portsmouth, New Hampshire, in 1749, excepting a few small craft. Whether or not anyone who had supervision of her construction was still alive in 1775–6 cannot be stated, nor can it be discovered whether any men who had been trained in any of the Royal Dockyards in England were available to the Continental service. In fact, even the men who designed each individual ship cannot be identified with certainty. The claim that the American naval architects were inexperienced can be neither supported nor denied until these questions are answered. It is from the few surviving plans of the Continental frigates, and from contemporary records of their accomplishments, that we must draw any conclusions, not only as to this claim but also to the skill of American ship-designers as compared to those abroad.

If the designers were without experience in man-of-war construction, the first thirteen frigates should have been the most severe test of skill in design. Therefore, it will be well to choose one of these as a subject of inspection and to discuss the qualities of others if possible. In looking over the accounts of the adventures of the first thirteen frigates, there are two that stand out for all-around good qualities; these are the *Hancock* and the *Alliance*. Since the plans of the former are available, she will be the one chosen.

There were a number of Americans who had held commissions as officers in the Royal Navy and who came home at the beginning of the Revolution. It is reasonable to suppose that the Congressional committee in charge of naval matters had obtained the aid of some of these men in fixing the type and rate of the new vessels. From the little correspondence between the shipbuilders and the various Congressional and marine committees that is available, it appears that the builders were always furnished the dimensions and specifications of the ships they were to build, and in some cases were also furnished the plans. In at least one case, sister-ships were built in widely separated yards, which must be accepted as proof that building plans were furnished some of the builders. In most cases, however, the builder either re-designed the vessel to suit his own ideas or was commissioned to do the design as part of his contract. It is possible that the builders received a preliminary design on which to base the plans they submitted as a part of their contract.

Newburyport, where the leading ship-building firm was that of Jonathan Greenleaf and Stephen & Ralph Cross, was an important ship-building center in Revolutionary times. A member of this firm, Greenleaf, was in the state legislature during the war, and through this connection, no doubt, the firm obtained contracts for a state ship and two of the Continental frigates, a 32- and a 24-gun ship. Whatever methods were used to obtain so much work for the firm, there can be no question whatever of the ship-building skill of the partners.

There is no record as to who designed vessels for the firm. In one case there is some evidence that the firm built from plans made by others. There is one man who must be considered in this connection: William Hackett of Salisbury and Portsmouth. Hackett was building the 32-gun frigate *Raleigh* at the same time the Newburyport firm was building the two Continental frigates. While there is no direct evidence that he designed the *Raleigh*, it seems highly probable that he did, for it is known that he designed the frigate *Alliance* and the liner *America* in 1777. The *Raleigh* measured, when her lines were taken off in England, at the Plymouth Dockyard in 1779, 131'-5" on the range of the lower deck, 110'-7¼" on the keel for tonnage, 34'-5" beam and 11'-0" depth of hold; her tonnage working out at 696⁸⁰⁄₉₄ tons. The similarity of these dimensions, as well as a resemblance in lines to those of the Newburyport 32-gun frigate, points to the conclusion that Hackett was the designer of both vessels. On the other hand, these features might have been dictated by the preliminary draught, and so a definite conclusion cannot be reached.

The firm of Greenleaf, Cross & Cross launched their 32-gun frigate in 1776, under the name of *Hancock*. Though the vessel was in the water in '76, it was impossible to get her ready for sea that year as guns, ironwork, rigging, sails, ammunition and stores were difficult to procure. Captain John Manly, who in command of the Massachusetts state schooner *Lee* had been a very successful officer, was ordered to her early in 1777 and sailed her to Boston to finish fitting out. Manly was much pleased with his new command as she seemed to be a very fast ship. He hurried the fitting of his ship and apparently sailed from Boston June 23rd, though some accounts state that she got away in May. British accounts being more accurate as to what followed, the dates given in them will be adhered to. The 24-gun frigate *Boston*, under the command of Captain Hector McNiel, sailed at the same time, under Manly's orders.

On June 27th the two frigates sighted a strange sail near the Grand Banks and went in chase of her. She was made out to be a small British frigate, and both ships cleared for action. After a little manoeuvering to test the sailing qualities of the contestants, the British ship, having discovered that she was overmatched, made sail to escape. The *Hancock* quickly outsailed the *Boston* in the chase that resulted and was soon alongside the Englishman. A running fight then began which lasted for two hours, in spite of the superiority of the American ship. Out-sailed and out-gunned, the English frigate was finally forced to haul down her colors and was made a prize. One of the features of this action was the sportsman-like behavior of the American commander; so close were the ships during part of the battle that the gun-wads of the *Hancock* set fire to the main channel of the English ship. When this was discovered, the *Hancock* ceased firing until the flames were extinguished and then resumed her cannonade. The British ship was found to be the 28-gun frigate *Fox*, Captain Patrick Fotheringhame, and was placed in charge of a prize-crew.

The three ships then laid their course toward Boston, but contrary winds forced them to the northwestward. On July 6th they were sighted by a British 44-gun ship, the *Rainbow*, commanded by Sir George Collier, with H.B.M. brig *Victor* in company. The British vessels made all sail in chase of the Americans but lost them as night came on. At daybreak on the 7th, however, the American ships were again discovered with a sloop in company, which they had taken during the night. As soon as the British ship and brig approached the American squadron, Manly formed his ships in line of battle ahead and set all sail, burning the sloop while his vessels were forming.

Then began a long and gruelling trial of speed. The *Rainbow* was only 6 miles away from the American ships when the chase began. At about 6 o'clock in the morning another sail was sighted to leeward, which was soon discovered to be under British colors. Though she did not reply to the signals of the *Rainbow*, Collier was quite certain that she was the British 32-gun frigate *Flora*, Captain John Brisbane. After crossing the bows of the *Rainbow* and coming about on the same tack, she was finally identified as that ship.

The lack of training on board the American ships now became apparent, as they then broke formation; the ships hauling up on different courses. The *Flora* chased the prize *Fox* while the *Rainbow* pursued the *Hancock*, the brig having fallen so far astern as to be out of the race. The rest of that day and all the following night the *Hancock* and *Rainbow* trimmed sail and shifted ballast in a desperate test of speed. The English ship was clean and in trim, as well as sailed by officers who had been in her long enough to know how to get the best speed out of her. The American ship had been afloat for about a year and was foul with grass; her officers and crew had been in her but a couple of months (of which about two weeks were spent under sail), and were unacquainted with her best points of sailing or best trim. During the night Manly threw overboard some of his spare spars and his boats and also started his water casks, to lighten ship. In doing this, he trimmed the *Hancock* by the head which, according to the pursuing British officers, did more harm than good. At daybreak of the 8th, the two ships being only a mile apart, the *Rainbow* began firing her bow-chasers. The wind gradually lightened, giving the cleaner ship an increased advantage, so that at half-past eight that morning the *Rainbow* was within hailing distance of the *Hancock*. Collier called on Manly to surrender, but the wind showing a tendency to strengthen, Manly sent men aloft to set studding-sails. Observing this, the British commander fired a broadside into the American ship whereat she hauled down her flag. This chase extended over 36 hours. The highest speed reached by either ship appears to have been about 6 knots, as the wind was rather light during the whole time.

Manly was afterwards exchanged and, no other Continental ship being available for him, he went in command of privateers until the end of the war. The *Fox* was retaken by the *Flora*, but the *Boston* reached home safely, where her captain was cashiered for not supporting Manly and for breaking formation. The *Hancock* was taken into the Royal Navy under the name of *Iris*, as a frigate of the same rate.

The career of the *Iris*, ex-*Hancock*, in the Royal Navy was by no means devoid of incident. She was a favorite ship and it has been said that she made a fortune for her officers on the American station by capturing so many privateers and other craft. She had the reputation among British officers of being "the finest and fastest frigate in the world." In 1780 she fought an indecisive action with the French frigate *Hermione* and would have captured her had not another French ship appeared. In 1781 she overtook the 28-gun American frigate *Trumbull* and captured her after an engagement lasting about an hour, the armed-ship *General Monk* assisting. Late in that year she was captured by a French squadron in the West Indies and was then taken into the French Navy. Here she remained for many years, first as a cruiser and then, old and rotten, as a powder-hulk in Toulon harbor. There she was found by the British when Toulon was taken in 1793. When the British evacuated the place later that year, the *Iris* was blown up. At the time of her destruction she was the sole survivor of the Continental Navy.

During the spring of 1779 the *Hancock*, while in British hands, was sent home to England to be repaired, cleaned and coppered. While she was in the Plymouth Dockyard receiving attention, her lines were taken off (June, 1779). The plans of this vessel shown in Plate I are copies of the draughts made for the Admiralty at that time. Comparing the dimensions given on the plans with those given earlier for the *Raleigh*, it will be noticed that the chief variation was in length, the *Hancock* being 5'-2" longer on the lower deck. The *Raleigh* had more tumble-home and less deadrise in the mid-section than the *Hancock*, but otherwise the ships were very similar underwater.

The *Hancock*, as can be seen in the plans, was a very handsome little frigate. For a full vessel, her model is excellent and shows why she was so fast. The speed of these frigates, however, is hard to estimate, the records being scant. The American naval historian Cooper says that "one of the traditions of the service (U.S. Navy) states that the *Alliance* was chased this year (1782) by an enemy's two-decker and that she ran 15 knots by the log with the wind abeam in making her escape." The *Alliance* was probably a frigate of the same size as the *Hancock;* a speed of 15 knots in a ship of her length seems extremely high, though not impossible. The speed of the *Hancock*, on the speed-length ratio, would be 14.6 knots and, judging by her lines, she might have been able to reach it. Tradition, however, is notoriously unreliable, and the reported speed of the *Alliance* should not be taken too seriously. There is no question but that the *Hancock* and *Alliance* were very fast ships, even judged by later standards. It cannot be doubted that they could do 12 knots easily, as the scant records show that this speed was reached a number of times. The lines of the *Hancock* are of such nature that there would be little reason to doubt the accuracy of these accounts.

The appearance of the *Hancock* as an American ship, according to a contemporary eyewitness's description, is interesting as it adds to the information shown on the plans. Before she got to sea for the first time an English agent made the following Intelligence Report: "Hancock,— A man's head with yellow breeches white stockings blue coat and yellow button-holes; small cocked hat with yellow lace; has a mast in lieu of an ensign staff with a lateen sail on it; has a fore-and-aft driver-boom with another across; two top-gallant royal masts (poles?), pole mizzen top-mast; whole mizzen yard and mounts 32 guns; has a rattlesnake carved on her stern; netting all around the ship; stern black and yellow quarter-galleries all yellow."

In some details the description is a little vague, both as to rig and to paint. It is evident that she was really four-masted since she had a lateen sail set on a mast at the extreme stern in place of the usual tall flag-staff;

RIG OF MIZZEN MAST SIMILAR TO *Hancock's.*

this was a good-weather sail and perhaps was not always carried. It is difficult to say whether she had a lateen mizzen yard or a gaff. From the description, however, it is likely that she had a lateen mizzen yard with a boomed fore-and-aft sail set abaft the mizzenmast in place of the usual gaff sail or spanker. The reference to "another across" in relation to the boom indicates a "ringtail" or studding sail set at the outer end of yard and boom. This light sail was set "square" instead of fore and aft as in the case of the later "ringtail," which developed from this earlier sail.

Unfortunately, the spar dimensions of the *Hancock* have not yet been found. Those of the *Raleigh* show that she carried both "crossjack" and

68

"mizzen" yards, which indicates that she had a rig much like that of the *Hancock*. The spars of the *Confederacy*, however, show she carried a gaff spanker. But the rigs of the frigates built in New England were not exactly the same, as the *Boston* had a gaff spanker, though she carried the lateen sail and mast in place of the ensign staff like that on the *Hancock*. All of the American frigates seem to have carried a spritsail and topsail under the bowsprit.

The description of the painting of the *Hancock* is not entirely clear as to whether or not her sides were yellow, and her stern black or black and yellow. If the stern were black and yellow, which seems unlikely, then the color of the sides is not given; therefore it is quite safe to conclude that she had yellow sides. Some of the American ships of this period had black sides with yellow mouldings, or just plain black.

The other Continental frigates were somewhat different in design than those described. The *Virginia* and *Randolph* were built on the same lines and were therefore sister-ships, even though the *Virginia* was rated as a 28 and the *Randolph* was a 32. Both had small beak-head bulkheads, a feature then obsolete in frigates in the British Navy. The *Confederacy* also had this feature of construction. The former two frigates were somewhat similar in general design to the *Hancock* but much smaller, being but 126'-3½" long on the lower deck and 34'-10" extreme beam. The *Confederacy* was quite a different ship from any of the foregoing; she was nearly as large as the later 38-gun frigates of the *Constellation* class, measuring 159'-9" on the lower deck and 37' beam. In spite of her greater size she drew a little less water than the *Hancock*; she had a great deal of freeboard, enough so that she could use sweeps on her berth deck, galley-frigate fashion, and handle her cables there as well. In one respect, however, she was not really a frigate at all, for she mounted no guns on her forecastle. All three frigates sailed well and were good seaboats. The frigates built in Rhode Island were said to be the slowest of all, but proof of this is lacking. The small frigates varied in size as much as the large ones. The 24-gun ships were from 114 to 119 feet long on the lower deck, while the 28-gun ships were from 126 to 132 feet long.

The American frigates of the 32- and 28-gun classes were usually fitted with long 12-pounders on the main-deck and long 9's on quarterdeck and forecastle. The 24-gun ships usually carried long 9's and 6's. The *Hancock* probably had 26 long 12's on her gun-deck and 6 or 8 long 9's on forecastle and quarterdeck. The *Confederacy* carried 28 12-pounders on her gun-deck, and eight 6-pounders on the quarterdeck. The *Deane* carried 4-pounders on forecastle and quarterdeck. The *Alliance* carried 28 guns on her gun-deck, 12's, and 12 guns on forecastle and quarterdeck, 9's. The ship-sloops usually had 6-pounders. The small craft were armed with a miscellaneous collection of guns running all the way from 2- to 18-pounders. The long 12-pounder was from 8'-6" to 9'-6" in length; the 9's were from 7 to 9 feet; the 6's were from 6'-6" to 9'-0"; 4's were usually between 4'-6" and 6'-6" in length while the 2-pounders and half-pound swivels were from 3'-0" to 3'-6" long. The 18-pounders were about the same length as the 12's, though a number of guns shorter than the standards just listed were put on board American ships during the war. Lack of room aboard some of the vessels sometimes made these short guns necessary. As far as can be discovered, the American naval guns were all mounted on trucks; the pivot gun does not seem to have been used, though the mounting of this class was used in Europe.

The types of vessels used on Lake Champlain during the Revolution cannot be passed by without comment, for they represented special designs to meet a particular war service. Having one American-built schooner, two captured British schooners and one sloop, General Arnold rapidly added to the American force on the Lake three large galleys, one small cutter-galley, eight or nine gondolas, and had a fourth large galley under construction by the early fall of 1776. All of this squadron, except one schooner and the unfinished galley, took part in the action in October of that year. At the time of Arnold's famous battle, the British had one quarterdeck ship-sloop, one large ketch-rigged radeau, two topsail schooners, one American-built and ketch-rigged gondola, a large decked cutter-rigged long-boat and some armed rowboats.

The large galleys of the American squadron are particularly interesting. There were, as just mentioned, four of these vessels built, apparently sister-ships. Their names were *Washington, Congress, Trumbull* and *Gates*. Because of the shortage of guns of any one calibre, their armaments were rather peculiar. According to her captain's receipt of Octo-

Washington, LAKE CHAMPLAIN GALLEY, 1776.

ber 2, 1776, the *Washington* carried two 18-pounders, two 12's, two 9's, four 4's, one 2-pounder, and eight swivels. The *Trumbull* had one 18, one 12, two 9's, four 4's and swivels as in *Washington*. The *Congress* had two 18's, two 12's and six 6's, with the swivels added. The *Gates* does not appear to have ever received her full battery before her destruction. Arnold seems to have been responsible for the building of galleys on the lake, but who actually did the designing is not recorded. Arnold felt that the geographical features of Lake Champlain, long and narrow with the prevailing winds blowing lengthwise of the lake, made the galley the most suitable type of war vessel for this body of water. The same opinion seems to have been held by both American and British in later years, for galleys continued in use on the Lake until after the War of 1812.

The *Washington, Congress* and *Trumbull* were all built at Skenesboro (now Whitehall), New York, during the summer of 1776. The *Trumbull* joined Arnold's squadron on September 30th while the *Washington* and *Congress* did not join until October 6th. The records of the American squadron are far from complete, and there are errors in official reports. As far as is known, Arnold's squadron was composed of the following vessels, at the beginning of the action of October 11th: the flag-ship, *Congress; Washington* and *Trumbull*, galleys; *Lee*, cutter-galley; *Royal Savage* and *Revenge*, topsail schooners; *Enterprise*, sloop; and the nine gondolas, *Boston, New Haven, Providence, New York, Connecticutt, Spitfire, Philadelphia, Jersey* and *Success*. The British fleet included the ship-sloop *Inflexible*, radeau *Thunderer*, topsail schooners *Maria* (flag-ship) and *Carleton*, gondola *Loyal Convert*, one large long-boat and two smaller ones, as well as seventeen one-gun rowboats. The British ships and gunboats were armed with guns ranging from 6- to 24-pounders.

The *Congress* was run ashore and burned to prevent capture and the *Washington* struck her colors during the 13th. The *Trumbull* escaped from the action but was captured by the British the next year and appears to have been destroyed in Brown's Raid, September, 1777. The *Gates* was blown up at Skenesboro, the same year. The *Washington* was taken into the British lake-service and re-rigged as a brig. Under the same name and her new rig, she seems to have been employed until the end of the war. While in British hands, her lines were taken off. Figures 10 and 11 are copies of the Admiralty draught as taken off, except the bowsprit added by the British when they changed her rig, which has been omitted, and the transom, shown in the body plan, which has been added. This last detail was reconstructed from contemporary pictures of the British schooners *Maria* and *Carleton*, since the sterns of these schooners were probably very much like those on the American galleys.

The design of the *Washington* was fixed by other specifications than

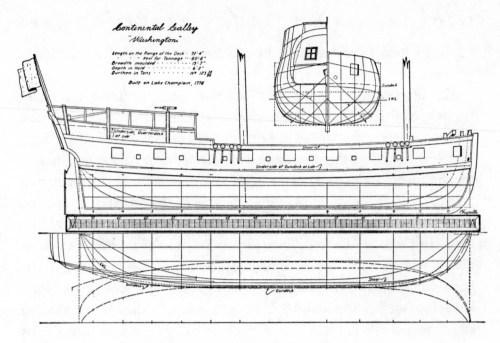

Figure 10. *Continental Galley* WASHINGTON *for Lake Champlain.*

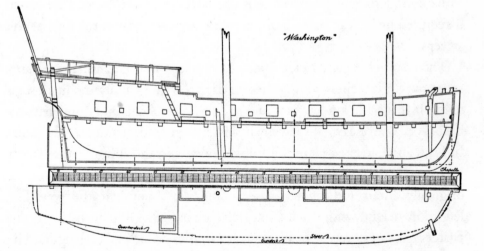

Figure 11. *Inboard profile and deck of the Galley* WASHINGTON.

73

the one which fixed her type. In building the vessels of his squadron, Arnold labored under great difficulties. Material, skilled workmen, ironwork, sails, rigging and guns were hard to obtain; practically everything required had to be brought from the coast. This naturally had much influence on the design of the vessels, as well as the necessity of getting a fleet in the water in the shortest possible time. Furthermore, men to man the ships were lacking. It can be easily seen how all these factors would limit the size of the vessels. On the other hand, the craft being built had to be large enough to carry as heavy a battery as could be procured for them. In the case of the galleys, there was also the problem set up by their method of propulsion. Sweeps were not particularly effective in large displacement craft with deep hulls. Then, too, shoal draft would be useful as it would enable the galleys to conceal themselves alongshore and to manoeuver in shallow water. Weatherliness was not particularly important, as the galley could be worked to windward under oars. A certain amount of speed, as compared with the usual sailing vessel, could be sacrificed for the same reason; still, too slow a hull must be avoided. In choosing a rig, the use of oars as well as the shortage of material had to be considered; for these reasons the lateen rig was decided on, since it required little gear and would interfere very little with the men at the sweeps.

The result of these considerations can be seen in the plans. The *Washington* was a judicious compromise in design, a gun-carrier modified so as to be manageable under oars and sail, having shoal draft and narrow beam, yet with heavy displacement in relation to dimensions. The short full run and entrance were skillfully formed and the speed of these craft was greater than would be expected at first glance. The *Washington*, as originally fitted and rigged, had two masts, about half the waterline length in height, with a yard on each. The yards, judging by very imperfect pictures, were about two-thirds the waterline in length. The plans show the simplicity of hull and fittings better than a lengthy description. The capstan, or "capstern" as it was often spelt, may have been a British addition.

The dimensions of some of the other vessels on Lake Champlain, both British and American, will give an idea of the size of some of the Revolutionary types of small men-of-war. The dimensions of the galleys can be obtained from the plates of the *Washington*. The cutter-galley *Lee* was of the following dimensions: length on the range of deck, 43'-9"; length

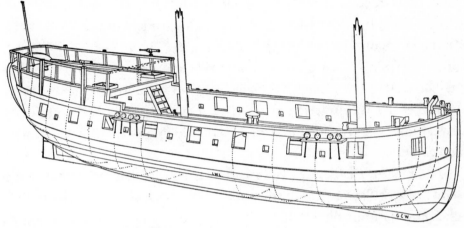

CONTINENTAL GALLEY *Washington*.

on the keel, 34'-0"; beam, 16'-3½"; depth in the hold, 4'-8". With four gun-ports and three sweep-ports on a side, and a short quarterdeck, the *Lee* was on a somewhat similar model to that of the *Washington*, reduced in size and fitted with a cutter rig (square-topsails).

According to the specifications that Arnold wrote himself, the gondolas were about 45'-0" long on the bottom, 16'-0" beam and 3'-6" deep in the hold. They appear to have been cutter- or hoy-rigged and to have had three guns. Arnold's specifications will be found in the Appendix. The dimensions of the *Royal Savage* and the other schooners and the sloop are unknown.

The dimensions of some of the British ships are as follows: the schooner *Maria*, length on the range of deck, 66'-0"; length on the keel, 52'-2¼";

beam, 21'-6"; depth in hold, 8'-2½". She had eight gun-ports on a side and five sweep-ports and was fitted with cutwater and figurehead. Her model was a little like that of the *Washington*, but deeper.

The schooner *Carleton* measured 59'-2" on the range of deck, 46'-10" on the keel, 20'-0" beam and 6'-6½" depth of hold. She showed seven gun-ports on a side, but had no sweep-ports and no cutwater or figure-head. She was much like the *Maria* in model and, like that ship, had a short quarterdeck.

The gondola *Loyal Convert* was a double-ender, measuring 62'-10" on the range of deck, 50'-8" on the keel, 20'-3" beam and 3'-7½" depth of hold. She had four gun-ports on a side and one on each side of the stem and stern-post. She was originally sloop- or cutter-rigged and had been built by the Americans on the St. Lawrence. She had a perfectly flat bottom, sides rounded in section, rather long quarterdeck and sunken forecastle.

The radeau *Thunderer* was a large example of her type. She was a scow, nearly flat on the bottom—about 6" deadrise—with raking ends like those seen on the ordinary scow of today. She had deep bulwarks all around and nine gun-ports on a side, with two in the transom and per-haps two in the bows. She had a very short high quarterdeck and was rigged as a bomb-ketch. Her sides curved, both in plan and section; her ends were about two-thirds the beam amidships. She was 91'-9" long on the range of deck, 72'-0" on the keel, 33'-4" beam and 6'-8" deep, in the hold. The dimensions of this strange craft, so contrary to the imagined picture of vessels of her period, show the surprising size of some of the "small" men-of-war of the Revolution.

The plans, dimensions and descriptions of some of these men-of-war are sufficient to give an idea of the problems in the design of war-vessels during the early period of United States history. Except for the annoy-ance they gave enemy shipping, the Continental frigates and small craft accomplished comparatively little. The failure of the Continental Navy as a whole, however, cannot be traced to poor ships, or even to the lack of war material. It was due primarily to the lack of trained seamen and of experienced and disciplined officers. So far as naval policy was concerned, the Revolution should have taught that it is quite impossible to build up a navy on short notice. Ships can be built, guns manufactured and war supplies gathered, but officers cannot be taught their profession in the short period of a few months, or even years. Nor can seamen, in a short space of time, be trained and given the education that will enable them to have confidence in their officers and in their service. So far as the art of ship-design and construction was concerned, the Americans had become aware of the advantages of large and fast vessels and had learned a little about the problems of their construction.

The years between 1784 and 1794 represent an experiment in that modern remedy for national ills, disarmament. The navy was totally disbanded in 1784 and the veteran troops, the "Continental Line," no longer had the status of a regular army. Fear of a possible military autocracy was the chief cause for this, though the loose confederation of the states and lack of money must be counted as contributing factors. The nation had no foreign entanglements, was tired of war and desired to "mind its own business." By its nature, the Revolution fathered that curious and unreasoning attitude of American thought, the "defensive war." The precepts of naval and military discipline are objectionable to a democratic people, which may account for the American's lack of sympathy for the military and naval profession in time of peace. In addition, the Revolution left the suicidal idea that, in time of war, the people needed only "to rush to arms to repel the invader" and thus win victory.

There was yet another consideration, which must be mentioned in order to understand the peculiar naval policy this country has usually followed. Though the confederation of states, later the United States, was a maritime nation, its people as a whole had neither interest in nor sympathy with naval affairs. Even in times of American naval activity only a small proportion of Americans was involved; those living along certain sections of the coasts and on the Great Lakes. The greater por-

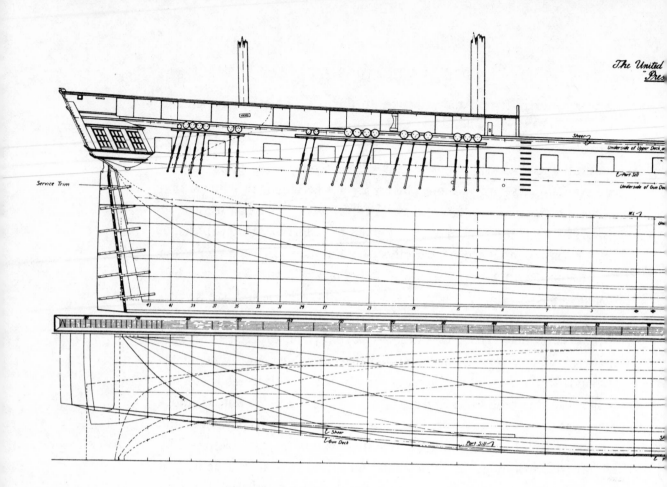

Service Trim

Sheer
Underside of Upper Deck
Port Sill
Underside of Gun De

WL

Shear
Gun Deck
Port Sill

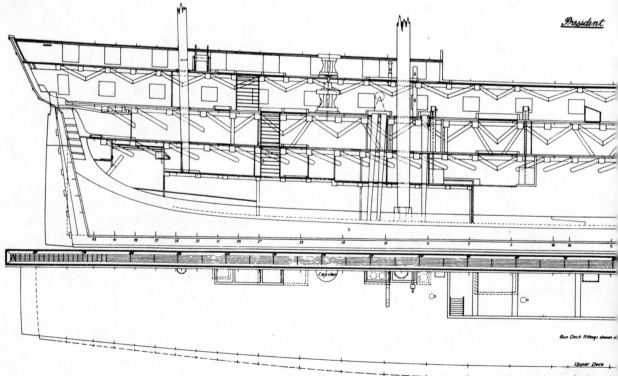

President

A

Capstan

Gun Deck fittings shown i

Upper Deck
Gun Deck

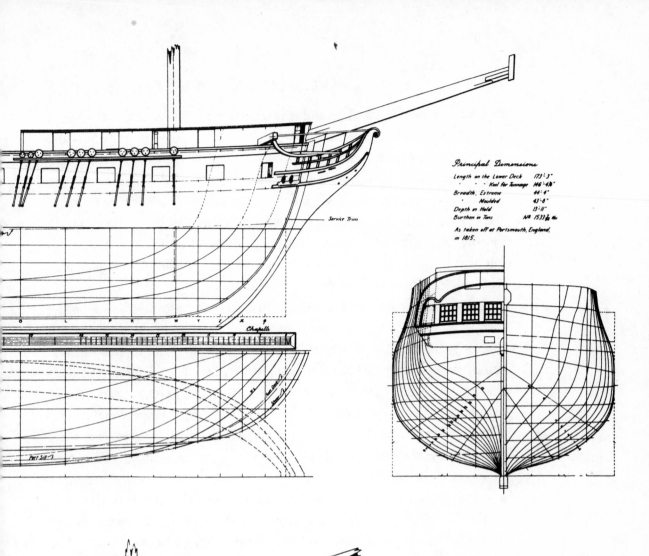

Principal Dimensions

Length on the Lower Deck	173'-3"
" " Keel for Tonnage	146'-4½"
Breadth, Extreme	44'-4"
" Moulded	43'-8"
Depth in Hold	13'-11"
Burthen in Tons	N° 1533 58/94 ths

As taken off at Portsmouth, England,
in 1815.

Service Trim

Chapelle

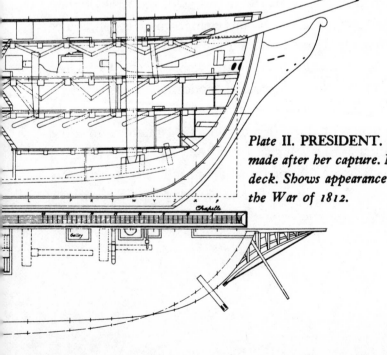

Plate II. PRESIDENT. Redrawn from a British Admiralty plan made after her capture. No reconstruction except in plan view of deck. Shows appearance of the American 44-gun frigates during the War of 1812.

tion of the people lived inland and therefore had no interest in such matters. People on the coasts, acting as individuals, could build ships and gain maritime prestige, but before the government could build and maintain a navy it had to have the voted permission of the majority living inland. Naturally it was always difficult to obtain this permission, since these voters felt the tax-money could be spent to better advantage in improvements close at home. This had considerable effect on the building of American men-of-war and, though rather a political matter than a nautical one, must nevertheless be appreciated.

The experiment was not successful and only proved that a nation merely courts war by weakening itself. It is not within the scope of this discussion to describe the steps by which the realization of this old and often taught fact was brought home to the people and government of the United States. By 1794 Congress had at last passed the necessary legislation to build naval ships and to reform the national navy. Arrangements were made for the building of six frigates; contracts were placed, supervisory organizations set up, designs decided on and appropriations made during this year. The resulting vessels were the famous 44- and 38-gun frigates of the *Constitution* and *Constellation* classes.

These frigates have been the subject of more mis-representation and mis-understanding than any other sailing ships in maritime history. The designers of the individual ships have been confused, the basis of their designs has been mis-represented, the various changes in their appearance and fitting have been garbled, and even their rating has been muddled; in fact, the confusion in accounts of these frigates seems endless. Even governmental and other supposedly authoritative publications have made serious mis-statements that have added to the tangle.

The basis of the design of these frigates offers a tempting subject as the first step in an attempt to get at the truth. For years there has been a parade of authorities telling glibly of the "French influence" on the design of American sailing ships as a whole, and on these ships in particular. Cooper, one of the first American naval historians, led the parade, and it has continued ever since. In fact age seems to have given the claim an air of sanctity. At the risk of committing heresy, however, it is time that the truth of this claim be examined.

In the first place, the truth of the existence of "French influence" could be proven in two ways, by specific reference to it in the writings of contemporary naval architects or by comparison of design features in American ships with those of the French. The statements of the numerous writers who have supported this claim may be divided into three classes. The first state that the lines of French frigates were taken off while they were in dry-dock in America during the Revolution and that these lines were used afterwards as the foundation of design, in men-of-war at least. On this basis, the claim has been advanced that the Continental frigates, as well as the later classes, were on the French model. The second state that the lines of French "luggers" were taken off on their visits to America, before or during the Revolution, and that these plans were the parents of the Baltimore clipper and all fast-sailing American craft. The third say that the designers of the *Constitution* and *Constellation* class of frigates modelled their ships on French lines without attempting to explain the source of such lines or plans.

There can be little question that the French took the lead in naval architecture during the last portion of the seventeenth century. Not only were French ships faster and better built than those of other nations, but they were larger in relation to their class. The reputed superiority of French design was founded on this fact; in time it became a tradition. Though the French maintained their lead well into the eighteenth century, their leadership was in jeopardy by the middle of the century. Examination of French and English plans shows very conclusively that the French superiority was, by 1750, a matter of relative size rather than of hull-form. The tradition of French superiority was so firmly established in England, however, that the copying of French ships continued for many years and resulted in some curious situations. For example, a small English frigate overtook and captured a much larger French frigate in

79

what appears to have been a fair test of sailing. This should certainly have proven the superiority of the English model in all but size. The Admiralty, however, permitted the copying of the French frigate in a new class, but because of service conditions, on a reduced scale. The result was that the Anglo-French design was uncommonly slow. Existing plans support the contention that English-designed ships were the equal of the French, with but few exceptions, from the time of the American Revolution on. But until the Americans began to build frigates in 1794, the French continued to lead in the size of their ships.

There was naturally much variation in French designs and it is not easy to find elements of hull-design that could be called "French" during the years between 1745 and 1810. However, examination of a large number of plans of French ships of all rates built during the period in question led to some conclusions. In nearly all large men-of-war, from the ship-sloop to the ship-of-the-line, built by the French during these years, the stem and stern-post were about perpendicular, with little or no rake. This gave very hollow waterlines in the lower portion of the under-body, one of the most noticeable features in French sailing men-of-war generally. The mid-section was nearly always like that of the *Swift* whose lines are shown in Chapter One, except that the French ships had an exaggerated angularity of section. The French brigs—and a few ships—had hollow garboards and much deadrise, as a rule, while the luggers, cutters and schooners had a straight, or nearly straight, rise at the garboards. These small craft also had the same lack of rake in the ends mentioned in regard to the large ships, though there was an occasional exception. Class for class, the French ships were usually the largest in all dimensions.

When the various statements concerning the "French influence" on the design of American sailing ships are studied, the fact that none of them ever give a definite example of an American ship built on French lines or identify any French vessel whose lines were ever taken off in America will be apparent. The mere fact that the statements are so vague and at variance shows a lack of real evidence. By considering each of the three classes of claims in turn, it will be possible to place a value on the tradition.

The writers who have claimed that the lines of French vessels were taken off while they were in dry-dock, either before or during the Revolution, can be quickly disposed of, for there were *no* dry-docks or marine railways, either private or government-owned, in the colonies or in the United States until after 1815. An inspection of the "American State Papers" will show that the lack of such facilities led to the first proposal for navy yards and docks in 1799. The first naval ship to go into a government dry-dock was the ship-of-the-line *Delaware* which was docked at the Gosport Navy Yard (Norfolk, Va.), June 17, 1833, and the private dry-docks and railways were not in use at New York, Boston or other ports until after the War of 1812.

Before dry-docks were built in this country, it was necessary to heave a ship down on her side at some convenient wharf to do any underwater repairs. It would be almost impossible to take off the lines of a large vessel in this position. When some naval ships were rebuilt during the early nineteenth century, they were hauled out on a wharf built for the purpose, but there is little likelihood that this was ever done in Revolutionary times because of the difficulty and expense. As a matter of fact, the only record of a French-built ship having received underwater repairs in this country before 1795 was that of the *Flora*, soon after the Revolution. This was a British frigate that had been taken from the French before the Revolution and that had fallen into American hands after being scuttled in Narragansett Bay. After the war, the Americans raised and repaired this vessel, and then sold her to her original owners, the French. There is no indication that she was hauled out, but she was hove down at Providence, Rhode Island.

To some extent, the foregoing remarks discount the claim that the French luggers were the parents of the fast American schooners of the Baltimore Clipper type. In addition to what has been said about dry-docks and hauling out, there is the fact that, as a matter of record, the lugger was not employed as a man-of-war by the French Navy until about 1775, some time after the American clipper-schooner had appeared. There is not the slightest evidence that luggers of the privateer type had operated on our coasts before the Revolution. To put the matter plainly, the attempt to show the connection between the French lugger and the American clipper-schooner is based on nothing other than ignorance. It is not difficult to prove that what foreign influence there was came, not from France, but from the Bermudas and so, indirectly, from the West Indies. The "Maryland Gazette" of August 27, 1761, printed the following advertisement: *"To Be Sold by Joshua Edmondson*, living in Vienna, the Hull of a Vessel, now on the stocks and nearly finished, of about 85 tons, built of exceedingly good well ſeaſoned white oak Timber and very much on the Bermudas mould." The specific mention of "mould" instead of "construction" leaves no doubt that hull-form or model is referred to, rather than a method of building. So conclusive is the evidence that further comment seems unnecessary.

Those writers who have stated that the *Constitution* and *Constellation* frigate-classes were designed under French influence rarely attempt to give any authority for the claim. As a result it is most difficult to offer any rebuttal. A careful search for the source of this claim has brought it to light, however. It is a report of Joshua Humphreys dated December 23, 1794, and may be found in the "American State Papers" (Naval Affairs), Volume XIV, page 8; it reads as follows:

"December 23, 1794"

"As soon as Congress had agreed to build frigates, it was contemplated to make them the most powerful, and, at the same time, the most useful ships. After the most extensive researches, and mature deliberations, their dimensions were fixed, and I was directed to prepare the draughts; which was accordingly done and approved. Those plans appear to be similar with those adopted by France, in their great experience in naval architecture; they having cut down several of their seventy-fours to make heavy frigates; making them nearly of the dimensions of those for the United States. ****** " The remainder of the report dealt with details of construction and material.

The third sentence of this report has been construed to mean that the American frigates were built on French ideas as to model, but the whole sentence points to a reference to mere size rather than to model. The specific reference to the cutting down of 74-gun ships and to "dimensions" can leave little doubt as to the true meaning of the sentence. It would be difficult to interpret the sentence as referring to "mould" or "model," except by disregarding the last portion of the statement entirely. Yet, on this interpretation, the claim for the "French influence" on the design of the American frigates was founded!

There is one piece of evidence in support of the theory of "French influence" that at first seems conclusive. In the John Paul Jones and Benjamin Franklin Papers in the Library of Congress there are some letters that refer to the matter in question. On March 25, 1780, the Admiralty Board at Philadelphia wrote to Franklin, who was in France, and in a postscript stated "the board would be highly obliged to your Excell'cy to send them drafts" of the latest French ships of war, as models for the American Master-shipwrights. This letter Franklin forwarded to Jones, June 1, 1780, and Jones applied to François Genêt on August 9th as follows, "P.S. I have received a request from the Honorable Board of Admiralty of Philadelphia that I should make a (sic) intrest with M. De Sartine for Plans of Ships of War and Frigates that have been constructed for the King since the Treaty of Alliance. I do not care to trouble the Minister again with my Letters before I sail; but I beg you to present my Best respects, and if he can Spare a few of the most Approv'd Plans I shall think it a great Additional Obligation confered on me." Jones also promised to take care that any plans given him would not fall into enemy hands. An unsigned and undated reply, erroneously attributed to La Vendahl in the Jones Callender, but in the handwriting of Genêt and probably of August 23, 1780, refuses the request and suggests that Franklin should make application instead of Jones. Nothing more is to be found among these papers relating to the matter. It would seem that the plans were not obtained; but if they had been, it is only necessary to point out that they would have come much too late to have any influence on the design of Revolutionary frigates and too early to be of use as guides for the *Constitution* and *Constellation* classes. There is no mention of the French plans in the naval records, and so it is highly probable that they were not procured.

During the early years of the French Revolution a few French shipwrights settled at Baltimore, and on this ground some writers have based a claim for the "French influence." The only contemporary reference to their influence is an advertisement in the "Maryland Journal and Baltimore Universal Daily Advertiser" of June 17, 1795, offering a schooner for sale "of pilot boat construction" which was "nailed and finished after the French manner." The distinction between type and finish in this advertisement is obvious, hence there can be no claim, based on this evidence, that these French shipwrights influenced the design of Baltimore craft. Furthermore, the draughts of schooners built near or in Baltimore, dated prior to the arrival of the French, show that the sharp American schooner had been fully developed by that time. A comparison of draughts of these schooners, dated before and after the coming of the French, fail to indicate any changes in basic design which would support the claim for "French influence" resulting from the arrival of the French shipwrights at Baltimore.

So far as the comparison of the plans of any American frigate or small vessel with those of the French is concerned, twenty-eight draughts of American vessels, of various types and sizes dated between 1775 and 1814, were chosen at random and compared with forty French draughts of vessels of the same general types and sizes. There could be but one conclusion, namely, that there were always marked differences in the designs of vessels of the two nations. The only feature that can be said to have been common to both was large size in relation to type or rate.

There would be no difficulty, after such a study, in separating the plans by nationality, without reference to titles or inscriptions. Comparison of the draughts of American ships with those of other nations shows the American to have been most closely related to the English designed ships not designed under "French influence."

In conclusion, it can be pointed out that the British, in copying our frigates, never confused the French with the American type and always made a distinction between them. Like the tradition of the "invention" of the schooner, or the "invention" of the clipper ship, the claim for "French influence" is based on the desire to find a simple and dramatic explanation rather than the less inspiring tale of a slow evolution.

It has long been customary to credit Joshua Humphreys as the designer of all the frigates built before 1812, except the *Essex*. This assumption is not based on fact. In 1794 a Congressional committee investigated the requirements for a navy and made recommendations. The Secretary of War, Henry Knox, was then ordered by President Washington to arrange for the design and construction of the required ships. It is impossible to follow by reference to the published State Papers the process by which this was accomplished, but it appears that the Secretary consulted numerous shipbuilders, merchants and Revolutionary naval officers, as to dimensions, armament and other features. One of the shipbuilders he consulted was the Philadelphian, Humphreys. Joshua Humphreys was a Quaker of Welsh descent, born at Haverford, Pennsylvania, in 1751. He seems to have served an apprenticeship as a shipwright, but whether or not he completed his "time" is uncertain. At any rate, in 1775 he was a partner of the Philadelphia shipwright Wharton, under the firm name of Wharton and Humphreys. This firm built the Revolutionary frigate *Randolph* and, possibly, some of the others that were laid down at Philadelphia. There is some question, however, whether or not the firm designed any of the Revolutionary frigates. By 1794 the firm was probably the leading one in the Philadelphia district. It has been stated that Humphreys was then the leading naval architect in the United States, but this

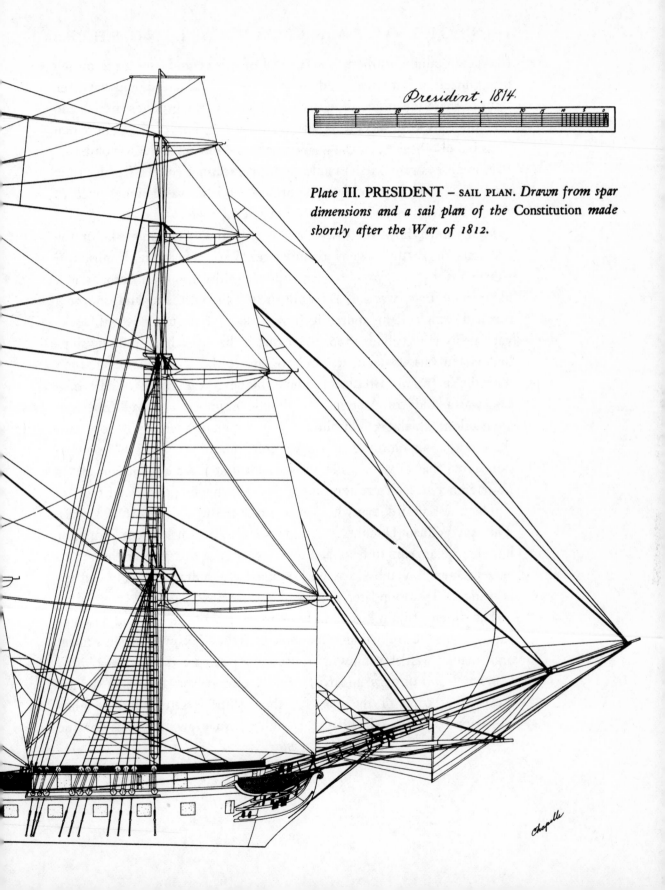

President. 1814.

Plate III. PRESIDENT – SAIL PLAN. *Drawn from spar dimensions and a sail plan of the* Constitution *made shortly after the War of 1812.*

Chapelle

is a mere opinion, as there is no record of this claim being made during his connection with the building of frigates. Hackett should have the right to share this distinction, it would seem, on the grounds that he had been not only very successful with the design of some of the Continental ships but also because of the quantity of his work since the Revolution.

Humphreys submitted a model and specifications for the frigates that, with some modifications, were approved, and he was commissioned to design the frigates and, later, to build one of them.

Humphreys, however, was not the only man so appointed, for the Secretary of War also went to another shipwright, a young Englishman named Josiah Fox. Fox was the son of a wealthy English merchant and, like Humphreys, was a Quaker. Born in Falmouth, England, in 1763, Fox had completed his apprenticeship as a shipwright in the Royal Dockyard at Plymouth about 1786. After that he had travelled, studying shipbuilding in various countries, and coming to the United States in 1793 with the intention of returning home the next year. His particular mission was a study of American shipbuilding timber. Fox had American connections which brought him to the attention of Secretary Knox, with the resulting appointment as a naval constructor. Humphreys' commission shows that Fox was to be his assistant, but Fox's commission makes no reference to such a relationship; this led to much friction later on.

There was a third man who played a part in the design of these vessels. This was William Doughty, born in Philadelphia. Little is yet known of him, but he appears to have had some experience as a shipwright and to have been employed by Fox and Humphreys as a draftsman. He will appear in this discussion later, as a naval constructor.

The papers of both Fox and Humphreys are in existence, and by comparing them the following facts come to light. Fox, who was a skillful draftsman as well as a shipwright, drew the plans for the frigates *United States* and *Constitution*, apparently under Humphreys' direction, though the existing copy of the plan for these ships is signed by Doughty and is probably an office-copy. Doughty also drew the plans for the

President and for the smaller *Constellation* and *Congress*. As a result there is some doubt as to the relative importance of the work done by each man in the development of these designs. It seems most likely that Humphreys should receive credit for the designs of *United States, Constitution, Constellation, Congress* and the first design for *President*. The best way to give the credit for the remaining frigates will be to describe each class and individual separately.

Theoretically the three 44's were sister-ships. The first one to go down the ways was the *United States*. She was built by Humphreys himself at Philadelphia and launched May 10, 1797 (State Papers). This frigate was said to be the heaviest built of the three 44's, as well as the slowest, and because of her lack of speed she received the nickname "Old Wagon." But after her spars were altered and masts shifted, some years afterwards, her speed was much improved. Yet she was never a fast ship, though a useful one. She lasted, with the aid of numerous rebuildings, until the Civil War, and was one of the ships scuttled and sunk when the Federals abandoned the Norfolk Navy Yard, April 20, 1861. She was later raised and used as a receiving ship until 1866 when she was finally broken up. Her chief claim to fame was her capture of the British frigate *Macedonian*, October 25, 1812.

The *Constitution* was built at Boston, Massachusetts, under the supervision of George Claghorne. She was built in the yard of Edmund, Joseph and Edward Hartt, though there is no evidence that they did any work on her. Perhaps they merely leased their yard, but on the other hand the quality of their workmanship, as shipbuilders, won them a later contract, and so it is quite possible that they acted as foremen in the construction of the frigate. The *Constitution* was launched October 21, 1797, after two unsuccessful attempts due to insufficient inclination of the ways. Her career is too well known to need further mention.

The third, and in some respects the most interesting of the 44's, was the *President*. This frigate was laid down at New York at the same time as the others of her class. The well-known New York shipbuilder, Foreman Cheeseman, was in charge of her construction. There was a joker in the law authorizing the six frigates which said that in the event of peace being made before the completion of these ships their construction was to cease. Peace having been made with Algiers in 1795, the work on all frigates stopped until Congress passed a supplementary act. This new act permitted the completion of the frigates that were far advanced in construction; these were the *United States, Constitution* and *Constella-*

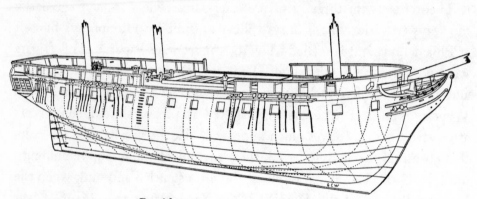

UNITED STATES FRIGATE *President.*

tion. But for lack of timber and other reasons, the *President* was not far enough advanced to warrant completion under the new act. At the time work ceased on her, the keel was set up and about one-fourth of her frames were ready. An important proportion of her live-oak timber had been lost when a schooner carrying them had gone ashore on Cape Hatteras.

It has been thought that the frigates built at this time were ships that were wholly satisfactory, but this was not quite the case. All of the new frigates were in the nature of experiments, for nothing approaching them in size and type had ever been built in this country, except the earlier *Confederacy* and the liner *America.* The result was much delay in their construction (the official explanation was difficulty in procuring timber, but changes in construction accounted for considerable lost time), and many changes in fittings after being commissioned. Officers and the naval constructors did not all agree that ships of such great size as these were the best for the service. Fox and Captain Truxton in particular were opponents of the big ships, while Humphreys and Captain Barry, with others, defended them. The disagreement between Fox and Humphreys on this matter was of long standing, as will be seen later.

In 1798 the impending trouble with France once more brought attention to the need of a navy and Congress made appropriations for more ships. Among the new projects was the completion of the *President*. Christian Bergh, a young and able shipbuilder of New York, was now made the master-builder and Doughty became the naval constructor. Doughty was permitted to make some changes in the lines of the new ship in order to increase speed. After some delay to make the necessary alterations, work started and the ship was launched April 1, 1800. When complete, the *President's* dimensions were the same as those of the *Constitution* and *United States*, but she was more lightly built and had slightly less freeboard.

Like her classmates, the *President* originally had a flush sheer from the stern to the foremast, as shown in the oft-published plan of the *Constitution*, with the same break down to the forecastle and gun-ports along the gangways amidships. The *Constellation* draught also shows this feature. At first the *President* had a figurehead representing Washington, but this was soon removed and a billet substituted. The *President* sailed on her first cruise August 5, 1800. She was a favorite ship because of her speed and appearance and served as flag-ship in the Mediterranean in 1801–2 and again in 1804–5. She was on the American coast from 1809 to the War of 1812. In 1811 (May 16th) she attacked the British ship-sloop *Little Belt* (ex-Danish) and shot her to pieces in ten minutes. There was much argument afterwards as to which ship fired the first shot, but both sides appear to have been anxious to fight. The Americans thus got revenge for the attack on the *Chesapeake* in 1807. During the War of 1812 the *President* was a flag-ship, first of Commodore John Rogers, then of Commodore Stephen Decatur, until her capture by the British.

When war was declared, the *President* with the *United States, Congress, Hornet* and *Argus* were in New York. Rogers put to sea on June 21st and cruised to the southeast hoping to meet the valuable "plate fleet" which was bound from Jamaica to England, with a British frigate and brig acting as convoy-guards. Early on the morning of June 23rd, however, the American squadron sighted the British 36-gun frigate *Belvidera* and went in chase. After a long pursuit in light weather, the *President* got within gun-shot, but, after firing a few shots with her bow-chasers, one of her main-deck guns burst, wounding the Commodore and killing and wounding many of her men. This accident caused some confusion in the American ship which, combined with some mis-management afterwards, allowed the English ship to escape. In the chase the American ships were led so far away from the course of the West Indian fleet that the latter escaped. After a short cruise during which a few unimportant prizes were taken, the American squadron returned home. The *President* made an uneventful cruise the next year and took 13 prizes, and only three in 1814.

In 1815 the *President* was again at New York with a squadron, this time under the command of Decatur. On the 14th of January she put to sea during a heavy snow storm which had blown the British blockading squadron off their station. Unfortunately, the *President* grounded getting out and pounded heavily for an hour before floating. In this situation she had torn her copper, sprung her masts and hogged her hull enough to leak badly. When the British reappeared on the morning of the 15th they sighted the damaged *President*. After an all-day chase one of the British ships brought the American to action. This was the 40-gun frigate *Endymion* which after two hours of a running fight was put out of action. Soon afterwards, the British frigates *Pomone* and *Tenedos* overtook the crippled *President* and, after a few broadsides from the *Pomone*, the American frigate surrendered.

The *President* was an interesting and valuable prize to the British, among whom her speed was common knowledge. In spite of her serious injuries she was taken into the Royal Navy, after some repairs had been made, but the ship was never serviceable. While she was in the Portsmouth dock being repaired, in 1815, her lines were taken off; these are shown in Plate II, her sail plan in Plate III. The *President* was broken up at Portsmouth two years afterwards. Subsequently the British built a frigate on her lines, slightly modified, and with the same name. This ship was also very fast and was one of the few older ships that could sail with the Symonds-designed ships of the Royal Navy in the 30's and 40's.

Comment on the plans of the *President* is required in view of the numerous published plans of her classmate *Constitution*. The plans of the *President* are valuable, as there are no other plans of these 44's that show their appearance during the War of 1812. There are numerous errors in the "restored" *Constitution* which can be found by comparing the plans of the *President* with those of the *Constitution* published by the government.

The question of how fast a ship the *President* really was cannot be answered, but contemporary accounts show that she was always looked upon as being faster than the *Constitution*; the latter is on record as having gone 13½ knots and could probably make 14. In light weather a frigate such as the old *Hancock* might outsail the *President* due to the easier run of the older ship, but in a breeze the bigger ship would overpower the smaller. In all but size the *President* represented the highest development in frigate-design, for she combined the desired features of her class to such a degree that no marked changes were made from her model in the best of the later frigates. Extra speed could be had only at a sacrifice of the fighting qualities of the type.

Returning to 1797, this year saw the launch of the first of the 36-gun frigates, the *Constellation*. She slid down the ways on September 7th at Baltimore, Maryland. David Stodder was the naval constructor in charge of her building, Captain Truxton assisting as naval superintendent. The *Constellation* had a long and distinguished career and is still afloat, though it must be admitted that there is little or nothing of the original ship left.

She has been completely rebuilt a number of times, from the keel up, as in 1805–12 when she was widened 14 inches and again in 1854 when she was lengthened and cut down one deck, each time her lines being altered to some extent.

The *Congress*, her sister-ship, was one of the frigates whose completion was delayed by the peace with Algiers. She was built under the supervision of the skilled James Hackett at Portsmouth, New Hampshire, and was completed in 1799, going to sea for the first time in December of that year. She was intended for the East Indian station, but was dismasted very soon after her start and returned home. This frigate had the most uneventful career of any American man-of-war of her date and after spending much of her life rotting in "ordinary" she was broken up at Norfolk, Virginia, in 1836.

These two ships, as first built, measured 163'-7" on the gun-deck, 40'-0" moulded beam and 13'-6" depth of hold. In appearance they resembled the 44's, reduced in size. Though built as 36's they were raised to 38's before being armed, as they were sufficiently large to carry the increased battery. It was originally decided that all of the 36's and 44's should carry 24-pounders on the gun-deck with long 12's on forecastle and quarterdeck, but this battery was discarded before the ships were fitted. The batteries of these ships varied a great deal from year to year, but the "establishment" was the following: the 44's carried 30 long 24-pounders on the gun-deck and from 20 to 22 carronades, 42-pounders, on the quarterdeck and forecastle. The *Constitution* was an exception, however, as she carried 32-pounder carronades in place of the 42-pounders. In addition, these frigates usually mounted a pair of long chase-guns on the forecastle. The 38's usually carried 28 long 18's on the gun-deck and 20 carronades, 32-pounders, on the forecastle and quarterdeck.

So far, five of the six ships of the two classes are accounted for. The sixth was the ill-famed *Chesapeake*. This frigate was originally laid down as a 44, like the *Constitution*. Because of the lack of labor and materials she was not far enough advanced in construction to be completed when the peace with Algiers was made, and so her building was cancelled; much of the timber intended for her was used to finish the *Constellation* at Baltimore. The *Chesapeake* was to have been built at Norfolk, Virginia, under the supervision of Josiah Fox and Captain Richard Dale. When she was again ordered to be put under construction she was reduced to a 38. Fox and others had long maintained that the other big frigates were so large as to be unhandy; they were also critical of the lines on which they had been built. There is some mystery as to whether or not Fox was ordered to re-design the vessel; at any rate he did. The *Chesapeake* was launched June 20, 1799, and measured 155'-0" on the gun-deck, 151'-0" on the berth-deck, 127'-5" on the keel, 40'-4" moulded beam and 13'-9" in the hold. She was a very handsome and fast ship, but was dogged by misfortune throughout her career. Her first serious misadventure was the attack upon her by the British *Leopard* in 1809, and her last was her capture on June 28, 1813, by the *Shannon* off Boston Light. She was taken into the Royal Navy and was broken up about 1820, another ship of the same name being afterwards built to replace her in the British Navy.

After the peace with Algiers, the American government had to build a 36-gun frigate, an 18-gun brig and an armed schooner as tribute to the Dey of Algiers. The frigate was the *Crescent* designed by Fox but built by Hackett. The brig was the *Hassan Bashaw*, which was designed and built by Humphreys. The schooner was named the *Skjoldebrand;* she was designed by Benj. Hutton, Jr., and built by Nathaniel Hutton, both of Philadelphia. These ships were all constructed between 1796 and 1798, and gave additional experience to American shipbuilders in the design of small men-of-war.

The building of frigates did not stop with the six 44's and 38's, for Fox designed the *John Adams*, 28-guns, which was built in 1799 by the citizens of Charleston, South Carolina, and presented to the United States. Fox also designed the 44-gun frigate (reduced to a 38) *Philadelphia,*

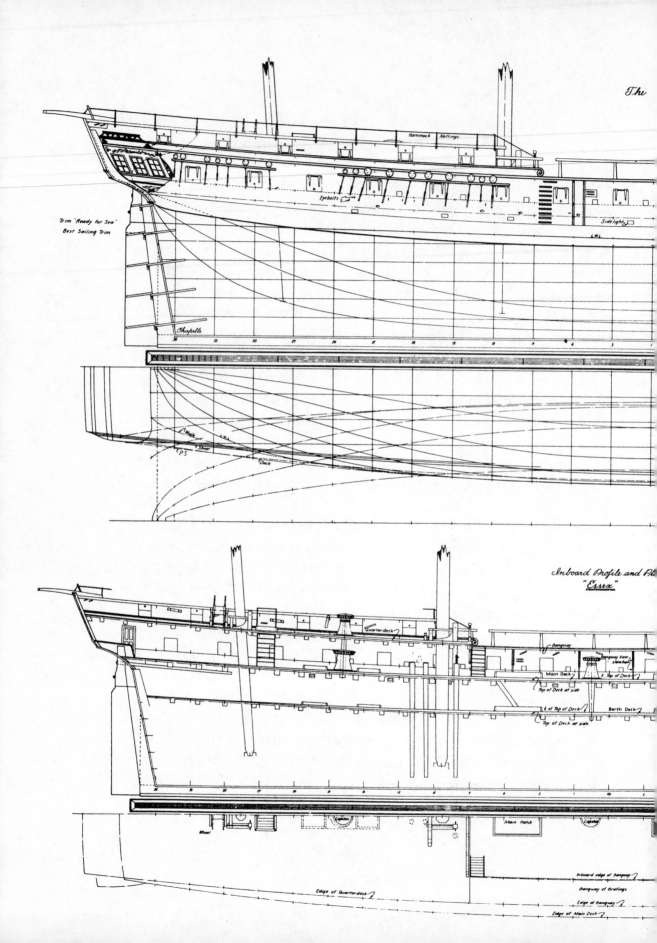

The

Trim 'Ready for Sea'
Best Sailing Trim

Hammock Nettings

Eyebolts

Sidelight

L.W.L.

Chapelle

Walk
L.W.L.
f.p.s.
Deck

Inboard Profile and Pl.
"Essex"

Quarterdeck

Gangway

Gangway knee
sheathed

Main Deck

Top of Deck at side.

£ of Top of Deck

£ of Top of Deck

Berth Deck

Top of Deck at side.

Wheel

Capstan

Main Hatch

Capstan

Edge of Quarterdeck

Inboard edge of Gangway

Gangway of Gratings

Edge of Gangway

Edge of Main Deck

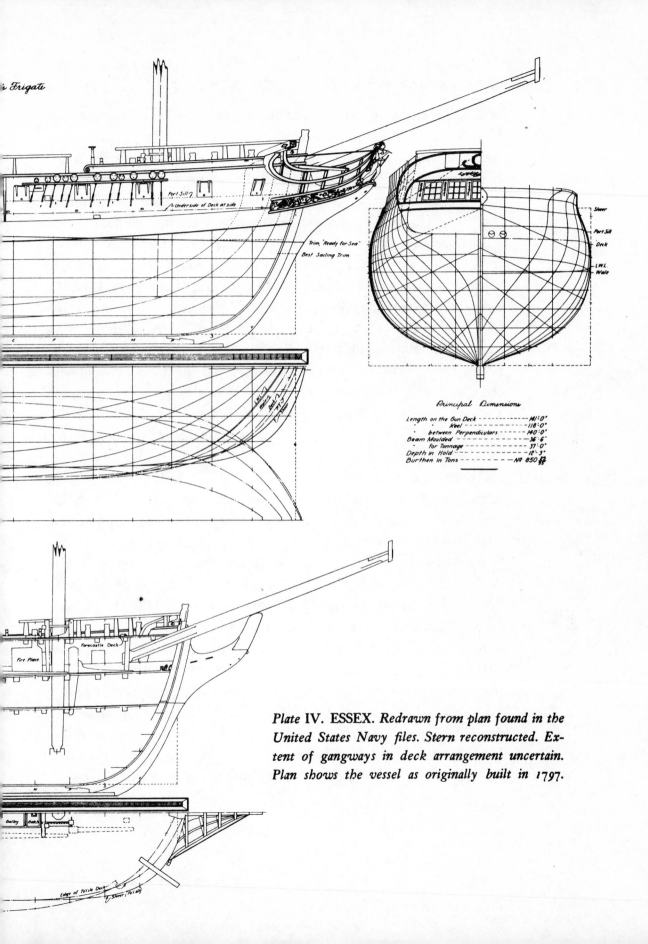

's Frigate

Port Sill 7
Underside of Deck at side

Trim "Ready for Sea"
Best Sailing Trim

Sheer
Port Sill
Deck
L.W.L.
Wale

Principal Dimensions

Length on the Gun Deck ------------ 141'0"
Keel ------------ 118'0"
between Perpendiculars ------------ 140'0"
Beam Moulded ------------ 36'6"
for Tonnage ------------ 37'0"
Depth in Hold ------------ 12'3"
Burthen in Tons ------------ N° 850

Forecastle Deck
Fire Place

Galley   Hatch

Plate IV. ESSEX. *Redrawn from plan found in the
United States Navy files. Stern reconstructed. Ex-
tent of gangways in deck arrangement uncertain.
Plan shows the vessel as originally built in 1797.*

Edge of Fo'sle Deck
T. Sheer (Fo'sle)

built at that city by its citizens and likewise presented to the government. New York citizens presented the beautiful 36, *New York*, designed by Samuel Humphreys, while Salem citizens went to Hackett for the design of a 32, the *Essex*, which was built by Enos Briggs at Salem, at the expense of citizens of Essex County, Massachusetts. She was launched September 30, 1799, having been built in a little less than six months.

Her plans are shown in Plate IV and Figure 12; these were redrawn from Hackett's original draught and Briggs' spar dimensions, the carving being reconstructed from a contemporary painting. The transom is wholly a reconstruction without authority, as no drawing or picture of it could be found. The reference to "nettings all around" in regard to the *Hancock* can be understood by referring to the sail-plan of the *Essex*. The Salem frigate was very much like a Continental frigate in lines and general appearance. Her history has been published so often that repetition is not required here. Considering her size, she was a fast ship, but her sailing was much hurt by a change in armament and other alterations before the War of 1812.

Citizens of cities and towns built a number of vessels for presentation, in addition to those just mentioned, including the 28-gun *Boston*, 24-gun *Merrimack*, brig *Richmond*, 20-gun *Maryland* and 20-gun *Patapsco*. The government also built the 28-gun *Adams* at New York, the 28-gun *General Greene* at Warren, Rhode Island, the 24-gun *Portsmouth* at Portsmouth, New Hampshire, the 24-gun *Connecticut* at Middletown, Connecticut, the brig *Norfolk* at Norfolk, Virginia, and the brig *Pinckney* at Charleston, South Carolina. The last two brigs are sometimes referred to as having been purchased, with six other ships. Nine small galleys were also built. In 1799, two 12-gun schooners were also built, the *Enterprise* and *Experiment*, at Baltimore. By 1800 there was a respectable navy, but the end of the quasi-war with France and the attitude of Jefferson's administration ended further improvement. Except for the *Constitution* and *Constellation* classes of frigates, the *Philadelphia, Essex, New York, Boston, General Greene, Adams, John Adams* and the schooner *Enter-*

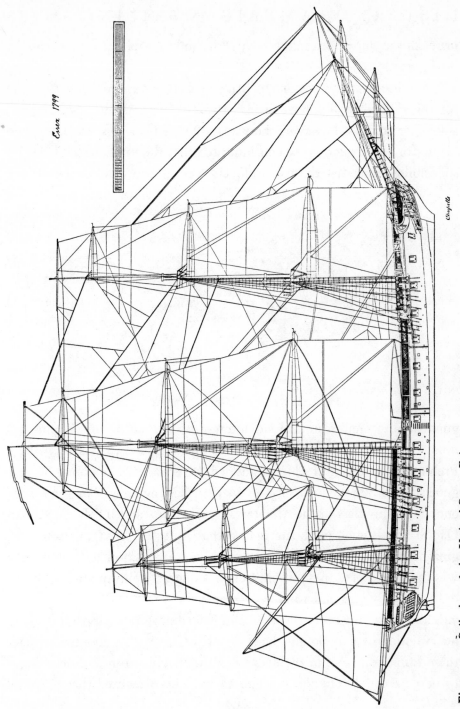

Essex 1799

Chirjetta

Figure 12. Sail plan of the United States Frigate ESSEX, *1799.*

95

prise, all the ships were sold out in 1801, and Humphreys and Fox were discharged.

It has been quite common to blame Jefferson for the reduction and for the ridiculous "gunboat-mania" that followed. The "State Papers" and other sources, however, show plainly that Congress was largely to blame for the reduction, which indicated that the public shared the responsibility, and that the naval officers were guilty of encouraging the

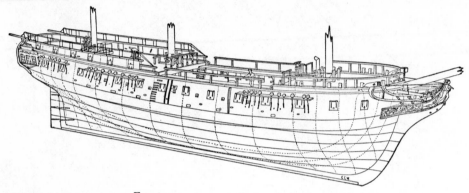

UNITED STATES FRIGATE *Essex*.

gunboat idea. Jefferson had no interest in the navy, nor did his administration; the only thought that Congress had was to save money. Preble and other naval officers advised Jefferson that gunboats were a good substitute for regular ships-of-war, an idea encouraged by the experience with this class in the Mediterranean in 1803 and by the success of Danish and French gunboats against the British at about this time. Beginning in 1803 with five experimental gunboats, a flotilla of about 168 was built by 1811. In 1799 an Act of Congress appropriated a million dollars for six 74's and for establishing navy yards. The frames for six 74's and their guns were obtained and placed in storage, apparently with no intention of completing the ships. The idea was, of course, to have these frames on hand in the event of war, at which time the ships were to be completed. Though it seems to have been realized that it would take nearly three years to build a 74, it does not seem to have been understood that three years, in time of war, is a long time, a period in which the enemy might take an unpleasant interest in the completion of the ships. However, the bright idea was never tried out, for the stores of seasoned timber represented by these frames proved too attractive to the gunboat builders and were converted to their use or to building other small craft. The loss in this operation was tremendous, but, after all, this has long been recognized as a necessary feature of American naval operations and policy.

The gunboats were an odd collection of different designs and sizes of galleys, cutters, sloops and schooners. The largest and last-built were schooners, about 75′ on deck. The earliest were only about 45′ long. Eight of these early gunboats crossed the Atlantic in 1805, on the way to the Mediterranean; they were Nos. 2, 3, 4, 5, 6, 8, 9 and 10. No. 7 also started but had to put back on her first attempt; on her second she went missing with all hands. The armament of these gunboats went through many changes, but usually they carried a 32- or a 24-pounder medium gun on a pivot and a small carronade on a truck carriage. No. 5 is shown in Figure 13 and gives some idea of the appearance of these little pots. When she crossed the Atlantic her gun was stowed below and her rig changed to a sloop. She also had a false keel added. It is said that when ready for the trip across, No. 5 only had about a foot of freeboard. Her crew consisted of a commander, a second officer, a steward, 15 able seamen, a corporal of marines and four privates. She left Washington for Hampton Roads May 1, 1805, and sailed for the Mediterranean May 15th. She reached Gibraltar June 17th and entered Syracuse July 8th or 9th. During August she operated with the American squadron off Tunis and then wintered at Syracuse. She returned home the next summer, arriving at Charleston, South Carolina, July 21, 1806, and was laid up at the Norfolk (Gosport) Navy Yard. It is interesting to find that she received 50 ash oars, 25 to 27 feet in length, when she was fitted out.

She cost $2,500.00 and was built under the supervision of Col. John Stricker and Master Commandant John Shaw. She was designed by Fox and built by Price at Baltimore.

The loss of only one of these little tubs is surprising and one must speak with respect of the seamanship and nerve of the officers and men

GUNBOAT NO. 5.

who took them to the Mediterranean and back. The designers of all the gunboats are not recorded, but Fox not only designed No. 5, but No. 3 and some of the later and larger boats; he may have designed them all. Only four plans of this class are known to exist, and so the details of the various designs are imperfectly known.

The reduction of 1801 stripped the navy of constructors, but Humphreys and Fox, though no longer regular employees, did work for the navy in 1803 and '04; in May of 1804 Fox was re-appointed a naval constructor. He remained in this position until he was discharged without cause in August, 1809. Joshua Humphreys was never re-appointed, for

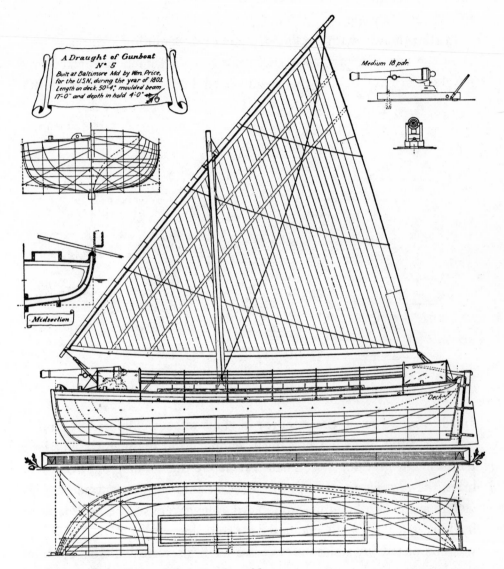

A Draught of Gunboat
Nº 5
Built at Baltimore Md by Wm Price,
for the U.S.N. during the year of 1803.
Length on deck, 50'-4", moulded beam
17'-0" and depth in hold 4'-0"

Medium 18 pdr.

Midsection

Deck

Figure 13. *United States Navy Gunboat No.* 5.

99

some reason, though during the last year of his employment he made a survey of certain locations in view of establishing navy yards, which led to later consultations.

In 1803 the war with the Barbary powers brought home to the government the fact that privateers could not be relied upon to replace small naval craft. Thus another theory advanced during the reduction of 1801

Vixen, 1803.

failed to work out in practice, for obvious reasons. The navy found itself, as a result, with but one small schooner and nothing else but large frigates. The need for more small craft led to the building of two 18-gun brigs, the *Hornet* and *Wasp*, the first at Baltimore by contract and the second at the Washington Navy Yard. They were sister-ships, designed by Fox, and were both converted to ship-sloops, the *Wasp* before she was completed. In addition, two smaller brigs were built by contract, the designs to be furnished by the builders to meet the approval of the supervising naval officer. The results were the brigs *Syren* and *Argus*, the former designed and built by Benj. Hutton, Jr., at Philadelphia, the latter by the Hartts of Boston, in whose yard the *Constitution* had been built.

Another pair of 12-gun schooners was ordered and, because of the success of the earlier *Enterprise*, it was proposed to build them on her lines. However, it was found that the plans of *Enterprise* were lost, and as a suitable schooner was found at Baltimore, she was purchased and named *Nautilus*. It is interesting to notice that in none of the correspondence relating to the schooners was the name of the designer of the *Enterprise* mentioned. He must have been known to the authorities, but there is no suggestion that another plan of the vessel might be obtained from him, though this would be an obvious course. It is difficult, for this reason, to decide why Benj. Hutton, Jr. was chosen to design the remaining schooner unless the unproven theory that he had designed *Enterprise* is accepted. The insistence of the Secretary of the Navy that the new schooner must be like the *Enterprise*, even in signing the contract for the vessel, is worth some consideration. Hutton got out a plan for the building of the new schooner which was sent to William Price at Baltimore, who had built the *Enterprise*. The new vessel was launched June 24, 1803, under the name of *Vixen*. Her draught is shown, re-drawn, in Figure 14. The various pictures of this schooner do not agree as to whether she actually carried the false quarter-galleries or not. She probably had a vixen (female fox) as a figurehead. The lines show the beauty of this little schooner and there can be no doubt that she was fast. The *Vixen* was a fore-and-main topsail schooner until about 1807, when she was converted to a brig and her sailing spoiled. Captain Tingey of the Washington Navy Yard seems to have been guilty of changing the schooners to brigs, but whether or not he had anything to do with the *Vixen* cannot be stated. The *Enterprise*, *Nautilus* and *Ferret* were all converted to brigs by 1811; the Fox-designed *Ferret* which had been built in 1804 even received a new name, *Viper*, as well as a new rig in 1810. The *Vixen* served in the Mediterranean and on the American coast until November 22, 1812, when she was captured by the British frigate *Southampton* in the West Indies. Both vessels were wrecked soon afterwards in the Bahamas.

The similarity of the *Vixen* to the *Enterprise* is a problem that cannot be solved. The *Enterprise* was completely re-built, from the floor-timbers up, at the Washington Navy Yard in the fall of 1811, and also received extensive changes earlier. After 1811 her hull form was very different

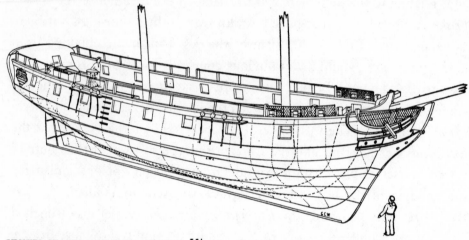

UNITED STATES SCHOONER-OF-WAR *Vixen*—14 GUNS.

from what it had been originally, and there was also much change in dimensions. Hence it is difficult to use the existing hull dimensions of *Enterprise* in a comparison with *Vixen*.

After Fox was discharged, there was no building until 1813. In that year, February 8th to be exact, William Doughty was made naval constructor. Apparently he had been operating a shipyard at Georgetown since the reduction of 1801. He was stationed at the Washington Navy Yard, and though never officially a chief-constructor, he acted in that capacity for many years. His first designs were for three new 44-gun frigates (six were ordered but apparently the money for three was used for ships built on the Great Lakes) and six large ship-sloops. The three frigates were within inches of being the same dimensions as the *President;* they

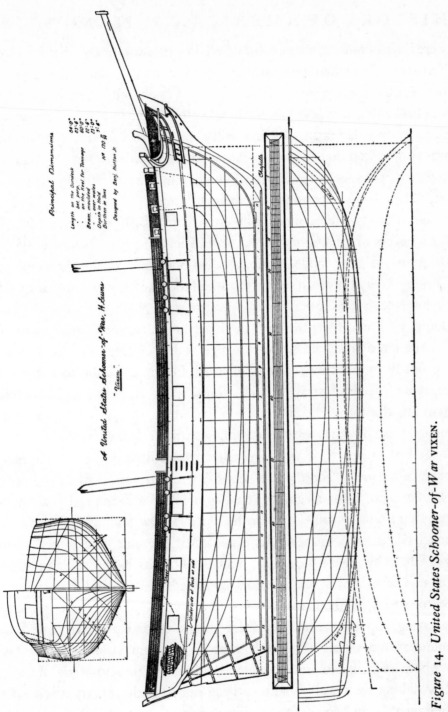

Principal Dimensions

Length on the Gundeck .... 84'-0"
    "   bet. perp. .... 83'-6"
    "   on the Keel for Tonnage . 60'-0"
Beam, moulded .... 22'-6"
    "   over wales .... 23'-0"
Depth in Hold .... 7'-6"
Burthen in Tons .... № 170 32/95

Designed by Benj. Hutton Jr.

A United States Schooner-of-War, N. Guns
"Vixen."

103

Figure 14. United States Schooner-of-War VIXEN.

were the *Columbia*, *Java* and *Guerrier*. The first was never finished, being burned in 1814 when the British took the city of Washington. The *Guerrier* was built at Philadelphia in 1814 by Joseph and Francis Grice; she was broken up in 1841 at Norfolk, Virginia. The *Java* was also built on contract by Flannigan and Parsons of Baltimore in 1814, and in 1842 was also broken up at Norfolk. These ships carried 33 long 32-pounders and 20 carronades, 42-pounders. Though on the same draught, these two frigates probably were different in appearance.

The six ship-sloops were built on two plans, three on each. Unlike his predecessors, Doughty was a firm believer in the advantages of the Baltimore Clipper model. Probably his long stay on the shores of the Chesapeake had given him a great admiration for vessels on this model. Seeing a chance to experiment on a large scale in the design of the new sloops, he drew one plan with the extreme Baltimore Clipper in mind. This design represented a ship with a great deal of drag to the keel, drawing nearly twice as much aft as forward. Her mid-section had about 23 degrees of deadrise, straight rising floors, and there was a slight tumble-home in the topsides. There was a little rake to the stern-post and a moderate amount forward. The ship was flush-decked and had a short topgallant forecastle. The design called for a ship 117'-11" on the range of the deck, 97'-6" on the keel, 31'-6" moulded beam and 14'-6" depth of hold; pierced for 22 guns, excluding bridle-ports, and rating as an 18-gun ship-sloop. On this draught the *Ontario*, *Erie* and *Argus* were to be built. The last was burned at Washington at the same time as the *Columbia*. The other two sloops were built by Thomas Kemp at Baltimore in 1813. The *Erie* was rebuilt and lengthened in 1820 and broken up at Boston in 1841. The *Ontario* was sold out in 1843, after some years as a receiving-ship at Baltimore. These sloops carried 20 carronades, 32-pounders and 2 long 18's. Both ships had the reputation of being fast, but because of the combined drag to the keel and the square-rig of a ship, they did not steer well. Had they been rigged as three-masted schooners they would have been much handier vessels.

In the second plan, Doughty used much less drag to the keel, but in other respects the draught was a duplicate of the first, even to general dimensions. From this were built the *Wasp, Peacock* and *Frolic*. The first was built at Newburyport, Massachusetts, during 1813 by Cross and Merrill. The latter gentleman is said to have invented the lift type of "half-model," but this is very doubtful. A model, reputed to be his original one, is still in existence; tradition has it that the model represents the *Wasp* but this is not true. The *Wasp* was one of the most noted of our men-of-war and after a very remarkable career was lost at sea with all hands; no trace of her ever was found. The second of the three on this draught was the *Frolic*, built by Josiah Barker at Charlestown, Massachusetts, at the same time the *Wasp* was building. She was a very handsome ship, and very well finished. The *Frolic* was captured, after a 60-mile chase, April 20, 1814, near Matanzas, Cuba, by H.B.M. frigate *Orpheus* and H.B.M. schooner *Shelburne*. Taken into the Royal Navy as the *Florida*, she was employed as a coast-guard ship for a while and broken up at Chatham Dockyard in 1819.

The remaining member of the trio, the *Peacock*, was built at New York by Adam & Noah Brown, who had a yard at Corlears Hook. The contract was signed July 26, 1813, and the vessel launched September 27th of the same year, and so it can be seen that the Browns could turn out a ship with little lost motion. She went to sea on her first cruise March 12, 1814. In building these ship-sloops, the shipyards were permitted much leeway in following the plans, with the result that the three sloops differed considerably in appearance and a little in lines. In the draught for these three, Doughty had introduced a little hollow into the garboards amidships which is believed to have been retained in the construction of all three ships. In the rake, sheer, profile of bow and stern and in the quarter badges and carving there appears to have been wide variation. Undoubtedly there was some difference in lines as well, for the three varied much in speed, the *Peacock* being the fastest according to reports. The lines and inboard works of this fine ship are shown in Figures 15 and

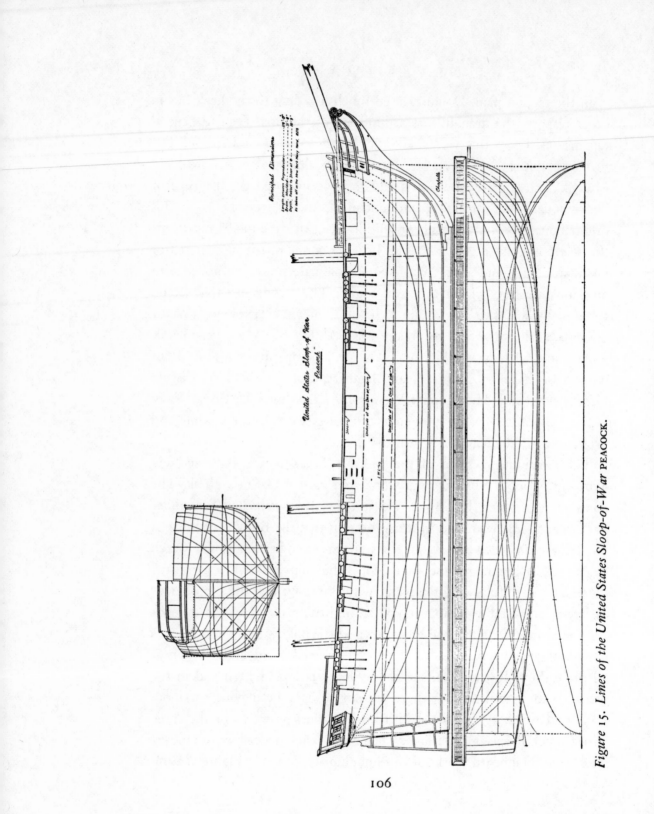

Figure 15. Lines of the United States Sloop-of-War PEACOCK.

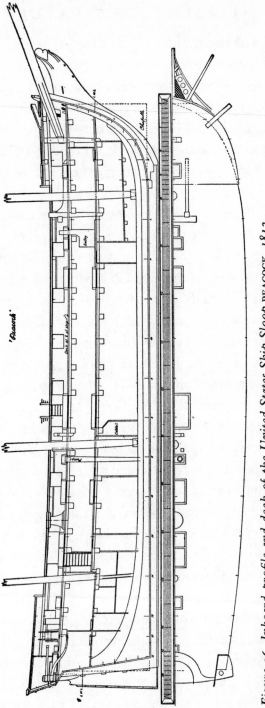

'Peacock'

Figure 16. Inboard profile and deck of the United States Ship-Sloop PEACOCK, 1813.

16; the contract and specifications are in the Appendix. These require little comment. The long and well-formed run combined with a somewhat full entrance indicate a ship that could stand hard driving. The powerful mid-section and low bilges gave great stability to carry sail in a breeze. The ability of the *Peacock* to outsail larger vessels in strong winds can be traced to these features. The *Peacock* and her two sisters carried the same battery as the *Erie* class, except that long 12's replaced the 2 long 18's of the latter.

The life of the *Peacock* was an interesting one. She not only survived the war, but lasted well into the '20's. She was broken up in 1828, at New York, where part of her timber was used to build a new and larger *Peacock*, which was lost on the Columbia River Bar in 1841 while engaged in surveying the Pacific Coast.

The *Peacock* got to sea on her first cruise under the command of Master-commandant Lewis Warrington. On the 28th of April, after a short action, she captured the British 18-gun brig *Epervier*, a new vessel. The English brig was sent home and was taken into the navy under the same name, to be lost with all hands shortly after the war. Incidentally Theodore Roosevelt, in his fine *Naval War of 1812*, called this brig "tubby." This description does not do justice to the British ship, for she was a very fine model. There is somewhat of a tradition that all the British ships of the War of 1812 period were slow, compared to the general run of American men-of-war, but this is quite untrue. There were frigates and ship-sloops, as well as brigs, in the Royal Navy that were as fast as any of the American vessels, with the possible exception of *President* and the ship-sloops of the *Erie* and *Peacock* classes. The American superiority in fast-sailing craft was in the schooner type, with which no other small vessels could compete in speed.

The *Peacock* returned from her first cruise October 29th, putting into New York. She had taken 14 merchantmen and had wrought much destruction in the Irish Channel and off the coasts of Ireland and Portugal and in the West Indies. In 1815 she again went to sea, still under Warrington, with the old *Hornet* and the store-schooner *Tom Bowline*. These vessels were to meet the *President* for an intended cruise in the East Indies, but the loss of the *President* prevented her from joining the squadron. The *Hornet*, after capturing the *Penguin*, was chased by a liner. She was

SHIP-SLOOP *Peacock*, 1813.

forced to jettison all her guns to escape, making her useless as a cruiser, and so she returned home. The *Tom Bowline* was sent away as a cartel with the prisoners taken out of the *Penguin*. This left the *Peacock* to proceed alone. She sailed around the Cape of Good Hope and cruised the Indian Ocean, where she took four very valuable Indiamen. She entered the Straits of Sunda and on June 30, 1815, she met with the Honorable East India Company's brig-cruiser *Nautilus*, 14 guns, which she took after two broadsides. As peace had been declared in the meantime, and as it was claimed that the British had informed the American commander of the fact before the action started, it has become fashionable among naval historians to deprecate Warrington's action. It has been suggested that "he could have kept the brig within half-pistol shot, until he could have inquired into the matter," quoting Roosevelt. Since Warrington believed the Briton's statement that peace was declared was merely a ruse to permit the escape of the brig, the question arises, on whose information could he rely? When it is considered that the *Peacock* was in hostile waters, far from home and in constant danger of being captured by the British East India station ships or squadrons, it is unreasonable to expect Warrington to do other than "shoot first and inquire afterwards." He would have appeared stupid indeed if the claim had been untrue and if he had followed Roosevelt's suggestion long enough for one of the heavy British men-of-war on the station to appear and gobble him up.

The career of the *Peacock* after the war was the usual round of the Mediterranean, North Atlantic and Pacific stations, with a short cruise in the West Indies during 1822–3, in the suppression of the West Indian pirates.

The importance of the *Peacock* in this discussion does not rest, however, on her history in wartime. Rather, it is the fact that her design influenced the ship-sloop classes in the American navy for the next 26 years. Because of her success as a cruiser, her speed and handiness, to say nothing of her fighting qualities, this ship was considered the proper model for her rate. Not only did the *Peacock* have a lasting effect on the design of American ship-sloops, but she raised the importance of that class in the estimation of the Navy so that, instead of having none, or at least very few (as before the War of 1812), a large number were built. The success of the *Wasp* was also a factor in this change, of course. Up until the time of these American ship-sloops, most foreign vessels of the class were quarterdecked ships, but afterwards the majority were flush-decked, as in the plan of the *Peacock*. It must not be assumed, however, that the Americans introduced the "flush-decked sloop" for this class of ship-sloop had been in use since 1790 or earlier, but they did make this type popular.

The experience of the War of 1812 resulted in an Act of Congress providing for the gradual increase of the Navy. In 1814 four ships-of-the-line were laid down but were not complete when peace came. Under this new act, these ships were completed. It is not certain who was responsible for their design, but it is possible that the lines of the 74's ordered in 1799, drawn by Joshua Humphreys, were altered and used. Doughty, on the other hand, may have designed them. They were built in the various navy yards and were named *Franklin*, *Washington*, *Columbus* and *Independence*. As a class they were complete failures, having insufficient displacement to carry their batteries, and were quick rollers to boot. None of them were employed as ships-of-the-line to any extent, and most of their lives were spent as receiving-ships or guard-ships. The only exception was the *Independence* which, after various alterations to fit her as a liner, was cut down to a frigate in 1836. To do this her spar-deck was removed and a larger spar-plan provided; this could be done as so much weight was taken out of her topsides by removing the spar-deck and its battery. The result was a class of ship known as a "razee," really a very heavy frigate. The *Independence*, as a razee, was 188'-0" between perpendiculars as against the original 190'-0", which made her a larger frigate than the *President* type.

The ships built on the Great Lakes and on Lake Champlain during the War of 1812 have not been mentioned. Unfortunately, very little is known about either their dimensions or lines, as but two plans have yet been found. One is of the corvette *Saratoga* (Figure 17), an enormous ship-sloop, flush-decked, 143'-0" on the gun-deck, 36'-6" moulded beam, 12'-6" from rabbet to gun-deck amidships. She was almost without sheer, little rake to the ends and was without figurehead or cutwater knee. She was built between March 2nd (when timber began to be cut) and April

11, 1814, when she was launched by the brothers Adam & Noah Brown who had been brought up to Vergennes, Vermont, from New York. The other plan was of the galleys built by the brothers at the same time; they were big open whaleboats, 75'-0" long, 15'-0" wide and 4'-0" deep, with a gun at each end and fitted to row and sail.

In view of the fact that the Browns also built Commodore Perry's brigs on Lake Erie (*Niagara* and *Lawrence*), it is probable that the *Saratoga* was very similar to them in appearance, though not in dimensions. This matter is worth mention as the *Niagara* has been raised and "restored." This "restoration" is so misleading, yet so widely publicized, that a misconception of the appearance of the Lake Erie men-of-war has resulted. It should hardly be necessary to point out that these two brigs were built very hurriedly and that no time was wasted on a cutwater knee or a billethead.

It is probable that Henry Eckford not only built the ships on Lake Ontario, but also designed them. He was a Scotchman who had settled in New York and had become well known for the rapidity with which he could build, as well as for the excellence of his designs and workmanship. For the present, at least, none of his plans of ships built on the Lake are available.

During the War of 1812 another naval constructor had been appointed. This was Samuel Humphreys, son of Joshua Humphreys, who received his appointment April 17, 1813, shortly after Doughty had been appointed. Samuel Humphreys was born in Philadelphia, November 23, 1778, and served under his father when the *United States* was being built. Before he was appointed to the Navy, he had been assisting his father in private work at Philadelphia. He was assigned to the Philadelphia Navy Yard, after his appointment, and built the liner *Franklin* there. He may have been the designer of the class, but this is doubtful, as has been mentioned earlier.

Francis Grice, born in New Jersey, was appointed later, May 7, 1817, and was assigned to the Gosport Navy Yard (Norfolk, Virginia). Little

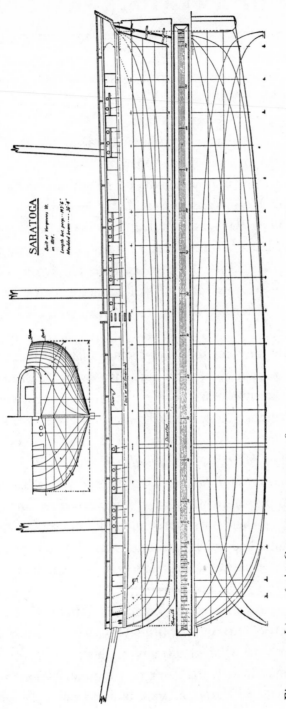

SARATOGA

Built at Vergennes Vt.
in 1814.

Length bet. perp....143' 6"
Moulded beam .....36' 4"

Figure 17. Lines of the Corvette SARATOGA, *1814.*

is known of his early life, except that he was a member of a shipbuilding family.

Henry Eckford was the next naval constructor to be appointed, being assigned to the New York Navy Yard July 13th of the same year. At about this time, Josiah Barker was placed at Boston Navy Yard. Barker, born at Marshfield, Massachusetts, in 1763, was a veteran of the Revolution, having served in the *Hague*. Apparently he learned his trade on the North River; in 1795 or thereabouts he started a shipyard at Charlestown, where the Navy Yard now is. Later he built ships near the old state-prison. Among the vessels he had built were the ship-sloop *Frolic* in 1813 and the liner *Independence*. Two other constructors were appointed before 1821, Samuel Hartt on June 1, 1819 and John Floyd, July 11, 1820. With this force of skilled men now available, building began along a predetermined plan, rather than in the haphazard policy of the past.

Doughty drew up plans for a new frigate class of nine vessels all laid down between 1819 and 1826. These ships were gradually completed during the next twenty years, so that the last launched were somewhat different in appearance from the early vessels because of numerous small changes during the intervening period. The vessels of this frigate class were *Brandywine, Cumberland, Columbia, Potomac, St. Lawrence, Raritan, Sabine, Savannah* and *Santee*. They were "double-banked" frigates, 175'-0" between perpendiculars, 45'-0" moulded beam and 14'-4" depth of hold. In general, their lines were much like those of *President* except that the new ships had an ugly round stern, combined with quarter-galleries. The *Brandywine* of this class was a noted sailer.

In 1821 the necessity of suppressing piracy in the West Indies and of maintaining ships to catch slavers led to the building of five schooners. By that time the few small clipper brigs and schooners built or purchased toward the end of the War of 1812 were rotten and worn-out, leaving the Navy without small craft. Four of the new schooners, the *Shark, Alligator, Dolphin* and *Porpoise*, were built on one plan which appears to have been furnished by Samuel Humphreys. They were small 12-gun schooners, varying somewhat in appearance. The fifth, the *Grampus*, a little larger than the others, was built at Washington and came from Eckford's board. Eckford apparently finished her plans in 1820, for he resigned June 6, 1820, but since he submitted plans afterwards, this is uncertain. Sometime late in the '20's Eckford went to Turkey as chief naval constructor and built a number of very large ships-of-the-line and frigates. While still with the American Navy, Eckford designed and built the 74 *Ohio*, of which more later. Eckford's ships were marked by great flare to the bows and, as far as his small craft were concerned, his work was obviously under the influence of the Baltimore Clipper. Eckford must be classed with the leading naval architects of his time.

When the new frigates were building, seven new 74's were also under construction. Six were designed by Doughty, the *North Carolina*, *New York*, *Alabama*, *Delaware*, *Vermont* and *Virginia*. The seventh, the *Ohio*, was designed and built by Eckford at New York, 1817–20. The *North Carolina* and the *Delaware* were launched the same year, the *Vermont* in 1848, the *Alabama* as a store-ship in 1864 and the *New York* and *Virginia*, still on the stocks when the Civil War began, were never completed. The *Ohio* was a fine ship, and very fast for her class, but the *North Carolina* and *Delaware* were not remarkable. The *Ohio* was the same size as the others, about 198'-0" between perpendiculars, but had a little more beam.

In 1825, ten new ship-sloops were ordered, which, with another ordered afterwards, were all in the water by 1830, and were all built in the navy yards. These vessels were mainly the design of Samuel Humphreys, who in 1826 was made Chief Constructor. Doughty ceased to be active at about that time though he did not resign until 1837. Under Humphreys' regime, it was the custom for the various naval constructors to meet as a board and iron out the conflicting opinions in regard to a plan. In many cases each one presented a design for the proposed ship or class, and the final result was often the incorporation of the ideas of a number of designers. For the new ship-sloops Humphreys, Floyd and Eckford submitted plans, though Eckford appears to have resigned earlier. After making two preliminary plans combining the ideas of these designers, Humphreys drew up the final building plan for sloops of the following dimensions: length between perpendiculars 127'-0", beam moulded 33'-9", 15'-6" in the hold. These vessels were merely enlarged *Peacocks* in many respects, but with round sterns. In some of the ships, as built, there were no false quarter-galleries, but most of the ships were given this useless feature. These vessels were the *Boston, Concord, Fairfield, Falmouth, John Adams, Lexington, Natchez, St. Louis, Vandalia, Vincennes* and *Warren*. The *John Adams* was officially the old 28-gun frigate of that name (1799) rebuilt. The appropriation made for that purpose was utilized to build a new sloop, as the old frigate did not contain enough sound timber and the appropriation was too small to rebuild her as a small frigate.

In 1825, Smith and Dimon of New York, later famous as builders of packet ships and clippers, launched a large 44-gun double-banked frigate for the Greek revolutionists named *Liberator*. She was 177'-10" between perpendiculars, 45'-0" moulded beam and 35'-1½" rabbet to rail. In lines she was an enormous packet ship with little overhang at the ends and a short heavy "head." The Greeks not being able to pay for her, she was sold to the United States and became the frigate *Hudson*. She was a fair sailer, but was built of poor timber and did not last long; in fact, she made but one cruise.

The old prize frigate *Macedonian*, captured from the British during the War of 1812 and taken into the navy, was rotten in 1830 and so it was proposed to "rebuild" her. In 1832 a new frigate, to mount 36 guns, was laid down at Gosport Navy Yard, as the first step in the operation. Designed by Humphreys, the new *Macedonian* measured 164'-0" between perpendiculars, 41'-0" moulded beam and 18'-0" depth of hold. She was a double-banked frigate and was launched in 1836, the old *Macedonian* being broken up in the meantime. The new frigate was armed

116

as a sloop in 1836 and had her spar-deck removed along with other changes in 1852.

The year after the launch of the *Macedonian* two new ship-sloops were built, the *Cyane* and *Levant*. These were designed by Humphreys and were similar to the *Boston* class, but larger, measuring 132'-3" between perpendiculars, 35'-3" beam and 15'-9" depth of hold. They had round sterns and were fine, powerful ships.

In 1839 a new *Congress* was built, to replace the old ship recently broken up. The new *Congress* was another Humphrey design, double-banked, with a round stern like the *Macedonian* but larger. She was a 44, 179'-0" between perpendiculars, 47'-8" moulded beam and 22'-8" depth of hold. Next to the big razee *Independence*, she was the biggest frigate in the navy.

Speaking of big ships, 1837 saw the launch of the great *Pennsylvania*, 120 guns, four complete, armed decks, measuring 210'-0" between perpendiculars, 56'-9" moulded beam and 22'-8" depth of hold. She drew about 22'-6" ready for sea and was originally armed with 32-pounder long guns. Without doubt, she was the most powerful ship of her time, and was a credit to Humphreys, her designer. She was laid down as early as 1822, taking about fifteen years to build. This ship has been given a bad reputation as a sailer, it being stated that she was slow, leewardly, cumbersome and crank. However, in spite of these claims, it appears that she could sail when in proper trim; the chief trouble with her was that officers, who had no experience in so large a ship, expected her to handle like a frigate. Although this great ship had a round stern and a flush sheer, she was not as ugly a ship as might be supposed by her description.

In reference to this ship and to the "French influence," it was interesting to find, in an inspection of plans collected by Samuel Humphreys, that the lines of the Spanish *Santisima-Trinidad* (in the Spanish fleet at Trafalgar, 1805) and those of the British 100-gun ship *Royal Sovereign* (also at Trafalgar) were used as references in designing the *Pennsylvania*. The omission of French plans is worthy of mention.

Some interesting small craft were also built in the '30's. The first were three sister schooners carrying eight 24-pounder carronades and two long 9's. These vessels, launched in 1831, were built in the navy yards, and were named *Enterprise, Experiment* and *Boxer*. They were mainly Humphreys' design, very much on the clipper model, and measured 88'-0" between perpendiculars, 23'-6" moulded beam, and 10'-6" depth of hold. They were converted to brigs or hermaphrodites in the '40's. They were designed for the suppression of the slave trade and for the West Indian station. They were fast but somewhat tender. The *Experiment* was built on an experimental plan of construction, the details of which have not been discovered.

In 1836 two more vessels of the same size were built, the brigantines *Dolphin* and *Porpoise*. These were almost duplicates of the 1831 class except that they had more beam and depth. Retaining the same length, they had a moulded beam of 25'-0" and a depth of 11'-0". The *Dolphin* was considered one of the two fastest sailers in the Navy.

In 1839, five 16-gun ship-sloops were launched, all alike. They were almost duplicates of the *Peacock* in appearance, but had more displacement and slight changes in dimensions. They measured 117'-7" between perpendiculars, 33'-10" moulded beam and 15'-0" depth in the hold. Armed with 16 carronades, 32-pounders, they were named *Preble, Dale, Decatur, Marion* and *Yorktown*. They proved to be handy ships with a fair turn of speed, but were no improvement over the *Peacock* in lines.

The '40's marked the last building for the sailing navy. Seven big ship-sloops or corvettes and five brigs were built. The new ship-sloops were on six different models, and were apparently designed by individual constructors, as follows: *Albany* by Grice, *Plymouth* by Pook, *Portsmouth* by Barker, *Germantown* by Lenthall, *St. Marys* by Brodie, *Jamestown* by Rhodes and *Saratoga* by Humphreys. Undoubtedly Humphreys also had some influence in the designs of the *Germantown, Portsmouth* and *St. Marys*. As a matter of fact, it is difficult to learn who really did the designing of all of this class except in the cases of the *Albany* and *Plymouth*.

The descriptions of each of these ships were the following: *Albany*, designed as a barque but rigged as a ship, clipper-built with much deadrise, flush-decked, with topgallant forecastle and very short poop, length between perpendiculars 147'-11", beam moulded 38'-6", depth in the hold 17'-9". She was the handsomest ship in the service and was the only first-class sloop with a square stern. The *Albany* was launched at Norfolk in 1846 and carried four 8" shell guns and 18 long 32's. She sailed from Aspinwall, now Colon, Panama, on September 28, 1854, and was never again heard from.

The *Germantown* was somewhat similar to the *Albany*, but with a round stern, and not so sharp. She was designed to be 148'-6" between perpendiculars, but was built 150'-0". She had 36'-0" moulded beam and was 16'-8" in the hold. The *Germantown* was built at Philadelphia and was launched in 1846; she was armed like the *Albany*. This sloop was an easy working ship and a good sailer. Her stern overhang was very short and she had no quarter galleries.

The *Portsmouth* was a very handsome ship, flush-decked and somewhat similar to the *Germantown* in arrangement. She was constructed on the lines of a ship built some years earlier by Josiah Barker, named the *Union*, which in turn was built on the lines of a privateer of the War of 1812. The *Portsmouth* was 151'-10" between perpendiculars, 38'-1" moulded beam, 17'-2" in the hold. Her battery was the same as that of the *Albany*. She was built at Portsmouth, New Hampshire, and launched in 1843, and was on the Navy List until 1915. The *Portsmouth* had a plain round stern and a great deal of rake to her stem combined with the usual heavy head.

The *Jamestown* was a larger ship than any of the foregoing, measuring 157'-6" between perpendiculars, 35'-0" moulded beam, 16'-2" depth of hold. She had a round stern with quarter-galleries and a short heavy cutwater, the stem having little rake. The *Jamestown* was launched at Norfolk in 1844 and was still afloat in 1932. She was one of the two ships of her class that was originally designed with a complete, but unarmed, spardeck. The other sloops were given this deck during the 50's and afterwards, except in the case of the *Plymouth* which had the deck originally and the *Albany* which had been lost. The *Jamestown* was a fast ship in a breeze, but required careful trimming, though she was not the all-around sailer the *Portsmouth* was reputed to be.

The *Plymouth* was somewhat like the *Jamestown;* she had a spar-deck as built, but she was a little smaller, 147'-0" between perpendiculars, 37'-3" moulded beam, and 16'-3½" depth of hold. She was built at Boston in 1843 and was burned at Norfolk during the Civil War. The *Plymouth* had a plain round stern with an exceedingly short overhang, and moderate rake to the stem. She was very weatherly and a fast ship, as well as being very handy.

The *Saratoga* was very much like *Portsmouth* in appearance and form, being 146'-4" between perpendiculars, 35'-3" moulded beam, and 16'-3½" in the hold. She had a plain round stern and moderate rake to the stem. She was launched at Portsmouth in 1842 and sold in 1907; she was used as a state training ship for many years. The *Saratoga* had the reputation of being a good sailer, weatherly and handy.

The *St. Marys* was a flush-decked sloop with a plain round stern and almost upright stem. She had much deadrise and was rather sharp-ended. Her measurements were 149'-3" between perpendiculars, 37'-4" moulded beam and 16'-6" depth of hold. She originally carried two more shell guns than her class-mates. The *St. Marys* was built at Washington and was launched in 1844. She was not sold until 1908. For many years she served as a school-ship.

As a whole, this was a very successful class of ships, but they show the extremes to which the "sloop idea" was carried. Nearly all the 44-gun frigates, such as the *Constitution*, *Cumberland* and *Congress*, were either cut down or re-armed as sloops during this period. The new sloops had replaced the frigate in popularity. But the new ships, called "first-class sloops," were not duplicated in foreign navies, except for a few old frigates that were razeed to sloops.

The brigs were an interesting class. They were designed for speed and were all more or less on the Baltimore Clipper model. Two of the five were sister-ships, the *Somers*, built at New York, and the *Bainbridge*, built at Boston. These brigs were built in navy yards and were launched in 1842. They were handsome little ships and attracted much attention, and a number of commercial brigs were built on their general lines as a result. The lines and inboard works are presented in Figures 18 and 19; the plans show the general practice in topside appearance and fittings of both sloops and brigs of their date. They were designed by Humphreys and measured 100'-0" between perpendiculars, 25'-0" moulded beam and 11'-0" depth in hold. These two brigs were very fast, and very much over-rigged; the *Somers* capsizing and foundering off Vera Cruz, December 8, 1846, with the loss of 40 lives and the *Bainbridge* foundering off Hatteras, August 15, 1863, when all hands but one were lost.

The brig *Truxton* was launched at the Gosport Navy Yard in 1842. She was 100'-0" between perpendiculars, 27'-3" moulded beam and 13'-0" in the hold. Her battery was the same as the other brigs of this class, 10 carronades, 32-pounders, and a pair of long or medium 32's. The *Truxton* was designed by Francis Grice and was the first naval vessel to set up her shrouds with any other method than the ancient deadeyes and lanyards. She had rollers in her chain-plates under which the shrouds passed. Apparently the shrouds set up on themselves, as in a stay. The *Truxton* had much deadrise and sharp ends, and was a very fast brig, with a high narrow sail plan. She was wrecked on the coast of Mexico, August 15, 1846.

The next year after the *Truxton* was launched, Grice had another brig in the water at Gosport, the handsome *Perry*. His new design was 105'-0" between perpendiculars, 25'-0" moulded beam and 11'-6" in the hold. She was first designed with a round stern, but the final draught showed

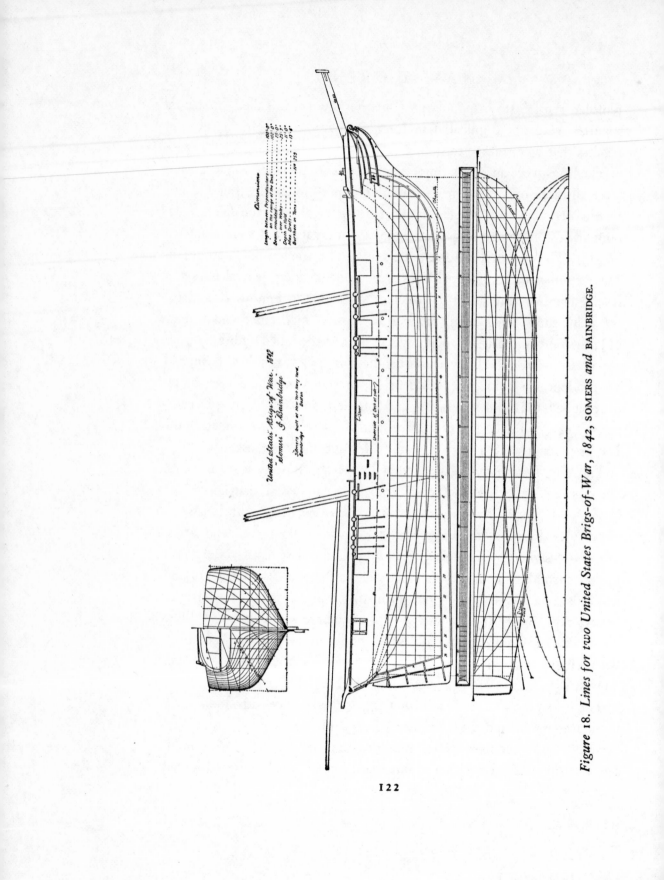

Figure 18. Lines for two United States Brigs-of-War, 1842, SOMERS *and* BAINBRIDGE.

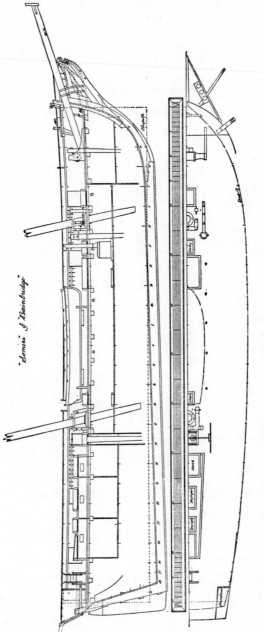

"Lewis & Bainbridge"

Figure 19. *Inboard details and deck plan of* SOMERS *and* BAINBRIDGE.

123

the usual transom. The *Perry* was much the sharpest of any of the brigs already mentioned, and was considered the fastest ship in the navy, surpassing even the swift *Dolphin*. When first launched, the *Perry* was considered a very dangerous ship, for she was somewhat over-loaded. When four of her carronades were taken out and the number of her boats were reduced, she proved to be a remarkable sailer and a stiff vessel. She was

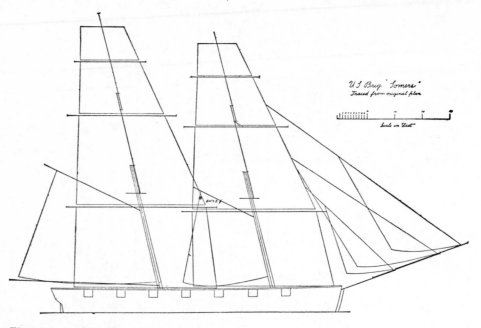

Figure 19A. *Sail plan of* SOMERS.

always somewhat wet, however. The *Perry* was sold out at Philadelphia August 10, 1865, bringing $6,500.

The last member of the class was the contract-built *Lawrence*, launched at Baltimore August 1, 1843. Little is to be found relating to this brig. She was built, and apparently designed, by Lawrence B. Culley, a famous Baltimore builder who later designed and built the famous clipper-ship *Architect*. The *Lawrence*—her draught is shown in Figure 20—was 114'-0" overall, 110'-8" on the waterline, 26'-2" moulded beam and 13'-3" in the hold. She carried the same armament as the others of her rig and was a

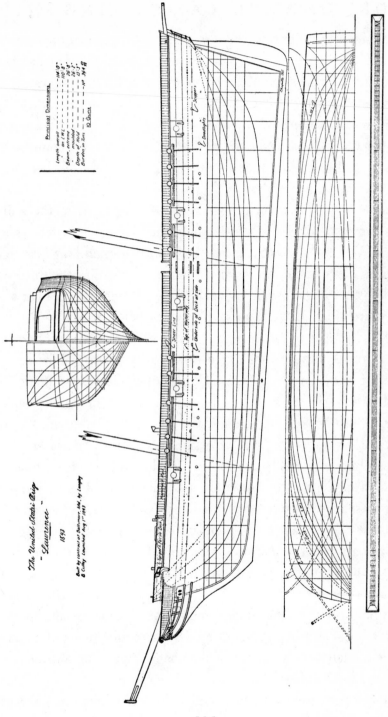

Figure 20. Lines of the United States Brig-of-War LAWRENCE, *built at Baltimore in 1843.*

handsome ship, as can be seen. She was the most extreme example of the Baltimore Clipper model in the navy; nothing approaching her had been built since the War of 1812. Because she drew a great deal of water, her usefulness was limited. She had the misfortune to be built of rather poor timber and was apparently rather lightly constructed as well. So far, no report of her qualities has come to light, nor has the survey, condemning her as unseaworthy in 1846, been found. Hence the reason for her sale in 1846, at New York, is not clear.

With these vessels, built in the '40's, the development of the sailing man-of-war ceased forever. A few sailing craft were purchased, as late as the Civil War, but their day as fighting ships was then long past. The United States Navy turned to steam at about the same time the European navies did. None of the naval powers designed sailing men-of-war after 1850, but merely completed those laid down earlier.

It would be proper to take one last glance back over the years of the evolution of the American sailing men-of-war and summarize the accomplishments of the American Naval Constructor. The introduction of faster and larger frigates and ship-sloops, the design of double-banked frigates and flush-decked ship-sloops, the use of the Baltimore Clipper model for small men-of-war, and the design of vessels to carry heavy batteries and still be fast; these must be listed as the accomplishments of the American Naval Constructor in the days of sail. It would be very rash to claim that these features were "invented" by Americans, but it can be at least said that they made them popular. Experience in designing and building sailing men-of-war had considerable influence on the design of later sailing merchant vessels. Without the lessons in design and construction of the big frigates and liners, the packet-ships and later clipper-ships would not have been possible. The combination of capacity and speed in men-of-war hull-forms, to say nothing of the requirements of size and strength, was related to the design of merchant shipping in a manner too obvious to require explanation.

Some of the men who were responsible for the designs of American sailing men-of-war have been referred to at length, others merely mentioned. The ability of some of the latter must, in all fairness, receive recognition by further comment. For the sake of clarity, the period of service of each designer and a list of the ships they are known to have designed, with other comment, will be given in chronological order of their appointment. Only the men who are definitely known to have designed individual ships will be mentioned, as many naval constructors were merely master shipwrights who did no design work as far as is known.

Joshua Humphreys, June, 1794 to October, 1801, designed the *Constitution, United States, Constellation, Congress, Hassan Bashaw*, 74's ordered in 1799, and a few galleys built in 1798.

Josiah Fox, June, 1794 to August 1, 1798, transferred to the newly formed Navy Department, displaced in 1801. Re-appointed May 4, 1804, discharged in August, 1809. Died in Ohio in 1846. Fox was a talented designer and introduced improved mould-loft practice while employed in laying down the *Constitution* and *Constellation* classes. His influence on the design of the American frigates of these classes, and the others, must be recognized. Undoubtedly he was the source of what foreign influence (English) there was in the design of these men-of-war. Josiah Fox designed *Crescent, Chesapeake, John Adams, Portsmouth, Hornet* and *Wasp, Ferret* (schooner), one or more early revenue cutters and a large part of the gunboats of 1803–7.

William Doughty, February 8, 1813 to October 2, 1837 (resigned). An able designer who was responsible for most of the ships of the United States Navy after the War of 1812. He was a fine draftsman, and had "boat-sense" which enabled him to design some very fine craft. Doughty designed *President*, probably with the aid of the elder Humphreys, and may have designed the *Independence* 74's. He was the designer of the *Peacock* class, *Erie* class, *Java* and *Guerrier*, *North Carolina* class of 74's, *Brandywine* class of 44's, some of the brigs built in 1814–15, and at least five revenue cutters. He introduced the use of the Baltimore Clipper model, of the extreme type, into the design of naval ships. From 1837 to

1842, Doughty and his son were timber contractors to the Navy Department.

Benjamin Hutton held a temporary appointment during 1803. He designed the brig *Syren* and the schooners *Vixen* and *Skjoldebrand* and may have designed *Enterprise* and *Experiment*. Hutton was a brilliant naval architect, a splendid draftsman and a practical shipwright. Too little is known of this very able man; he was the equal of Fox and Humphreys as a designer. As he was never a chief-constructor, he could be omitted from this list but his work deserves some recognition here.

Samuel Humphreys, April 17, 1813 to August 16, 1846 (died). Son of Joshua Humphreys and more talented than his father. An able designer, Humphreys was responsible for the design of *Pennsylvania*, *Macedonian*, *Congress*, *Boston* class of ship-sloops, *Cyane* and *Levant*, schooners of 1831, and *Dolphin* and *Porpoise* of 1836, *Somers* and *Bainbridge*, one first-class sloop and the *Morris* class of revenue cutters of 1831–2. He also designed other small craft and a number of steamers. All of his small sailing craft were on the Baltimore model. He was made chief-constructor November 25, 1826.

Francis Grice was appointed May 7, 1817, made chief about 1847 and went on sick leave in 1859. He died at Philadelphia in 1865. Grice was a firm believer in sharp-ended ships with much deadrise, and was the designer of *Truxton*, *Perry*, *Albany*, some small craft and also some of the later war-steamers. All of his men-of-war were very handsome ships, and his draftsmanship was of the highest order.

Henry Eckford was appointed July 13, 1817; he had been previously employed, however, as a master shipwright on the Lakes during the War of 1812. He was the designer of nearly all the men-of-war built on Lake Ontario during the war, *Superior*, *General Pike*, *Lady of the Lake*, *Mohawk* and others. He also designed the 74 *Ohio* and the schooner *Grampus*. Eckford resigned in 1820 and remained in New York for a while as a shipbuilder. He spent some years in Turkey where he designed the 247-foot *Mahmoudieh* and a few other very large ships. He was the builder under whom Isaac Webb served his apprenticeship. Like Hutton, he was never a chief-constructor, but was the designer of some very fine vessels. He was a man of great ability in the design of large ships and was a genius in organization.

The last of the great designers of sailing ships for the United States Navy was Samuel M. Pook, January 1, 1841 to August 15, 1866 (retired). He died December 2, 1878. His most important design among the sailing craft was the first-class sloop, *Plymouth*, and he was consulted in regard to the *Saratoga* and *Portsmouth*. He supervised the construction of many other vessels as well. He was the father of Samuel Hartt Pook, the famous designer of clipper-ships, who also became a constructor in the United States Navy. The elder Pook was not a believer in extreme deadrise and criticized the design of the *Albany*, Grice's design, very severely. He undoubtedly had much influence on the work of his son. The Pooks, father and son, were among the most talented of American naval architects. The elder Pook apparently received his early training as a shipwright in the Navy Yards and was employed in the yards as early as 1825. Constructor Pook did a great deal of responsible work during the Civil War.

The best comment on the skill of these men would be to say that, though the nature of their work often forced them to stand before that court which hands down its decisions in lost and foundered ships, there were very few judgments found against them.

Chapter Three PRIVATEERS AND SLAVERS

THE great American deity, "Speed," had no more devout worshipers than the designers and builders of privateers and of the small slaving craft that followed them. While in men-of-war, speed was subordinated in some degree to strength, capacity and other features, the ability to sail fast was the prime requirement of both privateers and slavers. The reason for this is obvious, for the existence of either class depended on this very ability. Though there was some distinction between the designs of privateers and slavers, because of the different nature and deadweight of the loads each carried, there was a close relationship between them. In fact, the slaver was merely the extreme development of the design used earlier in the privateer, and so the two classes can be considered together. The importance of these two classes in this discussion is due to their influence in the establishment of a trend of design, rather than to numerical or chronological considerations.

The privateer was a privately-owned vessel, armed and manned at her owner's expense for the purpose of capturing enemy merchant craft in time of war. International law of the time required that she have a commission or "letter-of-marque," as it was called, obtained from the government under whose flag she sailed; otherwise she was considered a pirate. Incidentally, the terms "privateer" and "letter-of-marque" were applied to vessels carrying the commission without discrimination in meaning. In order to obtain a "letter-of-marque," the vessel had to be bonded to the government, to satisfy any claims that might arise from illegal captures. Two bondsmen were needed for each privateer. Theoretically, the privateer had no right to her prizes until they were condemned by due process of law, but as the privateer could destroy vessels at sea, this was a mere formality.

The owner, officers and crew held "shares" in a privateering enterprise, much in the same manner as the Gloucestermen have done in the fishery. The rule of "no fish no pay" was applied to privateering because of the uncertainty and risk. The number of shares held by the owner, officers and crew was on an agreed ratio that varied with the size and reputation of the ship, the difficulty in getting men and the ability of the captain. Usually, "the owner and the ship" held about half the total number of shares and so received half the prize-money. When the national currency was inflated so as to be of trifling value, it was customary to divide goods in place of currency.

At the beginning of each war it was customary to fit out merchant craft of every description as privateers, though naturally fast-sailers were preferred. These vessels usually got to sea while the enemy was unprepared and so had some success until the enemy armed his merchantmen and sent his light cruisers to sea. When this came about the number of privateers became greatly reduced, as the slow ones were quickly captured or destroyed, and the small ones were too weak to cope with armed vessels. As a result, the second year of a maritime war was usually marked by the appearance of a class of privateer designed and built to meet the particular requirements of the business.

From the standpoint of the designer of privateers, speed was the most difficult problem. No designer of sailing craft, even nowadays, can be certain of how fast a design will be until the vessel is actually built and tried. To overcome this difficulty it has been the practice to use the model of a vessel known to be fast as the basis for a new design, and by making changes, to try to improve on the original. By the process of trial and error in each successive design, the naval architect gradually finds the right model for a given type and rig. The degree of "rightness" depends upon the intelligence, experience and observation of the designer. This statement is proven, today, by the fact that all designers of sailing craft cannot turn out fast vessels and even the most talented have occasional failures in spite of the accumulated knowledge and the "science" of modern naval architecture. Were the matter a simple one or merely a cut-

and-dried mathematical process, this would not be true, of course.

Aside from this particular problem, the design of privateers was not very difficult. The armament need not be heavy, as a privateer was not intended to fight a regular naval battle. She avoided the enemy's naval ships and privateers, for these would only give empty holds if captured, and hard knocks in any case; the privateersman was less interested in glory than in pelf. Hence the privateer carried at the most only enough guns to overawe the lightly armed merchantman into surrendering. Since a large crew was required to man the prizes that might be captured and sent home and, as merchant ships invariably carried small crews, the best privateering practise was to fire a shot or two from the battery, and if the merchant ship would not then surrender, to get alongside and overpower the small crew by boarding. Because of these tactics, the armament was of less importance than it was in the small men-of-war and could be subordinated to other features.

In the matter of strength, the privateer needed only to be strong enough to withstand the strains of carrying a heavy press of sail and the recoil of a light battery. Weight could be kept out of the ends of the ship, which enabled light construction to be used. As no great weights, such as cargo or stores, had to be provided for, the displacement needed only to be sufficient to support the light hull construction, a small battery, a small amount of provisions and stores, some ballast and a large crew. Because the cruise of a privateer was usually short and as the crew was rapidly reduced as prizes were taken and sent into port, the amount of provisions, water, stores and ammunition was not very great. And since only valuable goods would be taken out of a destroyed prize, and as such goods were commonly of little weight and bulk, there was little need for cargo capacity.

On the other hand, a privateer had to be a good all-around sailer, regardless of weather, and reasonably safe. In order to sail well in a breeze, she had to be stiff, and she had to be weatherly. In order to obtain high speed, particularly in light airs, she had to spread a cloud of sail. Though the ship, brig and brigantine rigs were used in privateers, the topsail schooner was the favorite rig of the class. The weatherliness of vessels rigged as schooners and the large spread of sail possible in the topsail-rig had much to do with the choice.

Toward the end of both the Revolution and the War of 1812 the size of privateers greatly increased, but they never reached the size of heavy naval frigates, in America. Only the French built privateers of such large dimensions. The largest American privateers did not exceed 120 feet in length, and so the schooner-rig could be used in the biggest craft. The fore-and-main topsail schooner was the favorite rig perhaps, but many of the largest craft were really "hermaphrodite-schooners" or "brig-schooners." The size of American privateers was fixed by the difficulty of obtaining large crews; the Americans were such enthusiastic priva-teersmen that the ports were quickly stripped of seamen. Not only did this condition have its effect on the size of privateers, but it caused serious embarrassment to the Navy.

The fitting out of privateers began very early in the Revolution; these early craft were merely converted merchantmen. The few small smug-gling craft were the best of the class, the others being slow sloops, brigantines, brigs and ships. As the war continued and the British Navy became active on the American coasts, these early privateers began to suffer heavy losses. The shortage of fast sailing ships of sufficiently large size for distant cruising, however, forced the Americans to build vessels to meet the new requirements as early as 1776; and so the inefficient con-verted merchantmen were rapidly replaced by specially designed vessels.

A great many of the newly-built vessels were schooner-rigged, a few were snows or brigantines, and some of the largest were rigged as ships. A good example of a large ship of the class was the *American Tartar* which the British captured in 1778. On survey she was found to measure 115'-0" on the lower deck, 95'-0" on the keel, 33'-3" beam and 15'-0" depth of hold; she was nearly as large as the Continental 28-gun frigates and just a little larger than the 24's. She was taken into the Royal Navy

Plate V. PRINCE DE NEUFCHATEL, PRIVATEER. *Redrawn from plans found in the British Admiralty files, original made soon after her capture. Position of galley shown in pencil on original may have been altered from original position.*

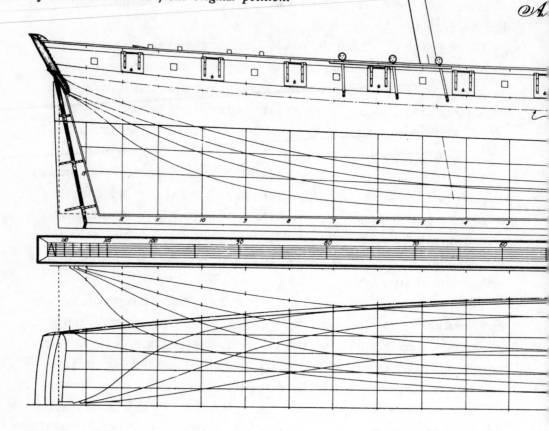

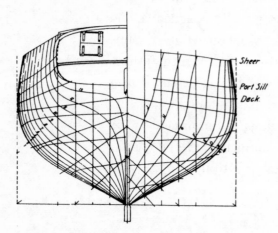

Sheer
Port Sill
Deck.

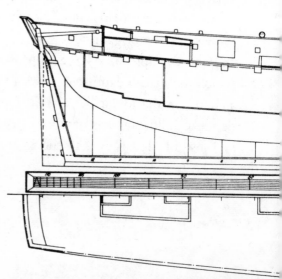

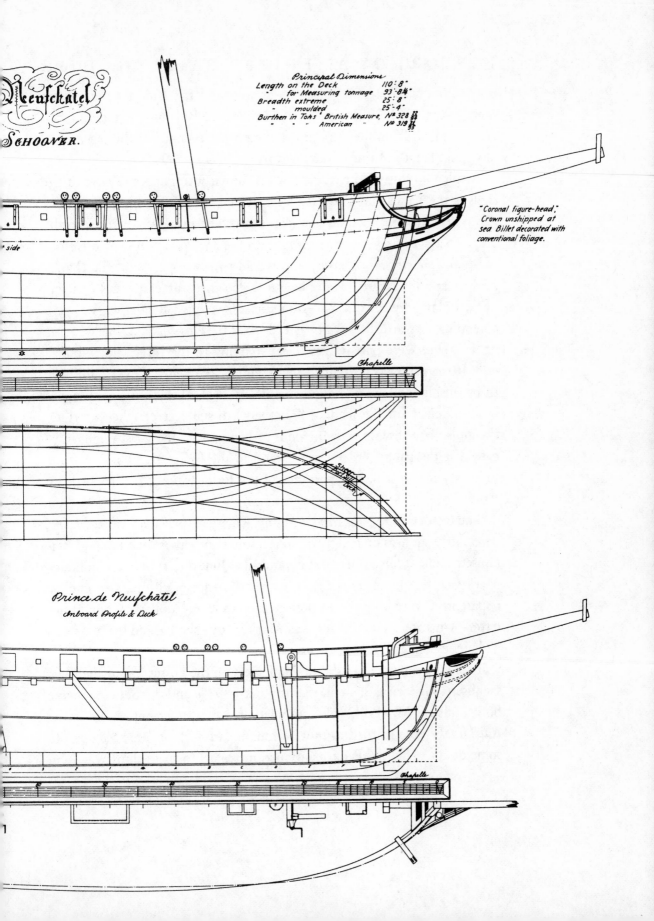

Neufchatel
Schooner.

Principal Dimensions
Length on the Deck .... 110·8"
" for Measuring tonnage ... 93·8¼"
Breadth extreme .... 25·8"
" moulded .... 25·4"
Burthen in Tons ' British Measure. Nº 328 33/94
" " American .... Nº 319 31/95

"Coronal figure-head,"
Crown unshipped at
sea Billet decorated with
conventional foliage.

'side

Chapelle

Prince de Neufchatel
Inboard Profile & Deck

Chapelle

as the *Hinchinbroke*, 28 guns. About a dozen large American privateers were taken into the British Navy during the Revolution, but like the frigates taken from the Americans, none were retained in the service for any great length of time after the war.

A splendid ship of the larger class is shown in Figures 21, 22, and 23. This is the handsome *Rattlesnake*, captured by the British 44-gun ship *Assurance* in 1781 on the American coast. The prize was taken into the Royal Navy as *Cormorant*, 14 guns; in 1784 she was again named *Rattlesnake* and shortly afterwards she was sold out. In appearance, the *Rattlesnake* was a miniature frigate, having a detached forecastle and quarterdeck. Judging by the original Admiralty plans, she had narrow gangways extending forward from the quarterdeck to the entry ladder, but whether or not there were narrow gratings extending to the forecastle is uncertain. If the gangways extended the length of the waist, they would have to be unshipped before the guns could be used, as the headroom would be insufficient for the loading "numbers" to stand erect when working the guns. The absence of stanchions or handrails in the waist might indicate that the gangways did not extend to the forecastle. There is some similarity in the general appearance of the *Rattlesnake* to the later frigate *Essex*.

The history of the *Rattlesnake* as an American privateer is vague, but apparently she was owned by John Andrews and others of Salem, Massachusetts, and received her first commission June 12, 1781. Her bonders, Mark Clark, John Andrews and Francis Boardman, all of Essex county apparently, were required to post twenty thousand dollars to obtain her letter-of-marque. Her master was Mark Clark; she carried 20 guns and had a complement of 85 men.

There is a statement in the Preble Papers, in the possession of the Massachusetts Historical Society, that the *Rattlesnake* and the *Belisarius* were both built by Mr. Peck. The authority for this statement as far as the *Rattlesnake* is concerned cannot be found, and so its accuracy is open to some doubt. The Mr. Peck mentioned in regard to these ships was John

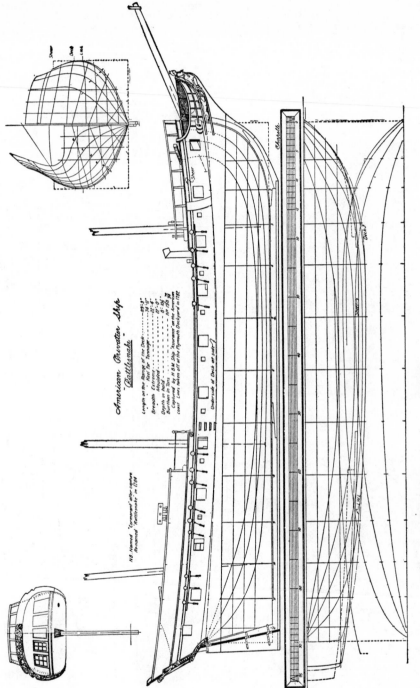

American Privateer Ship
"Rattlesnake."

Length on the Range of the Deck .... 89'3"
Kiel for Tonnage .... 74'10"
Breadth Extreme .... 22'4"
Moulded .... 8'0"
Depth in Hold .... 6'6½"
Burthen in Tons .... No. 198 94/95
Captured by H.B.M Ship "Assurance" on the American
coast. Lines taken off at the Plymouth Dockyard in 1781.

Underside of Deck aft side.

N.B. Named "Cormorant" after capture
Renamed Rattlesnake in 1794

Figure 21. Lines of American Ship-privateer RATTLESNAKE.

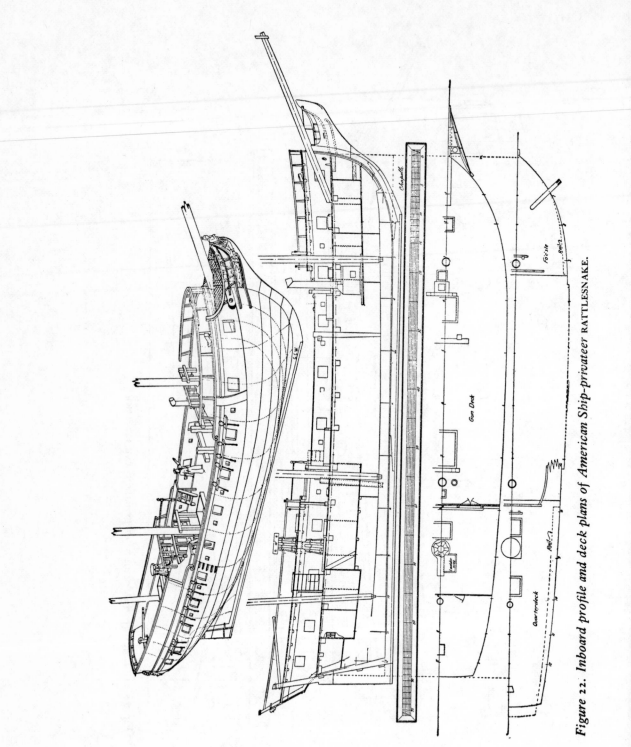

Figure 22. Inboard profile and deck plans of American Ship-privateer RATTLESNAKE.

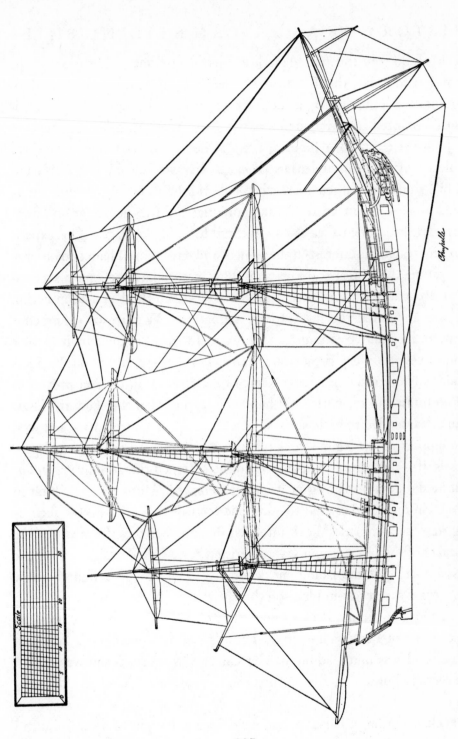

Figure 23. Sail plan of American Ship-privateer RATTLESNAKE.

137

Peck of Boston, the first American "naval architect" in the sense the term is used today, that is, a man who designs ships but who is not a ship-wright or shipbuilder. By some freak of history, the name of this man is usually omitted from catalogues of the great American ship-designers.

John Peck was born June 12, 1725, at Boston; he was one of the three children of William and Mary Peck, and was educated as a merchant. While studying mathematics, when still in school, he had become inter-ested in naval architecture. As an apprenticeship for the career of a mer-chant, he had gone to sea as a supercargo for a few voyages. This experi-ence increased his interest in the subject and gave him a chance to observe the action of a ship at sea. He seems, however, to have become a success-ful merchant, with ship-design as a hobby. When the Revolution began, he was appointed the inspector of saltpetre at Watertown, Massachu-setts, by a legislative committee of the state. In 1774 Peck had built a 20- or 30-ton vessel of very great beam, in order, as he said, to try out his ideas under adverse circumstances. Named the *Minerva*, this vessel proved to be both fast and seaworthy. When Peck learned that the state of Massa-chusetts intended to build some ships-of-war, he submitted plans and won the support of the legislative committee that inspected his plans and pro-posals. It is not certain whether or not he designed the 26-gun *Protector*, but he did design the brig or brigantine *Hazard*. This vessel was built in Boston in 1777, and carried 16 guns. She was called "Peck's Folly" accord-ing to some authorities. Peck intended to name her the *Minerva*, but the Speaker of the House, who was to christen her, upset Peck by naming the vessel *Hazard* at the launching ceremony, even though a figurehead of Minerva was already in place on the cutwater. There would have been a sly humor in naming "Peck's Folly" the *Hazard* that might have been the chief cause of Peck's annoyance. The *Hazard*, however, was a very fast vessel, and was much admired. Her career was short, as she was one of the vessels burned in the unfortunately-managed "Penobscot Expedi-tion."

Peck, according to his son, had never seen a draught of a ship, and had developed a method of his own for drawing the plans. According to the same authority, these early plans were almost unintelligible to Peck himself in later years. In view of the earlier discussion of the "French influence," it is interesting to learn from his son that the only book on naval architecture that Peck ever possessed was the 1711 edition of William Sutherland's *The Shipbuilder's Assistant*. It is not certain, however, that he even had this book as early as 1777.

As far as is known, all of Peck's vessels, except three, were built in various shipyards around Boston or at Plymouth and Newburyport. Two small vessels were built on Peck's own land under his personal supervision, and one was built abroad. At least two, perhaps three, were built at Plymouth in a private shipyard, Peck acting as inspector and supervisor. The other vessels were all built from plans and specifications, Peck acting merely as naval architect. The complete list of ships designed by Peck is not available; those listed by his son represent the more important, however, and they can be discussed in turn.

The *Belisarius* was built as a privateer. A large ship designed for speed, she was built by a Mr. Paul, apparently at Boston. This vessel was said by Joshua Humphreys to have been "one of the fastest sailing ships that swam the Seas." The original statement of Humphreys and his drawing of the body plan of the *Belisarius* are reproduced in Cutler's well-known history of the clipper-ships.[1] Humphreys gave the following dimensions: length on the main-deck 110'-10", length on the keel 93'-8", beam 30'-6" and depth of hold to the gun-deck 15'-6". Humphreys spelt her name "*Bellesarius*" and apparently his drawing was copied from the original draught by Peck.

The *Belisarius* was captured by the British in 1781. It was stated by Peck that the privateer had been sent to sea without sweeps and as a result was captured during a calm. She was taken into the Royal Navy as a 20-gun ship of the same name, but spelt "*Bellisarius*." Charnock, whose dimensions are not always trustworthy, gave the following measurements:

[1] *The Greyhounds of the Seas* (G. P. Putnam's Sons, New York, 1930).

length on the lower deck 104'-0", on the keel 91'-3½", beam 27'-6" and 10'-3" depth of hold to the lower deck. The difference in beam in the two sets of dimensions were either the result of taking the beam at the lower deck in Charnock's table, or a misprint in his book. This ship is often confused with a later merchant ship of the same name built at Salem in 1794, which was owned by the Crowninshields. There is a portrait of the later ship still in existence, but no picture or Admiralty plan of the Peck-designed ship has been found. Obviously the plan of the Peck-designed *Belisarius* cannot be reconstructed by the use of the portrait of the Salem ship, though it has been tried!

Peck also designed the famous *Empress of China*, built at Boston in 1783. She was owned by Robert Morris and others, of Philadelphia. Her fame rests on her feat of being the first American ship to arrive in China under the flag of the new nation. The *Empress of China* sailed from New York in February, 1784, under the command of John Green, and arrived at Macoa August 23rd. She came home in 134 days, making the voyage out and home in 14 months and 24 days. This vessel had the reputation of being a fast sailer, though she seems to have been a fairly full ship.

In 1782, Peck designed a full-lined ship named the *Gustavus*, carrying 16 guns. Little is known of this vessel except that Peck called her a "clump" and that she sailed well. She appears to have been given a letter-of-marque in 1782.

Peck also designed a packet-ship named the *Leda* sometime before 1786, as in January of that year she sailed for L'Orient, France. Peck claimed that her builder had deliberately changed her forebody to give him, the designer, a bad reputation. Peck seems to have incurred the dislike of all the builders, for whom he appears to have entertained the utmost contempt. During 1779 and 1780, Peck was at Plymouth, supervising the construction of the Continental ketch-rigged packet *Mercury*, which eventually fell into British hands. It is believed that the *Rattlesnake* was built at Plymouth during this period.

Peck claimed to have a "system" of design, which his heir offered to sell

American Ship-Sloop, ONTARIO, *built 1813*   (*Courtesy Peabody Museum*)

American Privateer of 1814, RAMBLER   (*Courtesy of Chas. H. Taylor*)

French Hermaphrodite LA GAZELLE, *designed by Marestier*

Six-Masted Schooner, MYRTIE B. COWLEY

to the United States government. The offer was not accepted. The details of Peck's system of design cannot be found among his son's papers, but it is probable that it amounted to little more than a mechanical method of fairing the lines, such as was then quite common, and mathematical formulae for finding displacement and fixing hull proportions. A great many of these "systems" have been proposed from time to time, but none

PRIVATEER *Rattlesnake*.

proves useful in practice. The originator of a "system" often turns out successful vessels in spite of his "system" rather than because of it.

To Peck belongs the credit of designing the first vessel to be built abroad from American plans. This was the *Maréchal de Cartries* of 390 tons, or thereabouts, which was built in France as an East Indian packet. This vessel is an interesting commentary on the theory of the "French influence" on American ship-design. The *Maréchal de Cartries* (Chartres?) was built about 1781–3. About 1785, or a little earlier, Peck retired to

Portsmouth, or Kittery, and operated a small shipyard there for a few years. He became ill in 1790 and his son brought him to Boston, where he died May 3rd of that year. John Peck's wife, who had been Hannah Jackson, died in 1770. His son, William Dandridge Peck, was a famous naturalist and a Harvard professor.

It is difficult to arrive at many conclusions regarding the influence of Peck. In character he appears to have been secretive, egotistical and easily discouraged; these would have had much influence in preventing the spread of his ideas. It cannot be denied, however, that he was a very clever designer. His ships, in all reported cases, were reputed to be swift sailers, easy rollers and very stiff under sail. Since his vessels were so successful, it is possible that they were copied to some degree, in New England at least.

Returning to the plans of the *Rattlesnake*, if this vessel was designed by Peck he was certainly following the hull-form that was popular in southern shipyards. The *Rattlesnake* is quite different in body plan from the *Belisarius*, and so it is possible that Peck was experimenting in his privateer designs. The *Rattlesnake* was very lightly built and was unusual in not having wales. In the Royal Navy she had a reputation for speed, which would appear to be indicated by her lines. There is certainly no "French influence" in this design, for the drag of her keel, her body plan and the extreme rake of her ends were quite contrary to the French practice of the time.

The schooner-privateers of the Revolution were generally too small or too lightly built to be taken into the Royal Navy when captured. Hence, plans of these vessels are very rare. Perhaps the best if not the only example of the type available for reference is the "Arm'd Schooner," purchased for the Royal Navy in the West Indies sometime in 1780 and named *Berbice*. But even this vessel cannot be identified as American-built with absolute certainty, for the records of her purchase and original name could not be found. A contemporary letter, written by a British naval officer on the West Indian station, speaks of her as being

"American-built" and refers to her reputation as a fast sailer. On this information and on the date of her purchase it seems safe to assume that she was one of the numerous American privateers that were captured in the West Indies and condemned there during the Revolution. Figure 24 shows a re-drawing of her draught, the latter being an unusually crude affair evidently made in a West Indian Dockyard.

The uncertainty in regard to the building-place of this fine schooner makes it hardly desirable to discuss her at great length, but her design is so interesting that a few comments can be excused. The *Berbice* shows plainly enough that the naval architect of the Revolution understood the design of fast-sailing fore-and-afters. The lines of this schooner, though quite different from a modern yacht, show a hull capable of high speed. The entrance, slightly hollow, is quite sharp; the "cod's-head and mackerel-tail" effect of the waterlines is more apparent than real because the after end of the run is a mere fin, due to the absence of a counter. If the load waterline was shortened aft and a counter worked onto the hull, the hollow buttocks and "tadpole-tail" would disappear in her lines. It is perhaps interesting to find that the S-shaped sections aft and hollow buttocks of the *Berbice* may still be seen occasionally on schooners designed on the shores of Chesapeake Bay. In spite of the doubt in regard to the building place of the *Berbice*, it can be said that she undoubtedly was representative of the sharp American schooners of her day.

Leaving the time of the Revolution and coming to the quasi-war with France, which began in 1798, we find that the same classes of privateers were employed that had been used at the beginning of the Revolution, the various types of converted merchantmen. Contrary to general belief a large number of privateers were fitted out during this rather peculiar war, but little was accomplished by these vessels, as few French ships were able to get to sea. The war, if it can be called that, did not last long enough for the specially-designed privateers to appear, and so to find another example of this type it is necessary to move on to the War of 1812.

The American schooner had begun to attract attention abroad as early as 1794, but the appearance of a class of large, fast and handsome schooners, almost without exception privateers, during the later years of the War of 1812, brought an increased foreign interest in the type. It was these vessels, and the American frigates, that really made the reputation of American ship-designers and builders abroad. The statement of James, the British naval historian, about these schooners will give some idea of the impression they made abroad. "None can compete with the Americans in the size, beauty, swiftness, or seaworthiness of their schooners. They will arm a schooner of 200 tons with seven guns, including a traversing 18- or 24-pounder, and give her a crew of at least 100 able-bodied men." After complaining that these schooners were usually spoiled by alterations after being captured and taken into the Royal Navy and pointing out that the fact that two vessels could have the same class-name, such as "frigate" or "schooner," without being the same size or power, James compares an American privateer schooner with one of the tiny Bermuda-type schooners in the British service. "The American privateer-schooner *Harlequin*, of Boston, measured 323 tons and mounted 10 long 12-pounders, with a crew of 115 men. Her mainmast was 84 feet and her foreyard 64 feet, in length. Her bulwark was of solid timber, and four inches higher, and two inches thicker, than that of the British 18-gun brig-sloop. The *Whiting* schooner and her class, on the other hand, measured 75 tons and mounted four 12-pounder carronades, with a crew of 20 men and boys; and her bulwark, if it deserved the name, consisted, with here and there a small timber, of an inside and outside plank." In commenting on James' remarks, it is hardly possible to accuse him of partiality toward the Americans, for his dislike of them is obvious throughout his *Naval History of Great Britain* and earlier *Naval Occurrences*. In comparing "typical" schooners, James chose the best class of American privateer-schooners and the worst class of schooner in the Royal Navy. The British had a number of fine schooners in their service, rising 150 tons, which were either purchased American-built vessels, or schooners built on the American model in England or Bermuda. There were also

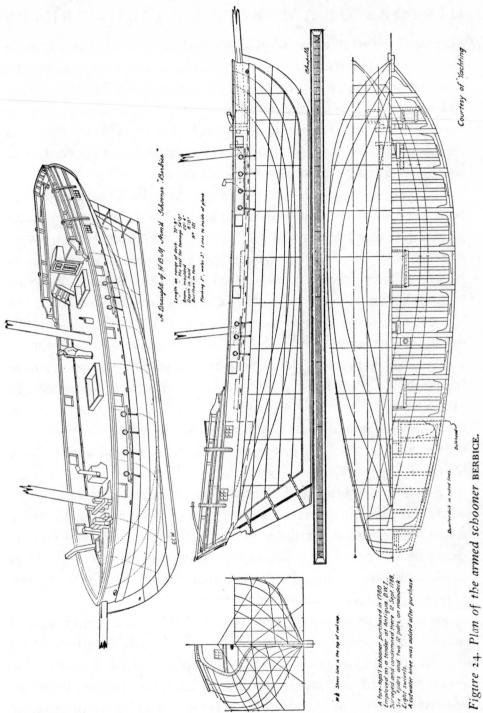

A Draught of H.B.M. Arm'd Schooner "Berbice"

Length on range of deck .... 76'3"
" .... the keel for tonnage 54'0'
Beam, moulded .... 20'4"
Depth in hold .... 8'0'
Burthen in tons .... No 121

Planking 1'. width 3'. Lines to inside of plank

GCW

Sheer line is the top of railcap.

A fore-topsl schooner purchased in 1780.
Employed as a tender at Antigua. B.W.I.
Surveyed and condemned there 12 Sept 1788.
Six 4pdrs and two 12 pdrs. on maindeck
Light swivels
A cutwater knee was added after purchase

Quarterdeck in raised lines.

Bulkhead

Figure 24. Plan of the armed schooner BERBICE.

145

some very remarkable English-designed and built experimental schooners in service. Therefore, it cannot be assumed that the tiny *Whiting* was wholly representative of the schooner class in the Royal Navy.

The *Harlequin* cannot be traced, but plans of a similar and more famous schooner are shown in Plate V and Figure 25. This schooner was the notorious *Prince de Neufchâtel*, whose story as a privateer can be found in almost any history of the War of 1812.

The *Neufchâtel* is believed to have been built by Christian Bergh at New York in 1812–13. She was owned by Madame Flory Charretton, an American citizen residing in New York. J. Ordronaux, her son-in-law and captain of the French privateer *Marengo*, appears to have been in New York during the early days of the War of 1812. Application having been made two days earlier, a letter-of-marque for the *Neufchâtel* was issued to Ordronaux at New York, October 28, 1813. The names of the sureties on her bond were F. Charretton, J. Ordronaux, C. G. Fontaine and Stephen Perpignon. The *Neufchâtel* was sent to France under the command of Ordronaux and fitted out as a privateer at Cherbourg. In March, 1814, she got to sea and took nine prizes in the English Channel. Madame Charretton died about this time, and the *Neufchâtel* passed into the hands of her trustees, Joseph Beyll, Peter Fresell and a man named "Benny."

Getting to sea again in June, she took six prizes in as many days. Throughout the summer of 1814, the *Neufchâtel* cruised in European waters, causing great damage to the enemy shipping. Though she was chased by seventeen British men-of-war during her cruises, her speed was so great that she had no difficulty in escaping them. Late in September, 1814, the *Neufchâtel* appeared at Boston and refitted.

She sailed again during the first week of October, and when four days out was about a half-mile to the so'th'ard of Nantucket Shoals, with an English prize ship in company. Here she was discovered, during a calm, by the British frigate *Endymion*. Though the frigate had the advantage of what little wind there was she could not get alongside the privateer by

146

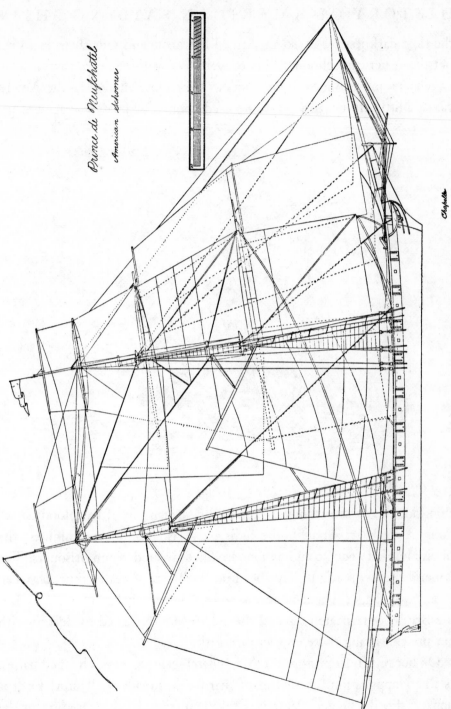

Prince de Neufchâtel
American Schooner

Chapelle

Figure 25. Sail plan of the American Privateer Schooner PRINCE DE NEUFCHÂTEL.

147

the time darkness set in, so she armed her boats and sent them in to cut out the American schooner. There were five of these boats carrying between 111 and 120 men. The attackers were close enough to the American at a little after 8.30 P. M. to be fired upon. The boats managed to get

Prince de Neufchâtel.

alongside the privateer, however, and then began one of the bloodiest actions of the war. Though the fight only lasted about 20 minutes, the British lost between 70 and 93 men in killed, wounded and prisoners. The American crew seems to have been unusually small at this time, between 37 and 40 men, of which 31 appear to have been killed and wounded. But the British were beaten off and the *Neufchâtel* returned to Boston with her prize, arriving there on October 15th.

On her return to Boston, the *Neufchâtel* seems to have changed hands, as a new application for a letter-of-marque was made by "John" Ordronaux, J. H. Beylle and Peter E. Frevall. In spite of the variation in the

148

spelling of the latter two names, it is apparent that Ordronaux joined two of Madame Charretton's trustees in the purchase of the schooner. From another source, it has been found that the price of the *Neufchâtel* was twenty-one thousand dollars. The new commission was issued December 12, 1814, and on the night of the 21st the *Neufchâtel* got to sea, under the command of Nicholas Millin ("a Jew by persuasion, a Frenchman by birth, an American by convenience"), and manned by 120 men, including 5 lieutenants. On the 26th she encountered a severe gale and on the 28th was sighted and chased by three British frigates, the *Leander, Newcastle* and *Acasta;* the first two were new frigates designed as a match for the American 44's and were big, fast ships. Though the high seas and strong wind were most unfavorable for the schooner, she managed to keep clear for most of the day but was finally overtaken. The *Neufchâtel* would have escaped had she not lost spars in carrying too much sail. According to the British officers on the *Newcastle,* their ship logged 13 knots for hours, with the American more than holding her own at this speed, running with the wind free. Taking the waterline length of the *Neufchâtel* as 107′-6″ and the maximum speed reached by her under these unfavorable conditions as 13½ knots, her speed-length ratio works out to be about 1.3. It is possible, therefore, that under favorable conditions she might have reached the ratio of the clipper-ship *James Baines* when she went at 21 knots, 1.355. From this the conclusion is drawn that the best of the privateer-schooners of 1812–15 were as well designed for speed as the clipper-ships of 40 years later, and also the old schooners could bear comparison with the fastest of modern trans-Atlantic racing yachts.

The commodore of the British squadron, Sir George Collier, was so impressed with the sailing and appearance of the *Neufchâtel* that, instead of sending her to Halifax to be condemned and sold as usual, he sent her to England with dispatches so that she might come to the attention of the Admiralty. On her arrival in England, she was taken into the Deptford Dockyard to be surveyed for purchase into the Royal Navy. In March she was put into dock and her lines were taken off, but in taking her out of dock she hung on the sill of the dock-gates and broke her back. Because of this accident she was not taken into naval service but was sold for a mere song. Lubbock, in his recent book, *The Opium Clipper*,[1] states that the lines taken off the *Neufchâtel* were afterwards used in the design of a famous opium-smuggler, the *Red Rover*, which in turn was the model for a number of other opium clippers. An interesting account of the connection of the design of the *Neufchâtel* with that of many of the opium clippers can be found in Lubbock's excellent study of the opium-smugglers. There was also an English schooner yacht named *Prince de Neufchâtel* afloat in the 1830's and '40's that may have had some connection with the American schooner, for the English yacht was 108'-0" long and 24'-10" wide on the waterline, about the size of the American.

The lines of the *Neufchâtel*, shown in Plate V, illustrate a beautifully modeled schooner, long, low and rather narrow. This clean-lined flier, with her striking rig, is bound to give a favorable impression of the ability of American schooner-designers of her date. It is not difficult to understand why these American schooners won approval abroad and wrung an admission of American superiority from the Yankee-detesting James. The lines of the *Neufchâtel* are sufficient explanation for her seventeen escapes from British men-of-war. The figurehead cannot be distinguished in the original plan, but the application for her letter-of-marque describes it as "a Coronal figurehead" and gives her American tonnage as $319^{88}\!/_{95}$ tons.

Though the *Neufchâtel* was pierced with 11 ports on a side, 22 in all, she carried but 18 carriage-guns. A search of the records of this schooner failed to show the size and type of her guns, but it is possible that her battery was made up of 12-pounder carronades, with two long 18's as chase guns.

There is a common belief among naval historians that the carronade was not popular among the Americans during the War of 1812. It has been also claimed that the War of 1812 doomed the carronade as a ship-gun. There is little evidence supporting these opinions, for the batteries of

[1] Brown, Son & Ferguson, Ltd., Glasgow.

American ships of all classes, naval and privateer, were mostly carronades during the war. After the war, ship-sloops, brigs and schooners in the United States, British and French navies were likewise armed with carronades, supplemented by a few long-guns. As far back as 1793, by which time the British Navy had armed nearly all classes of ships with whole or partial batteries of carronades, it was understood that long-guns were a necessary addition to the carronade battery, and so it cannot be claimed either that the Americans were the first to use the mixed battery. The ad-

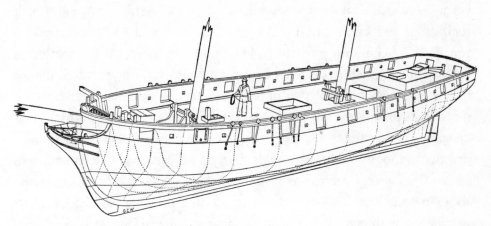

AMERICAN PRIVATEER *Prince de Neufchâtel*.

vantage of the carronade over the long-gun firing the same weight of shot was a saving of weight. Because of this advantage and because of its shorter length, the carronade could be fired somewhat more rapidly than the long-gun; on the other hand the carronade was useless at long range. In spite of the fact that the carronade has been given a reputation of being inaccurate, this gun was really more accurate than the long-gun up until the limit of range of the carronade was reached. This is a general statement, of course, and there were exceptions. The fact that the inventors of the carronade had attempted to overcome the handicap of using a short gun with a reduced charge of slow-burning powder by reducing the windage (clearance of shot in the bore) has been quite overlooked. The reduced windage prevented lateral movement of shot in the bore when the gun was discharged. The long-guns of the Americans were not as accurate as supposed, because of the underweight, and therefore increased wind-age, of their shot. The better shooting of the American gunners during the War of 1812 was not due to more accurate guns, but to better ac-quaintance with the range and accuracy of faulty cannon; the British guns and shot were superior, but their gunners were generally strangers to the qualities of their weapons.

The light weight of the carronade, combined with its destructive pow-ers at short range, made it an excellent gun for fast ships that could pick their range and a poor gun for slow vessels that could not. Since the car-ronade was accurate up to the limit of its short range, was effective in action and weighed less than the long-gun, and since it was desirable to have a light-weight battery in order to obtain the greatest possible speed, it is not surprising to find the privateers using this type of gun to a great extent. To illustrate the popularity of the carronade in American privateer-schooners, the privateers *Lottery*, *Decatur* and *Chasseur* will serve. The *Lottery* carried six 9-pounder carronades; the *Decatur* carried six 12-pounder carronades and a long 18 on a pivot; while the *Chasseur* was armed with eight 9-pounder carronades and six long 12's.

It must not be supposed that the *Neufchâtel* was unusually large or heavily armed for her class. Though she was one of the largest American privateers afloat in the War of 1812, there were many vessels as large as the *Neufchâtel*, a few larger, and many as heavily armed. The *Chasseur*, for example, was 115'-6" on deck, 26'-8" beam and 12'-9" depth of hold. The *Swift* was 110'-0" on deck and 25'-11" beam. The *Boxer* was 105'-4" on deck, 26'-6" beam, and 11'-5" depth of hold. The 17-gun *Herald*, built by Bergh in 1813, was 101'-0" on deck, 24'-8" beam and 10'-4" depth of hold. These were schooners or hermaphrodites; the ships were not much larger. The famous Salem privateer *America* measured but 114'-0" on deck and 31'-0" beam, and, though she carried 20 guns, her crew was no larger than that of the *Neufchâtel* when she had her full complement of

150 men. Of course, neither ship required that number to work or fight her, as a comparatively small crew could handle either.

The sail plan of the *Neufchâtel*, shown in Figure 25, is an interesting one. The picture of the privateer *Rambler* of the same period shows that the proportions and general appearance of the rig of the *Neufchâtel* were more or less typical of the whole class of hermaphrodites. The hermaphrodite-schooner differed from the modern brigantine rig only in having a schooner's foresail. The barren spritsail yard under the bowsprit, shown in the plan, was used to spread the shrouds of the jib-boom and flying jib-boom; the spritsail had dropped out of use in small American craft, though the barren spritsail yard remained in use in frigates and packet-ships for many years after the war. The most unusual feature of the rig of the *Neufchâtel* was the little royal carried on the pole of the maintopmast; it was undoubtedly a light weather sail and rarely set. The fore-and-aft main topsail bent to a short gaff was, apparently, a typical feature of American privateers, as similar sails are shown on the *Rambler*. As this cut of a topsail has not appeared on the plans of any foreign-built schooner, the sail was probably an American idea.

The history of American privateers shows many actions, like the fight between the *Neufchâtel* and the boats of the *Endymion*, which would have done credit to any armed force, but on the other hand, there were a great many tame surrenders. This record was not one that belonged to American privateers alone, but rather, it represented the experience of every nation that had privateers. As in the case of the American militia in the War of 1812 and the early volunteer regiments of the Civil War, who could fight brilliantly when they would but who usually preferred to give an exhibition of rapid foot-work, the privateersmen acted well or badly according to their discipline and training. The stories of the various American privateers too often illustrate sea-fighting as a highly specialized profession which required training not to be obtained on the deck of a fisherman, coaster or trader, and that victory was not to be bought by

153

"minute-man" preparation for war. If there was one lesson that might be learned from the naval War of 1812, it was that battles are usually won by the better ships and men, and not by mere numbers. Unfortunately, however, good ships and well-trained officers and men, in short, a good but not necessarily large navy, cost more and require more public interest than a small, ill-prepared navy, or even a navy dependent on mere numbers of ships and men.

In the development of fast-sailing craft, the slave-trade did not have any effect until after the War of 1812. In fact, the building of vessels designed to meet the requirements of the trade did not begin until about 1820. The period of the specially designed slaver can be placed as between 1820 and 1855. Though the slave trade was outlawed by both England and the United States before the War of 1812, it was not until the end of that war that the navies of either nation could take much interest in the business. The first step, after the war, was to clean up the West Indies which had become infested with pirates of the lowest type during the long years of the Napoleonic and American wars. Both the British and American Navies employed small men-of-war in this work. In addition to a small number of schooners, mostly purchased, and a few wartime-built brigs and ship-sloops of the regular navy, the United States employed a portion of the Revenue Marine in the suppression of piracy. The Revenue Marine was composed of small, fast schooners on the extreme Baltimore-Clipper model, manned by experienced seamen, and was quite effective. The British squadrons were made up largely of 10-, 16- and 18-gun brigs and ship-sloops. A few cutters and schooners, with an occasional frigate, were also employed. It took these forces about five years, 1820 to 1825, to discourage piracy in the West Indies, and there were even occasional outbreaks up until the late '30's.

The British were particularly efficient in taking pirates out of circulation, working on the old principle that a pirate rarely gave trouble after stretching hemp. It has been said that American naval officers, becoming disgusted at the affection and tender regard shown pirates sent to the

United States for trial, made a practice of turning over these vermin to the British naval authorities, who acted with common sense and dispatch.

At the same time that the campaign against piracy was being carried on in the West Indies and the Caribbean, a systematic attempt to suppress the slave trade was begun. In this service the British were the most efficient; political conditions and slave-owning sympathies prevented the Americans from making a whole-hearted effort to stop slave-trading. As a result, British cruisers were the first to affect the design of slaving ships and so may be considered first.

With their accustomed energy, the British went about the suppression of the slave trade by squadrons stationed in the West Indies, on the West African Coast and along the slave-trade routes. As it was soon found that there were some very fast slavers that could not be caught by the ordinary fast naval vessels, the Royal Navy attempted to obtain cruisers capable of high speed. The British Navy had a class of 10-gun brigs that had proven to be quite fast when in the proper trim and well-handled. These vessels were the notorious "Coffin-brig" class, which had been originally designed by Sir Henry Peake in 1807 as the *Rolla* class. These brigs were only 90'-0" long and 24'-6" extreme beam; they were very much on the Baltimore model and had sharp ends combined with a good deal of dead-rise. The fault of the design was the lack of displacement and stability to carry the heavy armament, eight 18-pounder carronades and two long 6's. The bulwarks were unduly high and much too heavy. The rig was large, which with the top-heaviness of the hull made the 10-gun brig class very dangerous and many were lost. One might think that the faults of the class would lead to early revision in the direction of reduced top-weight, but just as in the American naval schooners and brigs after the War of 1812, additional weights of boats, short quarterdecks and other fittings were added instead. In 1817, the 10-gun brigs were altered slightly by the increase of some sheer forward, and a large number of new members of the class were built.

As an experiment, some of these new 10-gun brigs were cut down and re-rigged as schooners, hermaphrodites and brigantines. Others were altered while being built. During the late 20's and early 30's the best-known members of the class used in the suppression of slaving were the *Buzzard, Lynx, Griffon, Brisk, Forester* and *Barracouta;* the latter was the only one rigged as a three-masted schooner (1829). It was found, however, that these experimental ships were not so fast as many of the slavers; hence new experimental craft were built. It is not necessary to follow the British in their efforts to build small naval craft capable of out-sailing the slavers; suffice to say that the British naval constructor Sir William Symonds, 1832–48, designed some small brigs and brigantines that were most successful in their work.

The Symondites were usually fast ships, but hard rollers. In model they were much like the American schooners, having great deadrise, but they differed from most of the Baltimore Clippers in having the turn of the bilge at or just above the waterline and their greatest beam at the height of the main deck. As a class, the Symondites were very unsteady gun-platforms, which destroyed much of their value as men-of-war. The Admiralty permitted other designers to compete with Symonds; perhaps the best of these outsiders was Joseph White of Cowes, a famous designer of yachts who also turned out some very fast opium clippers. One of White's best productions was the brig *Waterwitch*, originally a yacht. This brig, having shown great speed, was purchased as a slave-cruiser and was very successful in that capacity. She was a very lovely little brig and was widely admired.

Late in the 20's, the British were lucky enough to capture a very fast slaver-brig that had been built in Baltimore. This was the *Henriquetta*, taken by the *Sybille*, Sept. 6, 1827. The slaver had made six trips previous to her capture during which she had landed 3,040 slaves in Brazil, making $400,000 for her owners in less than three years. This vessel was purchased into the Royal Navy as the *Black Joke* and employed on the slaver patrol. The *Black Joke* was very successful as a slaver-catcher, but she was worn out in 1831 and was burned by order of the Admiral on the Cape of Good

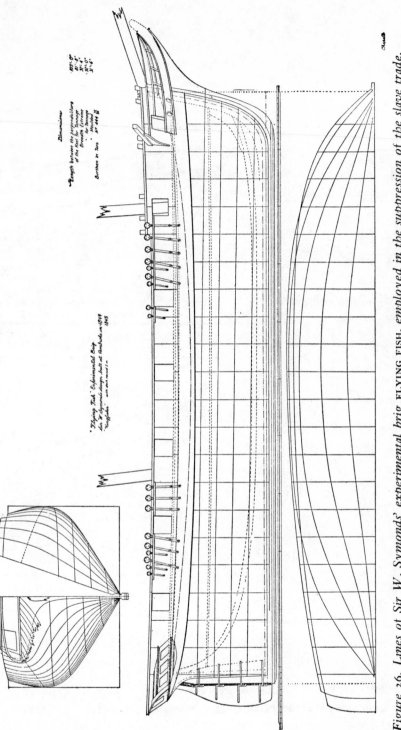

Figure 26. Lines of Sir W. Symonds' experimental brig FLYING FISH, *employed in the suppression of the slave trade.*

157

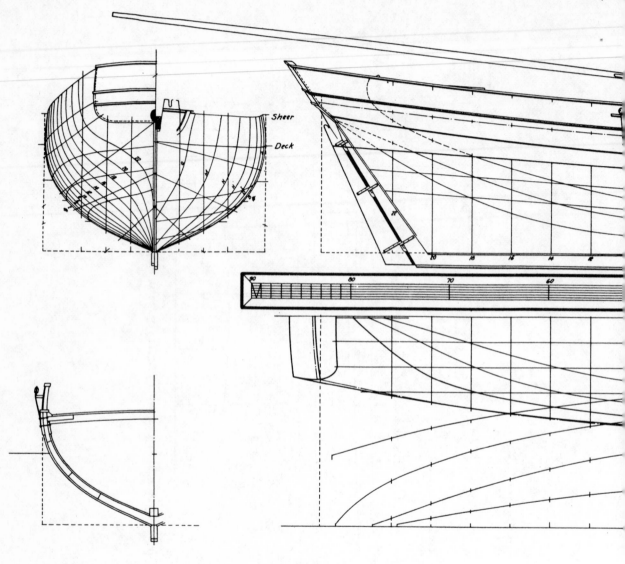

Sheer

Deck

Plate **VI. DOS AMIGOS.** *An example of a popular type of slaver, showing the peculiar gun mounting favored in this class of vessel.*

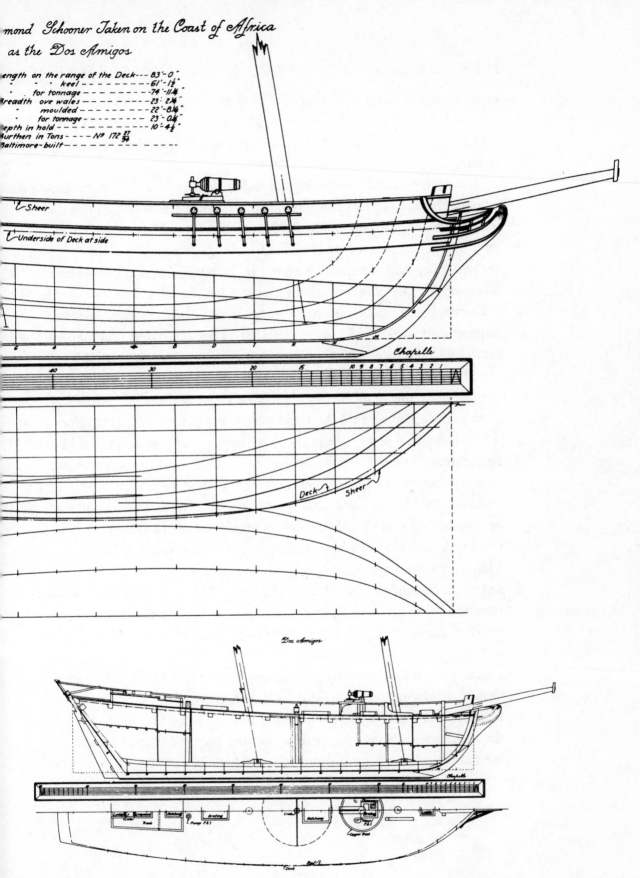

mond Schooner Taken on the Coast of Africa
as the Dos Amigos

Length on the range of the Deck --- 83'- 0"
  "   "   keel --------------- 61'- 1½"
  "   "   for tonnage ----------- 74'- 11¼"
Breadth ove wales ---------------- 23'- 2¼"
  "   moulded ------------------- 22'- 8¼"
  "   for tonnage --------------- 23'- 0½"
Depth in hold -------------------- 10'- 4½"
Burthen in Tons ----- Nº 172 $\frac{37}{34}$
Baltimore-built

Sheer

Underside of Deck at side

Chapelle

Deck Sheer

Dos Amigos

Chapelle

Hope station at Sierra Leone on May 3, 1832, and so her lines were never taken off. Her portrait shows a low-sided brig with very raking ends, a very handsome little ship. She was 90'-10" on the gun-deck and 26'-7" beam.

One of the slavers taken by the *Black Joke* was a Baltimore-built schooner named the *Dos Amigos*. This was a very fast vessel, and so she, too, was purchased into the Royal Navy, under the name of *Fair Rosamond*. Whether she was as fast as the *Black Joke* cannot be decided, as the particulars of her capture have not been found. Judging by her lines, however, the *Dos Amigos* was not captured because of any lack of speed.

Once it became necessary to design and build vessels to meet particular requirements of the trade, there appeared a class of slaving ship that was remarkable for speed. As the draught of a new slaver was being completed on the drafting-table, her designer had to consider every element pertaining to the trade. In the first place there was the matter of size. Most of the harbors on the African Coast where slaves could be purchased were small and not very deep. By 1820, large groups of slaves could not be purchased in one place, because of competition and for other reasons. A large ship would be hard to conceal, and as there was no legitimate trade on the African Coast that would give employment to a large ship, her appearance there would arouse the suspicions of the commander of a cruiser. A large ship would cost more than a small one and would require a large crew, thus adding unnecessarily to the expense. There was no reason, then, to employ large ships in the trade. The only question that determined the size of the ship, as far as the slaves were concerned, was how many could be crowded into her. Allowing for mortality from disease, filth and over-crowding, enough slaves had to be carried to show a big profit. Therefore, there was a minimum size for slavers, fixed by experience of the slaving captains, below which the slave-ship would be unprofitable. It was found that vessels between 60 and 100 feet in length paid the best, the exact figure depending on the pocket-book of the owner, the number of slaves his customers could handle, the particular requirements of the rig wanted by her captain, and the harbors she would be expected to enter.

The matter of rig was the next consideration. Often the captain or owner decided this matter, the choice usually lying between the schooner, either fore or fore-and-main topsail rig, and the brig. The brigantine and hermaphrodite rigs were also popular, particularly for large slavers. Because of the well-known advantages of the square-rig for deep water, all

AMERICAN SLAVER *Dos Amigos*.

slavers carried squaresails. The schooner and hermaphrodite each had the advantage that she was weatherly and easily handled by a small crew. The popularity of the brig seems to have been largely due to the number of light-sails that could be carried with that rig. As far as can be discovered, no ship or barque-rigged vessels were built for the trade while active efforts to suppress slaving were being made. A few ships were employed in the trade, it is true, but these appear to have been the ventures of amateur slavers rather than of the regular traders.

In the design of a vessel, the average conditions of weather and sea on the courses she would run in her trade had to be considered, particularly where speed was so important. The trade-lanes of the slave-ships were fixed by the locations where slaves could be procured on the African Coast, the location of the markets and the shortest and quickest course between these two points. The slave-marts on the African Coast were scattered along the western shore, from Cape Verde, in what is now Senegal, to Cape Morro in Portuguese Angola. This district included the "Grain," "Slave," "Gold" and "Ivory" Coasts and the lands adjoining the infamous "Bight of Benin." The markets for slaves during the period under discussion were largely limited to Cuba and Brazil. While it is true that great numbers of slaves were landed on the coasts of Florida and Georgia, and some smuggled into all southern ports, the bulk of these slaves were trans-shipped in Cuba. The slaves were rarely brought directly to the United States, as their importation was illegal and both the Revenue and Naval services enforced the law. Under these conditions it was difficult and risky, of course, to land large numbers of slaves and dispose of them. Therefore it was easier to land them in Cuba to be smuggled into the United States in small groups. Brazil, like the southern states, permitted slave-owning, but in addition allowed importation. The papers relating to the capture of slavers, between 1820 and 1860, show that practically all of the slaves were to be landed in either Cuba or Brazil. The most direct course from the slave marts of Africa to the markets in Brazil and Cuba was in the trade-wind area, which is marked by steady winds of moderate strength during most of the year. At other times, calms interspersed with short but heavy squalls might be met. Therefore the slaver ought to be designed so that she was fast in light and moderate weather but stiff enough to carry sail in a squall. These conditions made it desirable that the slaver be not only fast but weatherly to escape from cruisers. Although a vessel sailing the slave route would rarely meet an extremely heavy sea, she needed to be seaworthy enough for work in the open ocean.

The cost of a slaver was another factor. Like the more recent liquor-smuggler of the Prohibition period, the risk of capture, and the resultant loss of ship and cargo, was great; hence it was hardly wise to use an expensive vessel, that is to say, one that was unnecessarily costly. Therefore the slaver, like the later "rum-runner," was very plain and cheaply built, without decoration or "ginger-bread work." The cost of a slaver was fixed by her size and speed, not by her finish or construction.

The cargo of a slaver offered no great problem to the designer, as there was little deadweight involved that brought strains on the hull-structure. As a matter of fact, the only construction problem was to get the hull and rig strong enough to withstand the strains set up by carrying a heavy press of sail.

The necessity of speed in a slaver was obvious, once the cruisers became active. There was also the very high mortality among the slaves from over-crowding during a long voyage, and so speed and profits went hand in hand.

The armament on most of the slavers consisted of a single carronade or long-gun on a pivot, as the small crew of the average slave-ship made a battery useless. From the end of the War of 1812 to about 1830 there were some slavers that were sufficiently well armed to try to fight off a cruiser, but the lack of success taught the later slavers to trust to their heels rather than to their guns. The single gun of the slaver was enough to enable her to fight off a "hi'jacker" and to prevent attacks by the negroes when buying slaves.

The *Dos Amigos*, while in the Royal Navy as the *Fair Rosamond*, was placed in dry-dock at the Portsmouth Dockyard and her lines taken off during the summer of 1832. In 1837 the rig of the *Fair Rosamond* was cut down, in the process of which a drawing of her original rig was made. Plates VI and VIA were drawn from these plans. Little comment is necessary; the excellence of the design of the *Dos Amigos* is obvious. The mount of the pivoted carronade, a 32-pounder, is shown in the plans. Some idea of the great spread of sail carried by slavers can be obtained from Plate VIA. The *Dos Amigos* represented the most popular size of schooner-slaver, as can be seen by comparing her dimensions with two other slavers of the same rig. The *Bolivar*, later H.B.M. schooner *Nimble*,

161

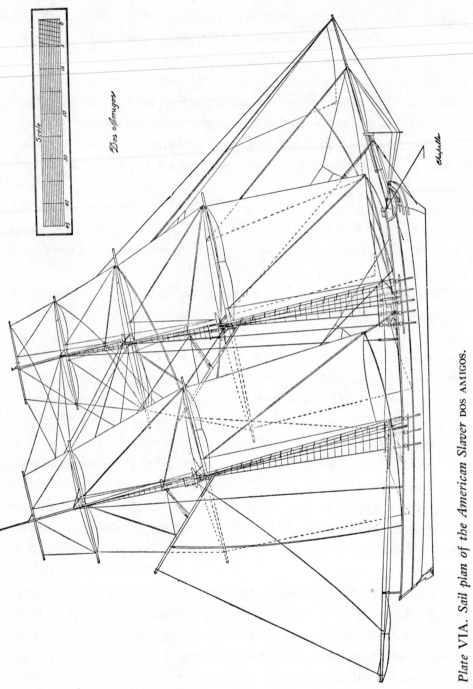

Scale

Dos Amigos

Chapelle

Plate VIA. Sail plan of the American Slaver DOS AMIGOS.

162

was 83'-7" on deck, 22'-2" beam and 9'-5" depth of hold. This schooner is said to have been built at Jamaica in 1822, but the statement is open to question. She was purchased for the Royal Navy in 1826. The schooner *Indagador* was 80'-6" on deck, 19'-6" beam and 10'-4" depth of hold.

Brig-slavers were usually larger than schooner-slavers, though this is no more than a general statement, there having been many exceptions to the rule. The brig *Diligente* was an excellent example of her type, being

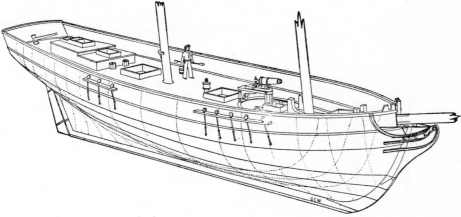

AMERICAN SLAVER *Dos Amigos.*

100'-0" long and 25'-0" beam. The only brig-slaver that was taken into naval service was the *Black Joke*, mentioned earlier, and so it is very difficult to find any plans of this particular class. A German shipwright, however, who was working in New York in the '40's, obtained plans of many American vessels which he took home as models to be copied; among them there was a slaving brig. These plans have recently been placed in the Peabody Marine Museum, by whose courtesy the plan in Figure 27 is shown.

This plan was marked "slaver brig" and is without name. She appears to have the "Golden Fleece" as a figurehead; this may eventually lead to her identification. In spite of her apparent bluffness, the brig was quite sharp forward, as there was a great deal of flare to the forward sections. The well-formed run indicated a fast sailer; the powerful mid-section, a stiff vessel. No spar dimensions for this vessel having been recorded; it is impossible to reconstruct her sail plan, but it was probably very large.

These two examples of slavers show the result of their designers' attempts to fulfill the requirements of the trade that have been discussed earlier. Since speed is an elusive factor of design, it was natural for the designers of slavers to turn to the fastest model known at the time the fast

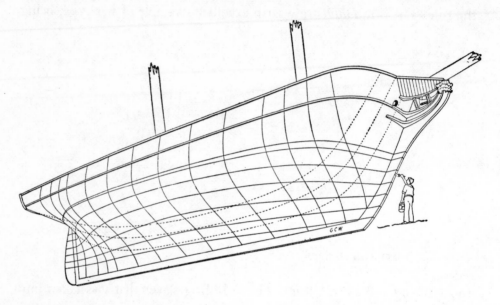

AMERICAN-BUILT SLAVER BRIG.

slaver came into existence, the Baltimore Clipper or privateer-model, as the foundation and inspiration for the new type.

From this it can be seen that though the British Navy must have the credit for putting a premium on the speed of slave-ships, beyond the requirements of profitable trade, the Americans receive credit for furnishing the model. The American Navy did not become active in the suppression of the trade, except along the coasts of the United States, until the '40's. Probably the largest part of the enforcement of the non-importation law fell on the Revenue Marine. By the time that the American cruisers became really active along the slave-routes, the model of the

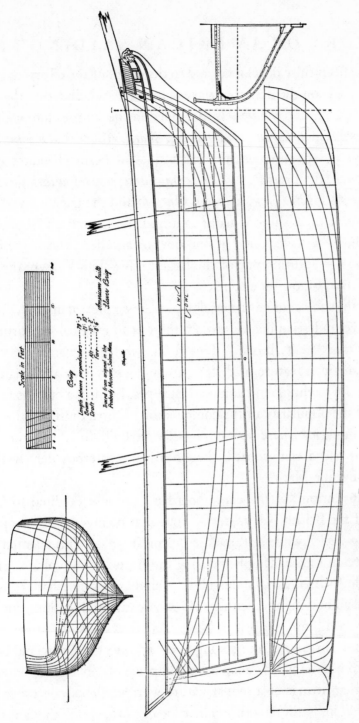

Scale in Feet

Brig

Length between perpendiculars ---- 79'-3"
Beam ---- 21'-10"
Draft { Aft ---- 11'-2"
       Fore ---- 8'-6"

Traced from original in the
Peabody Museum, Salem, Mass.

American-built
Slaver Brig

Figure 27. An American-built Slaver Brig.

slaver had been fully developed, and so the effect of the efforts to suppress the slave trade on the design of slave-ships came wholly from the British. The United States naval vessels that aided in the suppression of the trade were the schooners *Grampus, Porpoise, Shark, Alligator, Dolphin, Boxer, Enterprise* and *Experiment*, the brigantines or hermaphrodites *Dolphin* and *Porpoise*, the brigs *Perry, Truxton, Somers* and *Bainbridge*, also the *Spark*, the sloops *Peacock, Erie* and *Ontario* and the frigate *John Adams*. Not many of these ships actually captured slavers, but all were engaged in patrolling the slave routes at one time or another. The *Perry* had the distinction of capturing one of the largest slave-ships known, the American ship *Martha*, on June 6, 1850.

While the subject of naval vessels that were employed in the suppression of the slave trade is under discussion, there is an excellent opportunity to introduce the "centerboard." This fitting was, for many years, a distinctly American feature of design in schooners, sloops and small sailing boats of both yachting and commercial types. But it is a curious fact that, in spite of the popularity of the combination of shoal draft and the centerboard in America, there was no vessel ever built for the United States Navy that had a centerboard, though a few centerboarders were built for the Revenue Marine.

The "invention" of the centerboard is generally credited to Captain Schank of the British Navy. It is claimed that he invented a "drop-keel," or "sliding-keel," while stationed at Boston in 1774. This talented officer saw service on Lake Champlain during the American Revolution and was responsible for many ingenious ideas, including a single battery of guns that could all be fought on either side of the ship, and the introduction of the "drop-keel" into the British Navy. As far as the story of the "invention" of the "drop-keel" or "sliding-keel" is concerned, it would be more accurate to use the word "adaptation" in place of "invention," as there is evidence that fittings of a similar nature were previously in use in China and possibly in South America. The type of "drop-keel" thought to have been used in the Chinese vessels was what is now called a "dagger-board,"

166

a piece of plank dropped through a case and slot in the hull and reaching some distance below the bottom. The "drop-keel," "sliding-keel" and "dagger-board" would all answer to this description. The "jangada," mentioned in the first chapter, is thought to have used the "dagger-board"; as was mentioned earlier, this craft was a South American sailing-raft.

The "centerboard," "drop-keel" and "sliding-keel," "dagger-board," and the "leeboards" that were so typical of the Dutch sailing craft were all intended for the same purpose, that of preventing a shoal-draft hull from sagging to leeward when sailing with the wind abeam or when beating to windward. Previous to the adoption of these fittings, it was almost impossible to design shoal-draft vessels that could work to windward; this was the objection to the "radeau" and "gondola" of Revolutionary times.

Schank appears to have first tried a long plank, about three-quarters the length of his boat, working in a case and dropping a short distance below the keel. It could be raised when the boat got into shoal water by means of tackles at each end of the "keel"; these rove in the case, of course. Schank soon found that there was considerable difficulty in handling such a board because of its weight and its tendency to jamb in the case unless the tackles were very carefully handled. He also decided that the very long case necessary for this type of "keel" would be objectionable because of the room required, cutting the vessel's accommodations in two along the centerline. To overcome this difficulty he decided to use three or more small boards in separate cases, one at the bow, one amidships and one at the stern, except in large vessels where two "drop-keels" would be used amidship instead of one. These boards could be raised and lowered with separate tackles, as required by the depth of water in which the vessel was sailing, and could also be adjusted by the same means so as to help steering. The reason that Schank felt that multiple boards were necessary, with the use of the small "drop-keel," was that he had in view the design of square-rigged vessels. In this type of sailing ship, the "center of effort" or center of gravity of the area of the sails moved fore-and-aft a great deal as sails were furled or set (when compared with the fore-and-after). To meet this variation in the balance of the rig it was necessary to have a long keel, or in other words, a more or less rectangular under-body profile. Obviously the use of a single board or "drop-keel" amidships was the same as cutting away the profile under-water, at bow and stern, to an excessive degree, and the result was a vessel that would steer poorly at times.

Schank found it difficult to convince the Admiralty that his idea was practical. Finally he built a cutter 65'-0" on deck, 21'-5" beam and 7'-2" depth of hold, to mount 12 guns and fitted with three "drop-keels." This cutter, named the *Trial*, was built at Plymouth, England, in 1790 by Thomas Dunsterville. She was apparently privately owned, for she appears to have been purchased by the Admiralty in 1790. Before the *Trial* was built (1789), Schank had been permitted to build a small cutter-rigged boat in the Deptford Dockyard, which had given the Admiralty some confidence in the idea. After purchasing the *Trial*, the Admiralty put her into service for a time to see how she would meet the requirements of naval work. Judged from the reports of various observers and her officers, she was considered a success. Only a single British cutter had been able to outsail the *Trial* and this was a much larger vessel.

Having become satisfied with the usefulness of the "drop-keel," the Admiralty ordered the building of a ship-sloop with this fitting. The result was the *Cynthia*, built on the Thames in 1796, a ship-sloop mounting 14 guns and measuring 113'-2" on deck, 28'-7" beam and 12'-0" depth of hold. This ship was followed by two classes of gun-brigs built the next year, the *Hasty* class of 16 brigs, measuring 76'-0" on deck, 22'-6" beam and 8'-0" in the hold, and the *Assault* class of 17 brigs, measuring 75'-0" on deck, 22'-0" beam and 7'-11" in the hold. These brigs were fitted with two "drop-keels," one at each end of the ship, 10 or 12 feet in from the perpendiculars. All these vessels gave trouble, becoming leaky around the cases, and so eventually the "drop-keels" were removed.

Between 1796 and 1798, another English constructor named Samuel Bentham also built some men-of-war fitted with "drop-keels." Two of his vessels were double-ended ship-sloops of peculiar design, something like enormous whale-boats in model. These ships, the *Dart* and *Arrow*, were fitted with four "drop-keels." They were sister-ships, measuring 128'-8" on deck, 33'-10" beam and 7'-11" in the hold. The other vessels were four schooners, measuring from 80'-6" to 86'-6" on deck, one or two of which were fitted with "drop-keels." The Bentham vessels were very interesting craft, having a semi-circular mid-section and diagonally-planked bulkheads, built-in water tanks, hawse-holes at bow and stern and other peculiarities.

The difficulty of making the "drop-keel" cases water-tight discouraged the Admiralty from further experiment and the matter was forgotten for a while. But about 1810 the Americans began to take an interest in the idea. Around New York, particularly along the Hudson River, a large number of sloops fitted with the Dutch leeboards were in use. But the need for shoal-draft sailing craft with less cumbersome fittings than the leeboards was great, and so from 1811 on a number of patents were granted for types of centerboards. The "centerboard" differed from the "drop-keel," "sliding-keel" and "dagger-board" in being pivoted at the fore-end, with the hoisting tackle usually at the after-end. The first to receive patents for this type of board appear to have been the Swain brothers of New Jersey, who obtained a patent for some kind of a pivoted board in 1811. After the War of 1812, a number of rather large sloops were built with centerboards, some as early as 1815. Between that year and 1821, the use of the centerboard extended to the Chesapeake Bay, where the fitting was applied to schooners. The lack of plans of early centerboard craft has been particularly noticeable; hence the plans of the British naval schooner *Union*, shown in Figures 28 and 29, are of particular interest.

The history and origin of the *Union* are difficult to trace, but according to one account she was originally an American-built slaver. There

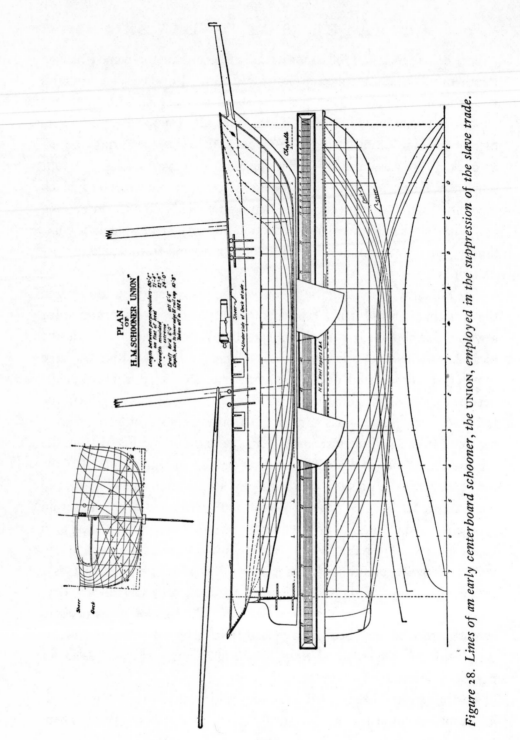

PLAN
OF
H.M. SCHOONER "UNION"

Length between perpendiculars: 80'2"
on flat of keel: 71'6"
Breadth moulded: 23'8"
extreme: 24'0"
Draft fwd 6'0" aft 6'6"
Depth, base to lower edge of rail cap 10'3"
Taken off in 1822.

Figure 28. Lines of an early centerboard schooner, the UNION, employed in the suppression of the slave trade.

170

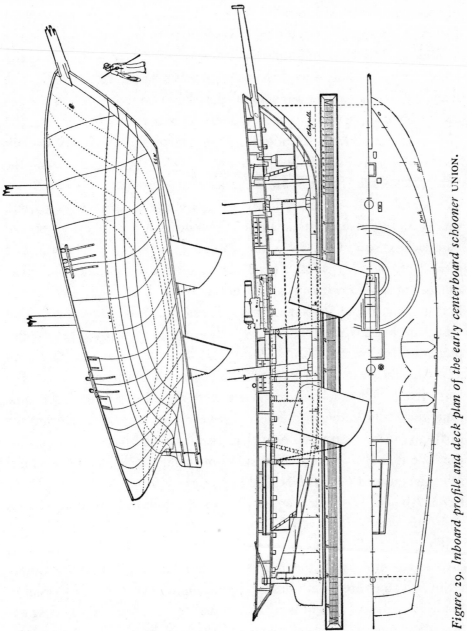

Figure 29. Inboard profile and deck plan of the early centerboard schooner UNION.

was a schooner named the *City of Kingston*, built at Kingston, Jamaica, in 1821, and purchased into the Royal Navy in 1823 under the name of *Union*, but this was a much smaller vessel than the one shown in Figures 28 and 29. The Kingston-built *Union* measured but 59'-9" on deck and 18'-3¾" beam, whereas the *Union* shown was over 80 feet in length. The schooner illustrated here was employed in the West Indies, as was also the earlier *Union*, operating against the slavers and pirates as the occasion dictated. With H.B.M. schooners *Lion* (formerly an American-built piratical schooner, 61'-8" on the gun-deck, 19'-4" beam and 5'-9" in the hold), *Renegade* (formerly the American-built piratical schooner *Zarragozana*, 76'-3" on the gun-deck, 19'-2" beam and 7'-4" depth of hold), and the West Indian or Bermudian-built schooners *Magpie* (53'-3" on the gun-deck, 42'-0" on the keel), *Monkey* (56'-0" on deck, 17'-10" beam and 9'-4" depth of hold), *Nimble* (ex-*Bolivar*) and the sister-schooners *Pickle*, *Pincher* and *Skipjack* (69'-9" on deck, 21'-9" beam and 9'-0" in the hold), with an old schooner named *Speedwell*, the *Union* made up a squadron that saw much adventure. Often working in pairs they fought pirates on the coasts of Cuba, Porto Rico, San Domingo and Haiti, and slavers in the Windward Passage, Old Bahama Channel and on the Bahama Banks. Though these schooners were not all in service at the same time, they were active in the years between 1823 and 1835. During the early '20's the United States Navy had a similar squadron operating against the West Indian pirates, consisting of eight small Baltimore-model schooners named *Ferret*, *Jackall*, *Fox*, *Beagle*, *Weasel*, *Grayhound*, *Terrier* and *Wild Cat*. These were all purchased vessels of from 47 to 68 tons and were very useful craft.

The plan of the *Union* is the earliest that has yet been found showing pivoted centerboards in the modern manner. The lines of this very interesting schooner are extraordinary, indicating an extremely fast vessel in moderate going. The run is of an unusual form, evidently the designer intending to combine a very fine run with a wide stern. The shape of this vessel, aft, is somewhat like that of some old schooners built on the Chesapeake Bay, and it is barely possible that the *Union* was built there.

The deck arrangement of the *Union* is also interesting, and shows an unusual fitting of the pivot-gun. The small deck openings, so few in num-

UNION, *1828.*

ber, are common in the few slaver plans that have been found, and support the claim that this schooner was originally a slaver.

The spar dimensions of the *Union* are missing, but she was rigged as a fore-topsail schooner. Sitting low in the water and having little sheer, the *Union* was a handsome and rakish vessel. The use of chain as centerboard pendants, though rare, is an idea that could be used to advantage in modern centerboard yachts.

The slaver gave designers much information on the models of fast ves-

sels, and undoubtedly had some influence on later craft, particularly fore-
and-afters. It would not be hard to trace the effect of the slaver on the
early schooner-yachts, for the pilot-schooners of New York and Boston
in the 1840's were on the same general model as the slaver, and from the
pilot-boat the best models of early schooner-yachts were copied. The in-

American Privateer of 1800.

terest in fast-sailing schooners and brigs in the United States during the
1830's and '40's ran high, and accounts for the rapid spread of the Baltimore Clipper influence along the coast. When it is realized that the
slaver-schooners and brigs reached a speed of 14 knots in many instances,
the high degree of development in their design can be appreciated. This is
why the type appeared in other trades, particularly the illegal ones requiring fast craft. It was perhaps fortunate for American designers that there
were so many illegal trades being carried on during the years between
1815 and 1845, for it is possible that the fast models of the privateer type

would otherwise have been quickly forgotten. The fad for fast vessels, that came from the interest in the slaver and pilot-boat type rather than solely from trade requirements, had much influence on the development of the big clipper-ships of the late '40's and early '50's. This fad also accounted for much of the interest that led to the building of the yacht *America*, and it is interesting, while early schooner-yachts are being mentioned, to find that an American-built slaver, the *Theresa Secunda* (said to have been built at Philadelphia), became a British yacht under the name of *Xarifa*.

It has been a popular idea that the Baltimore Clipper, as exemplified by the slaver, disappeared with the coming of the clipper-ships; the fact is, however, that the old model merely changed names, becoming the pilot-boat type of early American yachts, the "sharpshooter" type of Gloucester fishermen and the basic model of every fast keel schooner for another fifty years.

Chapter Four   REVENUE CUTTERS

THOUGH the amount of literature dealing with various phases of American maritime history is very great, there is surprisingly little to be found regarding the United States revenue cutters or their work. As a result the mention of the "revenue cutter" to anyone interested in old sailing craft automatically calls to mind the British one-masted revenue cutter rather than the American type. The lack of interest among American marine historians in the United States Revenue Marine is difficult to explain for the service has had a remarkable career, full of incidents of historical importance, and was founded some years before the Navy. During the sailing ship period the Revenue Marine was engaged in other work than mere enforcement of revenue laws, for its duties included suppression of the slave trade and piracy, life-saving and salvage work at sea, carrying of government dispatches and diplomats and assisting the Navy in wartime, all with their many incidental adventures. The Revenue Marine has had adventures in preventing smuggling similar to those for which the British service has become famous. No revenue service abroad has had a more interesting history than the American corps.

The only explanation for the neglect of the United States Revenue Marine history and of the cutters is that many of the records have been lost, including valuable plans of revenue vessels, and the tradition of the service does not encourage self-advertisement. Furthermore, the corps "has never produced a Marryat" to tell the unofficial adventures and incidents for which the service has been remarkable. In the matter of plans of cutters, these have been lost or destroyed since the Revenue Marine did not have its own bureau of construction until some years after the introduction of steamers; all construction work in sailing ship days was done either by the Navy construction corps or by private contractors.

In the early days the Revenue Marine suffered much from political control and resulting weakness of organization, but in spite of this the personnel has always been of very high calibre. This has been particularly true of the commissioned officers; probably because the Marine was so small during most of its career, that inefficient and unfit officers could be quickly identified and weeded out. The fact that the cutters operated singly increased the responsibility of the commanding officers, which in turn raised the requirements of the commissioned personnel.

The Revenue Marine also suffered much from the unfriendliness of members of Congress which was expressed in verbal attacks and reduced appropriations. Both the old Revenue Marine and the service in its modern form, the Coast Guard, have been subject to many attempts to either disband them or to merge them with the Navy. It has been a rather common idea, apparently, that the duties of this service could have been carried out by the Navy and that the Revenue Marine and present Coast Guard represented unnecessary duplication of ships, personnel and expense.

The training of officers for the Revenue Service and for the Navy differs in many respects, and both require a lifetime of study and experience. The naval officer is primarily a fighting man and the most important part of his training is naval tactics and gunnery; the increasing complication and mechanization of modern warfare, as well as rapid changes, makes the study of these matters a full-time profession. The naval officer's seamanship is directed toward the handling of fleets rather than toward handling small single ships in shoal water or in heavy weather. The revenue officer, on the other hand, is trained in salvage and life-saving work, as well as in policing; gunnery and naval tactics playing a comparatively small part in his requirements. He operates in a single small ship and, because of the demands made on his service, he must be a seaman of the highest order. As a result of the difference in training and in the resulting outlook of the two professions, there is considerable difference in their attitude toward the public; the revenue officer who is in constant contact must consider the public more than does the naval officer. These matters, however, need little discussion, for naval officers have

been employed in the Revenue Service on two occasions with unsatisfactory results. This is not a detraction of the naval man, but merely
an illustration of the difference in the requirements of the two services.

The complete history of the Revenue Marine, or Coast Guard, is not
yet available and little space can be given to it here. However, the evolution of the service can be recorded as the cutters are discussed.

Alexander Hamilton, first Secretary of the Treasury, received his port-
folio from Washington at the age of 32, soon after the latter's inaugura-
tion in 1789. Hamilton understood the necessity of employing watercraft
in the collection of revenue duties and in the enforcement of the revenue
laws. This is apparent by the fact that he wrote to the newly appointed
Collectors of the Ports on October 2, 1789, asking for information as to
local requirements and conditions.

The proposed service was carefully considered by Hamilton, for
though there was an obvious necessity for a revenue cutter organization,
there was a lack of funds and possible antagonism in Congress. The feel-
ings of the people and their representatives in Congress were not likely
to be friendly to an organization of this nature, for the enforcement of
the revenue laws by this means had been a great irritant prior to the
Revolution. Furthermore, the hard-earned liberty of the individual and
state was then highly regarded, and infringement of any kind was subject
to suspicion. On the other hand, the customs duties were absolutely necessary for the support of the federal government and, since the frailties
of human nature had to be taken into consideration, the collection of
these monies required a policing force. Furthermore, Hamilton had to
plan all the details of the service proposed for this work, its organization,
personnel and appointments as well as the size, class and station of the
vessels to be used.

As the Secretary received replies to his letters to the Collectors, and
gathered information, he gradually formulated a plan for a semi-naval
service, different in some respects from the revenue cutter services of
foreign countries. The United States had neither an army nor a navy at

178

this time; in fact, the central government had no means of law-enforcement other than those possessed by the states and the communities within their borders. It is highly probable that Hamilton, being aware of this condition, foresaw services exceeding the mere collection of custom duties and enforcement of the revenue laws, and planned the cutter service accordingly.

The first step was to get Congress to authorize the formation of the required organization. This was accomplished, after some difficulty, in an act passed March 4, 1790. Though the act permitted the use of revenue cutters, it gave neither authority nor funds for their construction. Therefore, on April 23, 1790, Hamilton asked Congress for a direct appropriation to build and maintain ten cutters, 36 to 40 feet on the keel, to carry six swivels and a crew of captain, lieutenant and six seamen each. He made the amazingly low estimate of $1,000 apiece for their construction and $18,560 for their maintenance. It is probable that this estimate was intentionally low in order to commit an economically minded Congress to the development of the new service. At any rate, on the plea that later information showed that many communities would require larger vessels than originally allowed for, Hamilton obtained an increased appropriation, a little later, for building cutters, and also an additional $2,000 for their boats. With this the foundation of the new service was laid, which was called by common reference, the Revenue Marine.

The ten cutters were contracted for in such a way that each was built within the limits of her proposed station, or if this were not feasible, as near to the station as possible. The choice of design and builder, in fact the whole contract, was largely in the hands of the local Collector until the captain was appointed, after which the latter took over the supervision of the construction in most cases.

Because of the manner in which these contracts were handled there are neither plans nor models that can be identified as having been used to build any of these cutters. There are only a few dimensions and incomplete descriptions which will help in visualizing these vessels. Though

179

the English term "cutter" was applied to these vessels by common consent, because of an association of this rig and type of vessel with the collection of the revenue in the public mind, all American revenue sailing vessels, with but about a half-dozen exceptions, have been schooners. This being the national rig, quite satisfactory as to speed and weatherliness, and a type that both officers and seamen would be well acquainted with, it was quite natural that the schooner should be employed instead of the English cutter in the American service.

The design of the sailing revenue cutter was a problem similar in most respects to that of the design of a privateer. The cutters could be lightly armed and manned, but speed was an absolute necessity if the vessels were to be successful. Since the cutters must spend much of their lives at sea, the need of reasonable seaworthiness was obvious. In order to catch smugglers and other law-breakers, weatherliness was also very important. On many stations a shoal-draft vessel would be most efficient, excessive draft in any case was undesirable. As the cutters were not expected to fight regular naval engagements, the bulwarks could be light, or omitted entirely. The dimensions of the cutters were first controlled by the small appropriations for their construction and the limited duties they were expected to perform. As the duties of the Revenue Marine expanded, however, there was a gradual increase in the size of new cutters. The station on which a cutter was employed also governed the size of the vessel to some extent. In general, the American revenue cutters ranged from 56 to 110 feet on deck, with a beam that was approximately one-fourth the length.

Returning to the first cutters built for the Revenue Marine, the following descriptions give what little information is now available concerning them. The *Scammel* was built at Portsmouth, New Hampshire, the contract for her being signed February 15, 1791. She was first named *Ferret* but this was changed to *Scammel* before she was launched. She was a two-masted schooner with a short quarterdeck, and open bulwarks composed of stanchions and caps on top of low "log" rails. She cost $1,250 to build and measured 57'-7½" on deck, 44'-0" on the keel, 15'-6" beam, 6'-6" depth of hold and 51⁸⁵⁄₉₅ tons burthen. She was sold out of service sometime late in 1797.

The *Massachusetts* was built by William Searle at Newburyport, Massachusetts, and was to cost $1,440. However, her captain had the builder alter the vessel during construction, without proper authorization, which led to greater cost. The government finally accepted her and paid the builder for the changes. The contract called for a vessel 48'-0" on deck, 18'-0" beam, 7'-0" depth of hold, and 63⁶³⁄₉₅ tons burthen; but as completed she measured 50'-0" on deck, 17'-8" beam, 7'-8" depth of hold and 70⁴³⁄₉₅ tons burthen. She was a two-masted schooner with deep bulwarks and a long quarterdeck. Her figurehead was a bust of an Indian and she had a square stern and carved quarter-badges. She was sold out of the service in 1798.

The cutter *Vigilant* was built at New York in 1791 and was a two-masted schooner 48'-0" on deck, 15'-0" beam, 4'-6" depth of hold and 33 tons burthen. She was sold in 1801.

The *Active* was built at Hampton, Virginia, for use on the Chesapeake and was a two-masted schooner pierced for 14 guns; measuring 40'-0" on the keel, 17'-0" beam, and 6'-6" depth of hold. She was also sold in 1801.

The cutter *Virginia* was of the same dimensions and built in the same place as the *Active;* it may be safely assumed that they were sister ships. Both were of 47 tons burthen. The record of the *Virginia's* service has been lost so it is not known what became of her.

No dimensions of the remaining four cutters are available; the *General Greene* was a sloop built at Philadelphia, her record is not yet found; the *South Carolina* was a schooner built at Charleston, South Carolina; her records are also missing as are those of the schooner *Diligence* built at New Berne, North Carolina, and the schooner *Pickering*, built for the Georgia station. The latter is omitted in the official "Record of Movements" of the United States Coast Guard.

As soon as these cutters were under construction, regulations were laid down for their service. These specified that the cutters were to cruise, not to anchor in a port, and were to patrol their stations in such a manner that their movements could not be calculated upon by law-breakers. Their officers were also officers of the customs, having the rights of search and seizure. In 1792 the Collectors were permitted to direct the movements of the cutters within the limits of their stations; previously they had been responsible for the cutter's supplies and repairs only. Officers were appointed by the Secretary of the Treasury and recruited their crews subject to the approval of that official.

These ten cutters were too small for the services required by the regulations, so sometime in 1797 the Secretary of the Treasury commissioned Josiah Fox to design a new class of cutter. It is not known how many of the cutters built in 1797–8 were on his lines, but it is certain that the *Pickering* and one built at Philadelphia were constructed from his plans, as Fox received payment for these draughts according to his papers in the Peabody Museum, Salem, Massachusetts. As the dimensions of at least seven of the new cutters seem to have been the same, it is probable that all of these were built from Fox's plans, though it must be admitted that this is not unquestionable evidence. As a result of this new construction, the beginning of the quasi-war with France found the Revenue Marine equipped with ten new cutters, the old *Vigilant* and *Active*, and also three purchased vessels.

Of the new cutters, the *Diligence, Eagle, Pickering, Scammel, Governor Jay, Massachusetts*, and *Governor Gilman* were fore-and-main topsail schooners, 58′-0″ on the keel, 20′-0″ beam and 9′-0″ depth of hold, carrying from 10 to 14 guns. James Hackett built the *Governor Gilman* at Portsmouth, New Hampshire; Nathan and Orlando Merrill the *Massachusetts* at Newburyport and Joshua Humphreys one of the two built at Philadelphia (*Diligence* or *Eagle*). The *Virginia* was slightly smaller than these cutters, measuring 50′-0″ on the keel, 18′-10″ beam and 8′-6″ depth of hold. She was armed with six 6-pounders on the main deck and four 4-pounders in the cabin. This cutter had a stern cabin and raised quarterdeck, though her sheer was probably without a break due to her deep bulwarks. This construction became popular about 1795 and was employed in the U.S.N. brig *Perry* as late as 1843.

The *General Greene* was built at Baltimore by William Price and was 150 tons burthen. In the newspaper account of her launch she was referred to as the "cutter" while in other and later accounts she was said to have been a sloop. It is possible that this cutter has been confused with the earlier vessel of the same name in these latter references and that she was really a schooner. The *Greene* carried 10 guns.

The purchased cutters, *Maria*, *Unanimity* and *North Carolina*, cannot be traced in the records of the service and no description can be found. The cutter *South Carolina* was a new vessel, but as her records are also missing it is not known whether she was built for a revenue cutter or not. In many government publications and records all of these cutters except the *Greene* are listed as having been of 187 tons burthen, but in the case of the *Virginia* this is an obvious error. During the war with France the schooner *Bon Pere* was captured by the cutter *Eagle* and taken into service as the *Bee*. The only contemporary picture of one of these cutters that has yet been identified is a rather poor drawing of the "jackass-brig" *Pickering* showing her as a fore-and-main topsail schooner of the Baltimore Clipper type with a flush, rather straight sheer. This picture was reproduced in *The Baltimore Clipper*.[1] The *Pickering* was the crack of her class, but her end was tragic, for she went missing with all hands late in 1800 while in the service of the Navy. The cutters built in 1797–8 were employed in the Revenue Marine for only a very short time as they were taken into naval service during the quasi-war with France; those returned to the Revenue Marine were sold after the change in administration that followed.

In 1801 the Secretary of the Treasury wrote the Collectors in regard to these cutters, requesting advice as to the smallest practical cutter for

[1] H. I. Chapelle, The Marine Research Society, Salem, Massachusetts, 1930.

their localities and asking if there would be any objection to the use of small pilot-boat schooners of the latest type. At about the same time the cutters received back from the Navy were sold; the Navy having retained the *Pickering, Scammel* and *Eagle.* As a result of the letter to the Collectors, new cutters of about 45 tons were ordered to be built to replace

UNITED STATES REVENUE CUTTER, 1815. 31-TON MODEL.

them. In spite of this pinch-penny policy, so typical of Jefferson's administration, the size of the cutters built between 1801 and 1812 rapidly increased with the passing of each year.

The revenue cutters in service during this period include a number of vessels, *Patriot,* 1800–05; *Collector,* 1803–06; *Argus,* 1804–09; *Union,* 1808; *Hazard,* 1808; *Mary,* 1808; *Potomack,* 1809; *Mary Ann,* 1809; *Independence,* 1810 and *George,* 1812, about which little is known beyond their period of service. Possibly they were all purchased or hired craft.

About 1800 the Revenue Marine employed a few galleys, particularly on the southern and Lake stations. These were vessels obtained from the Navy and had been built between 1798 and 1800. The Navy had built five classes of galleys: the *Senator Ross* class, 50'-6" between perpendic-

51-TON REVENUE CUTTER, 1815.

ulars and 13'-6" beam; the *Savannah* class, 51'-9" between perpendiculars and 15'-3½" beam; the *Marietta* class, 56'-0" on the keel and 14'-6" beam; the *St. Marys* class, 53' on deck and 16' beam, and a small class measuring 45'-0" between perpendiculars and 13'-0" beam built on the Mississippi. On the plans of either the *St. Marys* or the *Savannah* the galley *Governor Williams* was built; this vessel was in the Revenue Marine for a while as were some others. Incidentally, in planning these galley classes it was stated that they were intended for "protection of the revenue" as well as for naval duties.

One of the small cutters built after 1800 was the *Massachusetts* built in 1801. She remained in service until 1816 when she was sold. An inventory of this cutter, taken in 1816, gives some interesting information on the dimensions of revenue cutters built before the War of 1812; though cutters were not to exceed 45 tons according to the order of 1801, it is obvious that this regulation was never strictly adhered to, even at the time of the order.

Inventory of Revenue Cutter *Massachusetts*, April 10, 1816.

Length 58'-6½", Beam 17'-9", Depth 7'-0", 62⁴⁸⁄₉₅ tons, Draft 10'-0". Two masts, one bowsprit, one flying jib-boom, one main boom, one main gaff, one fore ditto, one squaresail yard, one topsail ditto, one squaresail boom, one main topmast, one fore ditto.

One mainsail, one lug foresail, one jib, one flying jib, one topsail, one squaresail. (Main gaff topsail and main topmast staysail were also carried. H.I.C.)

One cable, 80 fathoms, and anchor.

One cable, 80 fathoms, and anchor.

Two pumps with gear and two iron standards.

One deck tackle, one boom guy, two boats, two rudders and two oars for each, one jibstay, one flying jibstay, halyards, sheets and hanks for same, one pair of bowsprit shrouds, peak and throat halyards for the foresail, brails and sheets for ditto, one pair fore vangs with block and mast hoops for foresail, squaresail braces, lifts and footropes, topsail halyards and sheets, one pair of main shrouds, one springstay, one mainstay, one main topping lift, one jackstay for squaresail, main throat and peak halyards and sheets and two downhawls.

Hoops and blocks for the mainsail, one cat block.

Four patent lights in the maindeck, one cabin table and binnacle.

These do not represent a complete inventory, as much gear is obviously missing. It is probable that the cutter had two shrouds on the fore mast and a bobstay. The *Massachusetts* was noted for her sailing qualities and her general model and dimensions appear to have been popular in the Revenue Marine, as will be shown. The cutter *New Hampshire*, built at Portsmouth, New Hampshire, in 1802–3, was probably a sister ship; she too was sold in 1816.

The cutter *Louisiana* was a schooner of 60 tons, drawing six feet of water loaded for sea, built at Baltimore in 1804. The next year she fought

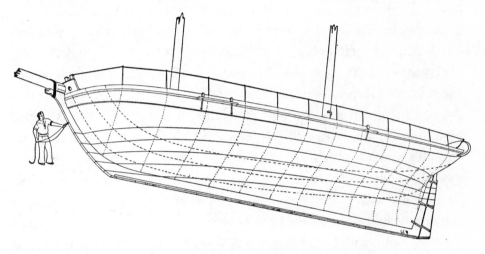

UNITED STATES REVENUE CUTTER 80 TONS, 1815, DESIGNED BY WILLIAM DOUGHTY.

an action with two British privateers out of Nassau, Bahamas, who had been committing depredations on the coast, and drove them off. In 1812 she fought two pirate schooners out of New Orleans, but could not capture them as they outsailed her. She disappeared from the records soon afterwards. The *Dolly* was a schooner purchased at New York for $17,817.48, in 1805; she was sold two years later. In 1806 the *Hornet*, formerly the schooner *Traveller* built at Newburyport, was received from the Navy, but was sold at Philadelphia the same year.

The cutter *Jefferson* was purchased about this time and remained in service until 1817. In 1812 she captured a British brig and schooner and in 1813 she took three British barges and their crews in the James River. In 1817 she captured a Spanish brig, the unlawful prize of a Buenos Aires privateer and, later, a Spanish ship that had also been taken by the same privateer.

The *Surveyor* was a cutter whose defense in 1813 won for the Revenue Marine the respect of the British squadron in the Chesapeake. She was a Baltimore-built schooner carrying six 12-pounder carronades that had been bought at Baltimore in 1807. In 1809 she captured a schooner that was without papers and in 1810 she took possession of a French privateer.

On the evening of June 12, 1813, the *Surveyor*, Captain Samuel Travis, U.S.R.M., was anchored close to Gloucester Point, in the York River near the Chesapeake. At eight o'clock the captain sent off a boat under the command of his brother, William Travis, to act as watch-boat. It was raining and there was a heavy mist; soon after leaving the cutter William found himself near three British barges which had not been discovered until the watch-boat was cut off from the cutter. Young Travis at once headed for the shore, firing five warning shots to inform the cutter of the intended attack. Her ports already open and the vessel ready for action, the watch officer called the remaining members of the crew and the captain. Five men were in the watch-boat which left on board a total crew of twenty, including officers. Soon after hearing the warning shots the officers of the cutter discovered two of the British barges approaching rapidly, but at such an angle that the cutter's guns could not be brought to bear. Captain Travis at once ordered each man to supply himself with two muskets and to fire them only when he gave the order. This order was not given until the barges were only a few yards away and the resulting musketry fire caused heavy losses in the British boats.

The hardy Britons hove alongside, however, and boarded the cutter, to be met by the desperate Marylanders in a fierce hand-to-hand struggle for possession of the deck. In the narrow space between the bulwarks of the schooner some ninety men fought with cutlass, dirk and pistol in the darkness and rain. The hoarse cheering of the British men-of-war's men was answered by the shrill, savage yell of the Americans, that became better known as the "rebel yell" in the Civil War. But the fight was a hopeless one for the cutter's men, and, outnumbered more than two to one, they were finally overpowered, the survivors surrendering when Captain Travis found that further defense was useless. The cutter's crew was taken on board H.B.M. frigate *Junion* and, on the following day, the commander of the British boats, Lieutenant John Crerie, returned Travis's sword to him with a letter expressing admiration for the defense of the *Surveyor*. The captured cutter was employed on the Chesapeake by the British, but does not appear to have been taken into the British Navy officially.

The cutter *James Madison* was built at Baltimore in 1807–8 and was stationed at Savannah. During the War of 1812 she captured a British ship, brig and schooner. On the 12th of August, 1812, she was captured by the British frigate *Barbadoes* after a long chase off Savannah. According to the Steel list of the Royal Navy for 1813 the *Madison* was fitting out at Halifax that year as the *Alban*. Under this name her plan was published in *The Baltimore Clipper;* she was a topsail schooner 94'-4½" long on deck, 24'-7⅛" extreme beam, 10'-6" depth of hold British measurement, built on the Baltimore Clipper model.

The cutter *Mercury* was built at Ocracoke in 1807; she was sold in 1807. The *Gallatin* was a schooner purchased at Norfolk for the Charleston station in 1807. In 1808 she chased a pilot-boat schooner, flying Danish colors, into St. Marys River after the Dane had made the mistake of firing at her. In 1812 this cutter captured a British ship and brig. The *Gallatin* blew up in Charleston Harbor, April 1, 1813, and a number of her crew were killed. The cause of the accident was never known.

The *Eagle* was a schooner of about 130 tons purchased at New Haven in 1809, in which year twelve new cutters were ordered to be built or purchased. The *Eagle* was captured by the British brig-of-war *Despatch* and a sloop-tender of the frigate *Pomone*, in October, 1814, after being driven ashore in Long Island Sound.

A schooner named *Pilgrim* was chartered for a while in 1811, as were

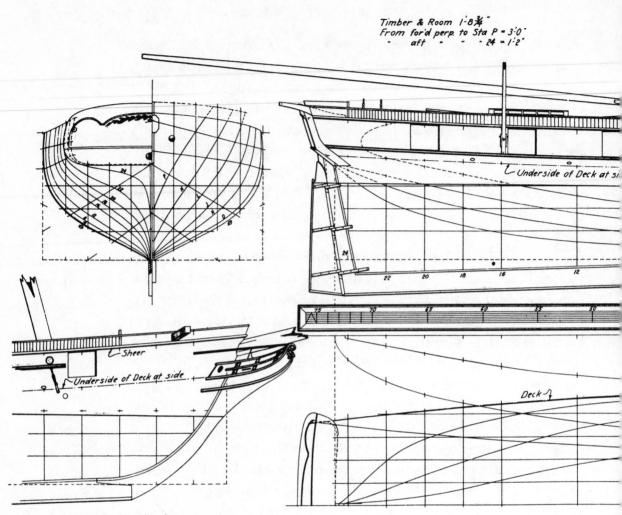

Timber & Room 1'-8¾"
From for'd perp. to Sta P = 3'-0"
" aft " " - 24 = 1'-2"

Underside of Deck at si

Sheer

Underside of Deck at side

Head for "Hamilton"

Deck

Plate VII. U. S. REVENUE CUTTER *MORRIS*. *Drawn from a plan
found in the Bureau of Construction and Repair, U. S. Navy Department.
An extreme "Baltimore Clipper" schooner of her date the Morris was the
"class ship" for most of the revenue cutters built in the '30's.*

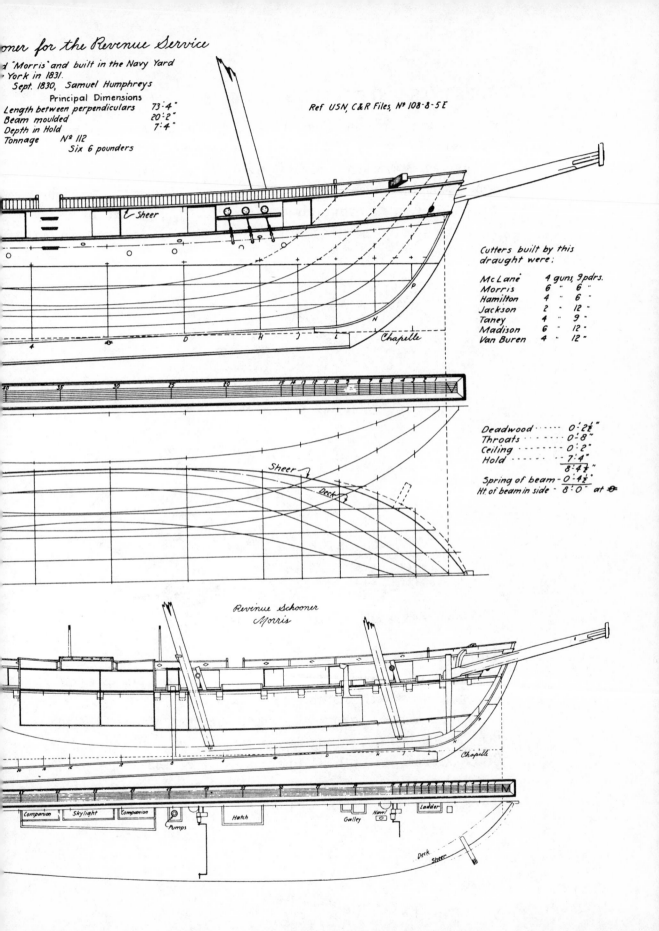

oner for the Revenue Service

d "Morris" and built in the Navy Yard
York in 1831.
Sept. 1830, Samuel Humphreys

Principal Dimensions

Length between perpendiculars   73·4"
Beam moulded   20·2"
Depth in Hold   7·4"
Tonnage   N° 112
        Six 6 pounders

Ref USN, C&R Files, N° 108·8·5 E

Sheer

Chapelle

Cutters built by this
draught were:

McLane   4 guns, 9 pdrs.
Morris   6   "   6 "
Hamilton   4   "   6 "
Jackson   2   " 12 "
Taney   4   "   9 "
Madison   6   " 12 "
Van Buren 4   " 12 "

Sheer

Deck

Deadwood ------- 0·2½"
Throats ------- 0·8"
Ceiling ------- 0·2"
Hold   ------- 7·4"
                 ‾‾‾‾‾‾
                 8·4½"
Spring of beam - 0·4½"
Ht. of beam in side - 8·0" at ⊕

Revenue schooner
Morris

Chapelle

Companion Skylight Companion   Hatch   Galley   Nav.   Ladder
Pumps

Deck   Sheer

the schooners *Active* and *Commodore Hull*. The *Active* was in the service until 1814; the *Commodore Hull* was captured by the British, August 3, 1813, and was taken into the British Navy as a tender according to some accounts. While in the American service the *Hull* was accidentally fired into by an American privateer, the *Anaconda*, January 16, 1813.

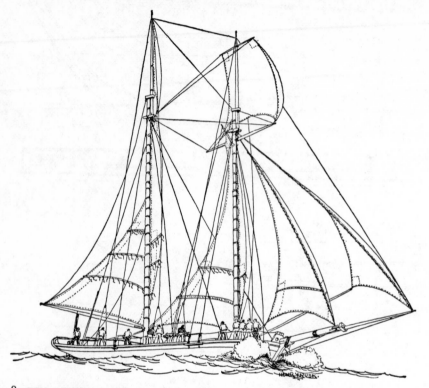

80-TON REVENUE CUTTER, 1815, DESIGNED BY DOUGHTY.

The employment of American-built schooners in the British Navy and the lack of recognition signals between government and privateer vessels were probably the causes of this serious mistake.

A cutter named *Vigilant* was built at Newport, Rhode Island, by Benj. Marble in 1812, costing $8,500. In 1813 this vessel captured the British privateer *Dart* off Block Island. In 1817 she seized a brig fitted out at Bristol as a privateer in behalf of one of the South American republics.

Principal Dimensions :

Length between perpendiculars	46' 3"
Length on the range of deck	48' 6"
Beam moulded	14' 6"
Depth in the hold	5' 0"
Custom House Tonnage	31 44/95 Tons

Spars

	Whole Length	Dia.	Head		Whole Length
Mainmast	43' 6"	12"	4' 0"	Topmast	14' 0"
Foremast	47' 0"	12½"	4' 0"	Topmast	14' 0"
Mainboom	29' 0"			Gaffs	10' 0"
Bowsprit	9' 0" outboard			Jibboom	9' 0" from cap
Squaresail Yard	29' 0"			Flying Topsl Yard	15' 0"

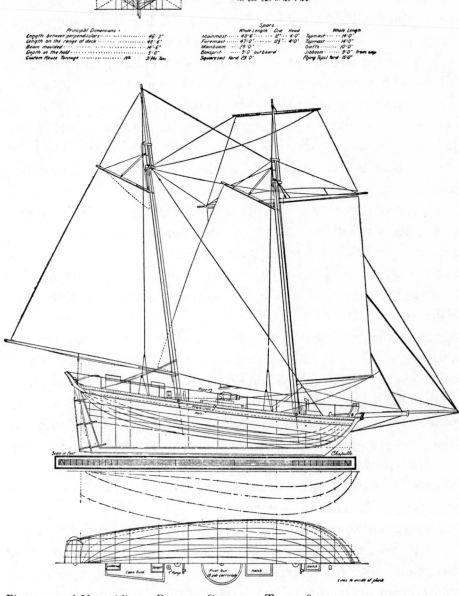

Figure 30. *A United States Revenue Cutter, 31 Tons, 1815.*

The next year the *Vigilant* captured a Spanish brig that had been hovering around Block Island, finding her to be the prize of one of the piratical South American privateers; the latter were usually armed schooners owned and fitted out in the United States and sailing under South American flags and commissions. The *Vigilant* was sold about 1825 for $2,800.

A cutter named *Diligence* was also in service during this period but her record has been lost and it is not known when she came into service. The cutters that were employed in conjunction with the naval service during the War of 1812 were the *Commodore Hull, Surveyor, Active, Jefferson, Mercury, Vigilant, Gallatin, Madison* and *Eagle*. The *Commodore Hull* is also called the *Commodore Barney* and *Commodore Barry* in many contemporary accounts.

The vicissitudes of war had seriously reduced the number of revenue cutters, so that, with the coming of peace, new construction was necessary. In 1815 William Doughty, the then naval constructor, was asked to design three new classes of cutters. Fortunately all three draughts were found in the archives of the Navy Department and are presented herewith. As was usual with Doughty's designs, these cutters were on the Baltimore Clipper model, but such extreme examples of the type are rarely found. The plans called for vessels of three sizes; the smallest was of but $31\frac{39}{95}$ tons burthen, 48'-6" on deck, 14'-9" extreme beam, and 5'-0" depth of hold. The next largest size tonned $51\frac{39}{95}$ Custom House measurement and was 56'-8" on deck, 17'-4" extreme beam and 6'-0" depth of hold. This plan was the one published in an abbreviated form by Marestier in his *Memoire sur les bateaux a vapeur des Etats-Unis d'Amerique* published in Paris in 1824; an attempt at restoration of this vessel was published in *The Baltimore Clipper*. The original draught presented now will correct the errors in those plans. The largest design called for a cutter of $79\frac{62}{95}$ tons burthen, 69'-6" on deck, 19'-4" extreme beam and 6'-9" in the hold. These cutters, as can be seen in Figures 30, 31, 32 were of similar design, differing but slightly in hull-form. Their armament varied, some having 12- or 18-pounder carronades, or long 9's, 12's or 18's. In

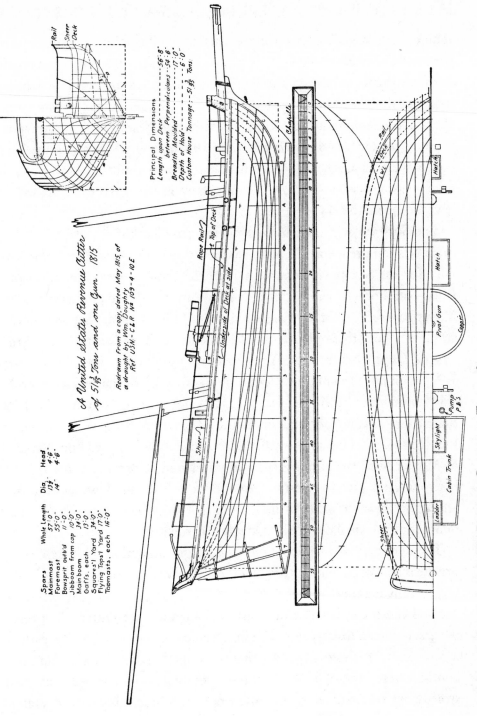

Principal Dimensions
Length upon Deck - - - - - 56'·8"
  "   between Perpendiculars - 54'·6"
Breadth Moulded - - - - - 17'·0"
Depth of Hold - - - - - 6'·0"
Custom House Tonnage - 51 3/95 Tons.

A United States Revenue Cutter
of 51 3/95 Tons and one Gun. 1815

Redrawn from a copy, dated May 1815, of
a draught by Wm. Doughty.
Ref USN - C&R Nº 109 - 4 - 10 E

Spars	Whole Length	Dia.	Head
Mainmast	57'·0"	13 3/4"	4'·6"
Foremast	55'·0"	14"	4'·6"
Bowsprit outb'd	11'·0"		
Jibboom from cap	10'·0"		
Main boom	34'·0"		
Gaffs, each	13'·0"		
Squares'l Yard	34'·0"		
Flying Tops'l Yard	17'·0"		
Topmasts, each	16'·0"		

Figure 31. A United States Revenue Cutter, 51 Tons, 1815.

addition, the larger boats sometimes carried one long 4 or 6; cutters' guns were usually made of brass. The plans all called for the pivot-gun amidships, which if not always the sole gun, was always the heaviest. Unfortunately, the plans do not give the names of any cutters built from them, but it is probable that the cutters *Detector* and *Search* built at Newport in 1816, the cutters *Alabama* and *Louisiana* built in 1819, and some later vessels were from the 56'-8" plan. The *Surprise*, built at New York in 1815, and her sister-ship *Dallas*, built there at the same time, appear to have been on the 69'-6" plan.

The *Surprise* was built in 90 days for the Charleston station, but her draft was too great for this place so she was sold in 1817. The *Dallas* was built for the Savannah station. In 1818 she took a South American privateer off Port Royal and in 1820 captured a slaver-pirate in the St. Marys River. The *Dallas* was sold in 1821. Other cutters that were probably built from these plans were the *Gallatin* built at Baltimore in 1816–17; the *Eagle*, built at New York in 1816; the *Monroe* built by Servant at Norfolk in 1817 and the *Alert*, built in 1818. These cutters were probably constructed from the two largest Doughty designs. The records of the cutters *South Carolina*, 1815, and *Hornet*, 1818, have been lost so they cannot be identified with these plans. According to the "Record of Movements" the cutter *Alert* was purchased at Baltimore in 1816 and her tonnage is given as 38 tons. As the records of purchase and tonnage are by no means reliable, it is possible that this cutter was one of those built from the smallest of the Doughty designs.

The cutters *Alabama* and *Louisiana* fought an action with a Mexican privateer in 1819. The cutters were on the way to their stations in the Gulf and had almost reached Mobile on August 31st. The day was very hot and there was little or no wind. About noon the cutters discovered three schooners directly ahead, lying very close together. Such a gathering of craft, in those days, was highly suspicious, for piracy and freebooting were rife. The two cutters wet their sails and got out their sweeps. At two o'clock in the afternoon the three schooners separated,

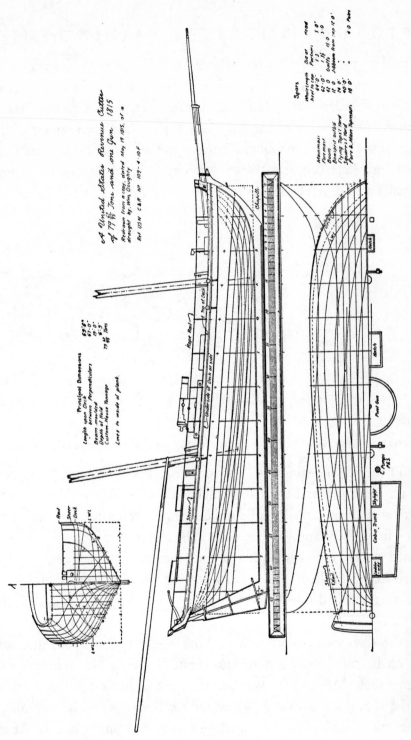

Figure 32. A United States Revenue Cutter, 80 Tons, 1815.

195

one standing toward the cutters. Fifteen minutes later the captain of the *Louisiana*, Loomis (senior officer of the cutters), fired a shot ahead of the stranger and ordered the *Alabama* to board her. It was found that she was an American schooner and that she had on board a number of passengers of the Spanish schooner *Filomena* out of Pensacola, a prize to the Mexican privateer *Brava;* both vessels being those ahead. The two cutters hastened on and at two-thirty the privateer came slowly around and

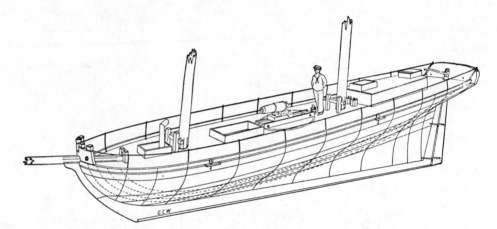

A UNITED STATES REVENUE CUTTER, 31 TONS, 1815, DESIGNED BY WILLIAM DOUGHTY.

headed for them, hoisting the "Patriot" flag. The *Louisiana*, being nearest, hailed and ordered the flag hauled down. On hearing this demand the privateer fired a volley of musketry into the cutter, wounding the cutter's first officer and three seamen. The annoyed cutter's men at once returned the compliment with a round from their pivot-guns, at which the privateersmen fled below. On boarding the *Brava* the cutter's men found that she had one brass 6-pounder and 18 men, besides officers, mostly negroes.

In 1820 these two cutters, still working together, destroyed Patterson's town on Breton Island, a notorious piratical hiding place. In 1822 the *Alabama* took three slavers, while in the same year the *Louisiana* cruised with the U.S. sloop-of-war *Peacock* and the British war-schooner *Speedwell* in the West Indies; the squadron taking five pirate vessels. At this

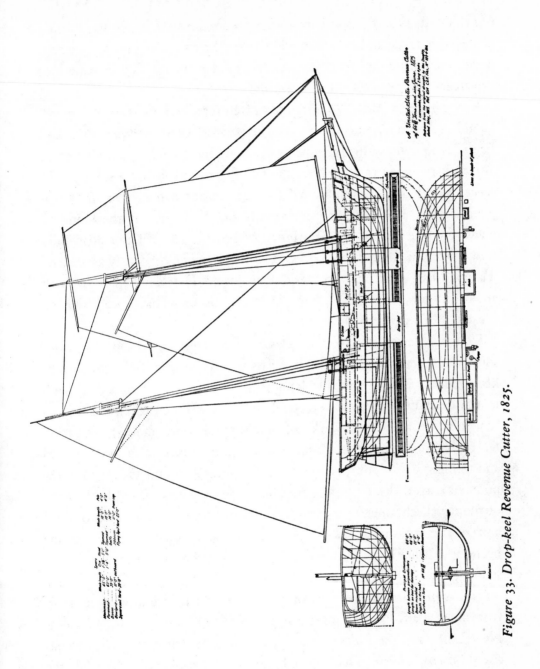

Figure 33. Drop-keel Revenue Cutter, 1825.

time all cutters on the southern stations were engaged in the suppression of the slave trade and piracy in addition to their regular duties. The robberies committed in American territorial waters by South American privateers also required their attention.

Between 1819 and 1826 a number of cutters were built or purchased, including the schooners *Sally*, 1819; *Lookout*, 1819; *Florida*, 1824 and *Eagle*, 1824, whose histories have not yet been found. A cutter named *Search* is reported to have been built at Boston, probably a sister of the earlier vessel of the same name. Another cutter named *Crawford* was built at New York in 1821, apparently on the largest of the Doughty plans; she was lost off the St. Marys, March 27, 1829. The *Dallas*, built as *Vigilant* in 1824 by Andrew Flannigan at Baltimore, was lost on Tampico Bar, September 21, 1836. The cutters *Detector* and *Wasp* built at Portsmouth, New Hampshire, in 1825, appear to have been built on the 56'-8" Doughty plan of 1815.

Doughty designed two more classes of revenue cutters in 1825 with shoal water stations in mind. One class was to be fitted with two dropkeels, which, judging by the draught, must have been inclined to jamb in the cases until rollers were used. This class of cutter was a topsail schooner with deep bulwarks of the war-schooner model, measuring 60'-0" between perpendiculars, 22'-4" extreme beam, 6'-0" in the hold and tonning $66^{55}/_{95}$ tons; armed with two long 4-pounders and four 18-pounder carronades (Figure 33). The other class was a shoal keel design of the naval schooner type, with deep bulwarks, armed as the drop-keel cutters and measuring 60'-0" between perpendiculars, 22'-4" extreme beam, 7'-0" depth of hold and $77^{64}/_{95}$ tons burthen (Figure 34). These schooners were rather bulky little ships but had big rigs and well-shaped hulls that promised a fair turn of speed. At least four cutters were built from these plans in 1825, probably the *Swiftsure* and *Louisiana* built at New York, and the *Pulaski* and *Marion* built at Baltimore. The *Pulaski* and *Louisiana* appear to have been built on the drop-keel model while the *Swiftsure* (renamed *Crawford* at Eastport, Maine, in 1835) and *Marion*

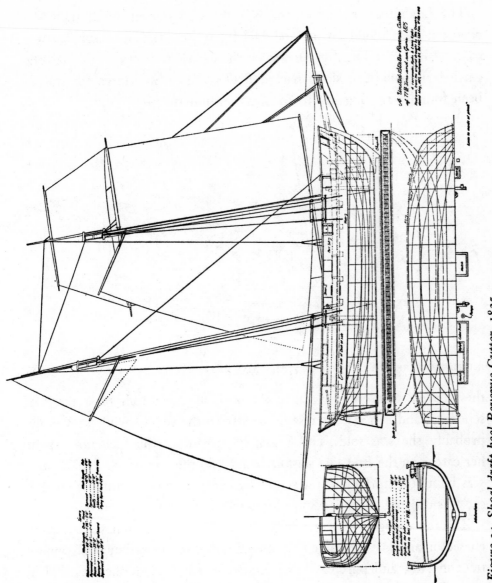

Figure 34. Shoal-draft keel Revenue Cutter, 1825.

were keel vessels. The *Erie* built in 1832 for Lake service is believed to have been on this plan also.

The *Louisiana* was sent to the New Orleans station; while there she captured the Colombian privateer schooner *Bolivia*. The *Louisiana* was sold out in 1830. The *Marion* was on the Charleston station; in 1826 she carried an American sloop named *Brilliant* into St. Marys for having been found wrecking in the Bahamas without proper permits. In 1829

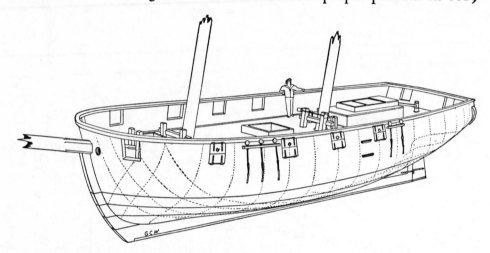

UNITED STATES REVENUE CUTTER OF 77⁶⁴⁄₉₅ TONS, 1825.

the *Marion* was cruising the coast of Cuba in search of a piratical schooner, and in 1833 she disappeared from the record while at Mobile, probably she was sold. The *Crawford*, formerly the *Swiftsure*, spent her career on the Eastport station, being sold there in 1838. The *Pulaski* was built for the Key West station where she stayed until 1833 when she was ordered to Philadelphia after which there is no record.

The remaining cutters in service before 1830 appear to have been purchased or hired vessels. The *Portsmouth* was a schooner built in Connecticut in 1825 and purchased at Portsmouth for $1,635; she was sold in 1833. The *Richard Rush* was in the service during 1829 but the record of her acquisition cannot be found. The schooner *Georgia* was chartered in 1829 for cutter duty. The plan of the revenue cutter dated 1829, Figure 35, cannot be identified as any of these.

Some of the problems of cutter officers of this period were rather peculiar. In 1826 the *Active*, Captain Webster, went to Havana with dispatches. While there Captain Webster was offered $10,000 to carry some officials to another port but refused the offer as he did not consider

UNITED STATES REVENUE CUTTER, 1825. SHOAL-DRAFT KEEL MODEL.

that he had the right to employ a national vessel for this purpose. On reporting the incident to the Treasury Department, he was told, to his disgust, that there would have been no objection if he had accepted the offer.

During the years between 1825 and 1832 a number of young naval officers obtained leave to serve in the Revenue Marine, among them many officers who later became famous; Stephen C. Rowan, who became a vice-admiral, for example. The slow promotion and lack of ships in the Navy made the smart schooners, active service and adventure of the

Revenue Marine attractive to spirited youngsters. However, the difference in training of naval and revenue officers made it difficult for them to work together, and the naval officers were disinclined to take orders from the civilian Collectors and Treasury officials, so it became necessary to discontinue the practise. An order, dated April 30, 1832, forced naval

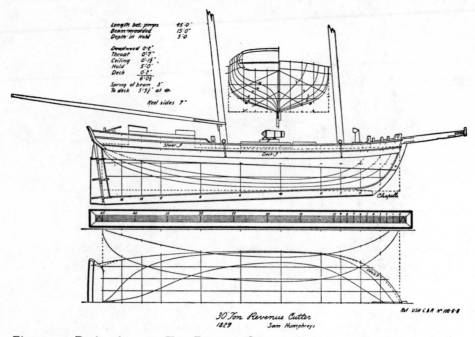

Figure 35. Design for a 30-Ton Revenue Cutter, 1829.

officers to choose between the Navy and the Revenue Marine; as a result about thirteen naval officers resigned their commissions in the Navy in order to remain in the Revenue Service, and the rest were displaced.

In 1830 it was decided to build new and larger cutters. The old vessels, though fast and seaworthy, were too small and lacked accommodation for the long cruises that were thought necessary on many stations. The usefulness of the cutters as dispatch-boats and as naval auxiliaries in time of war was recognized, so the new cutters were to be large and powerful enough to serve these purposes as well. The trend of official thought in regard to revenue cutters was away from the small pilot-boat type of 1815 toward the naval schooner type of 1798.

The Revenue Marine obtained the design for these cutters from the then naval constructor, Samuel Humphreys. It was first proposed to build all the new cutters in the navy yards, but this proved impractical because of the unfinished work in many yards, and because the work

30-TON REVENUE CUTTER, 1829.

done in the yards proved very expensive. Hence a few of the first cutters built were laid down in the navy yards at New York and Washington, but the majority were constructed by private yards under contract.

The class vessel was the *Morris* built in the New York Navy Yard in 1830–31; the *Alexander Hamilton* and *Gallatin* were built in the yard at the same time from the *Morris's* draught. This plan (Plate VII) called for a fore-topsail schooner 73'-4" between perpendiculars, 20'-2" moulded beam, 20'-6" extreme beam, 7'-4" depth of hold and roughly 112 tons burthen. The battery was to be six 12-pounder carronades or 6-pounder

long guns. In service, however, the cutters built on the lines of the *Morris*
varied greatly in armament. The design showed a beautifully modeled
schooner of the Baltimore Clipper model, with sharp ends, drag and
marked deadrise typical of that type. The *Morris* was built with the
unadorned pilot-boat stem, as were some of the other cutters, but most
had the naval head with billet, trail-boards and head-rails. The *Hamilton*
was the first to be so built; it is probable that all the class were similarly

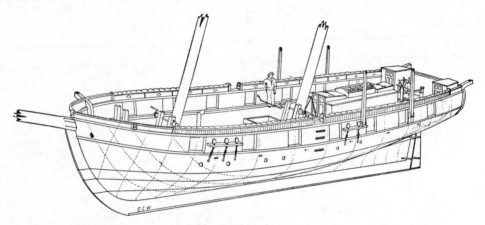

UNITED STATES REVENUE CUTTER *Morris.*

fitted eventually. While the new cutters were on the stocks they were
much admired and the plan of using one draught for the whole class was
carried out. Contracts were let to the New York firm of Webb and
Allen for the cutters *Louis McLane, Samuel D. Ingham, Richard Rush*
and, possibly, the *Oliver Wolcott;* all launched in 1832. The *Andrew
Jackson* was ordered to be built in the Washington Navy Yard; the
Campbell and *Dexter* were contracted for in New York, builders not
recorded. These were followed, in 1833, by the *Jefferson,* renamed
Crawford in 1839; the *Madison;* the *Roger B. Taney,* built by Webb
and Allen at a cost of $10,914; the *Washington* built at New York; these
were in turn followed by the *Levi Woodbury* built by L. H. Duncan at
Baltimore in 1836; the *Washington* built at Baltimore in 1837 and the
Van Buren, built there in 1839. This accounts for seventeen of the cut-

ters built in the '30's, the eighteenth was the little *Erie* of 65 tons built at Presque Isle in 1832, mentioned earlier.

These new cutters were employed with great success during the ensuing years. Their adventures would make a fascinating yarn, but unfortunately no more than a bare outline can be given here. The *Morris*, after the usual round of stations, was active in the Mexican War and was finally driven ashore three miles northwest of Key West in the hurricane of October 11, 1846, her crew being saved with difficulty. She was found to be bilged and a total loss when the storm was over.

The *Gallatin* was at Charleston in November, 1832, having been ordered there from her station at Mobile to act in the "Nullification Proceedings" of South Carolina. In 1840 the *Gallatin* was turned over to the Coast Survey, received back in 1848 and then returned to the Coast Survey again the next year.

The *Hamilton* was one of the best known of these cutters; for twenty years, 1831 to 1851, she was stationed at Boston. Here under the command of Captain Josiah Sturgis she was a local institution. The *Hamilton* made a cruise to Nova Scotia in 1839, to investigate the seizure of American fishermen by Canadian authorities, and was the first United States government vessel to enter Yarmouth. Like her sisters, the *Hamilton* was a very fine sailer and was used as the supreme test of any schooner claiming a reputation for speed. In races with opium-smuggling schooners, fast pilot-boats, fishermen, coasters and yachts, few vessels passed her either on or off the wind. After her transfer to Charleston in 1851 she was placed under the command of Captain T. C. Rudolph. Since 1792 the power to order the movements of the cutters within their station had been vested in the Collectors. These men were political appointees, usually complete lubbers having no knowledge of the sea or ships. The loss of the *Hamilton* could be traced to this condition, perhaps the most serious weakness in organization of the old Revenue Marine. The Treasury Department received a report from the Charleston Collector dated December 12, 1853, stating that the *Hamilton* had parted her chains in a

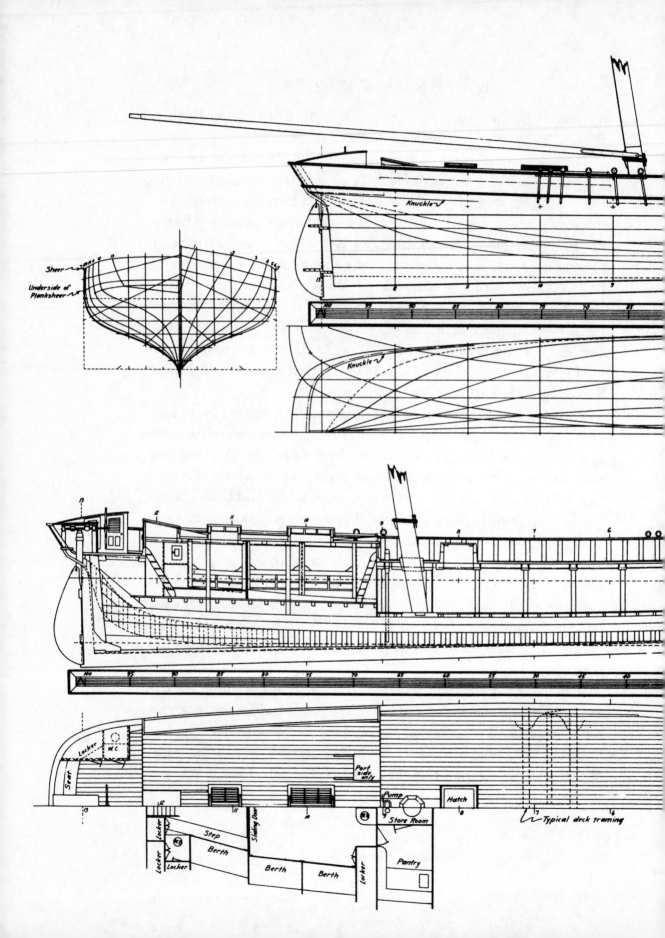

Sheer

Underside of
Planksheer

Knuckle

Knuckle

Seat

Locker

W.C.

Port
side
only

Pump

Store Room

Hatch

Typical deck framing

Locker

Locker

Locker

Step

Berth

Sliding Door

Berth

Berth

Locker

Pantry

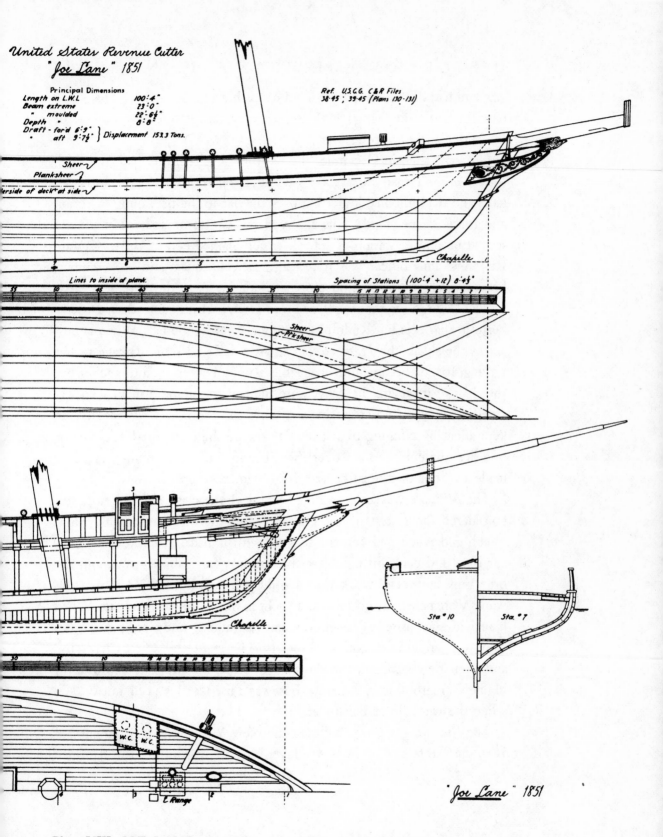

United States Revenue Cutter
"Joe Lane" 1851

Principal Dimensions
Length on L.W.L	100'·4"	
Beam extreme	23'·0"	
" moulded	22'·6¼"	
Depth "	8'·8"	
Draft - for'd 6'·9" aft 9'·7½"	Displacement 153.3 Tons.	

Ref. U.S.C.G. C&R Files
38·45 ; 39·45 (Plans 130·131)

Sheer
Planksheer
...erside of deck at side

Chapelle

Lines to inside of plank.

Spacing of Stations (100'·4" ÷ 12) 8'·4⅓"

Sheer
Plk sheer

Chapelle

Sta.° 10   Sta.° 7

W.C.   W.C.

L Range

"Joe Lane" 1851

Plate VIII. JOE LANE. *This plan is redrawn from plans found in the archives of the United States Coast Guard (Bureau of Construction and Repair). No reconstruction.*

gale and had driven onto a shoal, all hands but one being lost. This was a truthful statement that gave a false idea of what really caused the loss of the cutter and her crew.

For some time in December the weather at Charleston had been bad, the *Hamilton* remaining at anchor within the harbor because of the heavy gales and the difficulty in getting over the bar in the prevailing direction and force of the wind. This annoyed the Collector as he thought she should be on her station at sea, so he complained constantly to Captain Rudolph. This officer was noted for his recklessness and high temper; becoming angry at the Collector's attitude he made the statement "that he would go to sea that night or go to Hell." This occurred on December 9th; that evening Rudolph attempted to cross the bar. When almost across the shoals the *Hamilton* apparently suffered some damage to her rigging, for she became unmanageable. Rudolph attempted to anchor but the chains parted and she drove onto the bar, the single seaman who was saved was picked up at sea by a steamer some time afterwards, having kept afloat by clinging to a spar. The responsibility of the Collector for ordering the cutter to sea over the objections of her captain was never made a matter of official record, for obvious political reasons.

The *McLane* was another noted vessel of the class; she was not only considered the fastest of the class but also the most beautifully built. Webb and Allen had constructed her with unusual attention, her gun-carriages and deck fittings were fine examples of cabinet-work and her brass guns and metal work were highly polished. The inside of her bulwarks were panelled and she was a yacht in finish, inboard and out. When launched she visited Washington and attracted much attention from Congressmen, officials and local society. Her station was first Charleston and later New Bedford. On August 30, 1837, the *McLane* capsized off Hadley's Harbor in a tornado, but was raised and served until 1840, when she was sold at Baltimore.

The *Richard Rush* was built for the New York station. In January of 1840 she was frozen up in New Haven harbor. Apparently this damaged the vessel seriously for she was ordered sold soon afterwards, but the order was cancelled and she was turned over to the Lighthouse Service.

The *Campbell* was first stationed at Norfolk, then at Baltimore, and finally at Norfolk again. Here she was sold in 1834, on being found infected with dryrot. A small schooner was purchased to take her place and this vessel, in turn, was sold in 1839. Falling into the hands of slavers

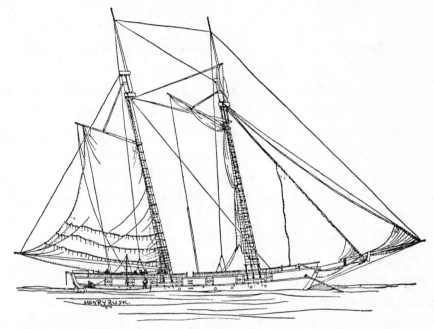

UNITED STATES REVENUE CUTTER *Morris.*

this ex-cutter went out to Africa under American colors, but owned by a Spaniard named "Blanco." Meeting with some slight damage on the voyage she put into Mesurado for repairs and here her crew, while ashore, became intoxicated, telling some men of a British naval brig anchored in the harbor the plan of the owner to load 250 slaves at Gallenas for Havana. As a result of this indiscretion, the British brig seized the schooner and the slaver-captain fled. This schooner was only 63 tons burthen. There is a tradition that some of the cutters of the *Morris* class became slavers after being sold out of service, but this is yet to be verified. These vessels would have been the proper size and model for the trade, and their speed would also interest slavers, and it is possible that there is some truth to the tradition.

The *Ingham* was built for the New Orleans station and was there until 1836 when she was sold. Her career was comparatively uneventful.

The *Dexter* made the usual round of stations until 1836, when she was placed under orders of the Navy for duty in the Seminole War in Florida. She saw service at Indian Key and on the west coast of the state, her crew being actively engaged in protecting the scattered settlements. The *Dexter* was sold at Charleston in 1841.

The *Jackson* also had an uneventful career until the Seminole War, in which she saw some service. Afterwards she was stationed at Baltimore, New York, New Orleans, Newport and elsewhere; finally she was sold in 1865 at Baltimore, where she had been stationed during the Civil War.

The *Wolcott* was at New Haven and New London until 1841, when she went to Wilmington, thence to Baltimore, returned to Wilmington, and then back to Baltimore again and finally, in 1844, to Mobile. Two years later she was dismasted and driven ashore in Pensacola Bay in a hurricane, but was hauled off and repaired. She then engaged in carrying government dispatches in the Gulf until the end of the Mexican War, and was sold at Mobile in 1851.

The *Jefferson* made the usual round of stations, her career unmarked by incidents of extraordinary nature until 1835, in which year she met with a serious accident, the nature of which has not been discovered. However, she was repaired for $1,700 and in 1836 was placed under orders of the Navy for duty in the Seminole War. She saw a good deal of active service in Florida waters until 1839, when she was repaired and renamed *Crawford*. On December 15, 1847, she was wrecked on Gardner's Point, while stationed at New London.

The *Madison* had a similar career, being seriously injured in 1836 and repaired. She was also employed in the Seminole War; in 1850 the *Madison* was delivered to the Coast Survey.

The *Taney* had no experiences that brought much attention to her until 1851, when she was ordered to Jacksonville, Florida, to prevent the departure of a filibustering expedition bound for Cuba. On August 3, 1852, she capsized in New York Harbor. Late in 1857 the *Taney* was struck by lightning near Tybee Island, Georgia, and was so badly damaged that she was sold on January 5, 1858, for $104.

The *Washington*, built in New York in 1833, was employed during the Seminole War and her crew had some exciting brushes with the Indians along the Florida beaches. In 1837 it was discovered that the vessel was badly infected with dryrot so she was sold out of the service. It is remarkable how quickly dryrot attacked cutters on southern stations, illustrating the effect of a warm climate on an oak-built vessel. The next cutter of this name was built at Baltimore in 1837. She was employed in winter cruising, from New York to the Capes of Virginia. An order dated December 16, 1831, required the cutters *Wolcott, Dexter, Hamilton, Morris, Swiftsure* and *Portsmouth* to cruise their respective stations during the winter months with the particular intention of aiding vessels in distress. By this order Secretary of the Treasury, Louis McLane, anticipated the Act of Congress of December 22, 1837, which ordered this service carried on by the Revenue Marine. In 1838 the *Washington* was rerigged as a brig. From 1840 to 1852 she was loaned to the Coast Survey, returned to the Revenue Marine in the latter year, she was in service until September 1, 1860, when she was seized by the authorities of the State of Louisiana at New Orleans.

The *Woodbury* cost $11,250 and was employed on the southern stations. In 1838 she was fired at by a French man-of-war near Vera Cruz, with resulting international complications. She carried dispatches in 1845 and during the Mexican War was employed in the Gulf of Mexico. She was sold at New York in 1847 for $550.

The *Van Buren* was employed in the Seminole War and in the war with Mexico. In 1846 she was found to be rotten and after being brought to New York was sold there the next year for $200.

The *Erie*, built on Lake Erie, remained in service until 1849. In 1838 and 1839 she was very actively employed in maintaining American neutrality during the rebellion in Canada. This was no easy task because of the activities of American sympathizers of the Canadian rebels. In the winter of 1838–9 the cutter's crew did duty ashore, patroling troublesome areas. The *Erie* was sold at Erie for $700, July 26, 1849.

The only other vessel employed in the Revenue Marine during the '30's was a purchased schooner or boat obtained in 1830 for harbor work.

In 1841 two more cutters were built. Their plans have not been found and their designers cannot be identified. From pictures and descriptions they appear to have been on the Baltimore Clipper model and enlargements of the *Morris* class. The *Thomas Ewing*, built at Baltimore, was a 170-ton schooner carrying six 12-pounders. She was employed in the Mexican War and went out of service sometime about 1852, being last recorded as on the San Francisco station. The *Walter Forward* was a 150-ton schooner built by William Easby at Washington in 1841–2; she carried four 9-pounders and was employed in the Mexican War, along with the *Woodbury, Ewing, Wolcott, Van Buren, Morris, Forward* and the new steam-cutters *Bibb, Polk, McLane, Legare,* and *Spencer*. The *Forward* remained in service until 1865, when she was ordered to be sold at Baltimore.

Requests for steam-cutters began as early as 1837; the steam-cutters just listed were built in 1844, except the *Polk*, built in '45. The other steamers built at this time were the *Jefferson, Dallas* and *Walker*. They were fitted with the "Hunter Wheel" or Ericson's screw propeller, but proved most unsatisfactory craft. As a result of their trials, sailing and side-paddle-wheel cutters were built subsequently.

The duties of the cutters, in addition to those incidental to the revenue laws, naval service and winter cruising, included the furnishing of food and water to lighthouses and the placing of channel buoys. In 1840 an attack was made on the Revenue Marine in Congress and a charge of extravagance was laid against it. It was proposed that the cutters be replaced with small boats, the fact that the cutters did a great deal of deep-water work being quite overlooked. When this was pointed out to the people's representatives the proposal was laid aside. In 1840 the following

UNITED STATES REVENUE CUTTER *Forward*, FROM A SAILMAKER'S ADVERTISE-
MENT IN THE COLLECTION OF M. V. BREWINGTON, JR.

guns were employed in the service, long 6's, 9's, 12's and 18's; 12- and 18-pounder carronades. The long guns were of brass, the carronades of iron. The armament of the cutters changed rapidly, but four or six guns were carried by most of the *Morris* class.

In 1844 the Revenue Marine was reorganized and many abuses which had grown up in the service were eliminated. The power of the Collectors over the cutters was little curtailed, however, and this remained a source of serious weakness. An officer, Captain Alexander V. Fraser, was made commandant of the cutter service, with Lieutenant George Hayes as his assistant. The commandant had control of the personnel, promotion and discipline being totally under his administration. As a result of the steam-cutter fiasco, the power of building new cutters was taken from the Secretary of the Treasury by Congress, who decided to have that power in its own hands.

In the '40's the number of cutters was gradually reduced until in 1849 only eleven vessels were left. Before 1848 only one small schooner was built, the *Vigilant*. She was built by William Webb in 1843 for the New Orleans station and was a centerboard schooner measuring 56'-0" between perpendiculars, 18'-5" beam, 4'-8" depth of hold and 50 tons burthen. She crossed a yard on her foremast; her lines and sail plan can be found in Webb's *Plans of Wooden Ships* obtainable in many large libraries. The plans of the famous steam-cutter *Harriet Lane* are also in this work. The *Vigilant* was lost in the hurricane of October 4 and 5, 1844, by being blown out of Key West harbor; all hands but two were lost. She had left her station in pursuit of runaway slaves, while under the command of an inspector, in disobedience of strict orders to the contrary. Another schooner, the *Nautilus*, was borrowed from the Coast Survey in 1843 and employed as a cutter until 1848, when she was returned to her owners.

In 1848 it was decided that new cutters were needed and seven were ordered, at least four of them being sister-ships. The records of construction for these cutters are very scant and many questions arise that cannot be answered. The plans of the new cutters called for very fast foretopsail schooners on the most advanced clipper model of the time. All these cutters were built by contract; their names being *Campbell*, *William J. Duane*, *Crawford*, *Morris*, *Lawrence*, *Samuel D. Ingham* and *Harrison*. The last two were built by John Carrick at Erie, Pennsylvania. The *Ingham* was sold at Detroit and the *Harrison* at Oswego in 1856. The *Lawrence* was built at Washington and was either a brig or a barque; the records refer to her as both. The *Lawrence* was wrecked at San Francisco in 1851.

REVENUE CUTTERS

The *Campbell* was built at Portsmouth, Virginia, during 1848–9 by Graves and Fenbie. In 1851 she was badly damaged when she was run down by a schooner during a gale and required extensive repairs. In 1855 she was renamed the *Joseph Lane* (referred to officially and in service usage as the *Joe Lane*). She ended her career on the Pacific Coast, where she was sold in 1869.

Her plans, found in the Bureau of Construction and Repair, U.S.C.G.,

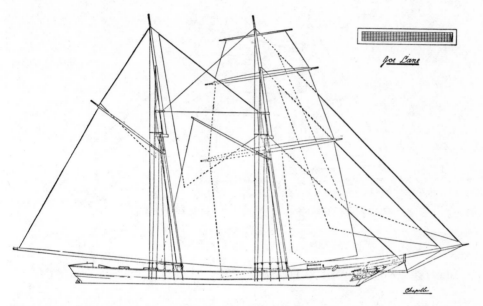

Figure 36. Sail plan of United States Revenue Cutter JOE LANE.

are the only ones available for her class; fortunately they are most complete. They were apparently made while she was on the Pacific Coast in the '60's, the date on them, 1851, being an error. She was a long, low keel schooner of about 102 feet on deck, 100'-4" on the load waterline, 23'-0" extreme beam and 9'-7½" draft (Plate VIII and Figure 36). The *Lane* represents, in a general way, the cutters built afterwards; the round stern, low freeboard and the beautiful clipper bow surmounted by an eagle with outspread wings, were characteristic features of the sailing cutters. The cumbersome hammock rails were usually omitted in this class, being replaced with hammock lockers on the quarterdeck; the heavy head of former classes was not used and the toilets were located in deck-houses. The sister-ships of the *Lane* were apparently the *Duane*, *Crawford* and *Morris*. The *Duane* and *Crawford* were built at Philadelphia by Jacob Tees; the *Duane* was seized by the Confederates at Norfolk in 1861, while the *Crawford* was sold at Newport in 1869. The *Morris* was built by John S. Brown at Baltimore and was sold in 1868.

UNITED STATES REVENUE CUTTER *Joe Lane*.

The last vessel obtained by the service in the '40's was a mere boat, the *Veto*, stationed at Castine, Maine, in 1849.

It is to be noted that the Revenue Service has always referred to vessels having names like *Samuel D. Ingham* by the last portion of the correct name, "*Ingham*," even in official records, as well as in everyday service usage.

The gold rush to California and the establishment of custom houses there made it necessary to have cutters in the Pacific. Until regular cutters could be sent out, local schooners were hired to serve the purpose. The first of these was the *Argus*, chartered in 1850, and again in 1851–53.

Another schooner, the *Frolic*, was hired in 1851, and was retained until 1853.

Ten new cutters were ordered in 1853, all built by contract, and all probably on the lines of the *Lane*, or at least similar to her in size. Six of the new cutters were built by J. M. Hood, a shipbuilder who had constructed eight clipper-ships between 1850 and 1853, including the noted *Raven* and *Archer*. Hood had two yards, one at Somerset, a small village on the Taunton River, just above Fall River, in Massachusetts; the other

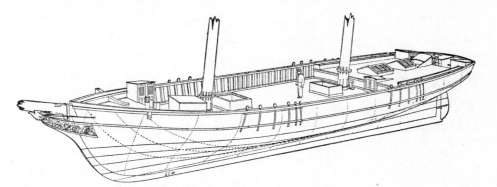

UNITED STATES REVENUE CUTTER *Joe Lane*.

at Bristol, Rhode Island. In the Somerset yard, Hood built the cutters, *James C. Dobbin*, *Caleb Cushing*, *James Campbell* and *Robert McClelland*; in the Bristol yard he built the *Jefferson Davis* and *William L. Marcy*. Page and Allen, of Portsmouth, Virginia, who built the clipper-ship *Neptune's Car* in 1853, also built the cutters *Phillip Allen*, *Lewis Cass* and *Henry Dodge* the same year. Another cutter, the *Sea Drift*, was built by Ivans and Grinnell at Stonington, Connecticut.

The *Dobbin* was captured by the State of Georgia authorities in 1861, but was sent north afterwards. She was the first cadet training ship, the present Coast Guard Academy being founded on her by Act of Congress, July 31, 1876. She was used as a school-ship through 1877 and was sold in 1881.

The *Jefferson Davis* was sent to the Pacific and became a marine hospital ship at Port Townsend in 1862. The *Caleb Cushing* was cut out of Portland Harbor on the night of August 26, 1863, by some daring Confederates and burned. The *James Campbell* was sold in 1875 and the *Phillip Allen* disappears from record in 1865. The *Marcy* was transferred to the Coast Survey. The *McClelland* was seized by the authorities of the State of Louisiana in 1861; the *Cass* by officers of Alabama and the *Dodge* by Texas at about the same time. One of these cutters that were seized by southern authorities appears to have been renamed *Petrel* and was sunk by the sailing frigate *St. Lawrence* during the early part of the Civil War. The *Sea Drift* was found to be unseaworthy while at Key West in 1857 and was condemned.

In 1853 the Revenue Marine purchased the fine Charleston pilot-boat *Eclipse* for $4,500; taking her into service as the *William Aiken*. This vessel was taken by the state officers of South Carolina in 1861, or, as the "Record of Movements" states, 1858.

In 1856, Merry and Gay of Milan, Ohio, contracted to build six cutters for $4,050 each; judging by the price these must have been small schooners. They were the *Jeremiah S. Black* who disappears from the record in 1868; the *Aaron V. Brown*, sold at New York in 1864; the *Howell Cobb*, wrecked in 1862; *Jacob Thompson*, sold at Baltimore in 1870; *Isaac Toncey*, sold at New Haven in 1869 and the *John B. Floyd*, sold at Detroit in 1858.

The only other sailing cutter built during the '50's was the *John Appleton*, built by Page and Allen at Portsmouth, Virginia, on the lines of the other cutters built by this firm. She was launched in 1857, and in 1861 she was delivered to the Navy at Key West.

Through the '50's and '60's steamers gradually replaced the sailing cutters, but as the latter were cheaper to maintain and were suitable for some stations, their building continued after the Civil War. Also, during the Civil War, a number of sailing schooners were borrowed or hired; the schooner-yacht *Henrietta* of New York was in the service for a time in 1861, and the schooners *Vixen, Thomas Corwin* and a few others were received from the Coast Survey temporarily. In 1863, the Revenue Marine was officially designated "United States Revenue Service."

In 1866 eight new sailing cutters, sister-ships measuring 110'-0" in length, 24'-8½" beam, 11'-0" draft and 227⁸⁵/₉₅ tons burthen, were ordered. J. W. Lynn built two of these at Philadelphia, the *Active*, sold

UNITED STATES REVENUE CUTTER *Alert* (*Active?*)

at New York in 1875 and the *Resolute*, sold at Philadelphia in 1872. W. H. Hathorn of Williamsburg, New York, probably the former partner of the famous George Steers, built the *Petrel* and *Racer*, both sold in 1872. Fardy and Brothers, of Baltimore, built the *Reliance*, sold in 1875, and *Vigilant*, off the record in 1871. Bierly, Hillman and Co., of Philadelphia, constructed the *Relief* (no record after 1867) and the *Rescue*, sold at Baltimore in 1874. Plans of these schooners have not yet been found. In 1869 a small schooner named *Search* was built at New York, costing $5,524. She was sold in 1896. The only other sailing vessel in the service during the '60's was the boat *Sunnyside*, employed at Waldoboro, Maine, 1863–8.

The last sailing vessels built for the Revenue Service were the *Active*, a small schooner built by David Blackburn and Co., at New York, in 1876, as a supply-boat for the Toms River, New Jersey, Life-Saving Station, and the famous Revenue Service training-ship *Salmon P. Chase*, built in 1877–8.

This little vessel was a barque-rigged clipper with a round stern and beautiful clipper bow. She was 103'-6" long on the waterline, between rabbets, 106'-3" on deck, 25'-6" extreme beam, 11'-0" draft and 294 tons displacement. The *Chase* was a remarkably handsome vessel having very sharp lines and was designed under the direction of Captain J. H. Merryman, U.S.R.M. This vessel was employed as a cadet training-ship for many years; many officers still in service received their service education in her. She was a much beloved ship in the service, and had much to do with the establishment of the traditions of the present Coast Guard Academy. Though somewhat overhatted, the *Chase* was a fast sailer and a fine seaboat. She was contracted to be built by Thomas Brown and Sons, of Philadelphia, but this firm was soon in financial difficulties, so the government had to complete her. When finished she cost in the neighborhood of $20,300. In 1895 the *Chase* was extensively repaired and apparently was lengthened amidships at the same time.

She was in collision with the Boston schooner *Richard F. C. Hartley* in the early morning of May 6, 1897, about 50 miles east of Charleston Bar and was completely disabled. The *Chase* was towed into Charleston, and then to Baltimore where she was repaired. In 1912 she was towed to Fortress Monroe from New London and became a marine hospital ship.

The spirit and traditions of the present Coast Guard were founded in the slippery little revenue schooners of the days of sail. These rakish topsail schooners, slashing through the heavy seas of a winter's gale, were the first to express the motto of the present service, *Semper Paratus* (Always Ready).

Chapter Five   # THE AMERICAN
                                  # SCHOONER

THE national importance of any type of merchant vessel is usually very difficult to decide to the satisfaction of everyone, for there are so many points of view from which the subject can be approached. The most natural way to judge, perhaps, is by the amount of cargo carried in a type, in proportion to that carried by others within the same period of time. The economic and historic importance of the cargoes carried by a type might also be a basis of judgment. On the other hand, the historic incidents in which a type of vessel has figured might be worthy of consideration. Then again, there is the technical viewpoint which, in the final analysis, is based on the degree of efficiency with which a type serves its purposes, in relation to natural and economic conditions. The span of existence and spread of popularity of a hull-form or rig are largely governed by this particular consideration. Size, beauty, sentimental qualifications or any one good feature alone counts for nothing against the economic and natural law of the survival of the fittest.

The application of any of these methods of judgment to American mercantile sailing craft causes no difficulty in arriving at a definite conclusion, however, for by any of these measuring-sticks the schooner must be accepted as the most important. Though square-riggers could usually carry more cargo than contemporary schooners, the ships have been far less numerous than the schooners from the time of the Revolution onwards. In spite of the fact that ships and square-riggers monopolized certain important trades, such as the packet and East Indian, and though they handled large and valuable cargoes individually, the total tonnage and value of such cargoes were small compared to that carried by the schooners engaged in the coasting and foreign trades. The square-riggers usually made long voyages, requiring weeks and months to make a round trip, whereas schooners, commonly employed in short, quick voyages, had a more rapid turn-over of cargo and valuation. In wartime, as during the War of 1812, or in times of maritime danger, as existed throughout the Napoleonic Wars, the schooners were able to carry the bulk of cargoes shipped in American bottoms because of their speed and ability to out-distance pursuing cruisers. In August, 1814, it was estimated that nine-tenths of the foreign trade of the United States was carried on in Baltimore Clipper schooners, and in 1815 it was claimed that one-half the total wartime trade of the country had been carried on by Baltimore vessels alone, the majority of which were schooners.

The economic importance of the wartime trade, as well as the regular schooner-trades such as the coasting and West Indian, requires no explanation. The lumber trade, the fisheries, much of the South American and African trades, sealing and considerable European trade were carried on in schooners, and the aggregate tonnage of their cargoes was enormous when compared to that of the square-riggers in the packet, East Indian, cotton and general trades.

The historic and economic implications of the slave trade, largely carried on by schooners, requires no discussion, but should not be overlooked. The employment of schooners as naval vessels, privateers, revenue cutters, pirates, slavers and illicit traders assured the type a notable part in a large number of important historical incidents.

From the technical point of view, the remarkably long existence of the rig and certain hull-forms in commercial work proves the efficiency with which the schooner met economic and natural requirements. The advantages of the schooners over the square-riggers rested in the smaller crews required by the former, as well as the schooners' greater handiness and surety in working in narrow channels and confined waters. There were disadvantages to the rig, particularly in very large vessels, but the relative importance of these can be gaged by the fact that the number of schooners rapidly increased at a time when other types of sailing craft were disappearing with great rapidity. The spread of the schooner's popularity was very remarkable. Beginning as an almost local type and rig,

ELSIE, *bow view*

ELSIE, *stern view*

ELSIE, *foreside of windlass showing fittings*

ELSIE, *after side windlass, showing it fitted for power*

ELSIE, *forecastle hatch and galley stack*

ELSIE, *knightheads and hawse*

ELSIE, *pumps and afterhatch*

ELSIE, *main deck, looking forward from hatch (circular hatch in background)*

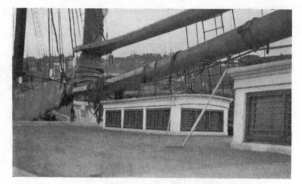

ELSIE, *foremasthead (foreside)*

Four-Masted Schooner, top of house looking forward

Four-Masted Schooner, fore end of forecastle

Four-Masted Schooner, forward end of quarter deck looking aft

Bow of Four-Masted Schooner

Stern of Four-Masted Schooner, showing method of planking stern

the schooner gradually became popular along the Atlantic seaboard to Canada, then in Europe and in Central and South America, finally in the Pacific and Far East. By 1790, if not earlier, the schooner was the national rig of both the United States and Canada.

The early development of the American schooner has been described in an earlier chapter, where the appearance of the sharp, fast schooner

SCHOONER *Marble Head.*

was also mentioned. The most rapid development of the schooner took place after the appearance of the sharp-lined hull, later known as the "Baltimore Clipper." As has been said, this model was in existence as early as 1746 at least. Though it seems definitely established that the type first developed in southern waters, it spread northward at an early date. The lack of definite information regarding the early evolution of the sharp-model schooner makes any attempt to trace this matter mere speculation. It is reasonably certain, however, that the sharp schooner did not at once become a distinct type, and also that there was no "first" sharp schooner. The process of evolution was gradual, and before the model was fully developed its construction had spread along the whole coast, from Maine to the Carolinas, wherever a fast schooner was wanted.

The Maryland and Virginia builders, however, specialized in this class of work and therefore developed the model more rapidly than elsewhere, with the result that the model became known as a Chesapeake type under the names of the "Virginia model" or "Virginia-built." Northern builders, having less constant demand for the sharp type, merely copied the more advanced southern builder when an order for a vessel of this class came to hand. By 1760 the "Virginia model" schooner was well-known along the coast and builders in Massachusetts, Connecticut, New York, New Jersey, Pennsylvania and the Carolinas were turning out excellent copies. Due to this and to the purchase of schooners at New York for the British Navy, the only plan of a pre-Revolutionary schooner of the Virginia model is now available.

Among the plans in the Collection of Draughts in the British Admiralty, there was this one of a sharp schooner, the *Marble Head*, titled "Built in New York in July, 1767." This vessel was probably one purchased there in 1767–8 for the Royal Navy, though it seems probable that her name was changed as she apparently was not carried on the Navy List as the *Marble Head*. She may have been purchased on the stocks, as some of the schooners were so acquired. The plan, redrawn in Figure 37 with the reconstructions noted, shows a schooner of good lines, considering the length and heavy displacement. It would be very risky to call this vessel "typical" of the "Virginia model" of the time, for she is the only example we have to judge by. However, she does give an idea of the stage of development reached, generally, in the construction of the sharp schooners of 1765–70. The original draught of the *Marble Head* does not show the deck arrangement, but it is probable that it was like the *Chaleur's*, shown in Chapter One, allowing for the difference in size of the two vessels.

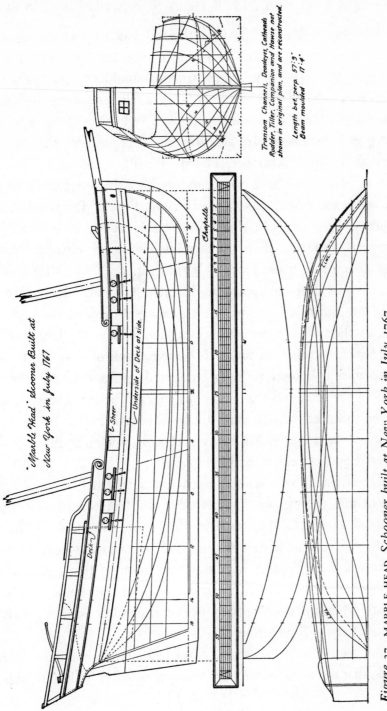

Transom, Channels, Deadeyes, Catheads
Rudder, Tiller, Companion and Hawse not
shown in original plan, and are reconstructed.

Length bet. perp   57'.9".
Beam moulded   17'.4".

'Marble Head' Schooner Built at
New York in July 1767

Underside of Deck at side

Sheer

Deck

Chapelle

L.W.L.

223

Figure 37. MARBLE HEAD, Schooner built at New York in July 1767.

The plan of the *Marble Head* is sufficient evidence that the advantages of sharp lines, great deadrise and drag to the keel, as well as a well-formed run, were not unknown to American builders prior to the Revolution. The model of this schooner is, generally speaking, a good one, and the *Marble Head* was undoubtedly a fairly fast vessel and a good sea-boat. No spar dimensions are available, but it is probable that she was a fore-and-main topsail schooner. Though a small vessel, the stern cabin of the *Marble Head* must have made comfortable living quarters; with slight modifications she would make a most practical yacht. Imagine the results of suddenly appearing at Marblehead in such a yacht during Race Week!

In general, this example of a sharp-lined schooner illustrates the features of design that made up the "Virginia model," or "Virginia-built" schooner which developed into the Baltimore Clipper. Cataloguing these features, we find that they include a great deal of deadrise at the mid-section; a rather strong rake to bow and stern, making the length on deck much greater than that on the keel; greater depth of draft aft than forward, or what is known as "drag"; rather deep draft; low freeboard to the level of the deck and sharply raking masts. The masts were probably first given this great rake to make the poorly made sails stand better, but finally it became a custom. In many craft with fine ends, the rake of the masts also may have eased the pitching.

In most of these early sea-going schooners, whether of the "Virginia model" or not, the rig was either that of the fore-topsail, or fore-and-main topsail schooner. The former rig had square-sail yards on her foremast only, whereas the latter had them on both main and fore, in addition to the fore-and-aft rigging. It is worth mentioning that many of these early schooners had booms on their fore gaff sails, but these went out of popularity when the over-lapping, or lug, foresail came into general use some time after the Revolution.

It would be natural to conclude, after reading contemporary seamen's accounts, that the term "schooner" was synonymous with these rigs dur-

ing the last half of the eighteenth century. However, there are contemporary pictures that show the true fore-and-aft schooner was not
unknown in this period. For the lack of information, it is impossible
to decide the comparative numbers of square-rigged and fore-and-aft
schooners. Since most of the evidence in the way of plans and spar dimensions refer to naval or sea-going schooners as having yards, it is possi-

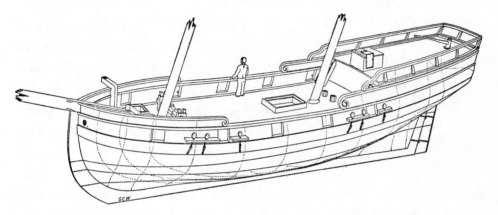

SCHOONER *Marble Head.*

ble that the fore-and-aft schooners in these early pictures are coasters and
fishermen. It is certain, in view of an existing picture, that the fore-and-
aft schooner rig was in common use on the Chesapeake before 1760.

The Revolutionary War made a greater demand than had previously
existed for fast schooners, not only for privateering but, when blockade
running became necessary, for commercial purposes. Plans of American
schooners of the wartime period are extremely rare and it is therefore
most difficult to learn much about their lines. The *Berbice*, shown in
Figure 24, Chapter Three, is the only example now available and, in spite
of the uncertainty as to her origin, probably shows the stage of development attained in this class. By the end of the war, the distinctive design
of the "Virginia model" had received refinements that marked the appearance of the extreme clipper schooner. Though there is a strong sim-

ilarity between the *Berbice* and *Marble Head*, the trend toward greater dimensions and reduced displacement in proportion to size, combined with greater deadrise, finer ends and longer runs, becomes apparent.

The demand for fast-sailing vessels after the Revolution, fostered by international and political conditions, enabled the "Virginia model" to continue its development. The unfriendly attitude of most of Europe toward the Americans was expressed by the arrest and condemnation of their vessels on the slightest excuse. To avoid this misfortune, the Americans had to depend upon their heels, for it was hopeless to expect a merchant vessel to fight successfully a man-of-war, and there was, of course, no American Navy for many years. Nothing is more conducive to the attainment of speed in sailing vessels than to have the owner's property and, perhaps, freedom depend upon this particular quality. As years passed and conditions became increasingly unfavorable to our infant merchant-marine, as they did in spite of the appearance of the very weak American Navy, the demand for speed became more insistent. The builders were ingenious and intelligent men, and when commercial considerations permitted them to make sacrifices to obtain high speed, they were not slow to experiment. They realized that high freeboard and bulwarks hurt sailing because of the extra weight necessitated in such construction, and it is probable that they had an inkling of the effects of the windage of these features. They also appreciated the fact that the greater the sail area in relation to displacement, the higher the speed would be. If one can judge by the designs that resulted from these experiments, it seems apparent that the advantages of light construction, combined with stability, were as well thought of by the designer of 1800 as by the modern yacht designer.

With greater freedom in design permissible, the builders began experiments with small schooners, and if the experiments were found to be advantageous, they were repeated in large vessels. As a result, the period between 1785 and 1800 saw the construction of many extremely sharp schooners; long, low and very fine-lined, and heavily sparred and canvassed. The freeboard of these schooners was extremely low; the effect of lowness and length was further accentuated by the use of the "log-rail" in place of bulwarks, this rail consisting merely of a square timber, 6 to 10 inches high, fastened to the top of the plank-sheer or covering-board. In comparison to their dimensions, the displacement of these schooners was small, and light hulls were obtained by using thin plank-ing and alternate double and single sawn frames of small scantlings in place of the usual heavy double frames. Everything was lightened: decks, deck-fittings, spars and rigging. The use of a hull-form having some initial stability combined with the heavy ballast possible on a given dis-placement, when hull construction was light, made it possible to carry a tremendous spread of canvas.

Most of the experiments were carried out in small schooners, as has been said; the small pilot-boats were usually the subjects chosen for test-ing the builder's theories. Since the builders along the shores of the Ches-apeake were particularly active in the production of fast vessels, it is not surprising to learn that the pilot-boats used off the Virginia Capes were usually the expression of some builder's experiment and were therefore, as a rule, extreme in design. This was particularly the case from about 1790 to 1815, and contemporary references to the "high-flying" Nor-folk pilot-boats are not uncommon. These schooners ranged from 45 to about 60 feet on deck; because of the speed developed by constant experimentation in design the Norfolk pilot-boat was not only used in the pilot service, but many of them drifted into trade, usually an illicit one.

Some of these craft were regular "racing machines" whose entry in a modern ocean yacht race would have been refused by the race-committee on grounds of their lack of safety. They were usually rigged as simple fore-and-aft schooners; having a large jib, a boomless and overlapping gaff-foresail, a boomed but loose-footed gaff-mainsail and a main-topmast staysail set to a short pole main-topmast. Most of them had no standing rigging whatever, neither stays nor shrouds. In these schooners the jib and main-topmast staysail were "set flying," that is, they were not hanked to a stay. If one of these vessels were to make a long sea-voyage, a square topsail and course were fitted to the foremast, which was then provided with a fidded pole-topmast like the main. Some appear to have been built as three-masted schooners, though this rig does not seem to have been used by the pilots.

When the War of the French Revolution began in 1793, the French and English purchased some of these pilot-schooners for dispatch-boats, light cruisers or privateers, for the reputation of the "Virginia Pilot-Boat" had extended abroad. During the war these little schooners were called upon to cross the Atlantic many times and, so far as is known, none of them was lost. So impressed were the British with the pilot-boats that they made a number of attempts to reproduce them, usually resulting in failure because of alterations made in the designs to convert them to miniature men-of-war.

One of the "Virginia Pilot-Boat" schooners obtained from the Americans by the Royal Navy was the *Swift*, whose plans are shown in Figures 38 and 39. This schooner was much less extreme in model than many of her type but appears to have been quite fast and remarkably seaworthy; probably this was one reason why the Admiralty bothered to have her lines taken off. The means by which the British acquired the *Swift* have not been learned but she was probably purchased by British officers in the United States. The open rails shown in the drawing of the lines were added by the British when she was fitted for naval service; the fitting of this kind of rail was done to others of the type when taken into naval service, as it was least harmful to the sailing qualities of the small schooners. The date that the *Swift* was built has not been learned, but since her lines were taken off in 1803, she was built some time previous to this year, possibly between 1795 and 1800. A somewhat similar vessel extracted from Knowles' *Naval Architecture* published in 1822 was reproduced in *The Baltimore Clipper*. This particular plan appeared earlier in Steel's *Naval Architecture*, which Knowles seems to have used without ac-

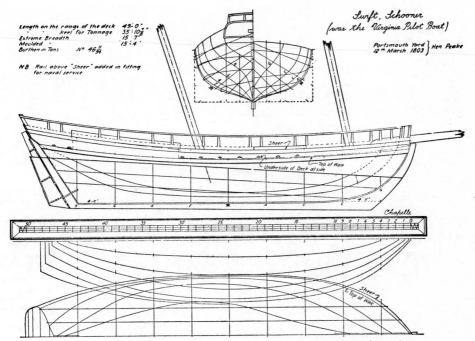

Length on the range of the deck 49·0"
   "   keel for Tonnage   35·10¾
Extreme Breadth   15 7"
Moulded   "   15 ·4"
Burthen in Tons   N° 46¹¹⁄₉₄

N B Rail above "Sheer" added in fitting
      for naval service

Swift, Schooner
(*was the Virginia Pilot Boat*)

Portsmouth Yard   } Hen Peake
12ᵗʰ March. 1803

Sheer
Top of Wale
Underside of Deck at side

Chapelle

Sheer
Top of Wale

Figure 38. *Lines of a Virginia Pilot-Boat, 1803, as fitted for naval service.*

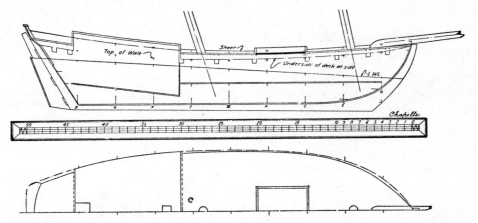

Top of Wale
Sheer
Underside of deck at side
LWL

Chapelle

Figure 39. *Inboard profile and deck of a Virginia Pilot-Boat of 1803, (as originally built).*

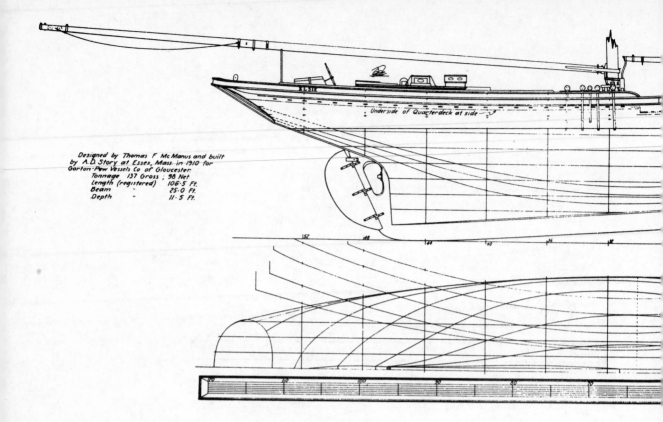

Designed by Thomas F. McManus and built
by A.D. Story at Essex, Mass. in 1910 for
Gorton-Pew Vessels Co. of Gloucester.
Tonnage   137 Gross ; 98 Net.
Length (registered)   106·5 Ft.
Beam   "   25·0 Ft.
Depth   "   11·5 Ft.

Underside of Quarterdeck at side

*Plate IX. ELSIE. The famous racing fisherman
built at Essex, Mass., in 1910. Drawn from designer's plan, builder's offsets and actual measurements of the vessel in 1933. No reconstruction.*

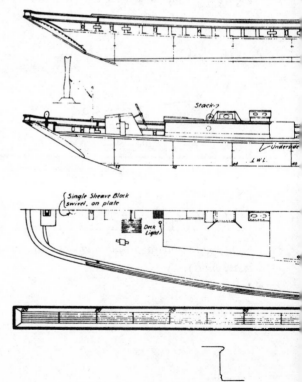

SECTION C

Stack·?

Underside

L.W.L.

Single Sheave Block
swivel, on plate

Deck
Light?

CABIN TRUNK

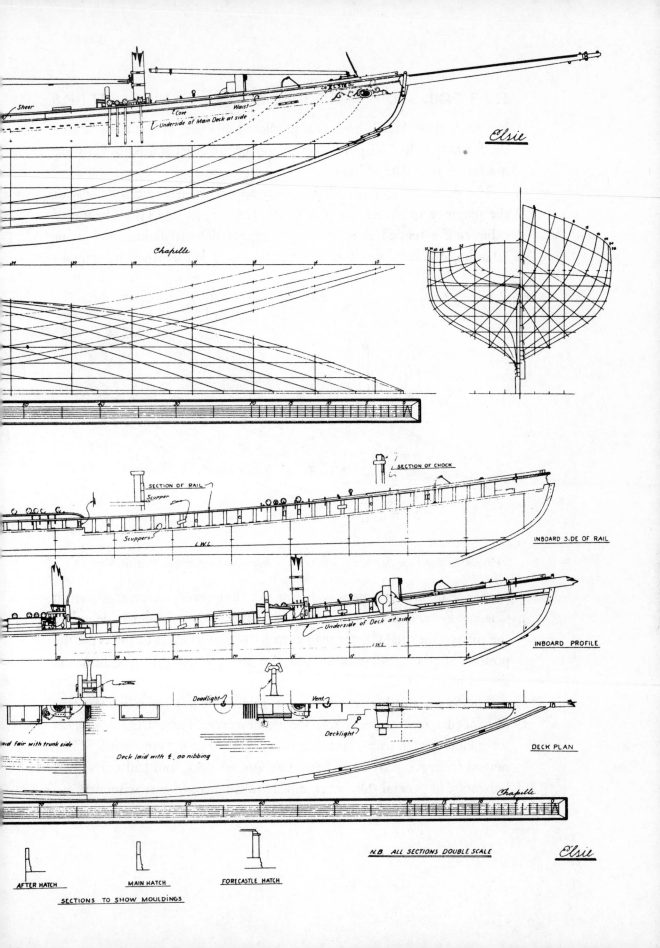

Elsie

Sheer

Cove   Waist
Underside of Main Deck at side

Chapelle

SECTION OF CHOCK
SECTION OF RAIL
Scupper

Scuppers

L.W.L.

INBOARD S.DE OF RAIL

Underside of Deck at side

L.W.L.

INBOARD PROFILE

Deadlight

Vent.

Decklight

DECK PLAN

laid fair with trunk side

Deck laid with t. oo nibbing

Chapelle

N.B. ALL SECTIONS DOUBLE SCALE   *Elsie*

AFTER HATCH   MAIN HATCH   FORECASTLE HATCH

SECTIONS TO SHOW MOULDINGS

knowledgment. Steel's book was published in 1805, so it is possible that the *Swift* and the "Virginia Pilot Schooner" of Steel and Knowles were not far apart in date of build.

The deck arrangement of the *Swift* appears to have been typical of the majority of American pilot-boats, from 1790 to 1830. The raised cabin roof extended clear across the ship, as did the sunken cockpit or "standing-room." The alternate arrangement of small American schoon-

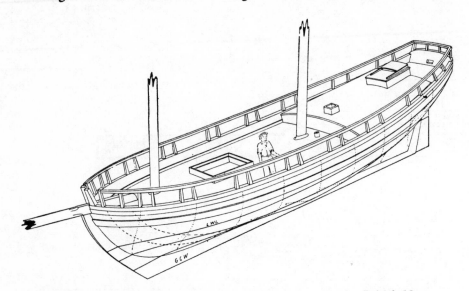

Virginia Pilot-boat Schooner SWIFT, *as a dispatch-boat in the British Navy.*

ers of the pilot-boat type was that of the 1815 revenue cutters shown in Chapter Four. Comment on the lines of the *Swift* need not be lengthy: the run is somewhat shorter than in many other examples of the type; the position of the greatest beam and also the greatest depth of buttocks should be observed.

The *Swift*, and her sisters, do not represent the large schooners that developed from the small pilot-boats, however. These large schooners were built for the over-sea trades, or at least for deep-water work. They ranged from about 65 to 95 feet in length, on deck, and had fairly high bulwarks; in general they were similar to the man-of-war schooners except in having sharper lines and less displacement. At the period under discussion nearly all sea-going merchant vessels, large and small, had gun-ports. The *Subtle*, shown in Figures 40 and 41, is an excellent example

VIRGINIA PILOT-BOAT SCHOONER *Swift*, AS RIGGED FOR NAVAL SERVICE.

of the application of the lessons learned by the American builders in the construction of the pilot-boats to large sea-going schooners.

The *Subtle* was an American-built schooner that the British captured from the Danes in 1808 and took into the Royal Navy. The early history of this vessel is not at hand. She served in the Royal Navy about four years as a cruiser; much of her service was in the West Indies. A British account stated that the *Subtle* had been built at Baltimore, but this cannot be verified.

In the latter part of November, 1812, the American privateer-brig

231

Jack's Favorite, under Captain Miller, put into St. Bartholomews, in the West Indies, to obtain supplies and water. A few days later the *Subtle*, commanded by Lieutenant Charles Brown, R.N., put into port and

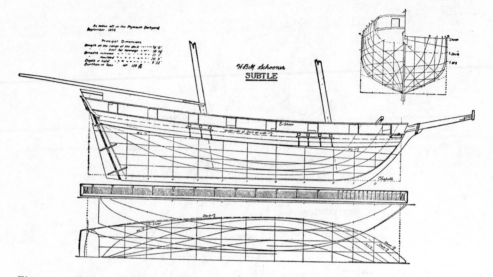

Figure 40. *Lines of the Schooner* SUBTLE, *1808.*

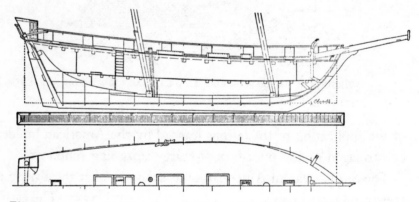

Figure 41. *Schooner* SUBTLE. *Inboard profile and deck plan.*

found the privateer at anchor in the harbor. It is said that Lieutenant Brown made the statement, ashore, that he would "follow and take that damned Yankee privateer if he went to Hell for her." On the 30th of the month the *Jack's Favorite* put to sea, the *Subtle* making sail after her.

THE AMERICAN SCHOONER

The privateer captain felt he could find a more pleasant occupation than battling a regular man-of-war, so he made sail to escape, with the British schooner in hot pursuit. The weather was squally as it was in the hurricane season, but soon both vessels had set "everything but the cook's shirt." The desperate race had not lasted very long before the American

Subtle, 1808.

captain noticed a white squall approaching. Though the fast British schooner was slowly gaining on the brig, the American decided that he must get sail off his vessel, for the squall looked particularly violent. He succeeded in getting his brig snugged-down just as the squall hit; his last view of the British schooner astern showed her to be still carrying sail. When the rain accompanying the squall had blown over, the schooner could be no longer seen. The *Jack's Favorite* hove around and retraced her course, for the privateersman was certain that the *Subtle* had capsized. Sure enough, the Americans soon sighted a few sailors' hats and

233

hammocks bobbing in the heavy sea, but not a man of the fifty officers and men of the *Subtle* could be found.

The plans of the *Subtle* show the remarkable degree of sharpness reached in the design of large American schooners before the War of 1812. The *Subtle,* because of her fine ends, apparently had a tendency to trim by the head when fitted as a man-of-war. This was a trait more common in brigs than schooners, but the *Subtle* was too sharp a vessel to make a safe war-schooner. The weight of a battery of guns on her deck, combined with her comparatively light displacement, made her a most dangerous vessel, and her capsizing can be traced to this fault. The *Subtle* had spars of the following dimensions: Mainmast, hounded length, 61'-2" diameter 17⅜" mast-head 5'-6"; Main-topmast, hounded length, 29'-0"; diameter 7½"; pole 2'-0", (total 31'-0"); Foremast, hounded length 56'-0"; diameter 17⅞"; masthead 5'-11"; Fore-topmast, hounded length 19'-0"; diameter 7⅝"; pole 11'-0", (total 30'-0"); Bowsprit, total length, 24'-2"; diameter 15⅜"; Jib-boom, total length, 27'-0"; diameter 7"; Main-gaff 21'-6"; diameter 5⅜"; Fore-gaff 21'-6"; diameter 5⅜"; Main-boom 44'-7"; diameter 9⅜"; Fore Yard 39'-11"; diameter 7¾"; Fore-topsail Yard 29'-0"; diameter 6¾"; Fore-topgallant Yard 18'-8"; diameter 4⅛".

From these dimensions it can be seen that the *Subtle* was rigged as a fore-topsail schooner, an extremely popular rig during the first half of the nineteenth century for sea-going schooners. The popularity of this rig, and that of the fore-and-main topsail schooner, was due to the all-around ability of these rigs. Though undoubtedly less weatherly than the fore-and-after, the square-rigged schooner had the advantage off the wind and on a reach. The modern trend in yachts toward rigs of remarkable efficiency to windward has been, to some extent, at the expense of speed on other courses, the trend itself being the effect of yacht-racing customs. The triangular racing course, with legs of equal length laid out in such a manner that one of them is a beat to windward, has placed a premium on windward work not met with in cruising or commercial sailing. A cruising yacht or any sailing vessel, aside from a racing yacht, does not beat to windward for a third of a voyage. Experience in ocean yacht-racing has borne this out to some extent, though the fixed destination and close competition in these races tends to place a high value on windward ability too. The perfect measure of comparative speed does not exist, it is true, but probably the old conditions of "catch me who can" did more to develop all-around speed in sailing craft than modern

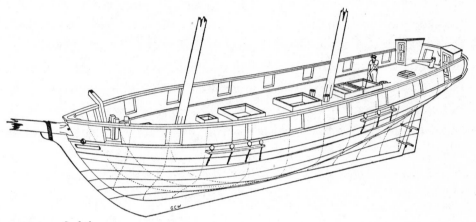

SCHOONER *Subtle*

yacht-racing. In the serious "game of tag" carried on between pursued and pursuer in the early nineteenth century, the former was usually put on her best point of sailing, either on or off the wind, and if the pursuer caught her it was usually by out-sailing her. Some vessels sailed best on one point, some on another, so the advantages of an all-around sailer as a privateer, naval vessel, or even as a trader, were obvious.

The rigging of the yards on the fore-topsail, or fore-and-main topsail, schooner was never standardized, but basically there were two methods employed in American schooners. The yards were as light as possible and in all but the largest schooners were fitted so that they could be lowered on deck. The upper yards were fitted in the same manner as a ship's topgallant yards, but the lower yards on a fore-and-main topsail schooner, or the fore yard on a fore-topsail schooner, had a special method of rigging. The problem of controlling these yards when they were being low-ered at sea made it necessary to use a "jack-stay." This was a heavy stay on the fore-side of the mast, passed around the mast-head over the trestle-trees and under the fore-stay, and leading to the deck or mast-bed, close to the foot of the mast, where it was set up with either deadeyes and lanyards or bull's-eyes from a ringbolt. The lower yard travelled on this stay by means of a lignum-vitae thimble seized to the yard and riding the stay. The stay was not used, usually, to support the yard when it was hoisted; this was done by a truss or parral line around the mast above the gaff-jaws and set up by a fall leading to the deck. This was necessary as the chafe of the yard on the jack-stay would soon cause an accident.

Large schooners, in which the lower yards were too heavy to be easily hoisted, had their yards rigged in the same manner as the lower yards of a ship. In small schooners such as the pilot-boats the course was not furled to the yard aloft, both being usually lowered on deck. In large schooners the course was rarely furled to the yard; it was hoisted by tackles rove through blocks on the yard. The head of the course was made to stand by a jackyard extending the middle third of the head; this came home to the yard when the sail was hoisted, one of the three tackles securing it. The other two acted as outhauls on the yard-arms. The bottom of the fore-course was spread by a boom, about equal in length to the fore-yard. This boom could be secured to the mast, rigging, or to the catheads, and canted as desired; by this means the course could be made to stand when braced up without the use of fore-tack boomkins or out-riggers, yet the foot of the sail could be very wide. This rig was very flexible and, except for the objection of the boom across the deck forward, was much simpler and handier than the rigs now used in yachts fitted with square-sails. The later hermaphrodite schooners had the fore-mast rigged brig-fashion, as far as the yards were concerned.

Sometime between 1800 and 1812 the names applied to the sharp schooners, "Virginia-built" or "Virginia model," were replaced in popu-

Inter-Island Trading Schooner, LANAIKA *in Honolulu*

West Coast Schooner BILL THE BUTCHER, *built 1871 at San Francisco*

Brig JAMES RAMSAY, *Baltimore 1830*

Schooner JUSTINA, *built Dorchester Co., Md., 1839*

Schooner, ST. MARY, *Baltimore 1847*

Schooner GEORGIA, *Dorchester Co., Md., 1853* (?)

Ship CORINTHIAN, *built at Baltimore 1822*

Brig G. P. STEVENSON, *Baltimore 1816*

lar usage by "pilot-boat" or "pilot-boat construction." These terms appeared much earlier than 1800, but did not at once become popular. The widespread use of the Virginia pilot-boat schooners no doubt accounted for this change. The local pilot-boats of Boston, New York and other ports differed but little from the older Norfolk model, so seamen hailing from anywhere along the coast knew what was meant by "pilot-boat"; these schooners having become synonymous with the sharp-model, in the public mind. Nevertheless, the old terms, "Virginia model" and "Virginia-built" did not disappear at once; they may be found in accounts dating as late as 1814. During the War of 1812, "pilot-boat" and "pilot-boat construction" appear most frequently, though "Baltimore-built" began to appear in wartime accounts also. The latter term was used a great deal after the war, particularly in regard to slavers, probably because so many vessels of the sharp model were being built in the vicinity of that city. The term "Baltimore Clipper," though sometimes employed before 1825, did not become common usage until the type was dying out, 1830 to 1850.

The word "clipper" seems to have been derived from an old slang phrase meaning to move fast; "to clip along" or "to move at a fast clip." The use of the term "clipper" seems to have started as early as 1815; the British used the term "American Clipper" in referring to fast vessels in the '30's while the Americans occasionally mention a "clipper-schooner" soon after the War of 1812, though the term did not at once become popular. The wide application of "clipper" to ships and to any type of fast-sailing vessel did not take place until about 1845.

The development of the sharp-model schooner reached a high plane during the War of 1812; the privateers of this war were among the best all-around sailers that were ever produced. The *Neufchâtel*, plans of which are reproduced in Chapter Three, is an excellent example. She was by no means an extreme vessel of her time, however. Plans of a number of American schooners of this class were published in *The Balti-*

more Clipper, among them the *Mosquitobit*, formerly the privateer *Lynx*; the *Sea Lark*, formerly the American *Fly*; and the *Grecian*, formerly a Baltimore-built letter-of-marque of the same name.

The trend toward extreme models of the clipper-schooner continued after the war. The rise of the illegal slave trade and the continued employment of privateers by some of the South American revolutionists, as well as the existence of a number of illegal trades, made a steady demand for fast vessels. Aside from these practical considerations, the psychological effect of the long years of constant demand for speed, that conditions had made necessary, must be appreciated. Speed had become a fad just as the rapid and lengthy development of machinery in recent times has made a fad of mechanization. Speed, whether required or not by the specifications of trade, was called "progress." A parallel in modern maritime history can be found in the recent developments in New England fishermen. Here the employment of high-powered engines is also called "progress," in spite of the fact that the average income of a fishing schooner, over a period of years equal to the usual life of one of these vessels, does not warrant the capital investment required by these engines or by the modern mechanized fishing craft. In the case of both the fast-sailing clipper-schooner and the modern heavily-powered fisherman, the result has been a rapid decline of the type under economic pressure. Economic laws are barriers which fads, even when masquerading as "progress," cannot hurdle. Speed and mechanism play an important part in true progress; it is the undue emphasis placed on them by fads that so often lead to financial failure in certain types of manufacturing and in transportation.

For examples of the extremely sharp vessels built after the War of 1812 one has only to inspect the slavers in an earlier chapter, and the 1815 revenue cutters. Since the similarity between naval and commercial schooners remained close, it will not be mis-leading to use the plan of a schooner designed for naval purposes as an example of the post-war trend of design.

THE AMERICAN SCHOONER

After the Napoleonic Wars, piracy was very common, particularly in the West Indies. A great deal of this piracy was committed by small pilot-boat schooners of from 50 to 60 feet in length which were almost impossible to catch with square-rigged men-of-war. The United States

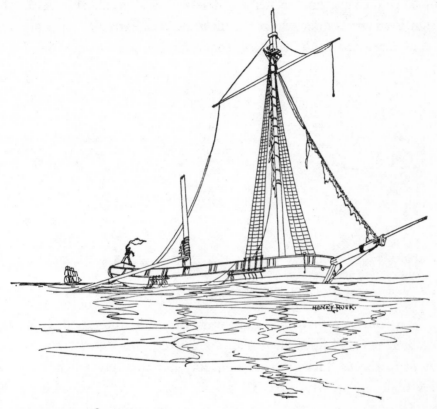

SCHOONER OF 1819.

Navy, at the end of the War of 1812, had no small craft suitable for suppressing these thug-manned craft, so had to build a number of schooners for the purpose. These schooners received mention in an earlier chapter. There appears to have been some uncertainty as to the size of war-schooner best suited for the West Indian service, for three plans of vessels of varying size were made, only two of which are known to have been built from. The design which was not used is reproduced in Figure

239

42 and was the work of Samuel Humphreys, made at Philadelphia in 1819. This design was for a large 14-gun schooner, based on the large privateers of the last war. The reason that the design was not used to build one of the schooners was probably the great draft proposed, 14'-9", which would have limited her usefulness in the service. However, the design is an interesting one for it illustrates the extremes of depth and sharpness reached in the large schooners of the post-war period. There

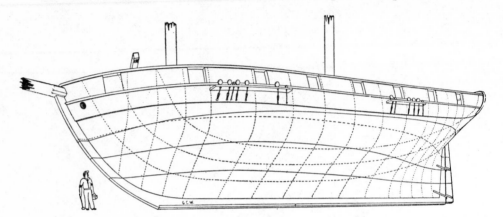

SAM HUMPHREYS' 1819 DESIGN.

can be no question that this design was faster than those built from, for she was larger and finer-lined than the *Shark, Alligator, Porpoise, Dolphin* or *Grampus*. Her draft, and possibly her cost, prevented her from being built, apparently. One of the examples, "No. 4," quoted by the French naval constructor Marestier in his *Memoires sur les bateaux a vapeur des Etats-Unis d'Amerique*, was this particular design. It is evident that Marestier was allowed to inspect a number of government draughts.

During the existence of the slavers, the deadrise and comparative depth of hull of the clipper-schooners reached their greatest development. Displacement, in relation to dimensions, was further reduced, brought about by means of finer ends and, in some cases, hollow garboards and extraordinary deadrise. The plans of two unidentified American schooners of this period, shown in Figures 43 and 45, illustrate the normal and ex-

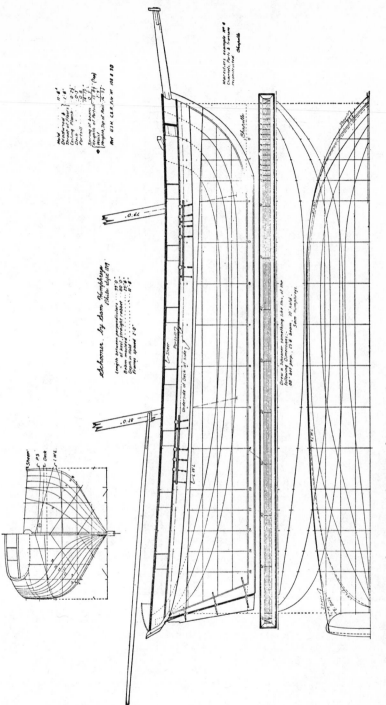
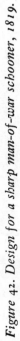

Figure 42. Design for a sharp man-of-war schooner, 1819.

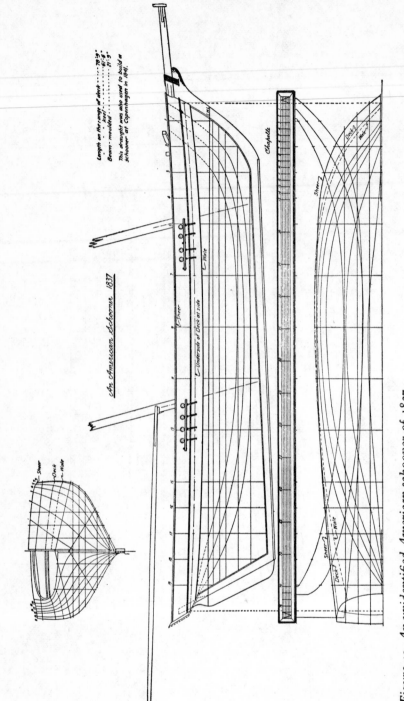

An American Schooner 1837

Length on the range of deck ...... 79'9"
           "   keel ...... 61'8"
Beam : moulded ...... 21'3"

This draught was also used to build a
schooner at Copenhagen in 1841.

Chapelle

Figure 43. An unidentified American schooner of 1837.

treme designs employed. These two plans, published by courtesy of the Peabody Marine Museum, Salem, Massachusetts, and "Yachting" magazine, were obtained in this country by a German shipwright named Mitzlaff. He seems to have visited this country prior to 1841, and again

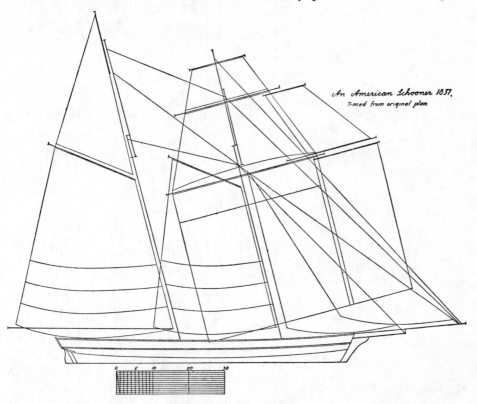

An American Schooner 1837.
Traced from original plan.

Figure 44. Sail plan of an unidentified schooner of 1837.

in 1844–7. He not only carried a number of American plans to Europe, but used some of them to build vessels. Not only did he build a schooner from the 1837 lines at Copenhagen, but he also built an hermaphrodite-schooner in Finland on an American model. Mitzlaff seems to have been an excellent draftsman and an educated naval architect. The vessels he built in Europe were much influenced by his American experience, but most of them cannot be called copies. Aside from the pilot-boat slaver, the *Dos Amigos*, the slaver brig, and possibly the *Union*, (which may

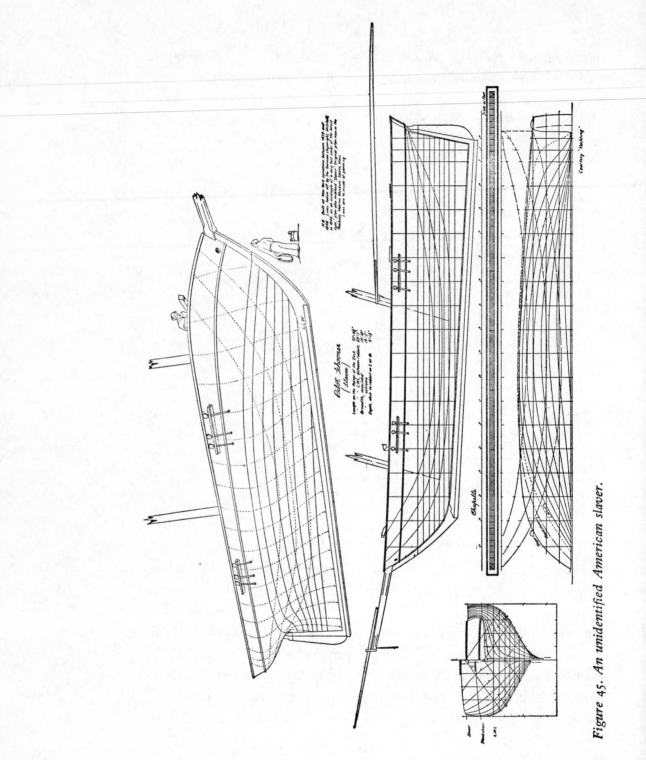

Figure 45. An unidentified American slaver.

244

have been a slaver too, according to one account; the plan seems to indicate slave-decks, by the way) which are published here, the only other
example is the *Diligente*, published in *The Baltimore Clipper*. Judgment
of the types employed in the slave trade must therefore be based on these
plans, though it is probable that not all vessels in the trade were as ex-

1837 AMERICAN SCHOONER SHOWN WITH FORE-AND-MAIN TOPSAIL RIG COMMON
WITH SLAVERS.

treme as these. The 1837 plan, shown as a fore-topsail schooner in her
original plan, Figure 44, could perhaps be accepted as the model of the
less extreme slavers, though most of these vessels appear to have been
fore-and-main topsail rigged.

The influence of the Baltimore Clipper on contemporary craft and
later types was most remarkable. Ships, brigs, sloops, naval craft, fishermen, coasters, yachts, pilot-boats and other craft adopted many features
of the Baltimore model, though sometimes the result was almost un-

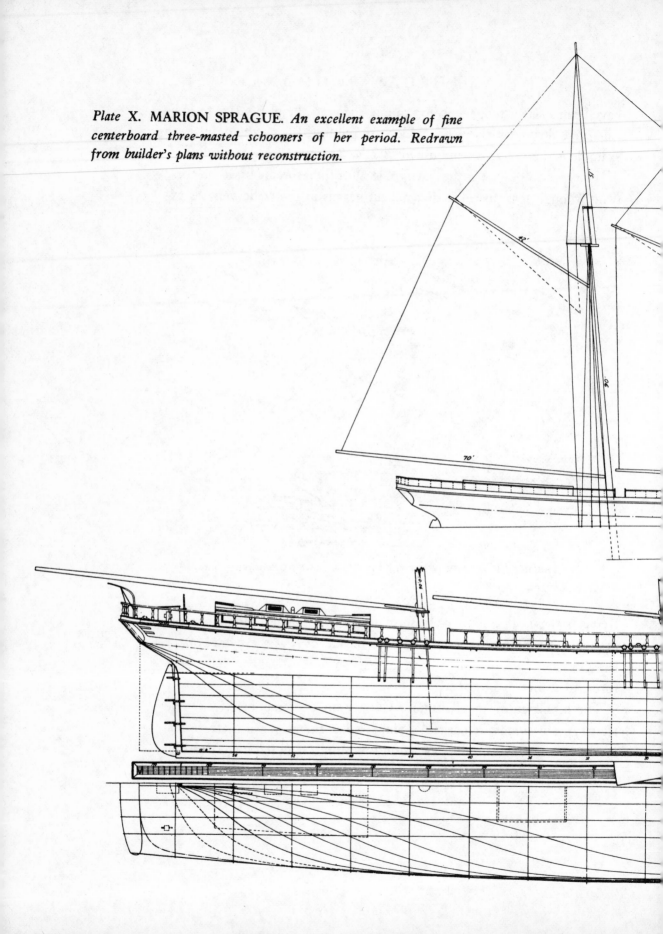

Plate X. MARION SPRAGUE. *An excellent example of fine centerboard three-masted schooners of her period. Redrawn from builder's plans without reconstruction.*

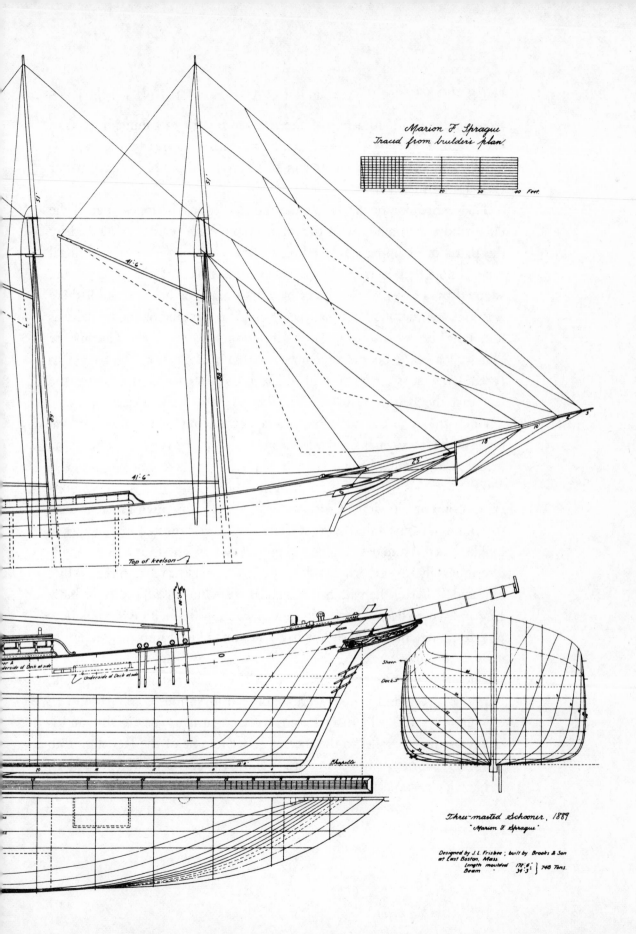

Marion F Sprague
Traced from builder's plan

0   5   10   20   30   40 Feet.

Top of keelson

Sheer
Deck S
Chapelle

Three-masted Schooner, 1889
"Marion F Sprague"

Designed by J.L. Frisbee; built by Brooks & Son
at East Boston, Mass
Length moulded   170'6" } 748 Tons.
Beam   34'5"

recognizable. The influence of the Baltimore Clipper cannot be said to have wholly disappeared even now, for many features of the type illustrated in the plans presented in this account can yet be seen in our yachts and fishermen.

The suppression of the slave trade and the gradual disappearance of the illicit trades, combined with the uneconomic cargo-carrier produced by the Baltimore Clipper model, doomed this class of vessel as a national type. Though it is true that the basic principles of the model were adopted by a great many classes of sailing craft, as has been said, there was so much modification that the original appearance of the model was lost. Possibly the last true Baltimore Clipper model is the Chesapeake "Pungy," a keel schooner type now fast disappearing from the Bay. This type, however, is purely a local one, and its existence does not alter the fact that the Baltimore Clipper has long ceased to be a national type. Though the type has not wholly disappeared, it passed out of general favor in the '50's; yachts and pilot-boats were the last types to employ the model in its original form.

The materials used in the construction of the early American schooners is of interest in view of the species of timber now used in yacht construction. Up until the War of 1812, or thereabouts, the Chesapeake builders used white oak, mulberry, pine, sassafras, chestnut and cedar indiscriminately. Northern builders used oak, hackmatack, birch, white pine and fir. After the war, oak and cedar were most used, except in New England where hackmatack, pine and fir were still much favored; yellow pine planking and southern live oak were introduced into this section as early as the '40's.

The painting of early American vessels was never standardized; black, red, blue, green and yellow were employed in various combinations. In colonial days the American schooners were usually painted in multi-colored stripes, parallel to the sheer. From the time of the Revolution to 1820 the favorite paint scheme was yellow topsides set off with a black stripe which was usually the first strake above the wales. In Revolutionary schooners the transom was often painted in different colors from the rest of the hull. The use of a wide stripe through the gun-ports first became popular in American naval vessels about 1808, and was generally adopted by large merchant ships afterwards. Philadelphia-built vessels were usually marked by having this band made up of multi-colored stripes. Black topsides came into use as early as the Revolution, but were not popular until after the War of 1812. Slavers and the Baltimore-built schooners were often distinguished by black paint without trim, even the copper above the waterline was covered with this funereal color. In the '40's and '50's dark green topsides became popular in schooners, usually in combination with a multi-colored band of red, white and blue, running the length of the vessel parallel to the sheer and extending from the planksheer, or covering board, upwards for about a third or half of the height of the bulwarks. Inboard, the vessels varied greatly, the inside of the bulwarks being red, brown, green, blue, white or varnished. The decks were usually left bright, or oiled. Deck-fittings were commonly white or gray, so that they could be easily seen in the darkness. However, there was rarely a standard scheme of painting in any type before 1845, except in naval or government vessels.

During the War of 1812 most of our naval vessels appear to have had yellow topsides and a black stripe, or the reverse, black topsides and a yellow stripe. The latter was replaced, after the war, with a white stripe, and large merchant craft followed suit.

The ballast of the early clipper-schooners was usually gravel or the coarser shingle, though sand and rock were also used. Some of the clipper-schooners could sail without ballast, because of their beam and flaring topsides, as evidenced by the letters of Captain Marryat, R.N., in regard to the purchase and loss of the New York-built hermaphrodite schooner *Samuel Smith*, of 180 tons, during 1829. These have been published in "The Mariner's Mirror," quarterly of the Society for Nautical Research, London, July, 1935, by E. H. W. Meyerstein, of the society. Marryat purchased the schooner while a wreck, because of her beauty of form and, as he thought, a good model for the Admiralty. However, after she was salvaged and fitted out by Marryat, she was driven to sea and lost with all hands; the letters are Marryat's explanation to the Admiralty.

The introduction of the American clipper-schooner abroad has been referred to. All the European maritime nations built copies of our sharp schooners during the first half of the nineteenth century. The British, in particular, built a large number of schooners on the American model and by 1840 had evolved a type of their own, which though having many features of the original model nevertheless was a separate type. In the '40's and '50's the British and Scotch builders turned out many fine clipper-schooners, for the opium and fruit trades, which compared favorably with the contemporary American schooners in speed, beauty and size. The British clipper-schooners were the first to use the flaring rabbet at the bow in which the rabbet followed the curve of the clipper-stem rather than curving upward as in the American schooners. This feature, combined with hollow waterlines, formed the "Aberdeen Bow" which was introduced by Alexander Hall, of Aberdeen, in the clipper-schooner *Scottish Maid*, built in 1839. Hall followed her with the fast opium clipper-schooners *Torrington*, 104.6 feet long and *Vindex*, 107 feet in length, as well as with other similar schooners.

The Dutch built similar schooners in the '40's and '50's, as well as schooners on strictly American lines. In spite of the popular idea that all Dutch-designed craft were slow, some very fast and very extreme schooners and brigs were built in Holland, as early as 1781. The importance of these foreign-designed vessels, as far as this discussion is concerned, is that they show the fallacy of the idea that only Americans were capable of designing fast vessels previous to the appearance of the well-advertised "clipper-ships."

The close relationship of the pilot-boat to the "Baltimore Clipper" has been referred to. Beginning with a common ancestor, the "Virginia model," the ports of New York and Boston had developed rather distinct types by 1840. At this time the chief difference between the two models was in depth, the Boston boats being much deeper than those of New York. In the '50's the two types again became more alike, so that by 1865 they were practically identical. Through a slow process of evolution the American pilot-boats, as represented by the boats of these two ports, had become almost standardized by this time. From 1865 to the time of the introduction of steam pilot-boats in the '90's and early 1900's, the sailing pilot-boats changed very little except for a gradual increase in size. The Boston-built New York pilot-boat *Phantom* of 1868 and the Boston boat, *Adams*, built at Essex in the late '80's, show two good examples of the type.

The *Phantom*, shown in Figure 46, was designed by the noted Boston builder and designer of pilot-boats, fishermen and yachts, Dennison J. Lawlor. She was launched in 1868, as has been said; a sister-ship, the *Pet*, was built soon afterwards. The *Phantom* was a beautifully modelled schooner; fast, seaworthy and weatherly. Her lines show the influence of the Baltimore Clipper in the great deadrise and drag to the keel, but otherwise her appearance has little similarity to the older model. The *Phantom* was a development of a New York boat built in the '50's, the *George Steers*, named after her famous designer. Plans of this vessel have been published in "Yachting" magazine, April 1935. The *Adams*, built by Moses Adams at Essex, Massachusetts, from designs by the distinguished yacht-designer, Edward Burgess, is reproduced in Figure 47. She was one of the first pilot-schooners built with the "spike" or pole-bowsprit. The *Adams* was not a particularly fast vessel, but she was a fine sea-boat. The *Phantom* and *Adams* represent the general characteristics of their class so well that detailed discussion is not necessary.

The subject of fishing schooners is a most interesting one but would require a volume to do it full justice. At least forty examples would be necessary to show each stage of development and every important change. A short outline of the development of this class has already appeared in print, ("Yachting" magazine, November and December, 1933, April, 1934), so this account can be limited to a general discussion.

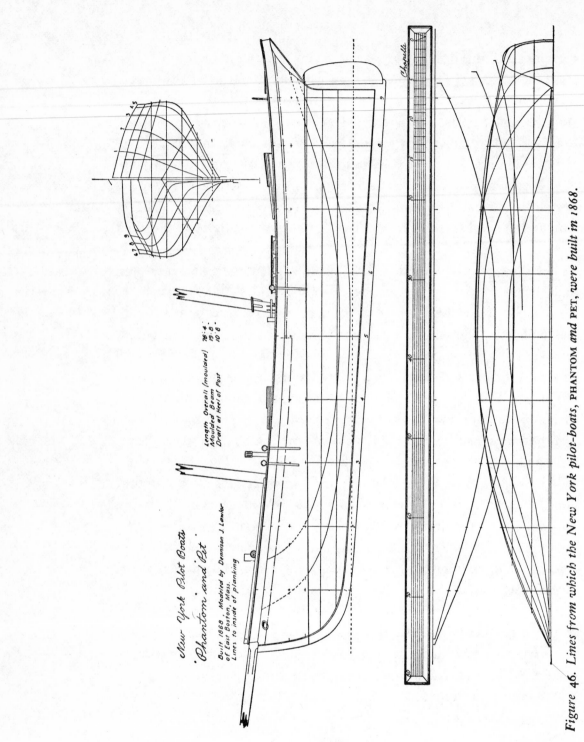

New York Pilot Boats
'Phantom and Pet'

Built 1868. Modeled by Dennison J. Lawlor
of East Boston, Mass.
Lines to inside of planking

Length Overall (moulded) 76' 4"
Moulded Beam   15' 8"
Draft at Heel of Post   10' 8"

Chapelle

Figure 46. Lines from which the New York pilot-boats, PHANTOM and PET, were built in 1868.

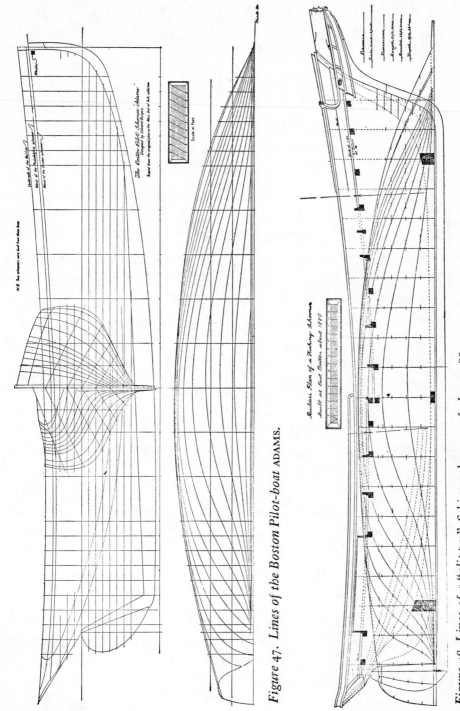

Figure 47. Lines of the Boston Pilot-boat ADAMS.

Figure 48. Lines of a "clipper" fishing schooner of about 1880.

251

The early New England fishermen, built at Essex, Ipswich, Gloucester, Newburyport and elsewhere, were small shore-fishermen, decked double-enders or square-sterned two-masters. The off-shore fishing in colonial times and up until after the War of 1812 was not a regular business as sufficient fish could be obtained nearer home. From prior to the Revolution, schooners were employed in the fisheries, but the greatest part of the business was carried on in the little "Chebacco-boats" and "Dogbodies." These appeared after the Revolution, growing out of the half-decked and open shallops of the colonial period. The "Chebacco-boat," named for the parish of Chebacco (now Essex) in the town of Ipswich where the type is said to have originated, was a sharp-sterned boat with a pink-stern; while the "Dogbody" was square-sterned. Both types had the same rig, that of the "cat-schooner," without bowsprit or jib. They were rarely over 40 feet on deck and usually had two or more cockpits or "standing-rooms" in which the crew stood when fishing. Some of the largest were flush-decked, however, and one of the "Chebacco-boats," the *Fame*, became a privateer in the War of 1812. These two types, "Chebacco-boat" and "Dogbody," remained in favor until about 1820, when the former developed into the "Jigger," later called the "Pinky." The "Jigger" was also referred to as "full-rigged" as it had a bowsprit and jib. The "Dogbody" was gradually replaced by the "Pinky" and the small square-sterned schooner. The off-shore fisheries, in the meantime, had employed a number of fair-sized schooners. The shore-fishermen, "Pinky" or schooner, rarely exceeded 52 feet on deck; the off-shore schooners were rarely over 65 feet long.

One of the interesting vessels built at Essex in the '20's was the three-masted schooner-rigged pinky *Spy*, launched in October, 1823. She measured 70 feet in length, 17 feet beam, 8'-6" depth and 91 $^{61}\!/_{95}$ tons burthen. The *Spy* was described as "pink-sterned, one deck, three-masts, no galleries, no head" and was built for Salem parties. She made a voyage to Zanzibar.

The square-sterned schooners first had short, high quarterdecks, and

Four-Masted Barquentine, JAMES TUFT, *looking forward*

Four-Masted Barquentine, JAMES TUFT, *looking aft*

Four-Masted Schooner, COPPER-FIELD, *looking forward*

JAMES TUFT *from her skys'lyard. (Center—four-masted schooner,* SAMAI. *Outside—four-masted schooner,* COMMERCE)

Down Easter, HENRY B. HYDE, *being re-rigged*

were known as "Heel-tappers" locally. In the late '30's the schooners were given longer and lower quarterdecks. These vessels were somewhat barrel-shaped in section, with short, full bows and runs; the bow adorned with a short and heavy cutwater. The rig was that of a simple fore-and-aft schooner, without light-sails of any kind except a main-topmast staysail. This was also the rig of the "Pinky." The latter type began to go out of favor in Massachusetts waters in the '40's, but existed in Maine until recent times, also in the Maritime Provinces. Three types, "Pinky," the small shore-fishing schooner and the larger off-shore or "Banker" schooner changed but little in model between 1830 and 1847.

In 1846–7 Andrew Story of Essex designed and built a schooner on speculation which was the expression of his own ideas of what a fisherman should be. He used the "Baltimore Clipper" model as an inspiration and launched a vessel having more deadrise and sharper ends than had yet been seen in the fishing fleet. This was the famous schooner *Romp*, but Story had much trouble selling her as she was considered too sharp for safety by the fishermen. However, when finally sold she was considered to be a great success and led to a complete change in the character of the New England fishing fleet. The copies of the *Romp*, built between 1846 and 1857, were known as "File-bottoms" or "Sharpshooters" because of their reputed sharpness in deadrise and waterlines.

These fishermen gradually grew shoaler, under the influence of a prevailing trend in design of schooners brought about by the writings of the American naval architect, Griffiths, and the influence of the then highly-advertised "clipper-ships." In 1857 the sister-schooners *Etta G. Fogg* and *George Fogg* were launched at Essex by Charles O. Story and these vessels marked the appearance of a new type, the "clipper" fisherman. The mania for speed, at all costs, took possession of the fishermen, and for the next twenty-six years the "clippers" gradually became increasingly shoal, with a corresponding decrease in deadrise; while the bows became very long and hollow at the waterline. The run became long and straight; the quarters increasingly heavy. Because of the tre-

253

mendous initial stability of the "clipper," the sail plans were very large, and as long as these schooners could be kept on their feet, a very high speed could be obtained. However, these vessels had the fatal ability to capsize when heeled beyond a certain point and there was much loss of life as a result.

The type is well illustrated in Figure 48 which shows the lines of a "clipper" schooner of 1880 as yet unidentified. This is a builder's plan and probably represents a vessel built at East Boston. This class of schooner was also widely known as the "Essex-model" and was popular in the fruit trade, sealing, coasting trades, and even in the whale fisheries. The two-masted coaster of New England was on this model from 1860 on. Though attempts were made to introduce the "pungy" schooner of the Chesapeake and the centerboarder in the '50's and '60's, particularly in the mackerel-fishery, the "clipper" remained the favorite.

The loss of life and property in the "clipper" model became a serious matter in the '80's and in 1884 a schooner was launched that brought about a revival of the deeper model. This was the *Roulette*, designed and built by Lawlor at East Boston. This vessel was much like Lawlor's pilot-boats but had more capacity. She was very successful and was followed by other vessels of the same type, some with the straight stem of the pilot-boat. Some of these schooners were the *Arthur D. Story, Grampus*, (built for the U. S. Fish Commission) and the *Carrie E. Phillips*. The latter, launched in 1887, was designed by Edward Burgess and introduced the spike-bowsprit into the fishing fleet, as well as many improvements in deck and rigging details. She was a fast and weatherly vessel and gained a great reputation by beating the famous Boston pilot-boat, *Hesper*, in a match race. The *Phillips* was followed by another Burgess-design of great fame, the *Fredonia*. She was a refinement of the *Carrie E. Phillips*, but had a clipper-bow. Other designers, George M. McClain, Thomas Irving and the Essex designers, Tarr, and Burnham, followed the lead of the *Fredonia*, turning out many very noted vessels of a somewhat similar model. This type remained in favor until about 1904.

THE AMERICAN SCHOONER

The introduction of the round-stem, seen in modern fishing schooners, took place in the late '90's and was the work of the great fisherman-designer, Thomas F. McManus of Boston. McManus was the son of a Boston sailmaker and was a fish-buyer who turned to design as a hobby; meeting such success with his first designs, in 1892, that he made design-

FISHING SCHOONER *Elsie*.

ing his business. The first schooners built with the round-stem were given Indian names, hence the round-stem schooners were known by fishermen as "Indian-headers." The greater number of McManus' designs were of this class of schooner, of which the *Elsie*, built in 1910, is probably the most noted. This schooner was built at Essex by A. D. Story for the Gorton-Pew Vessel Co., a subsidiary of the noted Gloucester fishing firm of this name. The plans of the *Elsie*, shown in Plate IX and Figure 49, show what was probably the highest development of

255

the New England fishing schooner, both in size and model. The *Elsie* is considered to have been the largest fisherman that would pay dividends without outside subsidy, such as has been received by the later "Racing Fishermen." Though not built as a racer, the *Elsie* was a very fast schooner and a dangerous competitor for the later, larger and more

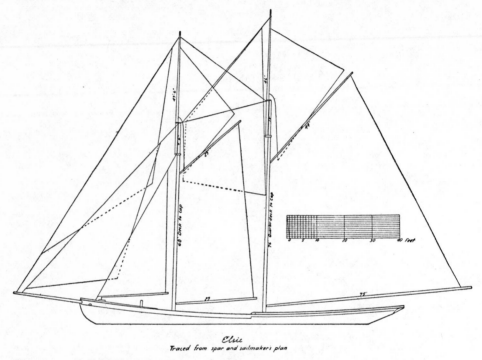

Elsie
Traced from spar and sailmaker's plan

Figure 49. Sail plan of the famous fisherman ELSIE.

yacht-like "Racing Fishermen." The *Elsie* has recently been lost at sea.

McManus also designed the first "knockabout" fishing schooners. These had long bow-overhangs in place of bowsprits and were designed to handle easily at the wharves and to avoid the loss of life caused by men being washed off the bowsprit when furling the headsails in heavy weather. The idea of the "knockabout" was obtained from some small sloop-yachts that had developed in Massachusetts Bay in the early '90's. The first fishing schooner of this type was the *Helen B. Thomas* built at

Essex in 1901–2 from McManus's designs; she was followed by others, the able *Shepherd King* designed by Oxner and Story in 1904 and the McManus-designed *Thomas A. Cromwell* in 1905. The type became quite popular during the years between 1907 and 1916, but like the "Indian-headers," was replaced by the present power-boats. The decline of the New England fishing fleet has been mentioned, the introduction of excessive power and the resulting operating expenses, as well as financial disturbance, were the contributing factors.

Another important group of fishing vessels are those employed in the

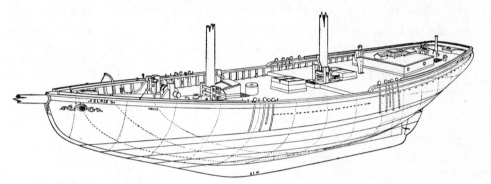

GLOUCESTER FISHERMAN *Elsie.*

oyster-fishery in Delaware Bay and on the Chesapeake. Most of the vessels in this business were centerboard schooners, though on the Chesapeake the work was done largely by the "bugeyes," a local two-masted, leg-of-mutton rigged and double-ended type of centerboard ketch. The smaller but somewhat similar log-canoes are also employed in the fishery. The oyster schooners were unusually fine types of centerboarders, somewhat like the schooner-yachts of the '60's and '70's, but with more displacement, flatter bottoms and harder bilges. This type of schooner developed on the Chesapeake Bay between 1835 and 1850 and spread along the coast as far north as Cape Cod. The early Chesapeake schooners had round-stems, as did some of the earlier Norfolk pilot-boats, but these were gradually replaced by the handsome clipper bow. The latest oyster schooners have returned to the early round-stem, however. The schooners used at New Orleans are similar to the Delaware schooners. Most of these schooners were built in the neighborhood of the Delaware, though some of those owned at New York and on Cape Cod were built at Essex, Massachusetts, and in Connecticut. The oyster schooner, like the fruit-trader, has not as yet been fully studied.

Coasters, in the United States, have been schooners since 1800, if not earlier. The early coasting trade was carried on in vessels of all types, square-riggers and fore-and-afters; but the schooner gradually monopolized the trade. Until about 1850 the American coasting schooner was a rather full-ended two-master, like the packets that ran between Maine ports and Boston. Most of them were fore-and-afters, but a great many of the Maine-built schooners were fore-topsail rigged. There were some sharp-lined coasters, particularly in the South. After 1860 the "Essex model" became common, differing from the "Bankers" of that particular model only in deck-plan.

As the length of coasting voyages increased the schooners grew larger. As large two-masted schooners required large crews to handle them and as the profits of the trade were rarely great enough to warrant this expense, the large schooners were rigged as three-masters. It was found that these schooners could be operated with very small crews and that they also sailed very well. The use of the three-master in the coasting trade seems to have started about 1850, though the rig was employed in sea-going schooners much earlier.

The date of the "invention" of the three-masted schooner has been variously placed, often as in the 1820's or '30's. Each shipbuilding community has a tradition of having built the "first" three-master some time within this period. Without pretending to fix the date of the first three-masted schooner, the rig can be traced back to 1800 or earlier. In 1800 the U.S.N. schooner *Experiment* was chased by two French privateer schooners, in the West Indies, one of which was a three-masted schooner. In *Greyhounds of the Sea*, by Carl C. Cutler,[1] there are references to a number of three-masted schooners of 1801–7.

There is more tangible evidence of the existence of three-masted schooners before 1806 than mere statements, however. This evidence is the plan of such a vessel, the Baltimore-built *Flying Fish*. This schooner was in the British Navy in 1806, in which year the Admiralty had her lines taken off for the construction of new schooners on the same model in Bermuda. The date and circumstance of the acquisition of the *Flying Fish* have not been learned, but it was obviously before the date of the order for the Bermuda-built copies. It seems reasonable to place the date of the launch of this vessel as about 1800. The original Admiralty draught states that the schooner was built in Baltimore, so there is no conjecture about that fact. Bulwarks were added to the schooner when she was fitted for naval service, according to a note on the draught, so it is probable that she originally had log-rails. Her model was that of the Norfolk pilot-boat. The plans of this schooner were published in *The Baltimore Clipper*, in 1930.

There is a reference to an earlier three-masted schooner, but this has not yet been verified from original sources. On page 267 of *The Corsairs of France*, by C. B. Norman,[2] there is a reference to "a three-masted schooner, the *Lincoln*" which was captured from the British by the French privateersman Thurot in 1759.

After the Civil War the three-masted schooner almost monopolized the coasting trades, particularly the lumber business. There were two types of three-master at this time, a rather deep-draft keel model and a shoaler centerboarder. These were satisfactory for specific trades, but were somewhat unsatisfactory for general work. The keel type was not very reliable in stays, when light, and the shoal model did not carry sufficient cargo; there were other objections as well. These difficulties

[1] C. P. Putnam's Sons, New York, 1930.
[2] Sampson, Low and Co., London, 1887.

were overcome, in the late '70's, by the development of the deep center-boarders. These were probably the most satisfactory coasting schooners ever built, for they combined the good features of both the keel and the centerboard model. The new type became very popular, particularly in New England and at New York.

Plate X shows the lines and sail plan of a three-masted schooner of this class, the *Marion F. Sprague*, built at East Boston in 1889 by J. M. Brooks and Son for E. H. Atwood, of Boston. She was designed by John L. Frisbee, who in addition to designing fishermen and coasters taught ship-drafting in the Charleston and South Boston "night-schools," with another draftsman, Albert S. Greene of Hanover. These two men were intelligent and practical teachers to whom many present marine-draftsmen owe much. Frisbee was a cousin of the shipbuilder of the same name in Salem, and designed large vessels for him as well as for the Brooks' firm. Some of the finest coasters built at Boston were designed by this very able man. As in the case of so many schooner designers in Maine, Massachusetts, New York and Maryland, Frisbee's accomplishments have been completely overlooked.

The *Sprague* was a very handsome vessel; the long quarterdeck shown in her plan is now rarely seen, though then very popular. The *Nathaniel L. Gorton*, built at Essex in 1916, and her sister-ship, the *Olivette*, were the last three-masted schooners so built in New England. Vessels of the *Sprague's* type were better sailers than modern three-masters because of their finer lines and the centerboard. The latter feature, as has been already mentioned, was most helpful in sailing and staying when the vessel was light. During the period of the *Sprague* the fitting of the coasting schooner with power hoisting machinery, winches and capstans, had not reached final development.

The three-masted coasting schooner has remained in existence in spite of the competition of steamers and power-boats. The handiness, low operating cost, comparatively low initial investment and general efficiency of the type has enabled it to survive. A number of such schooners have been built in New England, Maryland and the Maritime Provinces within the last thirty years, sometimes with auxiliary engines. Though hard-pressed by mechanical transportation, particularly the modern self-propelled barge traffic, the schooners still find work to do. It seems probable that there are still some trades in which the coasting schooners would show greater profits than the steamers or power-boats now used.

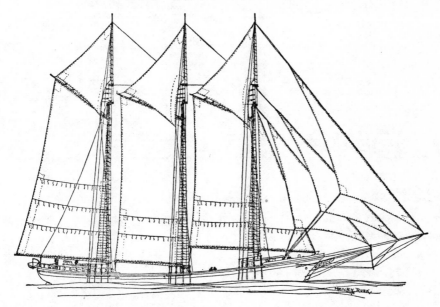

THREE-MASTED MAINE-BUILT SCHOONER.

An excellent example of the modern three-masted coasting schooner is shown in Figure 50; a design by J. J. Wardwell of Rockland, Maine. This designer, now in his eighty's, is still hale and hearty; during the many years he designed schooners he turned out a number of noted vessels, among them the first five- and six-masted coasting schooners that were built, in New England at least.

The old name for the three-masted schooner was "tern-schooner"; "tern" means "a series of three." This name was applied in the United States in the '50's, though apparently rarely employed in New England. In the Maritime Provinces, however, the term is still commonly used.

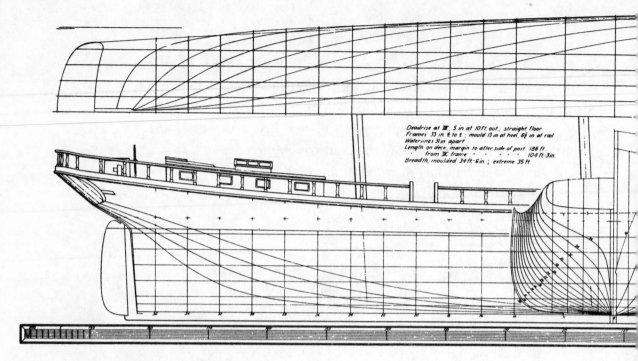

Deadrise at ℞, 5 in at 10 ft out, straight floor.
Frames 33 in. ℄ to ℄ ; mould 13 in at heel, 6¼ in at rail
Waterlines 3 in apart
Length on deck, margin to after side of post 186 ft
          from ℞ frame   104 ft·3 in
Breadth, moulded 34 ft·6 in ; extreme 35 ft

Plate XI. HOWARD SMITH. *Plan traced from
builder's plan. As these plans are not always followed
exactly as to details, and as no picture of the vessel
has been found, the accuracy of this plan in showing
the appearance of the Howard Smith is open to question. No reconstruction.*

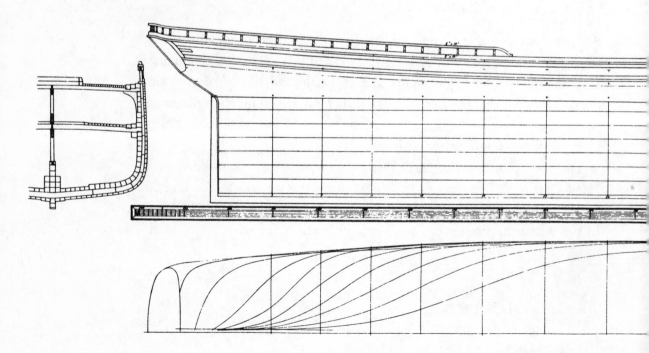

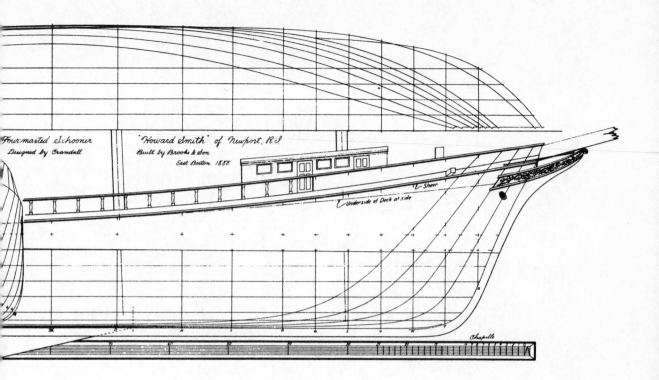

Four-masted Schooner
Designed by Crandall

"Howard Smith" of Newport, R.I.
Built by Brooks & Son
East Boston 1888

Sheer

Underside of Deck at side

Chapelle

Four-Masted Schooner [(Maine) marked "Healy's Schooner"]. The type of four-masted schooner employed in the coal trade. Vessels built on these lines during the World War proved too narrow to carry deck loads well.

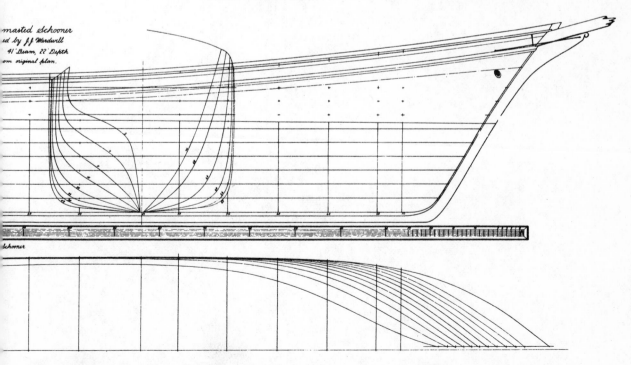

masted Schooner
ed by J.J. Wardwell
41' Beam, 22' Depth
om original plan.

Schooner

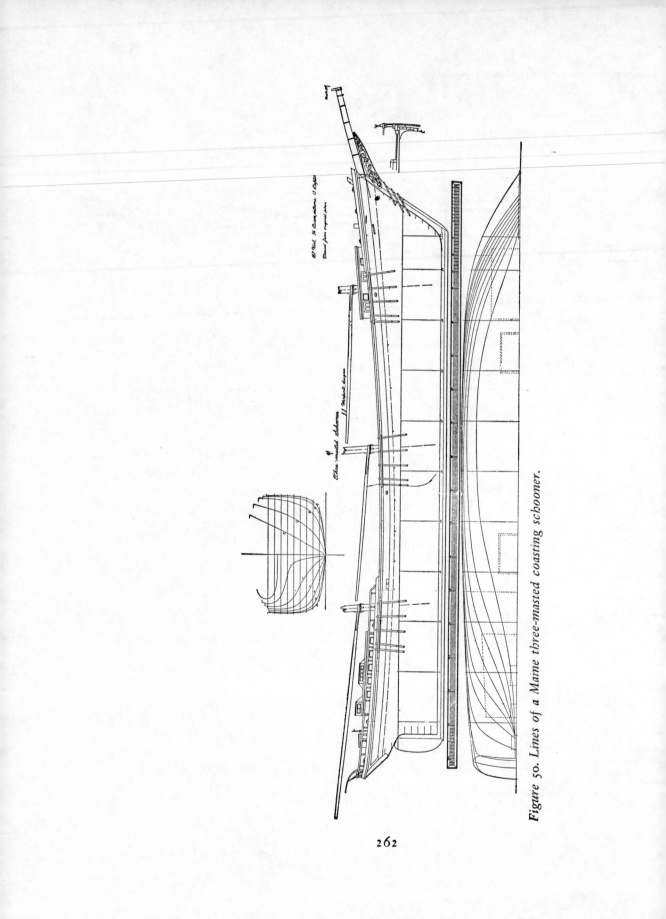

Figure 50. Lines of a Maine three-masted coasting schooner.

THE AMERICAN SCHOONER

The Nova Scotian builders developed a sharp-model three-master during the last European war which had the general model and the round-stem of the modern sailing fisherman. These vessels were built for the salt-fish trade and were designed for fast-sailing. Sharp schooners of this same general type, but with clipper bows, were tried out in the New England

FOUR-MASTED SCHOONER *Howard Smith*.

fisheries in the '70's and early '80's, but proved too large for the business; some of these schooners were changed to whalers.

The four-masted coasting schooners appeared in 1880, when the *William L. White*, of Taunton, was launched at Bath, Maine. This vessel was the result of the same demand that made the three-master popular, increased size and low operating costs. Most of the "four-posters" were centerboard vessels, ranging in length from 180 to 240 feet; the rig became popular with great rapidity, both on the sea-board and on the Lakes. Eventually the "four-posters," like the three's, dropped the use of the centerboard because of its additional cost in construction, loss of cargo space, and because tugs were available in every port and cheap to hire. Experienced coasters consider the older three's and four's much handier than the modern keel schooners, however. The four-masted schooner *Howard Smith*, shown in Plate XI, represents the better class of "four-poster" of her time, and was considered to be about the right type and dimensions for general trade. She was designed by Crandall and built by J. M. Brooks and Son at East Boston, in 1888, for the account of Gardner B. Reynolds of Newport, Rhode Island. While still a new vessel, this schooner was lost on Doboy Shoals, on the coast of Georgia. The *Smith* appears to have been a very handsome vessel, as can be seen by the plan. Flush-decked schooners were common in the lumber and coal trades. An example of a more recent four-master can be seen in Plate XI, a design by J. J. Wardwell for some schooners built in Maine during the last European war. These vessels were similar to a great many others built elsewhere during the war.

The schooners developed on the Pacific Coast have not, as yet, received the study that they deserve. Conditions on that coast were different than on the Atlantic; the strong winds and the need of windward ability to beat from the southern ports to the lumber ports, as well as the requirements of specific trades, created features not seen in the Eastern types. Most of the Pacific Coast two-masters were keel vessels, the model and appearance being similar to those in the East in the early period, 1850 to 1880. With the rise of importance of the Alaskan fisheries, the lumber trade, the Behring Sea seal-hunting and the South Sea Island trade, a number of special types and rigs came into existence. The Alaskan schooners appear to have been the first to adopt the leg-of-mutton mainsail that finally became so common on the Pacific Coast. As late as 1890, a great many of the Alaskan fishermen, and the sealers, were fishing schooners purchased in the East, or three-masted coasters. Auxiliary steam schooners appeared in the Alaskan and lumber trades in the '80's. The West Coast-built fishing schooners were much like the "Essex model" of 1870–86, but fuller-ended. The South Sea Island traders were a somewhat nondescript type, marked chiefly by peculiar deck structures, either very high quarterdecks or large deck-houses aft. In model they appear to have been somewhat like the Gloucester "Banker" of the '80's, though there were some that were much on the Baltimore Clipper model, particularly those built by Turner and by J. D. Spreckels.

The vessels built for the lumber trade, three-, four- and five-masters, were the most distinctive, however. The plans of the four-master *Caroline*, Figures 51 and 52, and those of the five-master *Inca*, Figure 53, show the interesting details of the lumber-traders. Both vessels were built by the Hall Brothers on Puget Sound, the *Inca* in 1896 and the *Caroline* in 1902. Specifications and contract for the *Caroline* can be seen in the Appendix; these contain much information on details of construction, as well as upon the method of financing. In view of the amount of information on these vessels further discussion is unnecessary.

The majority of the vessels built on the Pacific Coast after 1888 were finely constructed and finished; though earlier there were complaints that many were very poorly built. One of the most remarkable local types was the San Francisco scow-schooners; flat-bottomed and square-ended with the rig of the two-masted coaster. The Pacific Coast builders also produced a large number of very fine barquentines, which will be mentioned later. The rig of many of the West Coast-built schooners featured many details not seen elsewhere. The square course when set on schooners was furled up-and-down the mast rather than on the yard, the sail being on rings. When the sail was to be set it was hauled out along the yards by out-hauls to the yard-arms. There were many variations of this rig, but all on the same principle. Though this method of setting a square-sail is used abroad, it was not seen in the United States except on the Pacific Coast. The leg-of-mutton mainsails on schooners have been mentioned. The remarkable feature of the Pacific Coast leg-of-mutton rig was the topsail set over it, a triangular sail set on the topmast and sheeted to the boom-end, a combination of topsail and "ringtail." It is to be hoped that there will be an extensive and careful study of the West Coast types made in the future as they have been sadly neglected.

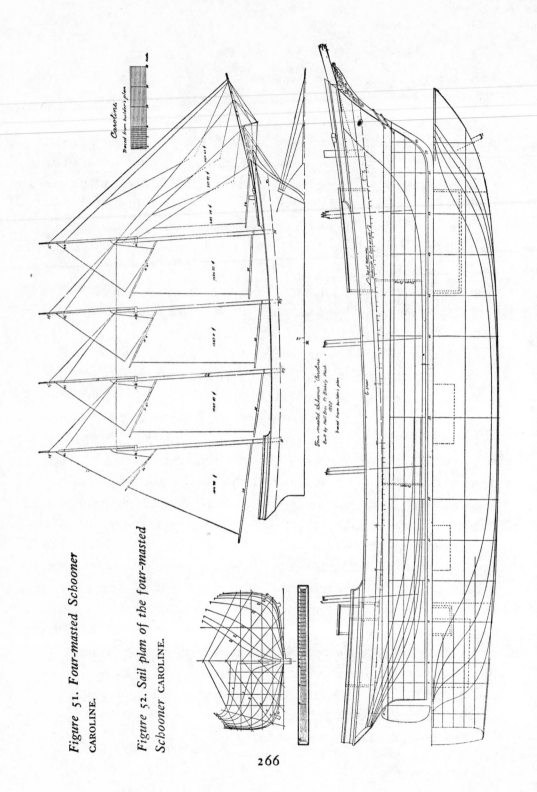

Figure 51. *Four-masted Schooner* CAROLINE.

Figure 52. *Sail plan of the four-masted Schooner* CAROLINE.

266

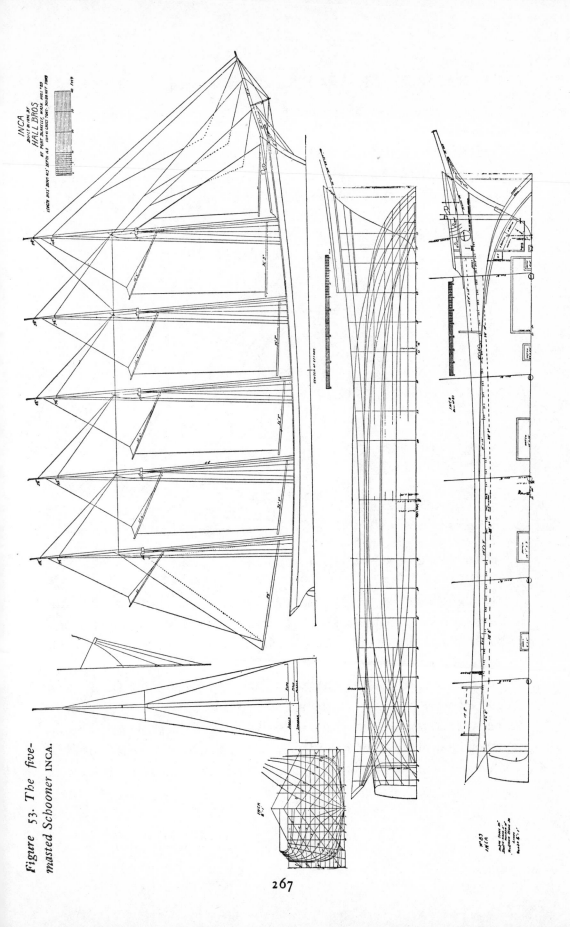

Figure 53. The five-masted Schooner INCA.

The development of schooners on the Great Lakes kept pace with that of the coastal schooners. Lake vessels, like those of other localities, had to be designed and built to meet certain natural and economic specifications. It is hardly possible to review these in the space available here; the important considerations were a limited draft and the restric-

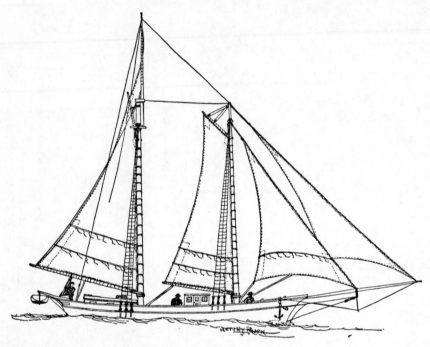

GREAT LAKES SCHOONER, 1852, THE *Challenge*.

tion in beam imposed by canals, as well as the requirements raised by the bulk-cargoes carried; ore, timber, grain and coal. It had been found early in the nineteenth century that the schooner, or the barquentine, was the most satisfactory rig for use on the Lakes.

Little is known about the early Lake schooners, aside from a few men-of-war, but from contemporary references they appear to have been shoal vessels somewhat on the Baltimore Clipper model. The introduction of the centerboard may have taken place as early as 1828, though this is very doubtful. The first distinctive Lake schooner type of which much is known was the centerboard "clipper" type introduced by William Bates, of Manitowoc, Wisconsin, in 1851–2. This was a shoal, rather flat-floored, sharp-ended schooner, often rigged with square-sails on the foremast. The first schooner of the new type was the *Challenge*, shown in Figure 54, which was built, as has just been said, at Manitowoc in 1851–2. While on the stocks, the model of this schooner raised much discussion, but after her launch she was admitted by all to be a great success. Her plan was taken to France by a French naval constructor as an example of a clipper centerboard schooner and is rather poorly reproduced in Admiral Paris' *Souvenirs de Marine*, Volume 5. The *Challenge* was noted for the regularity of her voyages and the ease with which she could reach the speed of 13 knots. Bates was one of the most advanced designers of his time and turned out a great number of fast Lake vessels that attracted much attention among the profession on the coast.

The *Challenge* was followed by the Bates-designed *Clipper City*, a handsome big schooner fitted with a centerboard and square topsails, built in '53. He also designed the *Montowoc*, another noted clipper of her time. For many years these centerboard two-masted "clippers" monopolized the Lake trade. Gradually the schooners grew in size until it was necessary to rig them as three- and four-masters, but the centerboard and usually the square topsails and course were retained. The rig of the Lake three-masted schooner differed from that used on salt-water; the ocean schooner had all three masts about the same in height, while the Laker had them of varying heights. A 600-ton ocean schooner, according to Hall's "Report on the Shipbuilding Industry of the United States," (10th U.S. Census), had spars of the following lengths: foremast 91 feet, mainmast 92 feet, mizzenmast 93 feet, all topmasts 56 feet; while a Lake schooner of the same tonnage, but somewhat longer and narrower, had: foremast 98 feet, fore-topmast 74 feet, mainmast 102 feet, main-topmast 74 feet, mizzenmast 86 feet, mizzen-topmast 57 feet. The Lake rig, therefore, was about the same in spar-plan as that used on three-masted schooners of 1806, as represented by the *Flying Fish,* mentioned earlier. The Lake builders turned toward five-masted schooners in 1881, in which year the first one, the *David Dows,* was built at Toledo, Ohio; she was 275 feet long, the largest schooner in the world at the time of her launch. In recent years, steamers and power-craft have driven the commercial schooner off the Lakes.

The five- and six-masted coasters of more recent times were developed to meet the competition of the early barge lines in the coal trade. They were, with few exceptions, rather unwieldy vessels, though often capable of high speed because of their great length. Only one seven-master has ever been built, the *Thomas Lawson,* but she was not a success as a sailer and was very unhandy. The wooden six-masters built in Maine were maximum in size that was practical in the schooner.

The centerboard is a small-boat "gadget" in the minds of many yachtsmen, and there is much prejudice against shoal-draft sea-going craft fitted with a board. It has been claimed that centerboarders are an unseaworthy type, and that the slot in the keel weakened the hull longitudinally. It can be seen that the centerboard has been used successfully in very large vessels. The largest schooner fitted with a board was probably the *Governor Ames,* a five-master 265 feet long and 50 feet beam. Her centerboard was off-center, and was 35 feet long; dropping 14 feet. In large schooners the board was usually alongside the keel, though in the small Hudson River brick-schooners and in some of the schooners used on Long Island Sound, the mainmast was off-center, alongside the centerboard-case. As for the slot, for the board, causing weakness, it should be obvious that the centerboard-case is a box-girder of great longitudinal strength; the reason that old centerboard-schooners do not hog in way of the board even though badly hogged elsewhere. The seaworthiness of schooners fitted with a centerboard was purely a matter of design with which the use of a board had no more to do than the color of the topsides. The fact that the marine-insurance premiums made

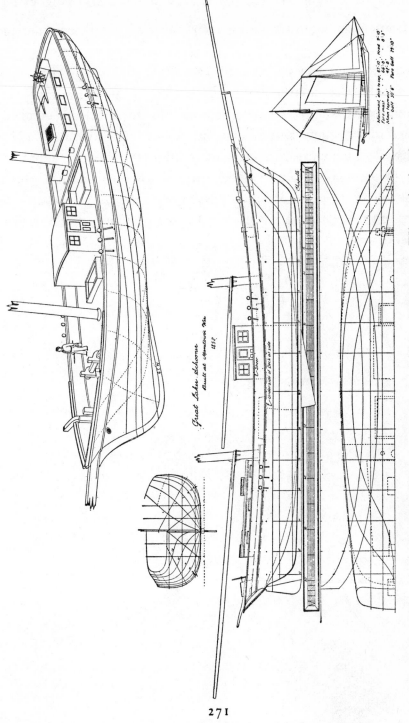

Figure 54. Great Lakes Clipper-Schooner CHALLENGE, *built at Manitowoc, Wisconsin, in 1852.*

no exceptions in regard to keel or centerboard is worth considering in this matter.

There are many types of schooners that have not been described, some of them of great interest, but space is lacking for a study of them. Though each passing year sees a gradual diminution in the number of commercial schooners on our coasts, it is to be hoped that they will not be allowed to disappear without an attempt to test them more thoroughly under modern conditions. Most American schooners have a "lucky" horseshoe nailed to their sampson-post or bowsprit-end, the open end is always upwards to "keep the good luck from running out." Will this be sufficient?

Chapter Six   MERCHANT CRAFT

THE development of the American square-rigger, particularly the ship, was never one of logical improvement in design. The question as to what constituted an improvement in design is a matter that must be settled, for this is the foundation of an understanding of the history of the American sailing ship types. The popular conception of a gradual improvement in the models of sailing ships, in which the appearance of the "first" improved design was followed by the wide acceptance of a similar class of ship, does not bear inspection. The mere passage of time between two periods of design by no means indicates that the later period produced the best ships. In a decision of what should be accepted as an improvement in design, economic and technical factors are of utmost importance. In short, these factors may be expressed as "cargo capacity, combined with speed and low operating costs." It might be assumed that the possession of these qualities was an obvious aim and that there would naturally be a steady trend in their direction. All trades, however, did not require high speed and not all required large cargo capacity; at certain times, when wages were extraordinarily low, the factor of operating cost was not of particular importance either. War, of course, was a period when large crews and heavy expense could be easily covered by freight-rates, leaving large profits for the owner. Because of these conditions, as well as of certain fads or psychological trends, it will be found that good and poor ships, from the point of view of the naval architect, existed side by side; and that periods of advance were often followed by retrogression in model.

An exaggeration of any one quality, such as cargo capacity or speed, at the expense of other qualities does not indicate an improvement in design. The ideal sailing ship could not be developed in any one trade; the requirements of a single trade were too narrow and always placed a premium on some one quality to the exclusion of others. For this reason the best models of ships, on technical and economic grounds, were produced when vessels were forced into general trade rather than employed in a single predominating trade. The uneconomic East Indiaman and clipper-ship illustrated two extremes developed by a combination of trade and psychological conditions; the exaggeration of single qualities at the expense of all others in these two classes of ship indicate the limitations of any one trade in advancing ship design. Exactly the same conditions, economic or political, are not repeated in history; nevertheless there is often much similarity. It is not surprising, therefore, to find that periods in which the bulk of American sailing ships were engaged in general trade produced somewhat similar ships, vessels of a fair turn of speed, good cargo capacity and low operating costs, differing only in appearance and detail. It is impossible, however, to make unqualified statements in regard to so confused a matter as the development of the American sailing ship types.

The colonial ships have already been described as slow, full-ended carriers. It would be imprudent, however, to assume that no merchant ships of this period were fast, sharp and weatherly. The records and other information are much too scant for such an assumption. Since it is known that some of the small men-of-war of the colonial period were well-designed fast-sailing craft, it is quite probable that merchant vessels of a similar type existed. However, in view of the information at hand, one may conclude that the fast merchant ship was a rarity. Fast-sailing requires sharp lines, which reduce cargo capacity. As long as the seas were too dangerous for merchantmen to voyage alone, the convoy system and fleet-movements, as applied to traders, effectively barred the demand for fast ships and maintained the predominance of full-lined ships. A convoy or merchant fleet could only proceed at the rate of speed of the slowest ship, therefore a fast ship could not make quicker passages or more numerous voyages and had to compete, economically, with the extreme cargo-carrier making the same number of voyages.

During the Revolution the American merchant ship received little attention; what little trade there was had to be carried on in the letter-of-marques. Legally these vessels were privateers, for there was no legal distinction between the expressions "letter-of-marque" and "privateer." However, common usage made a distinction, the "letter-of-marque" being applied to merchant vessels, with privateer commissions, who made seizures only when meeting enemy's vessels on their voyage between two ports; in other words, their seizures were incidental to cargo-carrying. "Privateers," on the other hand, cruised for prizes only; cargo-carrying was merely an incidental occupation. There was no distinction in their commissions or bonds because of this popular application of the two names. The ships that were engaged in the wartime trade were probably somewhat like the *Rattlesnake* in model, and were really men-of-war.

When the Revolution was over the sharp wartime ships that were left in American hands continued trading, but were rapidly replaced by the full-lined model. This was permitted by political and economic conditions in most trades. The years between the Revolution and 1812 saw but little change in the design of the bulk of the ship-rigged merchantmen, though an occasional sharp vessel was built, either for a special purpose or to suit an owner's whim. The plan of the Humphreys-designed *Illustrious President*, shown in Figure 55, is a tracing of the original draught found in the archives of the Navy Department, and represents the greater portion of the models used in American merchant ships of the period. Contemporary pictures in Salem, Boston, New York, Philadelphia and elsewhere verify this claim.

It was a somewhat peculiar fact that the years which saw the rapid rise of the sharp-model schooner did not see a parallel development in ship-rigged merchantmen. This can be traced partly to the difference in employment of the two rigs and partly to prejudice against sharp models, among owners of the ships, as well as to the economic factor that, in the final analysis, accounted for the difference in employment. It will be recalled that schooners were often employed in dangerous or illicit trades;

275

these created a demand for speed which developed the sharp model. The economic reason that schooners were used for these trades was that they were cheap to build, fit and man, compared to a ship. The practical result of this was the sharp-model schooner. Ships, however, because of their greater cost were not to be risked in such trades and therefore were employed only in such legitimate voyages as could be found. There were exceptions, of course, and a number of sharp-model ships are known to have been built before 1810, but owners were still largely under the influence of the old full-lined carriers so that the sharp type was a very small minority. Much of the work done by the merchant ship of this period necessitated long voyages, which tended to place much emphasis on cargo capacity.

Local historians, in their zeal to show the maritime importance of their particular section of the country, have made highly misleading statements as to the quality of the ships of their sections. The truth of the matter is that no section of the country, whether it was New England or Maryland, and no town or city, whether it was Salem or Philadelphia, monopolized the production of either well or poorly built ships. The quality of a ship, either in construction or finish, was in accordance to the value of its cargoes; the richness of the trade in which the ship was employed. It was to this condition that the reputation claimed for the merchant ships of Salem and Philadelphia can be traced; their excellence in construction and finish was due to the rich trades in which most of them were employed, the East Indian and China trades. It was not the superiority of the local shipwrights that produced these well-built ships, but rather the amount of money the owner could spend in their construction. The East India and China ships of Salem, for example, were no better than ships in the same trades hailing from other ports. Not only were vessels in the same trade on a par in construction, but also their models were about the same, no matter what their home port might be. As an illustration, the Baltimore-built China ships were not on the sharp model, but were about the same as the model used in the Salem ships in this trade.

The Baltimore builders seem to have built more ships on the sharp model, in this period, than builders elsewhere, but it must not be supposed that the builders outside of Baltimore were less capable. The Baltimore builders had the advantage because local ship-owners first developed the mania for speed, which grew out of their association with the Baltimore Clipper schooners. The sharp-built Baltimore ships of this period may be visualized by reference to the plans of the *Andromeda*, late *Hannibal*, in *The Baltimore Clipper*. The War of 1812 helped to increase the popularity of the sharp-model ship, but the type grew fashionable very slowly. The men-of-war, such as the 1813 ship-sloops *Erie* and *Ontario*, remained the extreme of the ship-rigged clipper model.

The rise in importance of the European packet trade after the War of 1812 gave employment to merchant ships of greater size than any except the East Indian and China ships. During the early years of the packet trade there was little improvement in model, but the short voyage and the possible increase and regularity of passages turned the packet-owner's attention toward an increase of speed. By 1825 a new class of packet had been evolved, an improved and sharper East Indiaman on the frigate model. Gradually the type became increasingly distinctive and reached its height about 1840-5, when steamship competition began to have its effects.

The requirements of the packet-ship made cargo capacity desirable, for the trans-Atlantic cargo trade was one in which all descriptions of goods were carried. The stormy North Atlantic and the hard winter passages, combined with the desire for speedy voyages, made the power to carry sail in heavy weather, seaworthiness, strength and speed prime requisites. Though the business was profitable, it was never one that produced tremendous profits; this prevented rapid development in design and the appearance of extremely sharp models. The desire for speed was

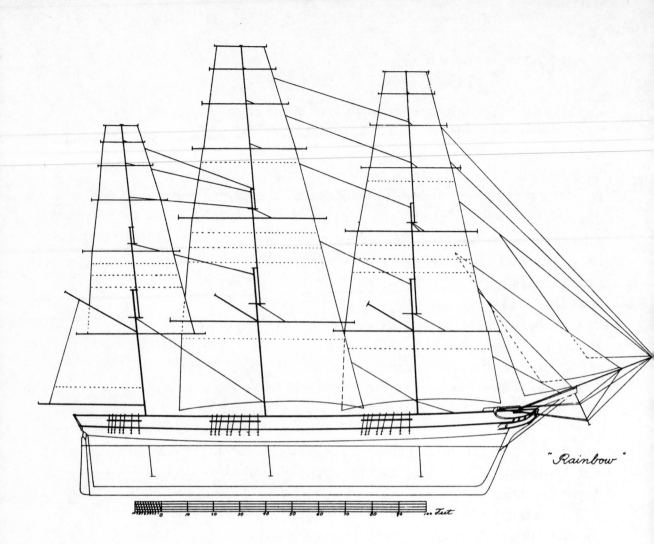

"Rainbow"

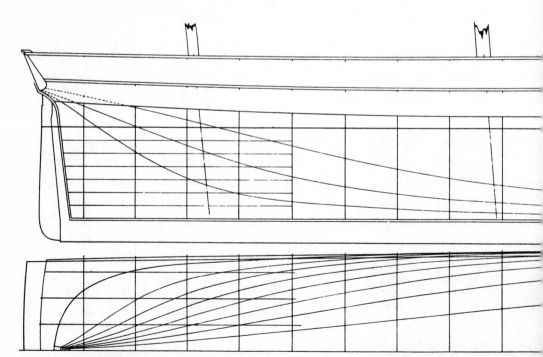

Plate XII. RAINBOW. Plan of the famous clipper ship, traced without reconstruction from builder's plan. Original in the Peabody Museum, Salem, Mass.

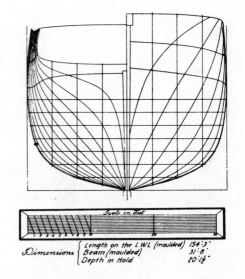

Canton Packet
'Rainbow'

Scale in feet

Dimensions		
Length on the L.W.L. (moulded)	154·3'
Beam (moulded)	31·8'
Depth in Hold	20·1½'

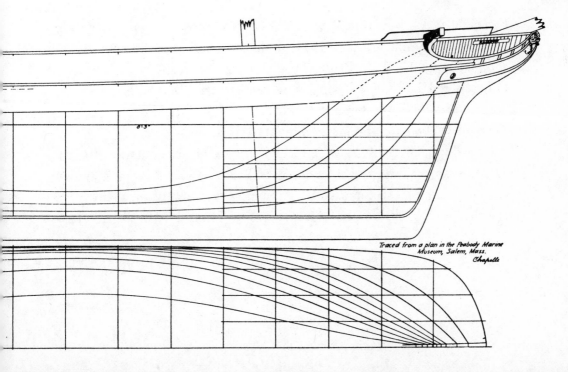

Traced from a plan in the Peabody Marine
Museum, Salem, Mass.
Chapelle

slowly gaining strength and the packets gradually felt its effect. A great part of the profits in the trans-Atlantic packet trade were obtained from the passenger traffic, and this was a factor in the design, construction and fitting of this class of ship. The plan of the *Queen of the West*, Plate XII, shows a characteristic design. This vessel was built by Brown and

PACKET *Queen of the West.*

Bell at New York in 1843. She measured 1168 tons and was a large vessel of her date and type. Brown, who designed her, was the nephew and adopted son of Noah Brown (builder of the ship-sloop *Peacock*). Other noted builders of packets were Christian Bergh, Isaac Webb, Stephen Smith of the famous Smith and Dimon firm, Henry Eckford, William Webb and, of course, Donald McKay.

The shipbuilders of New York achieved a great reputation for the construction of large vessels after the War of 1812. A very complete account of the most noted of these builders was published, many years ago, by G. W. Sheldon in "Harper's New Monthly Magazine," July,

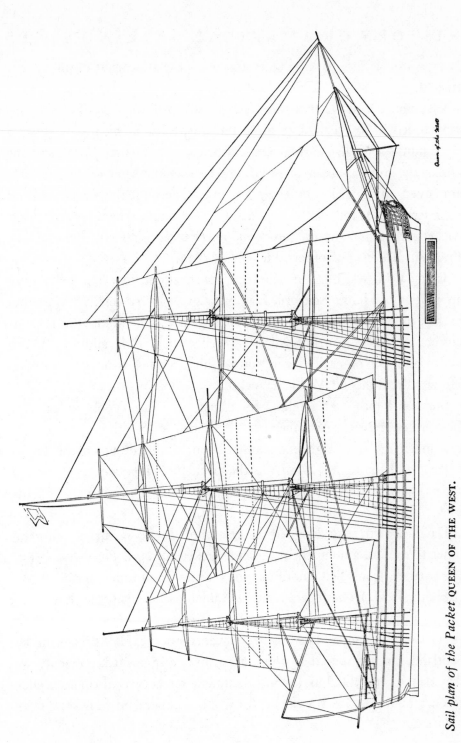

Sail plan of the Packet QUEEN OF THE WEST.

279

1882, (Vol. LXV, page 223) from which the following outline is extracted.

Christian Bergh was born in New York April 30, 1763. He was employed, it will be recalled, to finish the frigate *President*. He modelled a large number of sharp schooners and brigs, such as the *Gipsey* and the *Antarctic*, and a number of privateers. During the War of 1812 he was employed on the Lakes by the government; he built the vessels used on Lake Erie. After the war he returned to New York, where he built many packets, including the *Edward Bonaffe, France, Montano, Philadelphia, President, Rhone* and others. He died in 1843.

Isaac Webb was born in Stamford, Connecticut, in 1794, and was an apprentice of Henry Eckford. He built a great many vessels as a partner in the firm of Webb and Allen. This firm built a large number of revenue cutters, as has been mentioned in an earlier chapter. In addition, Webb built a number of packets and cotton ships, among them the *Natchez*. He was the father of William Webb.

Stephen Smith was a fellow-townsman of Isaac Webb and also an Eckford apprentice. As a member of the firm of Smith and Dimon, he was in charge of design and construction. Smith designed the frigate *Liberator*, later named *Hudson*; the packets *Independence, Virginian* and many other noted ships; he also built a number of clippers designed by Griffiths.

David Brown, who designed the *Queen of the West*, turned out many other fine ships, among them the fast packet *Roscius*. He died in 1850. His partner, Jacob Bell, continued the business for a time afterwards.

Henry Eckford has been mentioned in an earlier chapter. He came to this country from Scotland in 1796 and set up a yard at New York about two years later. He was only twenty-one years old when he left Scotland, but had served an apprenticeship in a ship-yard. Not only was this man a very able builder and designer, but he was also an excellent teacher of his art, as is evidenced by the number and fame of his apprentices.

William Webb entered his father's ship-yard at the age of fifteen to learn his trade. At the death of his father, in 1840, William took over the yard, the firm's name remaining as before, Webb and Allen. He was then but twenty-four. William Webb was probably the greatest ship-builder of his time, not only because of the number, size and quality of the ships he built, but also because of the extraordinary designs for which he was responsible. His accomplishments as a designer and builder of clipper-ships are well-known and will be mentioned later.

Donald McKay requires no introduction here for probably no de-signer has been the subject of as many discussions as he. Though making a reputation as a designer and builder of packets, his fame rests on his clipper-ship designs.

The packet type of ship was suitable for many trades and very similar vessels were built for the cotton trade and general purposes. It may be said that the *Queen of the West* represents the general model on which most of the American ships were built between 1825 and 1846.

The clipper-ships, which followed the packets, are unquestionably the most over-advertised type in maritime history. The quantity of literature dealing with the history of this class is greater than that dealing with all other types put together. Ranging from gushing sentimentality to statis-tics, this literature has covered nearly all phases of clipper-ship history, design and "romance." Overly enthusiastic writers, however, have painted a false picture of the importance of the type. The prevalent idea that the clipper-ship was the culmination of sailing ship design can be traced to these writers. The non-existence of the "first" clipper-ship has been shown by Cutler in *Greyhounds of the Sea*, but the fable of her appearance still persists.

The clipper was the outgrowth of the rising fashion for fast ships. Though the design of the clipper was closely related to the packet-ships, it also employed many of the principles of design that had proven suc-cessful in the early sharp-model vessels. One of the best known of the ship-rigged "Baltimore Clippers" was the handsome *Ann McKim*, built by Kennard and Williamson in 1833, at Baltimore. This ship was, in model, an enlarged clipper-schooner. It has been assumed that she was representative of her type, but this is most doubtful. The little information obtainable concerning these early sharp merchantmen seems to indicate that the *McKim* was far more extreme than her sisters, and that the *Hannibal*, mentioned earlier, was more typical. There is a slight similarity between the lines of the *Rainbow*, shown in Plate XIII, and those of the *Hannibal;* more noticeable than the similarity of the clipper to

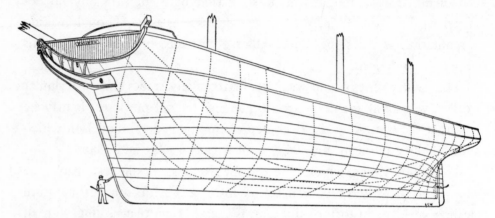

CLIPPER-SHIP *Rainbow.*

the *Queen of the West.* There seems little doubt that the earlier models of the clipper, such as *Rainbow, Samuel Russell* and *Witch of the Wave*, were developments of the type represented by *Hannibal*, rather than of the packet-ships.

The *Rainbow* has been often called the "first" clipper-ship, but the existence of such vessels as the ship-privateer *Rattlesnake*, the sharp-model *Hannibal* and the ship-sloops *Erie* and *Ontario*, as well as numerous others, makes this claim ridiculous. The reputed "hollow waterline" of the *Rainbow* is not evident in her lines and her sharpness has been much exaggerated. The *Rainbow* was the design of John W. Griffiths and was built by Smith and Dimon, in 1844–5, for Howland & Aspinwall. Griffiths was a very able designer and wrote a number of books on naval architecture. He was an opponent of the sharp-floored clipper type, though his early designs had much deadrise, as in *Rainbow*. Griffiths' theories founded the vicious shoal "clipper" schooners of the '70's. Griffiths, with Pook and Webb, developed the flat-floored clippers of the '50's best exemplified by the *Young America, Herald of the Morning* and the McKay-design, *Lightning*. It is hardly necessary to list the noted clipper-ships for these can be found fully described in *Greyhounds of the Sea*.

One of the favorite arguments among ship-lovers has been the relative merits of individual clipper-ships and their designers. It would be impossible to pick out the "best" clipper or designer, but this much can be said: from the point of view of the naval architect the early clippers, such as *Rainbow* and the handsome *Samuel Russell*, were models that were intrinsically faster than later ships, such as the *Flying Cloud*. The earlier clippers were too small to match the later ships in fast passages. Much of the increase in speed, in the later clippers, was due to increased length and harder driving. No naval architect can accept the short and full runs of the later clippers as indications of models capable of extraordinary speed in proportion to their length. The fast passages of the California-clippers were the result of great stability plus hard driving, rather than fast models. The choice of "best" ships by reference to shortest passages is erroneous, as was pointed out in an earlier chapter.

The choice of a "best" designer is another matter that is one of opinion. McKay is thought to be the "best" by many because of the success of some of his ships, such as *James Baines, Flying Cloud* and *Lightning*. Webb, however, turned out a greater number of clippers, which were undoubtedly as well formed as the McKay vessels; some were better, in fact. Griffiths and Pook showed the greatest originality; these two designers were probably influential in the evolution of the flat-floored clipper. Of all the lines of clippers that have been published, those of Pook appear to have been best formed for speed. From a naval architect's point of view, the clippers, *Rainbow, Sea Witch, Samuel Russell, Stag-*

hound, Lightning, Surprise, Herald of the Morning, Challenge, Witch of the Wave, Young America, Comet and the *Great Republic* are the best of the clipper-ship designs; though the choice of one or two of these individuals is perhaps questionable, in view of the comparatively few plans of clippers that are available.

There have been statements to the effect that the clipper-ship was the result of trade requirements. These were but partially true, for the clipper

CLIPPER-SHIP *Rainbow.*

was also the result of publicity and the mania for speed as expressed in "quick passages." The demand for speed was not the result of the California trade, for the fast merchant-ship had appeared earlier in the China trade; for which the *Rainbow, Sea Witch* and *Samuel Russell* were built. The mania for speed had slowly been infecting American seamen and shipbuilders since 1790. Fast passages made by driving the old packet type unmercifully were evidences of the disease that had appeared in the '30's, even earlier. The wild tales of these hard-driven ships seized the

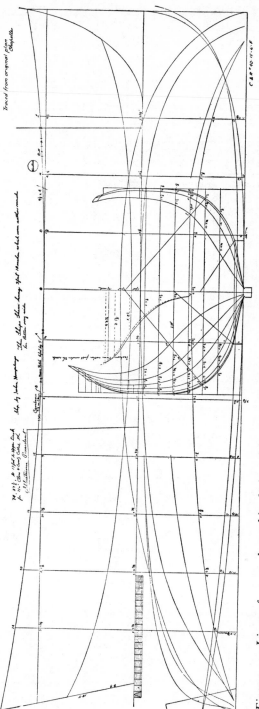
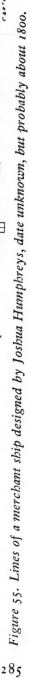

Figure 55. Lines of a merchant ship designed by Joshua Humphreys, date unknown, but probably about 1800.

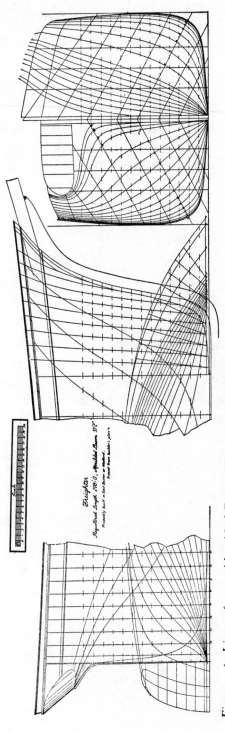

Figure 56. Lines of an unidentified Down Easter, built about 1880.

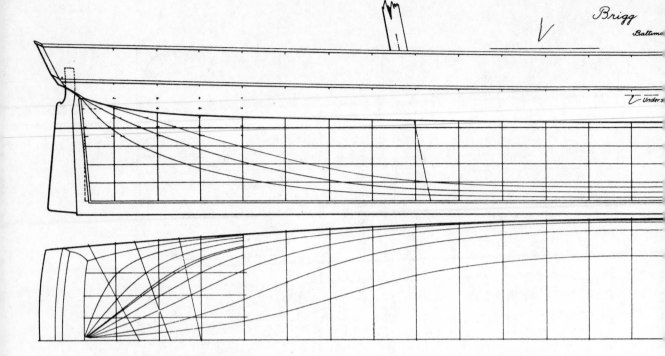

Unders

Plate XIII. QUEEN OF THE WEST. *Traced from builder's plan. An excellent example of a frigate-built packet, the Queen of the West may be said to represent all of her type in a general way. Original in the Peabody Museum, Salem, Mass. No reconstruction.*

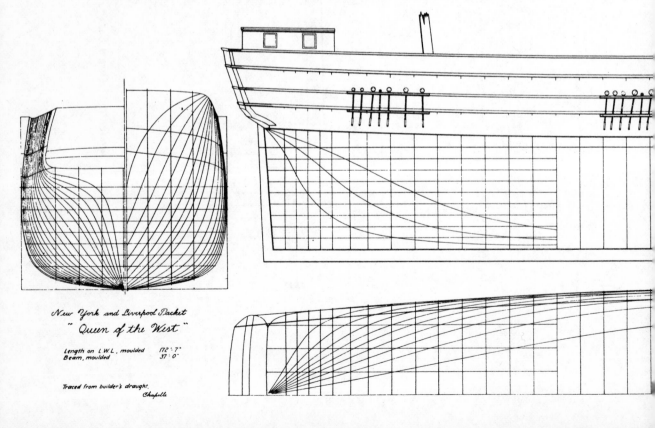

New York and Liverpool Packet
" Queen of the West "

Length on L.W.L., moulded   172' 7"
Beam, moulded   37' 0"

Traced from builder's draught.
Chapelle

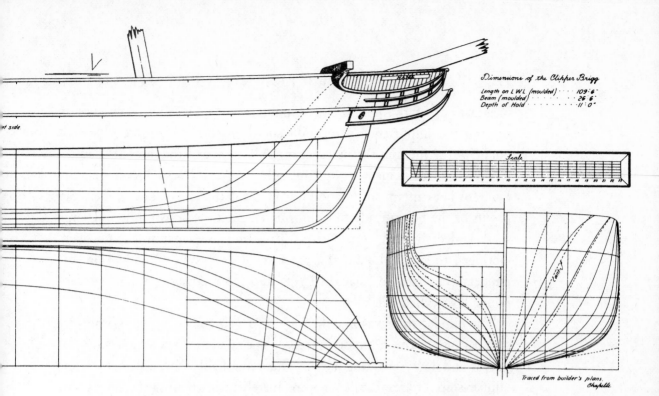

Dimensions of the Clipper Brigg

Length on LWL (moulded) · · · · · 109'6"
Beam (moulded) · · · · · · · · · · 26'6"
Depth of Hold · · · · · · · · · · 11'0"

Scale

Traced from builder's plans.
Chapelle

Brigg—Baltimore Clipper. Traced from a builder's plan of an
unknown vessel. It represents a variation in the Baltimore clipper
model insofar as drag and deadrise are reduced to a minimum.
It is probably a fast South American trader of large class. Original in the Peabody Museum, Salem, Mass. No reconstruction.

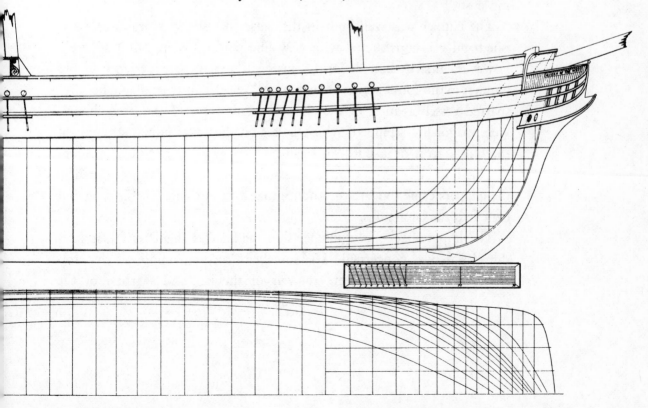

imaginations of the public and shipping men alike. The result was an accentuated importance placed on such passages and a great deal of publicity for them in the newspapers. As a result of the interest aroused, a reputation for being very fast brought cargo and passengers to a ship; fame for her captain and owner, but Hell for the crew. The tremendous profits of the boom-trade to California enabled the construction of large sharp-ended ships in which cargo space and low operating costs were sacrificed to speed. Under the pressure of competition, and pride, the clippers grew steadily sharper, larger and more costly, until at last economic laws called a halt.

The clipper-ship was not the highest development of sailing-ship design because of the emphasis placed on speed at the expense of cargo capacity and low operating costs. The remarkably short career of the clipper-ship (1846 to 1859 approximately) as a distinct type can be traced to the uneconomic design that had been developed by the fashion for speed. The hard driving necessary to get speed out of these ships required large crews, and also caused loss of spars, sails and gear, as well as straining the weakly built wooden hulls; all of which increased operating costs.

The clipper was well-built in the sense that she was beautifully finished and was constructed with very fine workmanship. She was weak, however, in structural design because of the lack of experience of her builders in the construction of such long, lightly-constructed and heavily-sparred vessels as most of the clippers were. Some of the later clippers were diagonally-strapped, which increased the longitudinal strength of the hull a great deal, but American builders were rather slow to adopt this method of construction. The lessons in structural design learned in the clippers came too late to produce many strong ships of this type, but benefited the later ships.

The importance of the clipper-ship model was small, as far as later ship-design was concerned. The so-called "medium clippers" that followed the clipper-ship were revivals of the last and sharpest of the packet-ship models; with the addition of the plain, unadorned bow and counter of the clipper. The medium-clippers were larger and better built than the earlier packets, and also had many of the improved fittings on deck and aloft that had been developed in the clippers. The movement of wooden shipbuilding away from New York in the '60's made Maine supreme in American shipbuilding in the '70's and '80's. The part of the Maine shipbuilders and designers in the history of American sailing ships has never received full recognition. The so-called "down-easters" that followed the clipper were almost wholly the work of these men. Some of these vessels were, without doubt, the highest development of the sailing-ship; combining speed, handiness, cargo-capacity and low operating costs to a degree never obtained in any earlier square-rigger. Some of the later ships were as full-ended as the packets, but most of the down-easters were medium-sharp. Though not as heavily sparred and canvassed as the clippers, the down-easters nevertheless had enough sail area to drive them at great speed. A partial history of the down-easters has been published, Lubbock's *The Down Easters*,[1] but a complete account of the type, illustrated by plans, after the manner of *Greyhounds of the Sea,* is required to do justice to this important class of ship.

Though space for a detailed study of the type is lacking here, two examples of the type can be shown. Figure 56 shows a tracing of a builder's plan of an unidentified medium clipper built at East Boston or Medford in the late '70's or early '80's. This vessel was a good model, having a moderately long and well-formed run and an entrance as sharp as some of the earlier clippers, but with her floor carried well fore and aft to give capacity. The lines of the *Henry B. Hyde,* shown in Figure 57, were taken from the builder's model by Mr. C. L. Douglas. The builder's model was for a ship 256 feet long, but the lines show her as built, 10'-8" longer than indicated in the half-model. The *Hyde* was designed by John McDonald and built by Chapman and Flint at Bath, Maine, in 1884. Her tonnage dimensions were, length 267.8 feet, beam 45 feet,

[1] Charles Lauriat Company, Boston, 1930.

depth 28.8 feet, 2,463 tons. In model, the *Hyde* was related to the famous clipper *Sea Witch*, designed by Griffiths, in that she had the flaring top-sides amidships. The *Hyde*, though fuller-ended than the extreme clippers, was a very fast ship, because of her fine run and easy lines. Her sail-plan was well-proportioned and handsome; the *Hyde* did not lack sail. This fine ship was justly considered the finest wooden vessel of the rig ever built in the United States. She was not only fast, but was an all-around sailer, as well as a carrier. The down-easters were designed for general trade, so had to carry all kinds of cargo, in all climes. The *Hyde*, and some of her sisters, illustrate the fine quality of ship turned out to compete in general trade. The failure of the down-easters to survive was due to the operating cost of the ship-rig, a handicap that led to the almost total disappearance of the brig and barque. This, with the competition of the steamer, doomed the full-rigged ship. Though ships continued to be built after 1890, they were full-ended carriers on the English iron and steel ship model, with no pretense to speed, sea-going barges to compete with steamers of equally ugly models in the bulk-cargo trades. It can be said, therefore, that the American ship ceased development about 1890, and shortly afterwards disappeared.

There were various ship-types whose classification was based on employment rather than model. Perhaps the best-known of these was the "whale-ship." This business employed a large number of barque and ship-rigged vessels, but during the greater part of the life of the trade the whale-ship was a converted merchantman of the general packet-model. After 1855 a number of medium-clippers were built particularly for the business, usually barque-rigged. These vessels were sharp-floored and easy-bilged to make them roll down when "cutting-out" a whale. The whale-ship has been described too often in books and magazine articles to require discussion here. Before leaving the whalers, however, it is worthwhile to mention that many of these craft were schooners of the "Banker" type, during the later years of the business.

The barquentine rig grew out of the ship and three-masted fore-

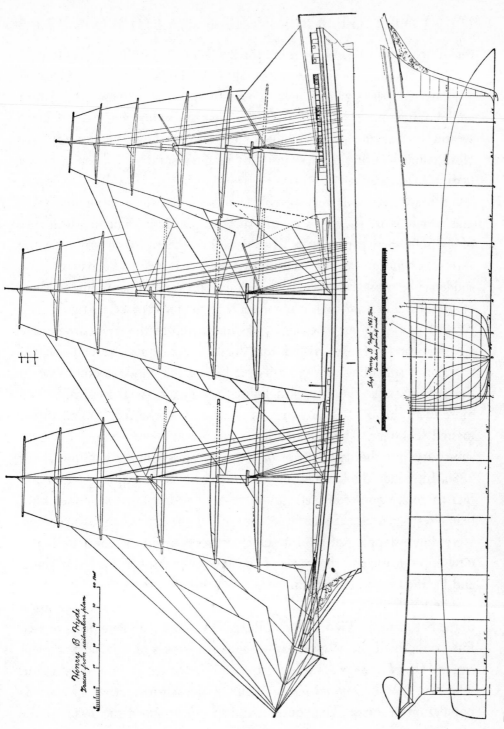

Henry B Hyde
Traced from sailmakers plan

Ship "Henry B Hyde" 3463 Tons
Lines taken from half model

289

Figure 57. Lines and sail plan of the Ship HENRY B. HYDE.

topsail schooner. The idea behind the development of the rig was to produce a combination of the advantages of the three- or four-masted
schooner and the square-rigger. It was found, as schooners grew larger
and required more masts than three, that the schooner was no more
weatherly than the average ship, for the latter had become increasingly
close-winded during the last years of its development. The ship, as she
became narrower, and as her spar iron-work became fully developed,
could brace her yards very sharply and, with the aid of improved staysails, would work to windward in a surprising manner. The disadvantages
of the schooner, particularly large vessels of the rig, when running before the wind at sea are well-known to all seamen. The danger of a
sudden jibe was the large schooner-captain's nightmare, under these
conditions. The fore-topsail schooner was the most practical rig for this
type of work; on large vessels it was but a step to the true barquentine
rig. By using a square-rigged fore mast, the barquentine had the advantage of spreading a larger sail-area before the wind, as compared to
the fore-and-aft schooner, and lighter rigging, as well as smaller and
more easily handled square-sails, as compared to the fore-topsail three-
masted schooner. The barquentine rig came into great popularity as a
substitute for either large three- or four-masted schooners, or ships, about
1880. In model, the barquentine was the same as the large schooners; in
fact there are numerous cases of three- and four-masted schooner hulls
being re-rigged as barquentines; the only important changes necessary
were the re-stepping of the fore mast farther aft, and the construction of
new upper masts and the yards. The rig became popular with the Maine
and Pacific Coast builders and, also, with those on the Lakes.

The Pacific Coast builders, in particular, gave a good deal of attention
to the barquentine. Figure 58 and Plate XIV show complete plans of two
fine examples of the West Coast designs for vessels of this very efficient
rig; the *W. H. Dimond*, three-master, and the *James Tuft*, a four-master.
The plan of the *Dimond* gives details of the leg-of-mutton spanker so
popular on the coast. The contract and specifications of the *Tuft* will be

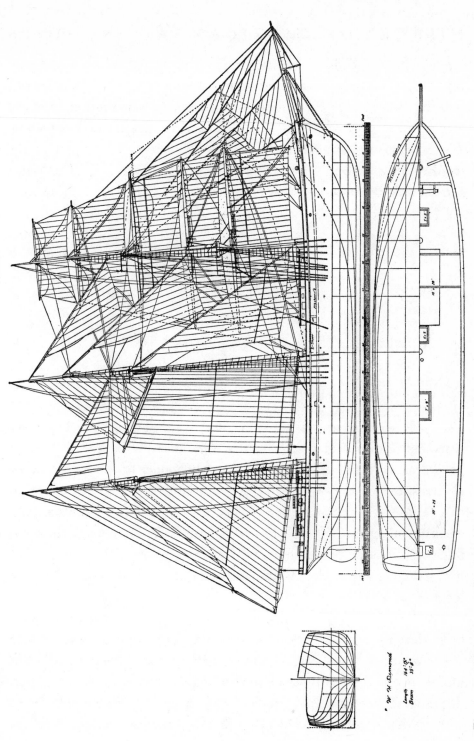

Figure 58. Barquentine W. H. DIMOND.

found in the Appendix. Extensive comment on these fine vessels is hardly necessary. The only possible criticism of them would be that they appear somewhat lacking in bearing forward, considering the weight of the fore-mast and yards; this fineness is particularly noticeable in the *Dimond*. These barquentines could run the large schooners out of sight in the Trades; in such voyages as to South Africa, or to the Islands. The Maine and the West Coast-builders estimated that the barquentine's fore mast

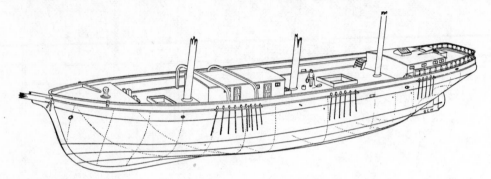

WEST COAST BARQUENTINE *W. H. Dimond.*

and yards, with the necessary rigging, cost as much as all the other masts, spars and rigging together. It will be seen that the barquentine was a good deal more expensive to build than a schooner of the same number of masts, but on the other hand, she was far less costly than a ship or barque. Many experienced sailors believe that barquentines, fitted with auxiliary oil-engines of small power and full sail-power, could be made to pay in some trades even now, providing they were not too large. The best size for such a vessel is said to be about 150 to 175 feet, tonnage length.

The two remaining types of square-riggers to be accounted for are the brigs and brigantines. These two-masted types were extremely popular with American seamen at certain periods and in certain trades. The models of these two classes of square-riggers, and of a third, the hermaphrodite, were generally much like contemporary schooners. Vessels of these rigs were employed in the South American coffee trade, the

African slave-trade, the Island trade in the South Pacific, the West Indian sugar and molasses trade, and in the lumber and coastwise trades. The popularity of the brig declined about 1840; she was succeeded in favor by the hermaphrodite and brigantine, whose popularity lasted about thirty years.

The brig was a close relative of the snow of colonial times and seems to have come into use in America about the same time as that rig. It would appear that the colonial brig was first called a "brigantine" in America. The distinction between the brig and brigantine, in colonial times, does not seem to have been closely drawn. This matter was discussed in the chapter on colonial shipping and need not be again explained. After the Revolution the brig became very popular in the overseas trades, as is evidenced by the numerous contemporary portraits of brig-rigged merchantmen preserved at Baltimore, Salem, Philadelphia, Boston and New York. These vessels were full-ended carriers in most cases, on reduced models of contemporary merchant ships such as the *Illustrious President*. There were, at the same time, a number of fast brigs on the sharp model, similar in some respects to the sharp-model schooners. Fast-sailing brigs were built during the Revolution; their lines were probably much like those of the ship-privateer *Rattlesnake* reduced in dimensions. After 1790, or thereabouts, brig-rigged vessels on the "Virginia model" became common in the West Indian trade, where the confused political conditions made speed necessary. The exact lines of these sharp brigs cannot be reproduced, for plans of them have not yet been found. In view of the extremes reached in sharp schooners in the same period, it is highly probable that some very remarkable brigs were built.

The popularity of the sharp brig increased at the time of the War of 1812. A great many were built for privateers and for blockade-running. These vessels were much like the "pilot-boat model" schooners in lines. So far no plan of an American brig of this type has been found, except men-of-war. In view of the similarity of merchantmen, privateers and

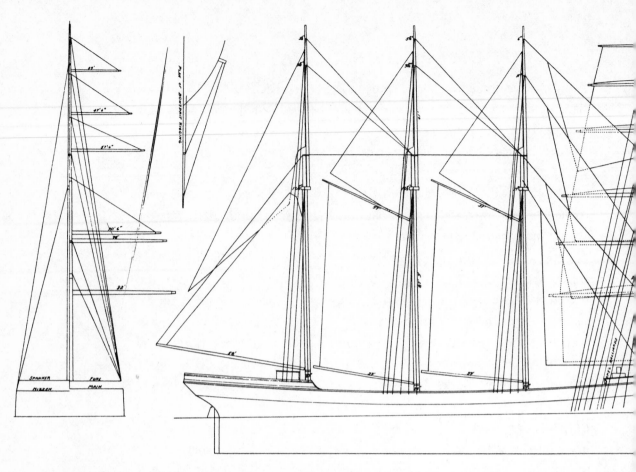

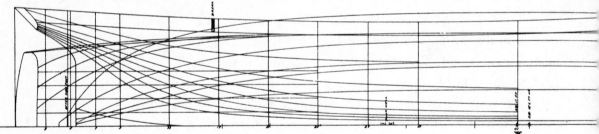

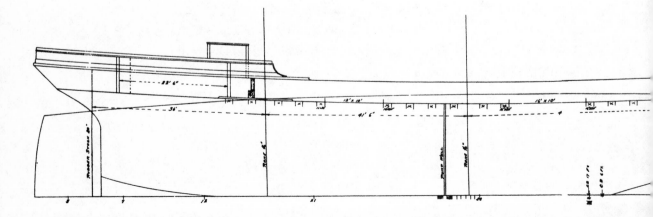

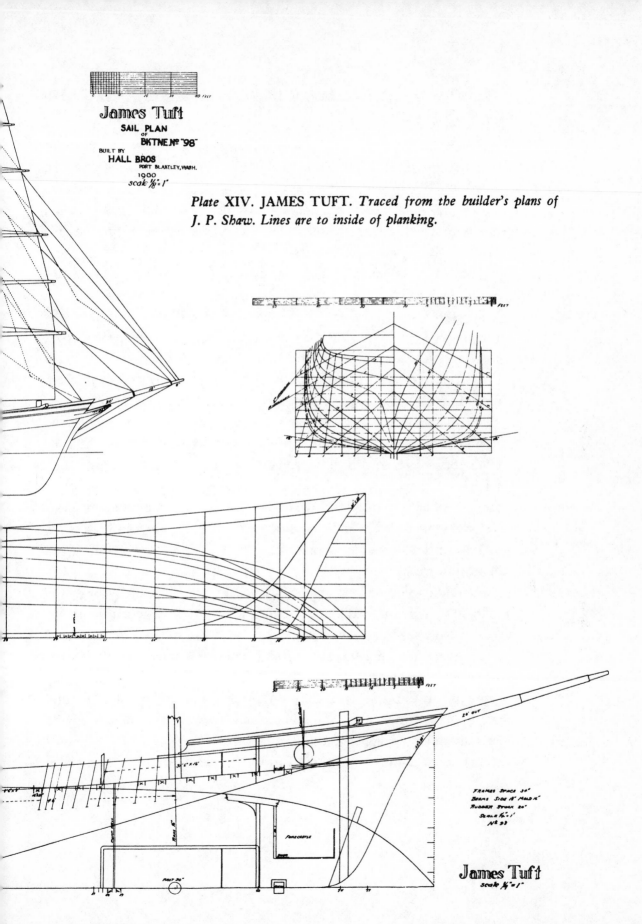

Plate XIV. JAMES TUFT. *Traced from the builder's plans of J. P. Shaw. Lines are to inside of planking.*

men-of-war schooners, during the same period, it is probably quite safe to assume that the sharp brigs showed a similar likeness. The plans of men-of-war brigs designed for the United States Navy during the last years of the War of 1812 show vessels on the "Baltimore Clipper" model with sharp-floors, heavy drag, raking ends, deep draft, low freeboard and fine lines. With the rise of the cruel slave trade, the sharp brig became increasingly popular, the fashion being set by the extreme slavers. From the end of the War of 1812, if not earlier, the merchant brig had followed the lead of the man-of-war in adopting the snow's trysail mast on which the spanker was set. This spar, later called the "spencer-mast," was adopted by ships about the same time. The use of the spencer-mast, and a fore-and-aft gaff sail set on it, spread to the other masts of ships; the rig may be seen in the sail plan of the clipper *Rainbow* on all three masts but most clippers and some of the later packets used the spencer on main and mizzen only. Strangely enough, the use of a spencer on the fore mast of an hermaphrodite brig is not indicated in any of the contemporary plans of this class that are at hand. So far as known, the spencer was never used on the fore mast of a fore-topsail schooner either, though it would seem that the spar would be feasible on both hermaphrodite and schooner. The sail plan of the U.S.N. brig *Somers*, Figure 19A, indicates that the spencer-mast was used on the fore mast of full-rigged brigs, however.

Full-ended slow-sailing brigs continued to be built, but by 1835 the brig most in favor was the Baltimore Clipper. The difficulty in obtaining a proper balance between clipper hull and square rig, mentioned in reference to the 1813 class of ship-sloops on the same model, the *Erie* and *Ontario*, caused these sharp brigs to have much less drag than formerly. At the same time, there was often a decrease in deadrise; until, finally, sharp brigs were built whose models were forerunners of the later flat-floored clipper-ships. A great many brigs of this new model were built at Baltimore; we are so fortunate as to have an excellent plan of one of this class, Plate XIII. This vessel has not yet been identified, but her model was probably much like that of the famous St. Michaels (Maryland) brig *John Gilpin* of 1830 and the fast Baltimore brig *Tweed* of 1834. The remarkably beautiful run and moderately sharp entrance of this brig are indications that she was very fast. Her lines show the probable relationship of the early clipper-ship model to the Baltimore Clipper merchantman, a matter mentioned earlier. There can be no claim that this Baltimore brig was in any way influenced by the clipper-ship, for she was built three years prior to the *Rainbow*. The plan of this brig was one obtained by the German, Mitzlaff, and is presented here by courtesy of the Peabody Marine Museum.

These brigs were losing favor at the time this example was being built; the hermaphrodite and brigantine rigs, on hulls of the same model, were supplanting them. These rigs were developed by the same urge that produced the later barquentine. The hermaphrodite rig has been described in discussing the *Neufchâtel*, a combination of schooner and brigantine. The merchant brigantine rarely carried any square-sails on the main; the same was true of the merchant hermaphrodite. The Baltimore brigantines of 1850 were remarkable for their flaring bows, a feature copied in the Maine-built brigantines. These vessels were usually between 100 and 112 feet long on deck; the Baltimore-built brigantines were often shallower than those built in Maine, reversing the earlier trend in Baltimore-built craft.

The exact reason for the change in trend in the model of Baltimore and Chesapeake Bay craft cannot be stated with certainty, but one may speculate that it was due to a change in conditions on the Bay. In early times the Bay, and its harbors, were probably quite deep, but as the surrounding country was deforested, a great amount of silt was washed down the many rivers and creeks, causing a gradual shoaling in the Bay, with the result that deep-draft craft became useless to a great extent.

The brigantine shares with the barquentine the possibility of revival in modern trade, for it has many of the same advantages on a smaller scale. A few square-rigged yachts, with this rig, have been built; in many cases the hulls have been too large for a two-masted rig, however.

Before leaving square-riggers, the use of the centerboard in vessels of this rig is an interesting matter that must be mentioned. Except for the drop-keel ships built for the British and Dutch Navies in the last decade of the eighteenth century, no centerboard ship-rigged vessels are known to the writer. Centerboard barquentines and brigantines were used on the Great Lakes, however, and centerboard barquentines were not unknown on the Atlantic Coast. Centerboard, or drop-keel, brigs were built for the British Navy, but as far as is known, no vessels of this type and rig were ever built in the United States, though a thorough research into Lake types may eventually bring such vessels to light. There have always been experimental craft built, so it is probable that American centerboard brigs and ships existed at some time in the past.

The colonial rigs, such as the ketch, lateen and the simple two-masted rigs, played a comparatively small part in later commercial types. The final manifestations of many early rigs were among the small local types; the gundalow, sharpie, Block Island boat, Chesapeake canoe and bugeye, for example. It would be a conservative estimate to place the number of local small boat types within the borders of the United States at a hundred, for every maritime district has produced one or more special types, ranging from an open skiff to a schooner. Most of these craft were employed as fishermen, though there are instances where some local types have appeared in the coasting trade. The old St. John, New Brunswick, wood-carrier that used to come to Boston with fire-wood was one of these local types, an enlarged "dogbody" in hull and rig. Many of these St. John wood-carriers were unbelievably crude; most of them engaged in carrying cord-wood to the lime-kilns at Rockland, Maine.

The only other colonial rig that survived was the sloop. This was a rig that was in great favor before the rise in popularity of the schooner. The use of this rig was not limited to the colonies on the North American mainland, for the sloop was a common rig in the West Indies as well. Very little information regarding early sloops is available, particularly in the way of plans. The rig came to the colonies from England; vessels rigged as sloops were often fairly large craft before 1700. It is probable that the *Ferrett*, illustrated in the first chapter, would serve as an example of the early sloops of large dimensions used in England and America, as has already been claimed.

The use of the sloop in the West Indies developed under conditions where speed was necessary. The lawlessness of this section of the New World during colonial times and afterwards, is too well known to require discussion. To meet the demand for fast craft, of moderate size that could be concealed in small harbors among the islands, which resulted from buccaneering and piratical activity, the West Indian builders, particularly those of Jamaica, developed a sharp-model sloop. This type had much deadrise, some drag to the keel, raking stem and sternposts, low freeboard and a raking mast; many were apparently rather sharp-ended. The "Jamaica Sloop" soon became a distinct type with a great reputation for speed and weatherliness. The advantages of such craft were obvious to West Indian merchants and the orders for new sloops of this model soon denuded Jamaica and nearby islands of suitable timber.

Faced with this situation, the builders moved from Jamaica, most of them going to Bermuda, where a species of red cedar known as "pencil cedar" was found in abundance. Here they continued the construction of their particular model of sloop, which soon took the name of "Bermuda Sloop." The period between 1690 and 1750 seems to have been the heyday of the type, in general favor at least. The type survived well into the nineteenth century at Bermuda, however, though the American schooner model was supplanting it by 1790.

The only plan of one of these Bermuda sloops, of a date prior to the Revolution, that has yet been found is the one in Chapman's *Architecturia Mercatoria Navalis* published 1763, a sloop of about 1750, probably.

This plan has been reproduced in *The Baltimore Clipper* and is a good example of the type, judging from contemporary pictures. An example of the final development of the "Bermuda Sloop" was published in "Yachting," (April, 1933); the *Lady Hammond*, which was purchased for the British Navy about 1804 and used as a model for twelve duplicates; all built in Bermuda by the famous Goodriche family of St. Georges.

The "Bermuda Sloop" model was probably adopted by the colonists along the shores of the Chesapeake during the early years of the eighteenth century, and was the prototype of the sharp-model schooners, as is proven beyond reasonable doubt by the newspaper advertisement of 1761 reprinted in Chapter Two. The disadvantages of the sloop-rig in large craft undoubtedly led to the evolution of the schooner, or brigantine, in Bay vessels. With the schooner-rig it was possible to increase length and capacity without a corresponding increase in beam and depth and so obtain a faster vessel.

After the schooner became popular in all trades, the sloops continued to be used on the large rivers and on the Chesapeake, as well as on Long Island Sound. The rig was also used to some extent on small coasters, particularly in trades in which short voyages were the rule. It must not be supposed, however, that the sloop did not make sea voyages of great length, for throughout the eighteenth century American sloops crossed the Atlantic regularly, and the Northwest voyage of the 90-ton *Lady Washington* in 1788–9 is well-known. Whaling and sealing voyages were made in sloops, particularly by New Englanders. However, the sloop became a rarity on blue-water after 1810.

In addition to the sea-going sloops, built more or less on the sharp model, there were also a number of packet-sloops which ran along the coast, carrying passengers and light freight. These were often fast craft, built on a good model and heavily sparred. A similar employment for sloops on the Hudson River produced large vessels of this class, though of a shoaler model than the coasting and sea-going sloops. The introduction of the centerboard increased the usefulness and popularity of the shoal-draft sloop at a time when the sea-going and coasting sloops had lost favor. The most important type of centerboard sloop, in point of influence and in setting a fashion, was the "North River Sloop," of the Hudson River packet-type. When the centerboard was introduced into these sloops they improved in weatherliness and speed. Their influence in setting a fashion for large sloop-yachts in the neighborhood of New York was undoubtedly great.

Another important class of sloop appeared on Chesapeake Bay, some time about 1815; at least Marestier found the type in use when he visited the United States about 1820–22. These were sloops built somewhat on the lines of the shoal Norfolk pilot-schooners, but with less draft of water. Like the pilot-boats, the sloops had no bulwarks, round stems and no head, little or no overhang to the stern and few deck structures. They had a slightly raking mast, with little or no standing rigging and a gaff-mainsail with a single jib. These boats were usually about 55 feet long, 20 feet beam and had a centerboard about 16 feet long. This type continued popular until about 1850, when a clipper-bow sloop somewhat similar to the New York sloop-yacht became popular; these in turn were replaced by the present V-bottom "skipjacks," leg-of-mutton jib-and-mainsail sloops, which came into fashion on the Bay some time after the Civil War.

The Hudson River sloops were gradually forced out of business by the river-steamers, but in the last years of their existence they became very large, between 70 and 90 feet on deck. The square-topsail of colonial days, and of the period before 1812, had ceased to be used in sloops by 1820, and was replaced by a fore-and-aft gaff-topsail, triangular in form, filling the space between topmast and gaff.

The Long Island Sound sloops were identical with those used about New York and were, in later years, on the same model as contemporary sloop-yachts, but somewhat more burdensome and built much heavier. Many sloops of this class were built at Noank and Essex, Connecticut;

most of them were about 50 feet long and were used in the fisheries or in hauling farm produce to market, as was the case on the Chesapeake also. The trading and fishing sloops of Long Island Sound were rapidly replaced by steamers in the '80's.

On the New England coast the trading and coastwise sloops made their last stands. Here, also, the sea-going sloops used in off-shore fisheries existed the longest. The stone, ice and cord-wood trades were, until a comparatively recent time, carried on almost entirely in sloops, as was much of the shore-fisheries. One of the most common classes of sloops were the scows, usually parallel-sided and not far different in shape from the ordinary harbor-barge of the sand-scow variety. These were very useful craft for river-trading as they could carry a very large cargo on a light draft of water. Because of this ability their use spread to the coasting trade, where they were often employed in the stone- and ice-trades. Most of the wood-trade on Maine rivers was carried on in this type of sloop, the boats were usually about 50 or 60 feet long and had either a centerboard, or a single lee-board (on the portside usually). Scow-sloops employed in the Quincy granite trade were called, locally, "square-toed frigates" in contempt, for they were usually very ugly, having no sheer and being roughly built. However, they were capable of astonishing speed under favorable conditions, particularly when light. Many of these scows were built in the neighborhood of Bath, Maine; particularly those used in the ice and cord-wood trades. With the passing of the demand for fire-wood and the introduction of modern refrigeration, both trades ceased and scow-sloops are now rarely seen. It is probable that the remarkable San Francisco scow-schooners were evolved from these sloops.

Not all the sloops in the granite-trade were scows, however, for many of them were fine centerboard vessels with good lines, clipper-bows and beautifully proportioned rigs. In addition, there was a class of smaller stone sloops, hailing out of Rockport or Quincy, Massachusetts. These were full-ended and flat-floored centerboard sloops with straight, unadorned, stems and short counters; built at Essex, Quincy or Newbury-port. An example of one of these, built at Essex about 1890, is shown in Figure 59. The larger sloops were handsome vessels; the finest and largest stone sloop was the *Albert Baldwin*, built at Essex in 1894 by Tarr and James. This grand vessel was 85 feet long, for tonnage, and 27'-3" extreme beam; her overall length was about 96 feet. Similar sloops, such as the *Mary White*, *William P. Hunt* and *America*, were built at Newburyport, Ipswich, Essex, Boston and Quincy, so it will be seen that the *Baldwin* was not purely a local type. In model, these big sloops (all over 60 feet on deck) were much like the "North River Sloops," having the same raking ends, easy lines and much the same deck arrange-ment, even to the short raised quarterdeck. The last two of these sloops afloat were the *Baldwin* and the handsome *America;* the *Baldwin* was allowed to sink in Gloucester harbor and the progressive citizens then permitted her to go to pieces. The *America* was, until recently at least, a water-boat at T-Wharf, Boston.

The fishing sloops were very popular in the shore-fisheries, out of Gloucester and Beverly, and were fine, able, keel-sloops. The type de-veloped at Gloucester is shown in Figure 60, much like the famed "Friendship Sloops" built in Friendship, Maine, and nearby towns. The Maine sloops were copies of the larger Gloucester sloops, which were called "sloop-boats" by the Gloucestermen. Though these sloops were commonly used in the shore-fisheries, they were capable of venturing off-shore to the Georges, and occasionally did so. The Gloucester sloops were built as large as 60 feet on deck, the Maine sloops rarely were larger than 40 feet. Though the same general model was used for both classes, the "Friendship Sloops" were much lighter built than the "sloop-boats" and were of a much cheaper construction. The "Friendship Sloop" is known to almost every yachtsman for the old fishermen have been con-verted to yachts in recent years, but the conversion usually consists of adding unsightly cabin trunks, and cutting down the sail-area until the sailing qualities of the type are lost.

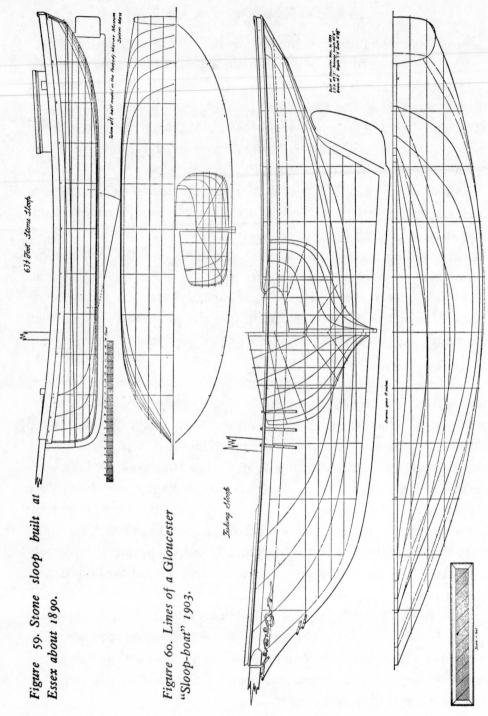

Figure 59. Stone sloop built at Essex about 1890.

Figure 60. Lines of a Gloucester "Sloop-boat" 1903.

63½ Foot Stone Sloop

Fishing Sloop

302

MERCHANT CRAFT

Centerboard half-decked sloops of various designs and models were common in the fisheries along the whole of the coast of the United States, but now these craft are rarely seen, commonly replaced by remarkedly ugly and inefficient motor-boats. The curious and interesting small sailing-boat types once so common in the United States have now almost disappeared; the period of sail in American commerce has passed.

Except for the Chesapeake Bay, sailing craft have nearly vanished in the waters of the United States. In some parts of the world, however, sail has held its own; the West Indies is such a place, close to our coast. China and the Far East are to be the last strongholds of the sailing merchant vessel, apparently.

Little has been done to preserve the American sailing craft, except in Maryland, where laws protect the type by not permitting the use of steam or power craft in "tonging" oysters on the banks. The intention of this law was not a sentimental one to preserve sailing craft, but was to enable the poor fishermen to compete with the wealthy ones, and to enable the lone independent fisherman to hold his own against the companies. The wisdom of this law is evident for the single independent fisherman is in the majority in Maryland waters, whereas the shore-fisheries of Massachusetts, for example, have slowly passed into the hands of companies or powerful individuals because the cost of the large and powerful motor-boats is now too great for an individual of moderate means.

To attempt to preserve sailing craft for purely sentimental reasons is a hopeless task, but it is yet to be proven that the sailing boat and vessel are no longer of economic value. The state of the New England fisheries, compared to that of Maryland and the West Indies, shows that mere increase of speed and mechanization do not constitute "progress."

THE evolution of the American sailing yacht can be said to have started in 1839–40 with the building of the 90-foot waterline schooner *Onkahye,* insofar as this vessel was a distinct departure from the then accepted hull-form for fast-sailing craft. Though a number of yachts, including the famous Salem brigantine *Cleopatra's Barge* (1816) had been built earlier in the century, all of them were constructed on either the Baltimore Clipper or the pilot-boat model; if sloops, they were duplicates of the contemporary commercial sloops or fishing smacks. The majority of these early yachts were schooners and were almost exact duplicates of the keel pilot-boat schooners in use at Boston and New York; in fact, some of them were converted pilot-boats.

A yacht is any vessel used for pleasure purposes, in the strict definition of the term; but since the time of the *Onkahye* the name has been applied to a type of craft quite distinct in hull-form and finish from commercial or naval vessels. In the early days of American yachting, the yachtsmen were untrammelled in their search for speed combined with seaworthiness, safety and reasonable accommodation. Most of the yachtsmen of the time were engaged in maritime affairs or had been to sea in their youth. Though desiring fast and smart yachts they also wanted practical vessels that could serve for other purposes when they were tired of them, not freaks or mere toys. These yachtsmen turned to fast commercial craft for inspiration and from them developed schooners and sloops that were excellent little ships in every way.

This condition could not last, however, when racing became an organized sport and not mere casual matches. It was soon found that racing boat for boat was unfair to the smaller yachts and that some method of handicapping was required. It was natural that this should be based on lineal measurements of the hull. All yachts were therefore handicapped on their Custom House tonnage, but this measurement was found to be very unsatisfactory in giving a correct indication of size. As a result, various measurement rules were developed, but each one tried eventually had to be changed. The difficulty with these rules was not in their failure to handicap fairly yachts already in existence at the time they were formulated, but in the trend of design they fostered by penalizing or placing a premium on some certain element of hull design, such as beam, depths, overhangs or waterline length. If the rule permitted wide shoal hulls of unlimited sail area and very light displacement, it followed that new yachts, built to race and to fit the rule, would grow progressively shallower and beamier and carry more sail until the racing fleet was composed wholly of such dangerous craft. Adding to the importance of the measurement rules, yachting history has shown that the racer sets the fashion for cruising yachts, and when the racer is of a vicious type, so is the cruiser. This is the reason that yacht design has never followed a normal course of improvement, but has gone from one extreme to another. It is also true that the science of yacht design, in more recent times as well as in the past, has not had the advantage of scientific experiment that has developed naval architecture; a condition that has been aggravated since commercial sailing craft have ceased to be in demand. It is impossible to trace each phase of the many changes of trend in yacht design in the limited space of a single chapter, but the important changes at least can be accounted for.

When the *Onkahye* was being designed, in 1838 and 1839, the sport of yachting was confined to New York and Boston, for only in these two cities were there men who had the wealth, leisure and interest or tradition conducive to owning pleasure craft. Furthermore, natural conditions in the neighborhood of these cities were suitable, particularly around New York.

Though yachtsmen of the period keenly admired the keel pilot-boat schooners, there were a number of them who were adherents of the shoal centerboard craft. When yachtsmen gather there is generally an argument over the comparative merits of competitive types of yacht, and it was natural that much contention arose over the comparative qualities of the keel and centerboard yachts of the time.

One of the supporters of the centerboard type of yacht was Robert Livingston Stevens of Hoboken who, with his brothers John Cox Stevens and Edwin A. Stevens, owned the schooner *Wave*. Built by Brown and Bell in 1832, the *Wave* was of the rather shoal keel pilot-boat model, 65 feet on the waterline and 72 feet overall, and was a very fast sailer. The Stevens brothers were the sons of Colonel John Stevens, the celebrated engineer who played a most important part in the early development of steamships. Robert L. Stevens followed in his father's footsteps as an engineer and had made a hobby of small boat design. The *Onkahye* was his first attempt at a large vessel.

Stevens apparently desired to prove that a centerboard vessel could be designed that would combine the advantages of both the keel and centerboard types and thus demonstrate the arguments of the supporters of the centerboard. Before constructing the new yacht, however, he wanted to verify his ideas, and his method of doing so has a peculiarly modern flavor. He first built an accurate scale sailing model of the *Wave* and then another of the proposed schooner and sailed these models against each other, making careful observations of the behavior of each. Incidentally, the half-model of the *Wave* in the model collection of the New York Yacht Club is one of the halves of this sailing model. As a result of his experiments, Stevens lengthened the model of his proposed schooner the equivalent of four feet to scale and from the lengthened half-model William Capes laid down the yacht in his yard in Williamsburg, opposite the Brooklyn Navy Yard, late in 1839.

Capes must have been somewhat shocked when he saw the half-model of the new schooner, for she was of an unorthodox form. Measuring 90 feet on the waterline, 96 feet overall and 23 feet beam, she had a deep forefoot, a slightly rockered keel, perpendicular ends on the rabbet line and her greatest beam and draft a little abaft the center of the waterline length. She had a large centerboard and was to have a very large spar plan on the square fore-topsail rig. The strangest thing about her was the shape of the mid-section; this showed a very thick keel structure, which had the appearance of having been attached to the hull of a very shoal vessel. This gave a hull with a very thick fin, high hollow garboards and topsides flaring strongly outward above the waterline.

Launched in 1840 the *Onkahye*, at first spelled *Oncahye*, drew about 13 feet with her board up when in sailing trim. In her trials she proved to be very fast and stiff, but rather slow in stays, as might be supposed from her description. In her deep-water cruises she was found to be a good sea-boat but a very hard roller; on one occasion she actually rolled her masts out and had to be towed home. Stevens tried out many ingenious ideas on the vessel, including the placing of much of her ballast outside in strips along her keel, the inside ballast being iron, and the use of mast tracks and sail slides of similar design to those in use today.

After using the *Onkahye* for a time the Stevens brothers sold her in 1843 to the government. The Navy took her in hand, removed her centerboard, strengthened her decks and put two guns into her with the usual number of heavy boats and cumbersome gear then considered proper in small naval craft, with the result that her sailing was much damaged. After about five years' service, including cruises to the West Indies and the coast of Brazil, the *Onkahye* was lost on Caicos Reef in the West Indies, on June 21, 1848, without loss of life.

Soon after the Stevens' had sold the *Onkahye* they commissioned young George Steers to model a new and smaller schooner for them. This yacht was also built by Capes during the early summer of 1844. *Onkahye* had been given a beautiful Indian name meaning "dancing feather," but the new yacht was named in Yankee slang, *Gimcrack*, meaning a "useless thing." The *Gimcrack* was about 51 feet overall and 49 feet on the waterline with 13 feet 6 inches beam. She drew about 7 feet 6 inches and, in the first part of her career at least, had a fin or fixed centerboard somewhere around 4 feet deep and between 12 and 15 feet long. The *Gimcrack* does not seem to have been a very successful experiment and the

Stevens' did not use her long. Her chief claim to distinction is that the New York Yacht Club was founded in her cabin, on the afternoon of July 30, 1844. So great has been the prestige of the New York Yacht Club since that time that it has generally set the yachting fashions for the rest of the country.

George Steers, the designer of the *Gimcrack*, was the son of an English shipwright, Henry Steers, or Steer, who came to the United States in 1819, and obtained work in the Washington Navy Yard. While there Henry Steers helped build a small marine railway, a ship-house and the war-schooners *Shark* and *Grampus*. It has been thought that he designed these vessels, but that was not the case. George Steers was born in 1820, while his father was employed in the navy yard; the third child of a family that eventually increased to thirteen children. The family moved to New York in 1824 and here Henry Steers built another marine railway and engaged in other mechanical and engineering projects until his death in 1841. The eldest son, James R. Steers, was also a shipwright and was employed at various times by Smith and Dimon and Wm. H. Brown. George was apprenticed to this brother and at an early age gave evidence of remarkable skill in design. Before he was twenty he had modeled a number of small boats and the *Manhattan*, 44'-0" long and 14'-8" beam, which went through successive changes of rig, cat, sloop and schooner. One of his small boats had been named in honor of John C. Stevens and the success of this boat had attracted the attention of the Stevens brothers, which led to the commission for the *Gimcrack*. Steers designed his first pilot schooner when he was twenty-one. This was the *William G. Hagstaff* whose sailing was so fine that she led to the later pilot-boats, the *Mary Taylor*, *Moses H. Grinnell* and the *George Steers*. Soon after building the *Hagstaff* he designed the 250-ton schooner *St. Mary the First* and the 247-ton schooner *Pride of the Seas*. During his career he designed the U.S. steam frigate *Niagara*, a very noted vessel, and three other steamers. He designed one clipper-ship, the *Sunny South*, built in 1854; a very sharp vessel 144'-8" long, 31'-4" beam and 16'-6" in the hold, which finally became a slaver under the name of *Emanuela;* after being captured she finished her career as a storeship in the British Navy on the Cape of Good Hope station. Steers would no doubt have designed other clippers had it not been for his untimely death on September 26, 1856, at the early age of 36.

It was in yacht design, however, that Steers gained undying fame. In addition to the *Manhattan* (later named *La Coquille*) and the *Gimcrack,* Steers designed over fifteen other yachts, including the schooners *Cygnet, Cornelia, Siren, Sybil, Norma, America* and *Haze;* the centerboard sloops *Una* and *Sylvia.* Steers also modelled the keel sloops *Ray, Sport* and *L'Esperance* and the centerboarder *Widgeon.* In 1854 he built the great centerboard sloop *Julia,* though the design of this yacht seems to have been the work of an unknown, one Nelson Spratt. While the Steers designs for keel craft were very successful, it is an interesting fact that his centerboard yachts were equally fine; an unusual thing in yachting history.

In 1855, the year after the *Gimcrack* was launched, Robert L. Stevens designed a large sloop for his brothers; the model for her being based on that of a very fast Hudson River sloop, the *Eliza Ann.* Capes built this sloop during the winter of 1844–5 and she was named *Maria.* When launched she was 92′-0″ on deck, 26′-6″ beam, 8′-4″ in the hold and her draft to shoe was 5′-2″. She had a shallow, round and flaring bow with a fine run aft; her deadrise was small. Her centerboard was 24 feet long and was not pivoted but was supported by coiled springs and counterbalanced. Five years later Stevens lengthened her 18 feet by the bows, giving her a very sharp entrance. She then measured 110 feet on deck, 107′-9″ on the waterline, and her spars were of the following dimensions: the hollow mainmast was 92 feet long, and her hollow boom 95 feet; she had a 61-foot gaff and her bowsprit reached outboard 38 feet, coming home underneath the deck forward. Among the "modern" features of this remarkable sloop were a rubber compressor on her mainsheet horse, mast track and slides, trusses in her hollow boom and a small "steering"

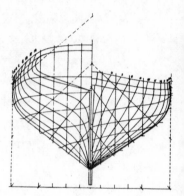

Length on Deck	95'6"
on Keel for Tonnage	79'6"
Beam, for Tonnage	22'6"
extreme	23'0"
Burthen in Tons, American Registry, Nº 171	
English Measurement } Nº 210	
Old Rule, or Builder's Tonnage	
Draught of Water Forward } 7'0" (6'0" m trim)	
Aft } 11'0"	
Depth of Main Keel	2'1"
False Keel	0'2"

*Original marked "Office Copy"
and "Yard Copy, Str. Coachman."*

Plate XV. *Schooner Yacht* AMERICA. *Redrawn from plans of this famous yacht made in England 1851–2. No reconstruction. The sail plan is drawn from the Admiralty draught and from George Ratsey's sail plan made at the same time. Scale ¼″ = 1'-0".*

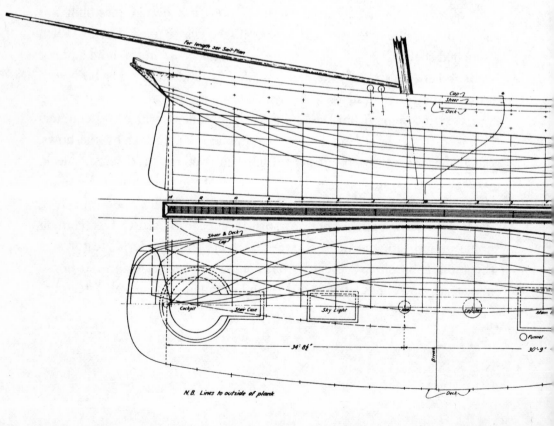

N.B. Lines to outside of plank

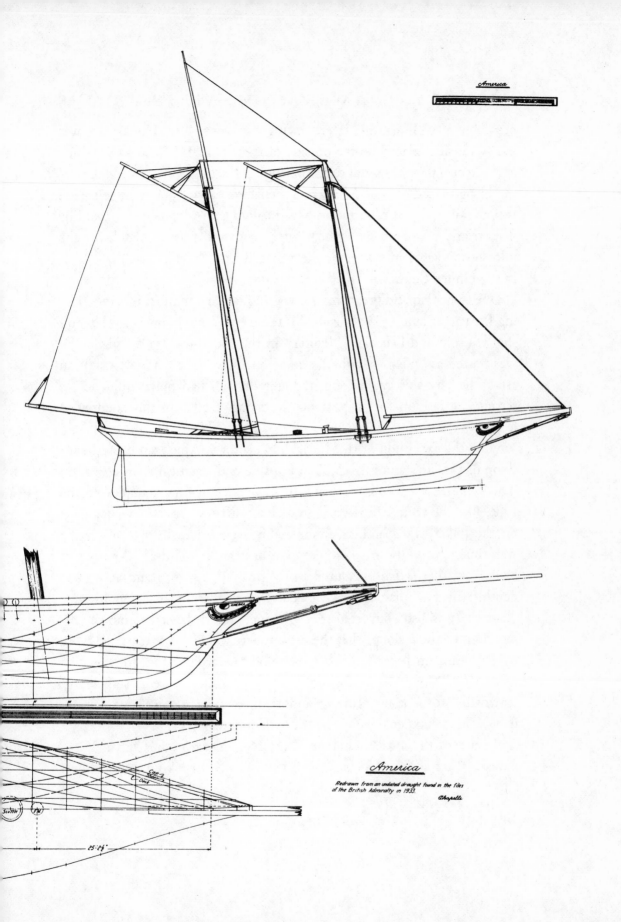

America

America

Redrawn from an undated draught found in the files
of the British Admiralty in 1933.

Chapelle

centerboard well aft. She steered with a 12-foot tiller. Her ballast was partly outside, placed on the outside of the planking in lead strips, thick at the keel and tapering out to a shim edge at the bilges, the copper sheathing being placed over it. As altered, the *Maria* carried about 7,890 square feet of sail, and was reported to have made over 16 knots under sail. She was strictly a smooth-water boat, of course, and was no match for the pilot-boat yachts in a breeze; she was the first "racing machine" built in the United States.

Due to her rig and great size she was dismasted a number of times during her career, and so she was finally re-rigged as a schooner. In the '60's she was sold and became a "fruiter" in the Honduras trade; finally she was posted as "missing with all hands" in October, 1870. The tradition established by this great sloop undoubtedly has had much influence in setting the fashion for large sloops as racing yachts, in this country at least.

With the exception of the *Maria*, however, the American centerboard sloop of the '40's and early '50's was a safe and practical cruising yacht. The centerboard sloops designed by Steers were fine examples of the type. One of them, the *Una*, lasted about fifty years, ending her days on the Lakes as a cruising schooner. She was originally 65'-0" on the waterline, 17'-10" beam, 6'-4" depth of hold and 6'-6" draft. Another of his sloops, the *Sylvia*, measured 81'-6" overall, 24'-6" beam and 7'-0" depth, rabbet to planksheer; her centerboard was 15'-6" long. In later years she was also converted to a schooner. It can be seen from the dimensions of these sloops that the centerboard yachts of that period were by no means small craft. They were good fast cruisers too, for the *Una* sailed from New York to Boston in 32 hours. They were all sufficiently seaworthy for coastal cruising and their owners would have felt no qualms in a summer crossing of the Atlantic.

Because of the shoal anchorage of the New York Yacht Club at Weehawken, later at "the foot of Cort Street" on the Brooklyn shore and on

the Jersey side from Commnipaw to Kill van Kull, the shallow centerboard yacht was most popular with club owners. The early racing courses
were also in shoal water, with the necessary result that racing yachts were
of light draft. Generally speaking, the yachts of the New York Yacht
Club members, particularly the sloops, grew increasingly beamier and
shallower each year after 1846. Schooners too followed the trend of the
sloops, and by 1851 the trend of design in the neighborhood of New
York was definitely toward the production of what later were called
"skimming dishes."

Conditions at Boston differed from those at New York, for the yacht
anchorages were in deep water, as were the racing courses and cruising
grounds. The Bostonian yachtsman therefore turned toward deep draft
yachts on the lines of the local pilot-boats. To Boston, perhaps, belongs
the honor of having the first professional yacht designer. He was a young
Dane, Louis Winde, (pronounced as the verb to wind) who was a
college graduate and a trained naval architect, educated in Denmark.
His first noted yacht was the schooner *Northen Light* built in 1839; this
vessel was followed by other successes, all on the Baltimore Clipper or
pilot-boat model. Some of the best known of these were the schooners
Pet and *Brenda* of 1845, the *Coquette* of 1846 (later the Boston pilot-
boat whose portrait is now in the rooms of the Boston Pilots' Association) and the *Volante* built in 1855.

The *Northen Light* was a sharp clipper schooner 62'-6" on deck,
17'-6" beam and 7'-3" depth of hold and 69$^{90}/_{50}$ tons burthen; she had a
short heavy head with trail-boards, billet and head-rails. Her deck arrangement was that of the pilot-boat, with a long low quarterdeck raised
about 8 inches above the main deck. The *Northen Light* was heavily
sparred; having a bowsprit reaching 16'-0" outboard, 67'-0" mainmast,
64'-0" foremast, 37'-0" mainboom, 18'-5" fore gaff and an 18'-9" main
gaff, with a short main-topmast. She was built by Whitmore and Hol-
brook and for many years was a popular trial-horse for any schooner,

whether yacht, pilot-boat, fisherman or trader that had any pretensions to speed; sharing this particular honor with the revenue cutter *Hamilton*.

The *Coquette* was Winde's masterpiece and was somewhat similar to the *Northen Light*. Her dimensions were 62'-3" on the waterline, 18'-8" beam, 8'-8" depth of hold and 9'-4" extreme draft. The *Coquette* was celebrated for weatherliness and for having beaten the big sloop *Maria* in a match race. In appearance she was a long, low pilot-boat schooner with a long graceful cutwater.

The smaller schooner *Brenda*, built the year before *Coquette* was launched, was 48'-0" overall. This schooner went to Bermuda in May, 1849, and while there she won a race against a cutter, the *Pearl*, which was the first international race so far as American yachting records show. Winde went into partnership with a shipwright named Clinckard in the '40's and the firm built most of the yachts designed by Winde as well as a number of pilot-boats and other craft. In his designs, Winde held very closely to the Baltimore Clipper models; his vessels having high rising floors, sharp convex waterlines, moderately hollow buttocks and much drag to the keel, the turn of the bilge being at the load-waterline. His few existing models show a good deal of flare in the topsides. It cannot be said that Winde introduced any great innovations in design, but, like Steers, his designs had much influence on contemporary craft.

For some years previous to 1850 the idea of an international race between the crack yachts of the United States and England had been in the minds of the Stevens brothers, in fact it has been said that the *Onkahye* was built with this in mind. It was not until the great industrial exhibition of 1851 in London, however, that the idea became reality. The suggestion of an American merchant in England that an American schooner be sent over to try conclusions with English yachts enabled the Stevens' to interest their friends in the matter. The result was the building of the famous schooner-yacht *America* by William H. Brown. George Steers who was then employed by Brown, his own shipbuilding firm of Hathorne and Steers having been dissolved in 1849, was commissioned to furnish the model and to supervise the construction. His reputation for being able to turn out fast schooners and his former association with the Stevens' made the choice of his design a natural sequence of events. It is hardly necessary to repeat the history of this distinguished vessel for accounts of her career have been published in great

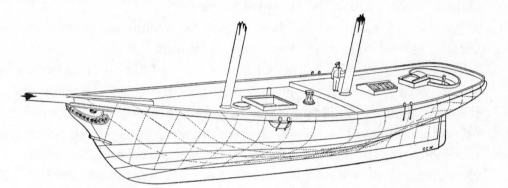

YACHT *America.*

detail, not only in histories of the America's Cup, but also in yachting magazines during each year in which a race for the Cup was held.

Certain comments on the *America* are necessary, nevertheless, due to the mistaken ideas prevalent concerning her model and her designer In the first place, the statement has often been made that this schooner was the first to have a hollow entrance. The plans in earlier chapters are sufficient to refute this claim. There is also the impression that the *America* was the fastest American schooner yacht then in existence. This is really nothing more than conjecture for the vessel was not tried against any of the contemporary cracks, apparently because of a lack of sufficient time. The fact that the *America's* greatest beam was abaft the middle of her waterline length has been hailed as an innovation of Steers', but this too is untrue for vessels had been so built before 1800. In 1794 the British captured a French frigate so constructed, the *Pomone* and many of the Virginia pilot-boats had the same feature. A large number of American

313

schooners built before 1850 were also designed in this manner, so the position of the *America's* greatest beam cannot be said to have been exceptional. In view of the fact that Griffiths in the United States and Scott Russell in England had both published theories in regard to hull forms having the features of design just mentioned, previous to the building of the *America*, it is obvious that Steers was not an originator of the basic principles of design used in the famous schooner.

A great many plans of the *America* have been published in the past; unfortunately, however, no two agree. The plans published herewith (Plate XV), by courtesy of *Yachting* magazine and Mr. W. P. Stevens, are proposed as being the only ones that show the vessel accurately in the original form. The *America* was built from a model, but even if the original model could be identified with certainty, it would not follow that the correct lines might be obtained, for it is tradition that Steers changed her lines somewhat in laying her down on the mould-loft floor. In collecting the various published plans, it was found that all of them that had any claim to authenticity were based on four sources, the dates of which are prior to 1876. The earliest one of the four may be the lines published in Griffiths' *Marine Architecture*, for they are probably taken from the original half-model, in view of the close friendship that appears to have existed between Griffiths and Steers. The only plan that is known to exist which can be dated as having been made while the schooner was in her original state is the one found in the records of the British Admiralty and reproduced here. It is an undated plan, probably made in the Portsmouth Dockyard in 1851 or 1852. The reason for this identification is that the sail plan was made in '52 by George Ratsey, the English sailmaker, from measurements of the vessel, while she was in the dock at Portsmouth. The similarity in details of the hull in both lines and sail plan indicate some relationship between the two drawings. One thing is certain, the lines were taken off prior to 1856, for in that year the *America's* name was changed to *Camilla* and had her lines been taken off after this change the plan would show the new name. When the undated Admiralty plan is compared with the contemporary prints and paintings such as the H. Sargent picture belonging to the British yacht designer Charles E. Nicholson, the Brown and Severin print of 1851, the Ackerman & Co. print of 1851, and the Robins' lithograph in the New York Yacht Club, it will be found that pictures and plan agree in detail. The pictures mentioned are reproduced in the standard history of the yacht, *The Yacht America*,[1] by Thompson, Stephens and Swan. When it is also considered that the Admiralty plan was made by men trained and experienced in taking off lines, and (if the vessel were measured in the dockyard) working in a drydock specially fitted for the purpose, the likelihood of the plan being accurate is greatly enhanced.

There are two other source plans, one made in Pritcher's yard at Northfleet, England, just prior to the rebuilding of the *America* in 1859. The other was made by Captain L. Braine, U.S.N., while the yacht was on the Navy List after the Civil War. Neither plan shows the care in detail evident in the Admiralty plan, nor do they agree in important particulars with the prints and pictures just mentioned. The rigged model in the Model Room of the New York Yacht Club is obviously in error and is not deserving of serious consideration. The half-model there requires further identification before being acceptable as evidence. In passing it may be added that most published plans have been "restorations" or very poor copies of the Admiralty plan by way of the Ratsey plan, which was a hasty and incomplete copy of the plan made in the dockyard as far as hull was concerned.

The advent of the *America* did not bring about any immediate change in the trend of design of yachts in the United States, except to increase the popularity of the hollow bow. As new yachts were launched, it was noticeable that they became increasingly sharp forward after the launch of the *America;* though the trend in this direction can be traced as far back as 1846. The success of the *America*, however, was effective in accentuating this feature of design and in spreading the principle outside

[1] Charles E. Lauriat Co., Boston, 1925.

of New York. The fact that this celebrated schooner was a keel boat and that nearly all her immediate successors were centerboarders serves to show how little she influenced the trend of design around New York, so far as type was concerned.

The effect of measurement rules was becoming apparent at about this period. The first method of handicapping yachts employed in the New York Yacht Club was the use of the Custom House Tonnage Measurement, which was followed by comparison of displacement, as found from measuring the half-model or by actually weighing the yacht in some kind of a balance dock. In 1848 the club returned to the Custom House rule; handicapping being on the basis of from 35 to 45 seconds per ton by either Custom House or displacement as the existing rule required. In 1850 the rule was changed to a formula that measured length, beam and depth somewhat after the Custom House method of measurement; in 1856 the sail area was measured for handicap but in 1859 this was replaced with a measurement based on length of waterline and beam. Other clubs followed suit, though some employed length overall or the mean between length on the waterline and overall as a basis for handicap as early as 1856. Measurement rules based on these factors remained in force until 1870. Sail area and displacement are the two factors of measurement that have the most to do with the comparative speed of yachts having the same overall length; the proportion of one to the other controls speed to a very great extent once length is used as a basis of comparison. It is obvious that all these early rules left much to be desired in the measurement of this ratio. Measuring displacement alone put no limitations on sail area, so it was only necessary to put as big a sail area as was possible on a hull of minimum displacement to "cheat" the measurement and handicap. The sail area rule had no effect on fixing any minimum on displacement and the length or mean-length rules were equally open to "cheating." The length-and-beam measurement was also meaningless as far as the two important speed factors were concerned. The particular difficulty in all measurement rules, as said before, has not been in their

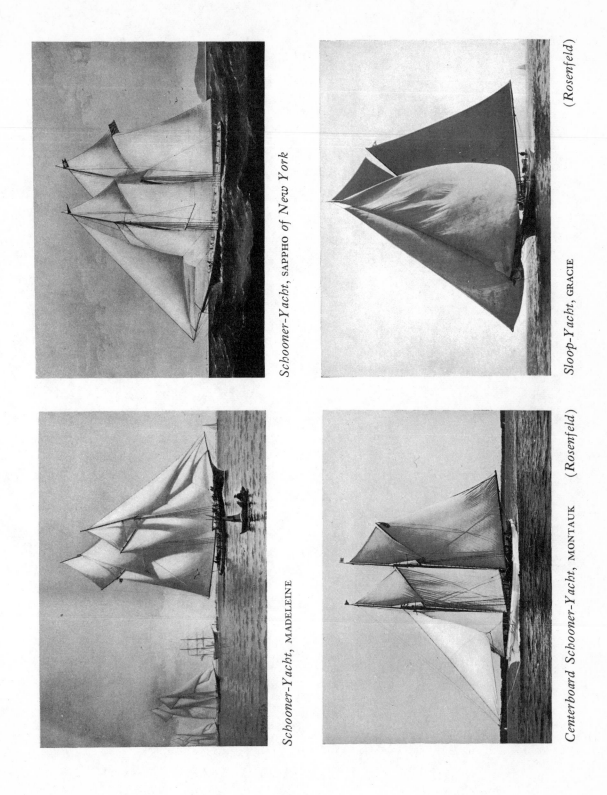

Schooner-Yacht, SAPPHO of New York

Sloop-Yacht, GRACIE　　　　(Rosenfeld)

Schooner-Yacht, MADELEINE

Centerboard Schooner-Yacht, MONTAUK　　(Rosenfeld)

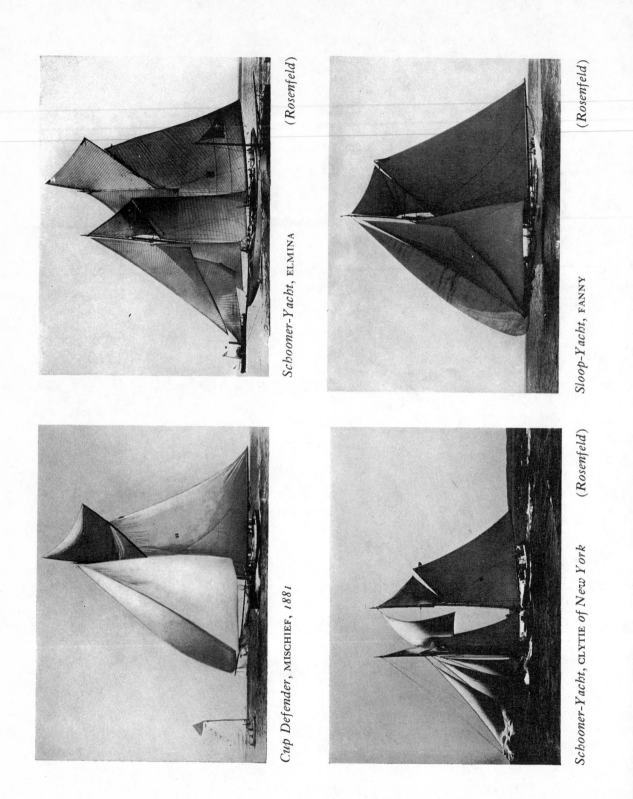

Schooner-Yacht, ELMINA (*Rosenfeld*)

Sloop-Yacht, FANNY (*Rosenfeld*)

Cup Defender, MISCHIEF, *1881*

Schooner-Yacht, CLYTIE *of New York* (*Rosenfeld*)

inability to fairly rate existing yachts but rather in the trends of design set up in the models of new craft built to "fit" the particular rule in force. In early days of American yachting the practical considerations of stability and ballast also had much effect on the trend of yacht design.

In the early yachts, rock and pig iron ballast, stowed inside the hull

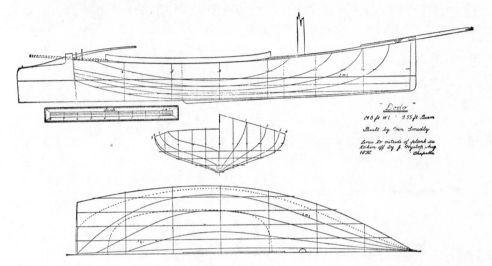

Figure 61. Lines of the sand-bagger DODO.

between the floor-timbers, was common. While some yachts, such as *Onkahye* and *Maria*, tried lead outside, these experiments were very rare. Iron, moulded to fit between the frames, as was used in the *America*, was the highest development of inside ballast. It had been the practice, since the days of privateers and slavers, to use shifting ballast when by the wind to carry a heavy press of canvas in a breeze. Unless very large crews were carried, there were practical objections to the practice in large seagoing yachts, but in small half-decked boats, where one man could handle enough ballast to make an appreciable difference in the amount of sail that could be carried by the wind, shifting ballast had great possibilities as long as it was not barred by the racing rules. Even in fairly large craft of the light displacement and beamy type the shifting ballast could be effectively used. When this kind of ballast was to be used it

317

was customary for the racers to agree as to whether the ballast was to be brought "home" or was to be thrown overboard, if desired, during the race.

The result of the early measurement rules and the use of shifting ballast may be summed up in the so-called "sand-baggers." These were sloops or cats 18 to 28 feet in length, racing under a length or mean-length rule, and were popular racers in New York waters as early as 1855. Their popularity finally extended to Boston, the Lakes, as well as to southern

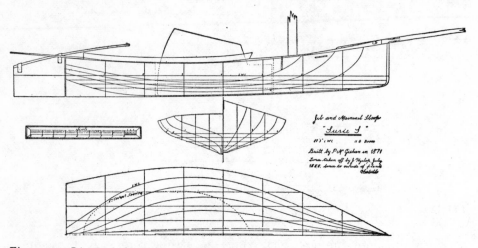

Figure 62. Lines of the famous sand-bagger SUSIE S.

waters. The "sand-bagger" developed from the small half-decked boats of the New York watermen, used for commercial purposes and as party-boats. The watermen were keen sportsmen, willing "to bet their shirt" on their boats. As a result of the competition between these early boats, local builders gradually developed a class of wide shallow centerboard craft designed to carry an enormous amount of sail by means of shifting ballast and great beam. Most of these boats had perpendicular ends and two rigs, sloop and cat; two mast steps being fitted so that they could race under either rig on short notice. No better illustration of the type can be given than the plans of five boats, built by noted builders of the class, *Dodo, Susie S., Pluck and Luck, Comet* and *Truant*. The sail plan

318

of *Susie S.* gives some idea of the big rig carried by these "racing machines." The early boats of the class were less heavily canvassed and some of them had short counters or fantail sterns. The only early builder of these sloops whose name is known, aside from "Bob" Fish, was a man named Ingersoll, who turned out a number of fast boats, one of which went to France. It is rather interesting to discover that the most recently

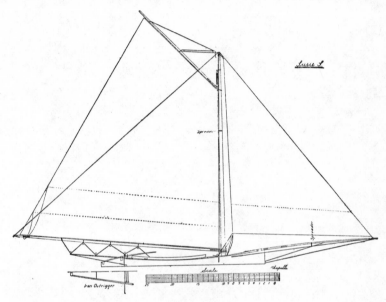

Figure 63. Sail plan of the sand-bagger SUSIE S.

built racing dinghies are reversions to the "sand-bagger" in design; though the shifting ballast of the dinghy consists only of her crew. The period of the "sand-bagger" lasted until the late '80's; the height of their popularity around New York and Boston was between 1865 and 1885.

The *Dodo* (Figure 61) was a "Penny-Bridge Boat," so called because it was built in the neighborhood of Penny Bridge on Gowanus Creek, Brooklyn. She was built by "Hen" Smedley, a carpenter by trade who was not only a clever builder of this type of craft, but an excellent boat sailor as well.

The *Susie S.* (Figures 62 and 63) was considered to have been one of the best of the type. She was built by "Pat" McGiehan, a celebrated builder whom W. P. Stephens has described as having been "an excellent judge of bad whiskey." The *Susie S.* was somewhat notorious because of her part in a gambler's race that received some undesired publicity. Her career was varied; before becoming the *Susie S.* she had raced in New Orleans' waters as the *Albertine*, before which she had raced in New

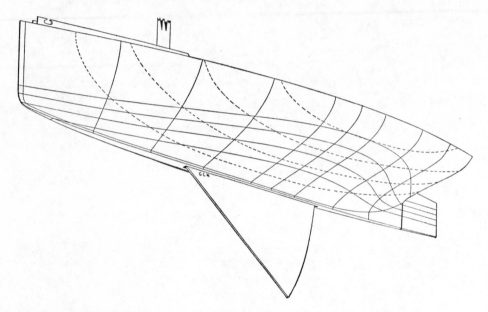

SAND-BAGGER *Susie S.*

York regattas as the *Bella*. A "sand-bagger" of her size had American Elm frames spaced 12 inches apart, sided 2 inches and moulded an inch and a half. The planking was three-quarters of an inch thick; stem and stern-posts sided about 3 inches. The mast had a diameter of 10 inches at the deck, 5 inches at the truck. From 25 to 28 sand-bags formed the ballast, each weighing about 45 pounds. Racing crews of the 28-foot boats numbered as many as seventeen, who were mostly engaged in handling the ballast. The crews of "sand-baggers" were usually made up of water-front toughs and the races could hardly be classed as "gentlemanly."

The *Comet* (Figure 64) was one of the smaller examples of the type;

she was modelled by the clever A. Cary Smith, while an apprentice of the great "Bob" Fish. Both of these men acquired fame in the design of large yachts and will be mentioned later.

Pluck and Luck (Figure 65) was modelled by "Jake" Schmidt of Williamsburg who was a hatter by trade. In spite of this doubtful training

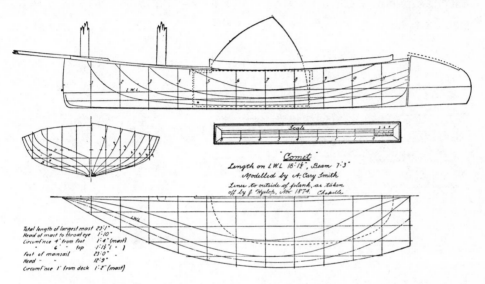

Figure 64. Lines of the sand-bagger COMET.

for yacht design, Schmidt was a great builder of "sand-baggers" and an able boatman to boot. Among the cracks of the "sand-bagger" class built by this man were the *Dare Devil* and *Parole. Pluck and Luck* was one of the favorites of her particular size of racers.

Truant (Figure 66) was built from a model made by William Kyle of Harlem Kills and was usually raced as a cat. Kyle, like Fish, could design larger yachts with reasonable success. This was something that most of the "sand-bagger" designers could not do, for they were uneducated men who had developed one model which they used over and over again with only minor changes.

The "sand-baggers" were extraordinarily fast boats in smooth water. Their flaring topsides enabled them to carry their ballast farther out from the centerline than a boat having topsides more nearly vertical, a thing recently rediscovered by the dinghy designers. Were it not for the trend of design fostered by the "sand-bagger" there would have been no serious objection to the type, for they satisfied the class of yachtsmen who wanted speed at all costs. However, because of their speed, the "sand-bagger" models were adapted to larger yachts and their dangerous characteristics became accentuated; it was the class of yacht which developed

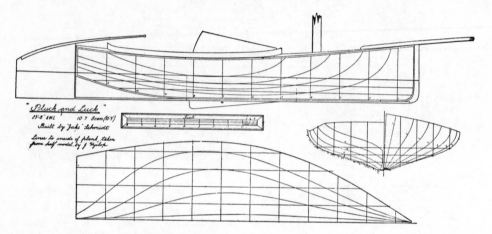

Figure 65. Lines of the sand-bagger PLUCK AND LUCK.

from the "sand-baggers" that has given the centerboard yacht a bad reputation that should have been credited to poor design rather than to inherent qualities of the type.

It would be improper to assume that only the modellers just mentioned were successful in turning out the "sand-bagger" for there were a great many other builders of local reputation, such as George Roahr, known as "Buckshot," who was a shell builder and a noted "sand-bagger" designer too; there was also C. A. Willis, nicknamed "Neef," of Port Washington, who turned out the crack *Cruiser* in 1868. Most of the builders of this class of boat made their reputations soon after the Civil War.

The best way to show the trends of yacht design is to follow the changes of racing rules and to discuss the most distinguished yacht designers of each period in yachting history. A great many designers and builders have turned out successful craft, but only those whose careers were particularly notable can be mentioned.

Robert "Bob" Fish, born in New York City in 1813, was the son

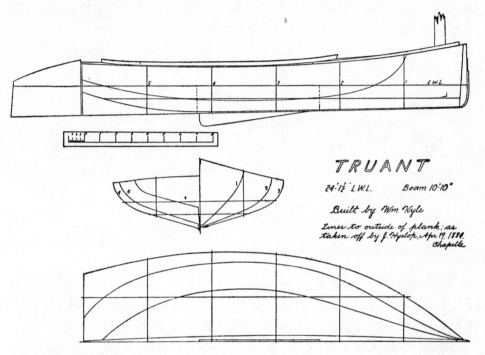

TRUANT
24.1½" L.W.L.   Beam 10·10″
Built by Wm Kyle
Lines to outside of plank; as
taken off by J. Hyslop. Apr. 19. 1886.
Chapelle

Figure 66. Cat TRUANT.

of David Fish who had a boatshop at the foot of Roosevelt Street, East River. "Bob" Fish learned the trade of boatbuilding and for some time had a shop on South Street. While there he modelled his first boat of large size, the sloop *Newburg* in 1845. Fish moved to Pamrapo, New Jersey, about 1850 and there became active in yacht construction. Among the yachts built by him soon after his removal to Pamrapo was the very handsome centerboard sloop *Bianca* built in '51. He also built the centerboard sloop *Truant* which crossed the Atlantic in 1853 and the centerboard sharpie sloop *Luckey* in 1855. He built the first cat-boat seen in

323

England, the *Una*, for the Earl Mount Charles in 1852; later he sold one of his cats in Germany where the type became known as "Bubfish" boats in his honor. Others of his yachts include *Undine* and *Gertrude* built in '52, *Victoria*, 1856, (later a blockade-runner, during the Civil War), *Eva*, 1865, and *Coming*, 1868; all centerboard sloops when first built. He turned out a few schooners, the handsome *Meteor* in 1869; the splendid big keel schooner *Enchantress* (Plate XVI) in 1870; the second *Wanderer* in 1871, (the first was the schooner that became notorious as a

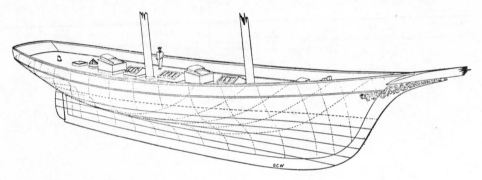

SCHOONER-YACHT *Enchantress*.

slaver and which was designed by W. J. Rowland of Port Jefferson, L.I.) and he altered the big *Sappho* in 1869. Fish commanded the *Enchantress* for some years and was a good seaman as well as a designer.

Many of his contemporaries considered Fish to be nearly the equal of Steers as a designer, but generally speaking, the yachts designed by Fish were of the shallow centerboard type following the undesirable trend of his time. His work on *Sappho's* alterations in '69 apparently interested him in the keel type, however, and *Enchantress* was the result. It cannot be said that his conception of a keel schooner, as represented by *Enchantress*, was strikingly original for she was very much like the *Sappho*. Comparing the two, *Enchantress* was a little deeper, somewhat narrower, a little longer overall, but somewhat shorter on the waterline. Though she was evidently a very fast schooner, the *Enchantress* was not a very successful racer. In her campaign in England, lasting three seasons (part of the time under the command of Fish), she suffered from break-downs from trying to carry too much sail. While in England she had 8 feet added to her stern, which lengthened her waterline a few feet and increased her overall length to about 144′-0″. In spite of her size and power, she appears to have been somewhat overhatted. At the time she was being lengthened, the English newspapers reported the following spar di-

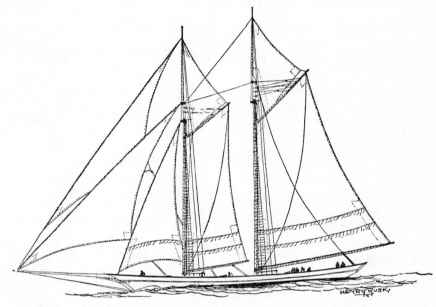

SCHOONER-YACHT *Enchantress* OF NEW YORK.

mensions; main mast, deck to hounds, 69′-0″; masthead, 11′-0″; maintopmast, 50′-0″; fore mast, deck to hounds, 64′-0″; masthead, 10′-0″; foretopmast, 48′-0″; main-boom, 82′-0″; main gaff, 50′-0″; fore gaff, 26′-0″; main jackyard topsail yard 44′-0″ and fore jackyard topsail yard 35′-0″. It is not clear whether these were her original spars or not. The *Enchantress* was built by S. Pine of Greenpoint, N.Y., and was beautifully finished inside and out. She had the reputation of being extremely fast on a reach, but was very difficult to get into trim. She required a crew of sixteen to handle her. Next to *Sappho* she was considered the fastest keel schooner in the United States.

Richard Fanning Loper was born in Philadelphia in 1800 and went to sea in his youth. He was second mate to Captain N. B. Palmer in the sloop *Hero* on a voyage to the Northwest Coast. He was a member of an old Philadelphia family and related to one of the Stonington, Connecticut, shipping families, the Fannings. Loper was the inventor of a screw propeller, the "Loper Wheel," used in some of the early American screw men-of-war and revenue cutters. He was a keen yachtsman and was interested in naval architecture and marine engineering. His business interests were varied; he controlled a steam packet line between Philadelphia and Hartford, Connecticut, and was connected with the Harlan and Hollingsworth and the Cramps shipyards. An amateur designer, Loper turned out a number of successful yachts, all on one model slightly altered from time to time. His method of designing can best be described as the "cut and try" method; in spite of his engineering ability he appears to have blindly followed the methods of design that were prevalent among the "sand-bagger" builders. His first yacht was the *Madgie*, a centerboard sloop built for him in '57 on his model. Loper also modelled a second yacht of this name, another named *Josephine* and the fine centerboard schooner *Palmer* which was a candidate for the America's Cup defense in 1871. Loper once stated that all of these yachts were on the same model, progressively altered for each successive vessel.

The *Madgie* (Figure 67) went through many changes which will serve to illustrate the state of yacht design after the death of Steers. She was built by Byerly and Son in Philadelphia and launched early in '57. After two seasons, Loper put a new stern on her and changed her to a schooner (in 1859). In 1860 he gave her a longer bow and finally sold her in 1864. The new owner renamed her *Magic* and she sailed in her first New York Yacht Club race in 1865. In 1869 she was placed in the hands of David Carll at City Island and completely rebuilt, and again changed owners. The next year, 1870, she was one of the fleet that defended the America's Cup against the *Cambria*, not only beating the challenger, but also the fleet, made up of such noted racers as *Halcyon, Fleet-*

326

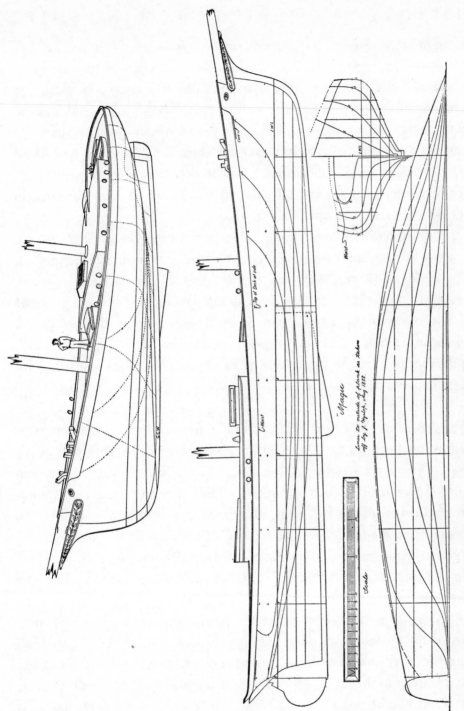

"Magic"

Lines to outside of plank as taken off by J. Peploe, Aug. 1888.

Scale

Figure 67.- Lines of the Cup Defender MAGIC, *of New York.*

wing, Idler, Madeleine, Sylvie, America, Rambler and *Phantom*. In 1873 the *Magic* was again rebuilt and eventually she was sold to Key West where she was used as a pilot-boat, and also as a supply-boat for the sponging fleet for many years; only recently becoming worn out. In spite of the bad reputation given most yachts of her type and date she was a fast and seaworthy vessel after her alteration in '69; the Key West pilots thought very highly of her capabilities. It is quite apparent that her numerous changes had left but little evidence of Loper's work in her design by 1870. Loper died in 1880.

Halcyon, one of *Magic's* competitors in the 1870 Cup race, will serve to show that the latter was no exception in design to others of her period. The *Halcyon* (Figure 68) was built by J. B. Harris of Port Jefferson, Long Island, in 1866; apparently he also designed her. Little is known of Harris save that he altered the Steers-designed sloop *Widgeon* to a schooner. *Halcyon* was not the equal of the fast *Magic*, finishing ninth in the race of 1870. Her poor showing can probably be accounted for by her comparatively full run.

Another modeller of great fame during the years following the Civil War was "Phil" Ellsworth. He was one of five brothers, oystermen, who had come from Little Egg Harbor, New Jersey, to Pamrapo about 1840. One of the brothers, "Joe," became a noted racing skipper, and sailed the yachts modelled by brother "Phil" with great success. Among the yachts turned out by "Phil" Ellsworth were the centerboard sloops *Fanita, Kangaroo, Elephant, Crocodile, Penquin, Tigress* and the big sloop *Atlantic* designed as an America's Cup defense candidate in 1886. He also turned out a number of centerboard schooners, among them the *Grayling* and the big *Montauk*. His designs were marked by having very long sharp bows and short full runs; the ill-formed run probably prevented his models from ever reaching the speed promised by the fine entrance. *Elephant* (Figure 69) was one of his most successful boats and has a better run than most of the Ellsworth models. She was built in 1879 by Alonzo Smith at Islip, Long Island, and shows the characteristic mid-

328

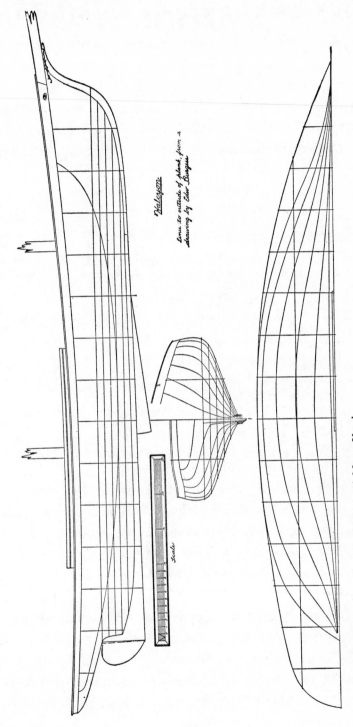

Halcyon

Lines to outside of plank, from a drawing by Edw. Burgess

Scale

Figure 68. Schooner-Yacht HALCYON of New York.

329

section and entrance of this designer's yachts. Ellsworth was also known as "Capt'n Phip." *Atlantic* was his last yacht of note.

Joseph B. Van Deusen was prominent as a modeller from about 1851 to 1876. He was the designer of the centerboard schooner *Columbia* built at Chester, Pennsylvania, in 1871, as well as of the centerboard schooners *Fleur de Lys* and *Phantom* built in 1865 and of the keel schoon-

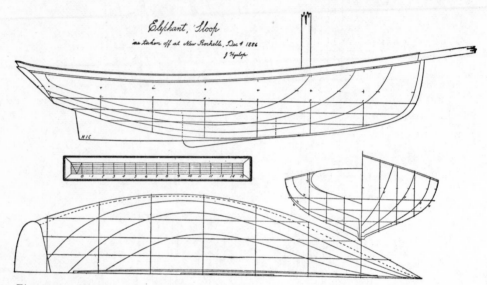

Figure 69. Sloop-yacht ELEPHANT.

ers *Alarm*, 1864, *Fleetwing*, 1865, and *Rambler*, 1865. The *Columbia* was one of the fastest centerboard schooners ever built, though she had the very doubtful honor of having been the first American yacht to lose a heat in an America's Cup race (1871, against *Livonia*); but she also had the distinction of holding the record for thirty-miles in these races that was not broken until 1934. Her record has been mistakenly accredited to the later cutter *Columbia* who defended the Cup in 1899 and 1901. Van Deusen designed the big centerboard schooner *Mohawk*: 121'-0" waterline, 30'-4" beam, 6'-0" draft and 235 feet from her boom-end to the tip of her flying-jibboom. This big schooner capsized and drowned her owner, an accident which attracted attention to the faults of the extreme "skimming-dishes" among the large yachts. Van Deusen also re-designed the schooner *L'Hirondelle*, that afterwards became famous as the ocean racer *Dauntless*. This designer appears to have been a man of great intelligence and some education; unfortunately little is known of his career, outside of his work in yacht design.

The brothers C. and R. Poillon were shipwrights who specialized in the construction of yachts and pilot-boats; they had a shipyard and sawmill on the Brooklyn waterfront, later moving to Gowanus Creek. Their foreman, William Townsend, did all their designing except for a few yachts built from the designs of "Bob" Fish, "Phil" Ellsworth and A. Cary Smith. Among the yachts modelled by Townsend were the centerboard schooners *Peerless*, 1871 and *Clio*, 1873; and the keel schooner *Sappho* built in 1867. He also modelled many pilot-boats.

Sappho (Figure 70) was probably the best-known yacht modelled by Townsend for she was a Cup Defender and the subject of much contro-versy. She was built by the Poillons on speculation and was the largest schooner yacht that had been built at the time of her launch, in '67. Her builders sent her to England to be sold, with strict orders, it is said, that she was not to race. However, her skipper disobeyed orders and raced her in cruising rig and improperly ballasted, with the result that she was soundly thrashed by the British schooners *Cambria* and *Aline*. It was this race that led to the first challenge for the America's Cup, for it gave the *Cambria's* owner, James Ashbury, the idea that his schooner could beat anything in the United States. Not being sold, the *Sappho* was brought home. Here she was eventually sold and, in 1869, her new owner put her in the hands of "Bob" Fish to be altered, in spite of the fact that she had never had a fair trial in her original form. Though Townsend and the Poillons protested, Fish "hipped" the *Sappho* out below the water-line, padding her frames at the turn of the bilges 7 inches on each side, in such a way that her measured beam was not increased; altered her rig and rearranged and increased her ballast. The *Sappho* was undoubt-edly a faster boat after the alterations, but it seems to have been in spite

331

of the "hipping" rather than because of it, for the *Sappho* never lacked stability. Her original trouble was due to a poor rig and having her ballast too high and improperly distributed. In 1871 the *Sappho* was considered to be the fastest keel yacht in America and is the yacht referred to in the discussion of "speed-length ratio" in Chapter Two. Much of her speed was undoubtedly due to her very large rig as well as to her lines; many critics thought that a longer and slightly wider counter would have made her even better than she was. Her successful defense of the America's Cup in '71 and her races abroad gave her an important part in American yachting history. Her lines show her before the alteration made by Fish.

Among the lesser known modellers active between 1851 and 1885 was D. D. Mallory, of Noank, Connecticut. He turned out many fast centerboard sloops, including the *Mystic* in 1856, *Richmond* in 1857, *Haswell* in 1858, *Plover* in 1859 and *Zouave* in 1861. There was also J. B. Voorhis, or Voris, who modelled the sloop *Madeleine*, built by David Kirby at Rye, New York, in 1869. In 1870 she was changed to a schooner; her hull was altered in 1871, and again in 1873, after which she became one of the fastest centerboard schooners in the New York Yacht Club fleet and successfully defended the America's Cup against the Canadian challenger *Countess of Dufferin* in 1876. Voorhis also designed the keel schooner *Tarolinta* in 1870. D. O. Richmond, of Mystic, Connecticut, won some fame when he modelled and built the noted centerboard sloop *Fanny*, (72'-0" overall, 68'-0" waterline, and 23'-9" beam) in 1873. "Dave" Kirby also modelled some fast yachts including the celebrated centerboard sloop *Arrow*, 61'-8" waterline, in 1874, and the earlier but less successful centerboard sloop *Addie V.* of 1867. He also modelled the centerboard sloop *Pocahontas* as an America's Cup defense candidate in 1881, but she was so slow as to receive the opprobious nickname "Pokey." John F. Mumm was another designer of centerboard sloops; one of his best yachts was the *Daphne* built in 1885.

There were a number of fast yachts in existence during the '60's and

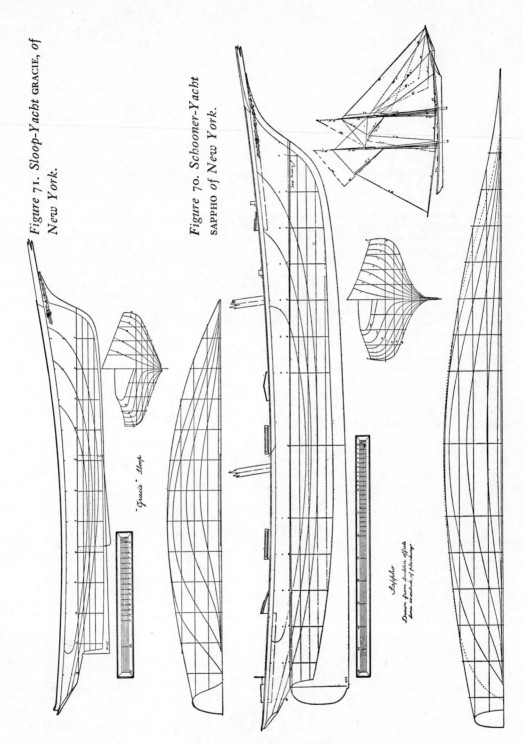

Figure 71. *Sloop-Yacht* GRACIE, *of New York.*

Figure 70. *Schooner-Yacht* SAPPHO *of New York.*

"Gracie" Sloop

Sappho

Drawn from builders offsets
Lines to scale of plankings

333

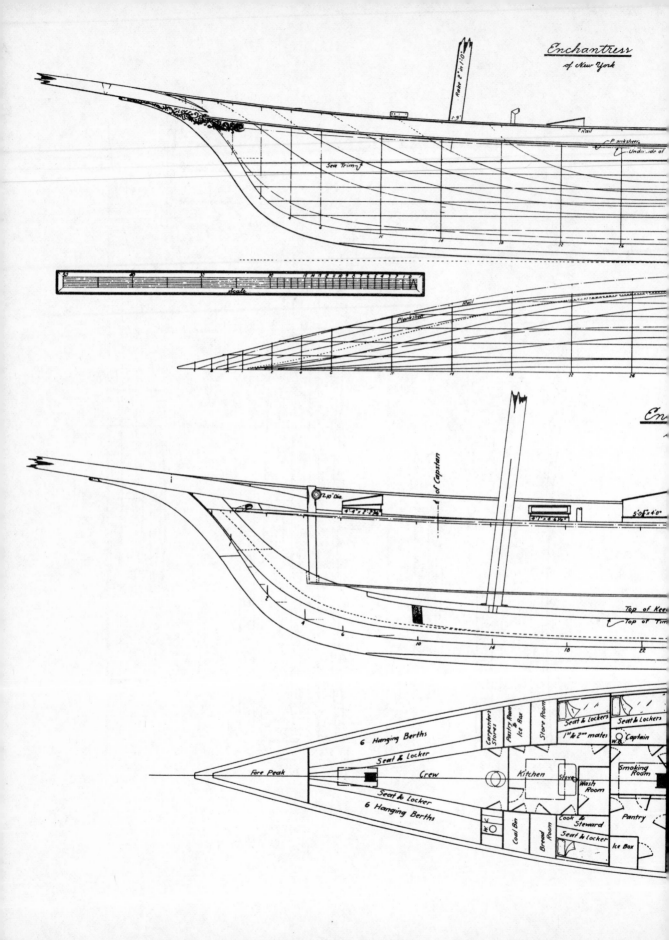

Enchantress
of New York

Rake 2" in 1'0"

1-9"

Rail

P. sinksheer
Underside of

Sea Trim

Scale

Plankshear

Rail

En

£ of Capstan

2.10" Dia.

5'0" x 4'0"

Top of Keel
Top of Tim

Carpenters Stores
Pastry Room to Ice Box
Store Room

Seat & Lockers
Seat & Lockers

1st & 2nd mates
Captain
W.C.

6 Hanging Berths

Seat & Locker

Fore Peak
Crew

Kitchen
Stove
Wash Room

Smoking Room

Seat & Locker
6 Hanging Berths

Coal Bin
Bread Room

Cook & Steward
Seat & Locker

Pantry

Ice Box

Plate XVI. Schooner Yacht ENCHANTRESS. Plan showing vessel before alteration in England. No reconstruction.

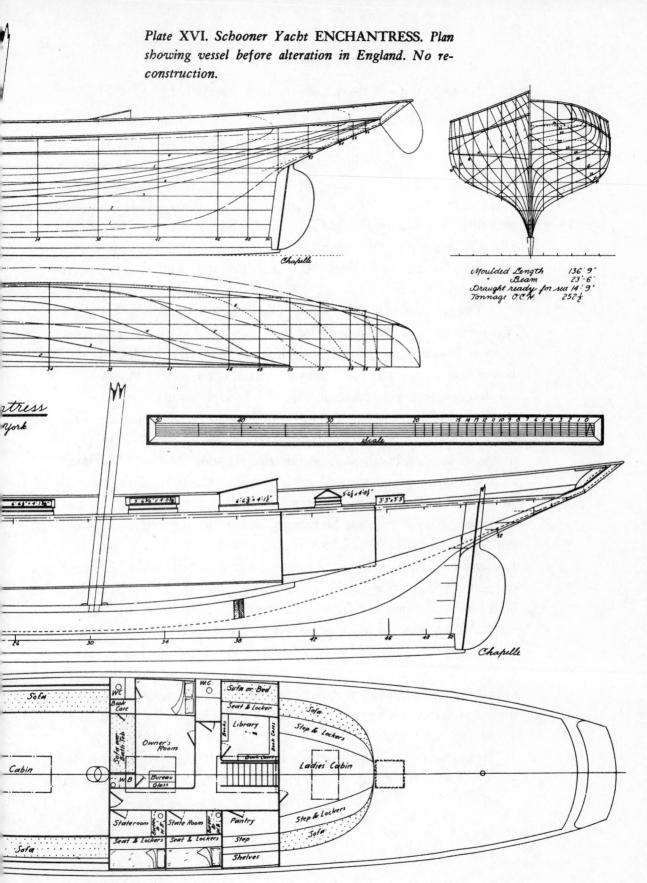

Moulded Length   136' 9"
Beam   23' 6"
Draught ready for sea 14' 9"
Tonnage O.C.H.   252½

Chapelle

Scale

Chapelle

Sofa · WC · Book Case · Sofa over Berth Tub · Owner's Room · Bureau Glass · Cabin · W.B · Stateroom · State Room · Seat & Lockers · Seat & Lockers · Sofa · W.C. · Sofa or Bed · Seat & Locker · Library · Books · Book Cases · Pantry · Step · Shelves · Sofa · Step & Lockers · Ladies' Cabin · Step & Lockers · Sofa

'70's that were modelled by men little known as yacht designers. The *Idler* schooner, built in 1864, was designed by Samuel Hartt Pook of clipper-ship fame; apparently the only yacht designed by this able architect. Among the yachts designed by men who were little known as yacht designers were the centerboard schooners *Vesta*, 1866, built, and probably modelled, by Daniel Carll, and *Tidal Wave*, designed by A. A. Scank. There was also the sloop *Gracie* (Figure 71), modelled by A. Polhemus of Nyack, New York. All these schooners and the sloop were shallow centerboarders.

In Boston, during the years that followed 1851, Dennison J. Lawlor was rising to fame as a designer of fast pilot-boats and schooner-yachts. New Brunswick born, Lawlor began modelling and building in East Boston about 1850. He is said to have been an apprentice of Winde's, but this has not been verified. Not only did Lawlor model some very fast yachts and pilot-boats, but also some very noted fishing schooners. One of his earliest yachts was the 73-foot keel schooner *Olata* built in 1853; five years later she became a New Orleans pilot-boat. In 1856 *Olata* went from Boston to St. Thomas, West Indies, in seven days under mainsail and jib only. Lawlor was probably best known for his pilot-boats and fishermen, and he will long be remembered in Boston waters as the designer of the great Boston pilot-boat *Hesper* and for the fishing schooners *Roulette* and *Sylph*. Probably no designer has left a more lasting influence on fishing schooners than this man. He was the adviser and friend of both Edward Burgess and the well-known designer of fishermen, Thomas F. McManus. One of the handsomest of Lawlor's models that exist is that of the pilot schooner *Dancing Feather*, 68 feet overall, built in 1853. Lawlor was well-read, an excellent draftsman and had the education required of a naval architect. Among his many famous designs is that for the brigantine *Newsboy*, a very fast vessel of her day. Not even Steers or Townsend had a wider experience than this great Boston designer.

The changes in measurement rule must again be referred to. The rule of 1859 had remained in force until 1870, when the old displacement measurement was tried again. In 1873 the "Cubic Contents" rule was tried; this measured the hull's volume below the lowest point of the covering board (deck at side). The weakness of the earlier rules, in controlling the trend toward shallow, beamy hulls, was not corrected by any of these new rules. The large cabin trunks and low freeboard of the "skimming dishes" were the causes of serious weakness in strength, in spite of the box-girder formed by the centerboard case. If a piece of paper is folded boat-shape and then bent upwards and downwards the movement of the sides inward and outward shows the effect of cutting the deck beams with the long cabin trunks. The plans of yachts of the period show better the results of these rules than any amount of description, however.

1880 introduced marked changes in the British rule. Without entering into a detailed account of the rule in force in England, it is sufficient to say that the trend in design there had been toward very narrow and extremely deep draft hulls, usually cutter-rigged. These yachts were wall-sided, flush-decked and very heavily ballasted. In the opposite extreme, they were as unhealthy a type of yacht as the shoal centerboarders. The change in the British rule was the first attempt to stop the trend in the direction of excessively narrow and deep yachts.

Rule changes are always marked by hot arguments as to what the intent of the rule-makers should be: whether they should aim at speed at all costs or whether they should try to produce a racer that will be suitable for a cruiser after her racing days are over. Seventy-five years of racing rule measurement have shown that there are grave difficulties in trying to legislate the racing-cruiser into existence.

While the English were tampering with their rule, the Americans were also trying to find a more perfect rule. The years between 1875 and 1889 were marked by furious arguments between American yachtsmen favoring the deep English type, known as "cutter-cranks," and those supporting the "skimming dishes." The introduction of the "cutter" type into America, and the change in measurement rules that resulted in a new trend in American yacht design can be traced to a book by P. R. Marret,

Yacht Building, the first book ever published on yacht design. This work was published in England soon after the *America* raced there, and ran through a number of editions. An American yachtsman, Mr. Robert Center, brought a copy of the book home with him in 1870 and, with A. Cary Smith, designed a cutter by means of directions given in the work. This vessel was of iron and was built somewhat on the lines of the cutter *Mosquito* which were published in the book. The *Mosquito* having been built of iron, and very successful in her day, probably influenced Center and Cary Smith in their choice of material. The new cutter, named *Vindex*, was the first iron yacht built in this country.

Archibald Cary Smith was born in New York City in 1837, the son of a Presbyterian minister in "Chelsea Village." When eighteen he was apprenticed to "Bob" Fish at Pamrapo, but learned little boatbuilding as he and Bob spent most of their time racing "sand-baggers." Later Cary Smith paid Leonard H. Boole, a former Webb apprentice, twenty-five dollars for instruction in mould-loft work and drafting. After trying yacht-designing for a while, Cary Smith turned to marine painting with much success, but eventually returned to his profession. After helping Center design *Vindex* he designed the schooner *Prospero* in 1873, the first American schooner to have the English pole bowsprit. The spar was held in such contempt, however, that it was soon removed, not to be seen again until Edward Burgess reintroduced the spar some years later. In 1879 Cary Smith designed the second iron yacht built in this country, the very able *Mischief*.

The *Mischief* (Figure 72), built by Harlan and Hollingsworth at Wilmington, Delaware, was a most successful yacht. She was narrower and deeper than the sloops of her time and had a few of the English cutter characteristics in her rig. She defended the America's Cup in 1881 against the second Canadian challenger, the sloop *Atalanta*, and was the first defender built from plans. The *Mischief* was 61'-0" on the waterline and had a cabin trunk 30'-0" long, 1'-6" high and 13'-10" wide; her cockpit was 9'-0" long. Her spars measured as follows: mast, deck to hounds

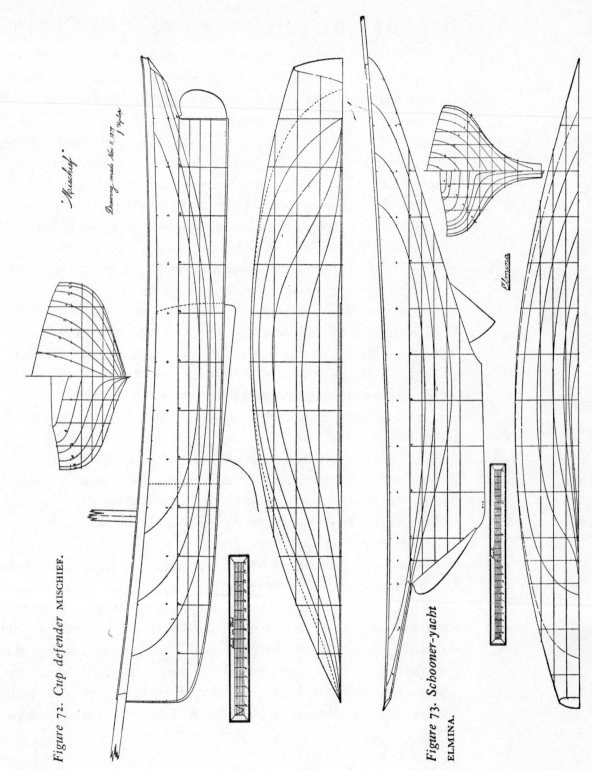

'Mischief'

Drawing made Nov. 11, 1877 J. Taylor

Figure 72. Cup defender MISCHIEF.

Elmina

Figure 73. Schooner-yacht ELMINA.

337

63'-6", topmast 41'-6", mainboom 62'-6", and she swung a 43'-8" spinnaker pole. At the time the *Mischief* defended the Cup she was, curiously enough, English owned. In the Cup trials she beat the fast *Gracie* and the sloops *Hildegard* and *Pocahontas*.

Cary Smith designed a great many other successful yachts, among them the schooners *Iroquois*, *Intrepid*, *Yampa* (one-time the German Emperor's yacht), *Fortuna*, *Lasca*, *Amorita* and *Elmina* (Figure 73). He also designed the unsuccessful America's Cup defense candidate *Priscilla* in 1885. The *Priscilla* was afloat in 1932, doing duty as a power mailboat running between Nassau and Great Abaco in the Bahamas. Cary Smith designed a great many commercial craft during his long career including a number of Long Island Sound steamers.

One of the chief supporters of the cutter type in this country was C. P. Kunhardt, editor of the then leading yachting magazine, *Forest and Stream*. He was an able writer, well educated, a designer of no mean ability and a fine sailor as well. He was succeeded by W. P. Stephens, a writer and designer of the same calibre, also a "cutter-crank." The introduction of deep draft yachts into American waters, particularly in the neighborhood of New York, was due to some extent to the efforts of these two men. As the fray grew hotter, the opposing sides took to extremes, the "cutter-cranks" defending the "plank on edge" yachts, and the "skimming dish" supporters, the "sand-baggers."

After the launch of the *Vindex* the number of American-built cutters steadily increased. In 1876 John Hyslop, an able amateur, designed the centerboard cutter *Petrel;* a modified keel cutter, the *Volante*, was built in 1877 from a design by Center and she was followed by two extreme cutters, the *Muriel*, designed by the English designer John Harvey in 1878, and the *Yolande* built the next year. None of these cutters could do much with the centerboarders, but in 1881 a cutter appeared that gave the centerboard camp a shock. This was the imported Scotch cutter *Madge*, 46'-0" overall, 39'-9" waterline, 7'-9" beam and 7'-8" draft, built in 1879 from designs by G. L. Watson. In seven matches with fast

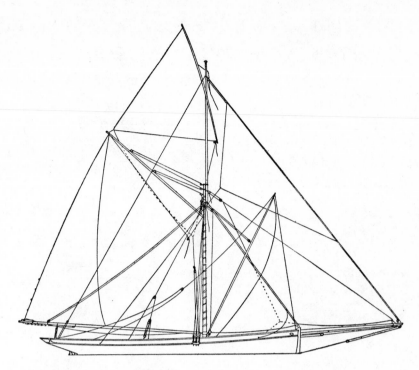

CUTTER (*after Dixon Kemp*).

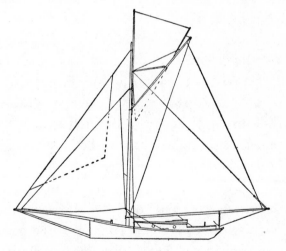

SLOOP (*after C. P. Kunhardt*).

339

centerboard sloops she lost but one. The *Madge* was followed by other importations: the *Clara* in 1885 and the famous *Minerva* in 1889, both of which met with success.

The difference in design of the cutters and sloops can be illustrated by the *Gracie* and the *Bedouin* (Figure 74). The latter was designed by Harvey in 1881 and built at City Island that winter. She had the reefing bowsprit and mainmast placed well aft, typical of the English practice.

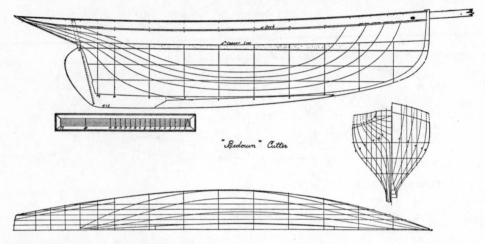

Figure 74. Cutter-Yacht BEDOUIN.

The *Gracie*, after her launch in 1868, had undergone many changes. When first built she was 60'-3" overall and 18'-8" beam. In 1869 she was lengthened 2'-0" aft and in 1874 she was again lengthened so that she was 72'-9" overall. In 1879 she was completely rebuilt by David Carll so that she was about 80' overall and 22'-6" beam. Her lines (Figure 71) show her after this rebuilding. In her new form she had the following spars: mast heel to truck 74'-0", topmast 36'-0", mainboom 63'-0", gaff 31'-0" and her bowsprit was 19'-0" outboard. Like *Mischief* she had the double-headsail rig, with her forestay coming to the gammoning. The *Gracie* and the *Bedouin* raced against *Priscilla* and *Puritan* in the Cup trials of 1885; the *Puritan* being chosen to defend the Cup against the

British cutter *Genesta*. *Gracie* was more than a match for *Bedouin* and was about the equal of *Mischief*.

The success of the *Madge* had given American yachtsmen the idea that their sloops were not the match of the crack English cutters, so when *Genesta's* challenge was received in 1885 they built yachts specially for the match. The lengthy and bitter arguments between the advocates of shoal centerboarders and narrow cutters had created an intermediate class of "compromise" deep centerboarders, following the *Petrel* and *Mischief* in principle. Cary Smith of New York and Edward Burgess of Boston were probably the leading exponents of the type.

Edward Burgess, the son of Benj. F. Burgess, a Boston sugar importer, was born at Sandwich, Cape Cod, in 1848. He studied at Harvard and became a naturalist. In 1883 he went to England and his love of yachting led him to study designing as a hobby. On his return home he found that, due to financial reverses, he had to earn a living, so he and his brother set up as yacht designers. He not only proved himself an able yacht designer but was also a fine racing helmsman. In his short career as a designer, lasting only seven years, he designed 137 vessels, including eleven fishermen, three pilot-boats and thirty-seven steam yachts. He died at the early age of forty-six, July 12, 1891. Many of his ideas were the result of his studies in England and his association with D. J. Lawlor. Among the yachts designed by this great Bostonian architect were the three America's Cup defenders, *Puritan*, 1885, *Mayflower*, 1886 and *Volunteer*, 1887. He designed the famous fishing schooners *Carrie Phillips* and *Fredonia*, and the racing cutters *Gossoon*, *Tomahawk*, *Harpoon* and the 70-footer *Titania*, as well as the schooner-yachts *Sachem* and *Constellation*. The *Titania* (Figure 75) was an excellent example of his work. This fine "compromise" sloop was built in Brooklyn in 1887 and was similar in many respects to his Cup Defenders, *Puritan* and *Mayflower*. Her rig was much like that of the English cutters, but her bowsprit did not reef.

The rule changes in 1882 had brought about another trend of design, as can be seen by *Titania*. The Seawanhaka Yacht Club introduced a rule in 1882 that took sail area into consideration combined with the waterline length. The next year the club altered the rule slightly, and in 1884 the New York Yacht Club adopted a rule using about the same factors of measurement. In 1890 the latter club adopted the 1883 Seawanhaka rule without change. These rules were designed to encourage the deep yacht of the "compromise" or cutter type. As usual, they seemed to fit existing yachts of this type very well, but the possibilities of "cheating" were not appreciated by yachting authorities.

In spite of the good intentions of the rule-makers, these new rules eventually developed a trend of design as vicious as the old "Cubic Contents" rule. So rapidly did the new trend develop that by 1895 any connection between the ideal racing cruiser and the existing racers had been lost. The years between 1885 and 1890 had produced a healthy class of racing cruisers, similar to *Titania* in America and to *Minerva* in England. The *Minerva* had made the 40-foot class very fashionable after her arrival in 1889, but by 1891 the class had been raced out, leaving *Gossoon* and *Minerva* the undisputed cracks of the rating. Attention then turned to the next largest class, the 46-footers, that year.

The Herreshoff shops in Bristol, Rhode Island, turned out a new sloop, or rather cutter, that year for the class. While building she was much ridiculed, but after her launch she became a sensation. This yacht was the *Gloriana*, a beautifully modelled cutter of moderate power and a much cut-a-way profile. In cutting away the forefoot the overhang of the bow was much lengthened as compared to contemporary yachts. The shorter waterline thus obtained in this design permitted an increase of sail under the rule, which accounted for some of her speed, good hull lines accounting for the rest. However, her speed was attributed to her bow, as in the case of the *America*, and the "Gloriana-bow" was tacked onto everything, including Cape Cats. The Herreshoffs, however, had discovered

342

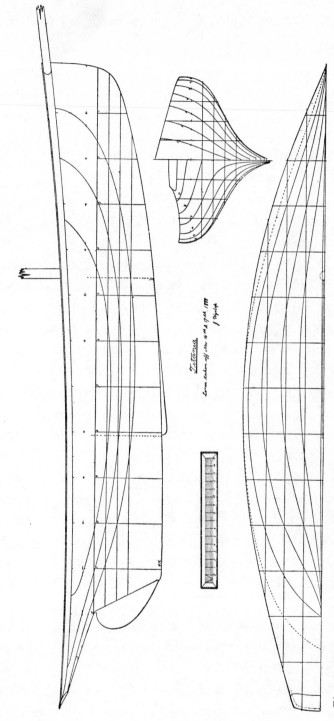

Titania

Lines taken off the 16th of Aug. 1888
J. Ogilvie

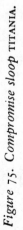

Figure 75. Compromise sloop TITANIA.

the weakness of the rule; a big boat could be produced on a short water-line, capable of carrying enough sail to beat a hull of normal type.

In the fall of that year, the Herreshoffs turned out a radically different boat which, while obtaining the advantages under the rule that were had in *Gloriana*, went a step further and reduced displacement to a minimum. This was the "fin-keel" sloop *Dilemma*, 25'-0" on the waterline and 7'-0" beam. Her hull was spindle-shaped, shallow and with long overhangs, stability being obtained by a steel plate fin weighted at its lower edge with a cigar-shaped bulb of lead weighing about two tons. It will be remembered that the fin had been tried in *Gimcrack* many years before, but the Herreshoffs were working on a different principle than Steers, which led to more successful results. The *Dilemma* was a fine boat for pleasure sailing in comparatively smooth water, but when the same idea was applied to large yachts the result was the development of as undesirable a class of yacht as the "skimming dishes," mere smooth water racing machines.

In *Dilemma* ballast had reached its final evolution. Beginning with the early yachts of the *America's* time, with all ballast inside, the intervening years had witnessed a gradual increase in the amount of outside ballast. The English cutter craze had done much to increase confidence in the idea and by 1885 many yachts in America had all their ballast outside. Most of these yachts were of the narrow "plank-on-edge" cutter type, however, which lacked initial stability so that much of the effectiveness of this form of ballast was required merely to keep the hull upright when at rest. The result was that these craft lacked power to carry sail in a breeze, as a rule, and were at their best in light going. In *Dilemma* this objection was overcome to a great extent by using a hull with some initial stability and increasing the effectiveness of the outside ballast by reducing displacement in the neighborhood of the keel by means of the thin metal plate fin, as well as by concentrating the ballast as low as the draft permitted. The *El Chico* (Figure 76), built by the Herreshoffs the year after *Dilemma*, illustrates the type and shows how effectively this class of yacht utilized outside ballast. A great many similar yachts appeared in America and England, and for a time were in great vogue. The smaller craft of this class were rigged as jib-and-mainsail sloops; the large craft were usually given a modified cutter-rig. The fin-keel type survives in many modern one-design classes, such as the "Star-Boats."

When the Dunraven challenge for the America's Cup was received for races in 1893, four candidates were built for the defense. Two of

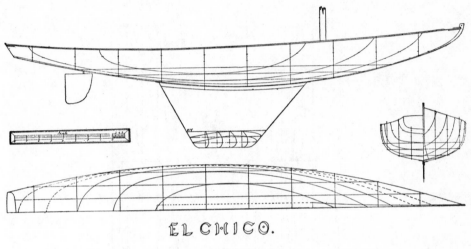

EL CHICO.

Figure 76. Fin-Keel sloop EL CHICO.

these were designed by Herreshoff, the keel-and-centerboard cutter *Vigilant* (Figures 77 and 78) and the fin-keel cutter *Colonia*. Boston produced the other two, both on the fin-keel model, the Paine designed *Jubilee*, and the *Pilgrim*, designed by the successors of Burgess, Stewart and Binney. All four were real racing machines, in the neighborhood of 124 feet overall, with waterlines measuring from 84 feet to 86 feet in length; their rigs were of the cutter-type, with fidded topmasts but with fixed bowsprits. The fin-keel yachts suffered much from structural failures and the *Vigilant* was chosen to defend the Cup against *Valkyrie II*. After a successful defense the *Vigilant* raced for a couple of seasons, one

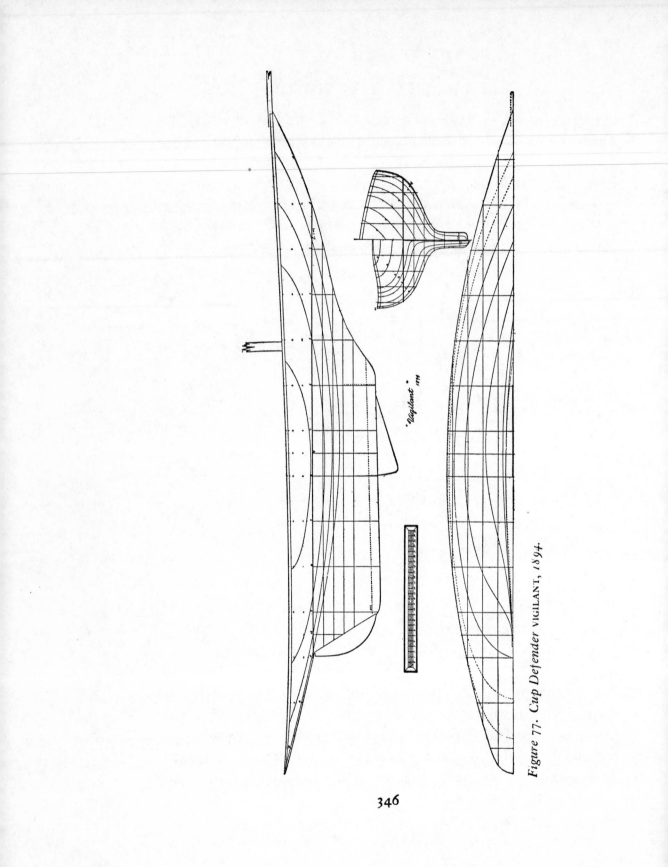

"Vigilant" 1894

Figure 77. Cup Defender VIGILANT, 1894.

abroad. In England she did not do as well as was hoped, for the racing courses there, made up of comparatively short legs, were unfavorable to a boat as slow in stays as the *Vigilant* proved to be. She was a fast boat, however, and was the first defender to have a bronze bottom.

The Herreshoff-designed yachts were chosen to defend the America's

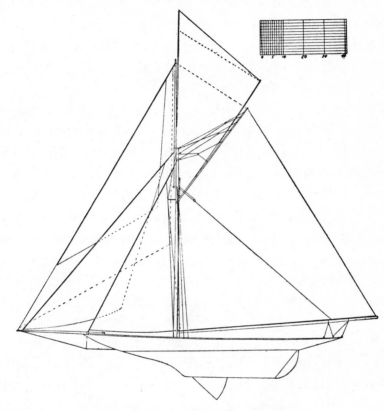

Figure 78. Sail plan of the Cup Defender VIGILANT.

Cup in all the races from 1893 to 1920. The defenders of 1930 and 1935 were designed by the son of Edward Burgess, W. Starling Burgess, but built by the Herreshoff yard.

The Herreshoff designs were the work of Nathaniel Herreshoff, born in 1848, the descendant of a Prussian engineer who came to America in 1770. Nathaniel, nicknamed "Capt'n Nat," was educated as a mechanical engineer at the Massachusetts Institute of Technology and was employed by the Corliss Engine Works of Providence, Rhode Island, at the time of the Centennial Exposition, 1876, in the erection of an engine in the mechanical exhibition. A brother, John, was also a mechanical engineer, though blind from youth. This brother and a partner had a boat-yard at Bristol, Rhode Island, operated as the firm of Herreshoff and Stone. Both Nathaniel and John were keen yachtsmen; Nathaniel very early in life developed a keen interest in designing. The firm of Herreshoff and Stone built some early yachts of the rather deep centerboard type: the sloops *Kelpie* and *Qui Vive* in 1864, *Clytie* in 1865, *Sadie* in 1867 and *Orion* in 1870. They also built the schooners *Triton, Ianthe* and *Faustine*. Nathaniel eventually joined the firm and in 1871 he designed the deep centerboard sloop *Shadow* that beat the *Madge*. The firm turned to the construction of steam vessels, engines and boilers under the name of The Herreshoff Mfg. Co., and did very little work on sailing yachts for some time. Nathaniel, however, did design and build small yachts for himself or friends, such as the noted cat, *Gleam*, built in 1877 and the cat-yawls *Consuelo*, 1884 and *Clara*, 1887. In 1890 he designed *Penquin* and *Gannet*. Since that time he has designed, in addition to those yachts already mentioned, the Cup Defenders *Defender*, 1895, *Columbia*, 1899, *Reliance*, 1903 and *Resolute*, 1914 (race of 1920). He also designed the unsuccessful defense candidate *Constitution* of 1901, the sloops *Navahoe* and *Niagara*, the New York Yacht Club's one-design classes (the 30, 40 and 50-foot classes), and the noted racing schooners *Ingomar* and *Westward*, along with a great number of other yachts great and small. Nathaniel Herreshoff retired from active designing some years ago but two of his sons are following in his footsteps. L. Francis Herreshoff, one of his sons, has been most successful as a designer of racing craft and is noted for the ingenuity of his hull and rigging fittings. His recent cruising yachts have been marked by the reintroduction of the clipper bow and carved work.

As the measurement rule developed the principle of a big boat on a

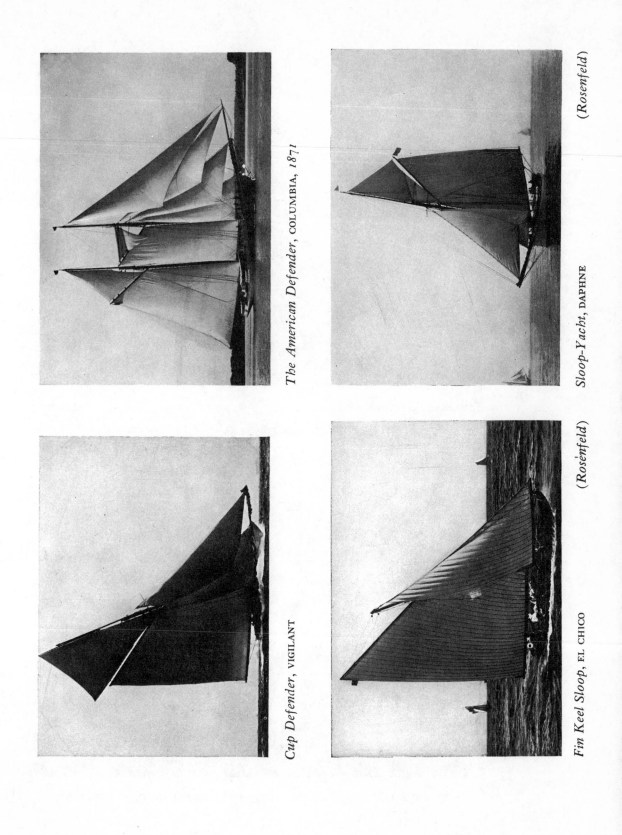

The American Defender, COLUMBIA, 1871

Sloop-Yacht, DAPHNE   (*Rosenfeld*)

Cup Defender, VIGILANT

Fin Keel Sloop, EL CHICO   (*Rosenfeld*)

Schooner-Yacht, EMERALD   (*Rosenfeld*)

MAYFLOWER *with topmast housed and a single reef in strong breeze, 1886*

short waterline length, the scow type came into existence. The idea expressed in this type was the obtaining of great increase of length on the waterline, combined with a marked decrease in beam, when heeled under sail. This feature of design, combined with very light displacement and big spread of sail and the use of the weight of the crew as shifting ballast, resulted in some of the most astonishing freaks that have appeared in yachting history. In model, these scows were really punts, in that their sides were not parallel. The more extreme had saucer-shaped midsections, very flat on the floor and sides strongly flared outward. The bow and stern both ended in transoms in many cases. The type came into being in the 15-foot waterline class which became fashionable in 1895. The first step toward the extreme scow was probably the 15-footer *Question*, designed and built by Larry Huntington in 1895. She was really a development of the New Haven Sharpies and the flat-bottomed skiff. The scow reached its greatest extremes in the 21-foot class that raced for the Quincy Challenge Cup on Massachusetts Bay. On a 21-foot waterline, these boats had an overall length of from 40 to 52 feet, with the sail area of an earlier 40-footer. These scows were so lightly built that they went out of shape, some going to pieces after one hard-sailed race. Most of the scows were centerboarders, but eventually two boards, one in each bilge, took the place of the large single board; the double-boards are known as "bilge-boards." Some of the scows, particularly the ones so large that the weight of crew was insufficient to keep them on their feet, were fin-keelers.

The largest scow-type yacht ever built was the *Independence*, 140'-10½" overall, 90'-0" waterline, 23'-11½" extreme beam, 20'-0" draft and 146.75 tons displacement, carrying about 14,373 square feet of sail, that was built as an America's Cup defense candidate in 1901. She was designed by Bowdoin B. Crowninshield of Boston and was a fin-keel scow; though a brute of a boat she was very fast under certain conditions. However, she was too uncertain in her behavior to be chosen as a defender. The Herreshoff-designed defender *Reliance* of 1903 was of a somewhat similar model. Among the designers who played a part in the development of the scow were Thomas Clapham, Charles Mower, W. Starling Burgess, Arthur Keith, Clinton H. Crane, Edwin T. Boardman, the Wisconsin firm of Jones and La Borde and the other Middle West designers, Arthur Dyer, Gus Amundson, W. L. Davis and C. M. Palmer.

Some of these designers turned out other types equally well, Burgess, Boardman, Mower, Crane and Crowninshield, for example. The last-named was also a noted designer of fishermen and commercial schooners, as well as a distinguished designer of yachts of all types.

The scows were probably the fastest single-hull sailing boat that could be designed, though they were smooth-water racing machines. One of them, the *Seeress*, sailed a 15-mile triangular course in 2 hours, 7 minutes and 45 seconds. The scow survives today, on the inland lakes of Wisconsin, Minnesota and Canada and on Barnegat Bay, New Jersey. The modern scows are built under strict limitations, however.

When the steam yacht became fashionable there was a decline in the popularity of the schooners, particularly after the rig ceased to be used in America's Cup races. Nevertheless, the schooner did not wholly go out of use and a few schooner racing classes remained fairly active. In the late '90's and early 1900's there was a small class of large racing schooners, of modern design, that saw hard racing. These schooners were of a rather mixed type, but the *Elmina* (Figure 73), designed by Cary Smith and built at Shooter's Island, New York, 1902, will give an idea of the wide divergence in model between a schooner yacht of her date and the keel schooners of earlier years, such as *Sappho*.

In 1905 there was something of a revival in interest in large schooners of the seagoing type, as a result of a cup offered by the German Kaiser for a trans-Atlantic race. The entries were of various rigs, there being eleven starters: one three-masted topsail schooner, two three-masted fore-and-aft schooners, five two-masted schooners, one barque, one ship and one yawl. The race was won by the Gardner-designed three-masted schooner *Atlantic*, who averaged 10.32 knots over the 3,013-mile course.

She was then a new vessel, of the cruiser-racer variety, and a fine example of her type.

William Gardner, designer of the *Atlantic*, was one of the leading American designers, on the same plane of achievement as Steers, Lawlor, Cary Smith, Burgess and Herreshoff. He was born at Oswego, New York, and was a graduate of Cornell University. Gardner, after graduating, was employed in the John Roach shipyard for a while, leaving to go abroad. While in England he entered the Royal Naval College at Greenwich and made advanced studies in naval architecture. While in England he became acquainted with some of the leading English yacht-designers, who turned his interest to yacht-design. In 1886 Gardner returned to New York and opened an office as a naval architect. His first yachts were the 40-foot cutters *Liris* and *Kathleen;* the former brought him much fame. During the ensuing years, Gardner turned out a great many fine yachts; the schooners *Alcea, Quisetta* and *Radiant* and the cutters *Norota, Syce, Neola, Aspirant* and the Cup defense candidate *Vanitie*, of 1914, among them. The *Vanitie* was one of the handsomest of her class and is too well known to modern yachtsmen to require comment. Gardner retired from active designing in 1925; during his career he had designed, in addition to yachts of all descriptions, a number of commercial craft. His retirement and subsequent death was a great loss to his profession.

In 1901 the Seawanhaka Yacht Club had changed its rule so as to bar scows and fin-keels, by measuring the area of mid-section and waterline plane. Other clubs did not at once follow suit, but in 1903 the New York Yacht Club revised its rule in response to expressions of dissatisfaction by yachtsmen with the current trend of racing yacht design. The new rule was the first stage of development of the present "Universal Rule." This rule measured the length of the hull at a point one-fourth the beam outboard from the centerline and also measured displacement and girth. The relation of sail area was taken into consideration and limitations placed on excessive draft, sail area, hollow garboards, wide sterns, scow bows and light displacement. Since 1903 there have been alterations in the rule, further limitations on minimum freeboard, length of mast and minimum weight of that spar, sheer, tumble-home of topsides, camber of deck, scantlings and use of centerboards. The "Universal Rule" has been accepted generally, except in handicap racing of cruising yachts and in ocean racing. While this rule has developed a fairly useful class of racing yacht, it has fallen short of the ideal in producing a racing-cruiser.

Yachting history proves that the evolution of yacht-design has not been a logical and steady series of improvement; not only is this true of racers, but also of cruisers. This fact has already been pointed out, but the effect of the "Universal Rule" on both racers and cruisers again illustrates the relation of measurement rule to trend of design. In racers, under this rule, the tendency to combine a full mid-section with fine ends as required by the quarterbeam and girth limitations has resulted in the concentration of the heavy displacement necessary under the rule in a comparatively small proportion of the length amidships. The result has been a slow hull and an uncomfortable sea-boat. The rule has also nullified the value of overhangs as far as any gain in heeled waterline or stability is concerned, resulting in high sharp overhangs of little value beyond serving as a bowsprit and an outrigger for a standing backstay. The "Universal Rule" racer has a hull that cannot be driven efficiently at high speeds, so that, in spite of tremendous improvement in the manufacture, cutting and design of sails and highly efficient rigs, the all-around speed of the sailing yacht has not shown a comparative improvement.

Though the rule was intended to produce a cruiser-racer it has not done so. Under its influence the centerboard yacht has disappeared as a class racer under the rule. In general, the "Universal Rule" racer has been a distinct reversion to the undesirable "plank-on-edge" cutter; this was so much the case that the rule required some tampering to prevent extremes. The rule requires that centerboards must be beneath the cabin floor, a highly undesirable feature in a wooden yacht from the structural standpoint, and effectively bars the shoal draft required in many local-

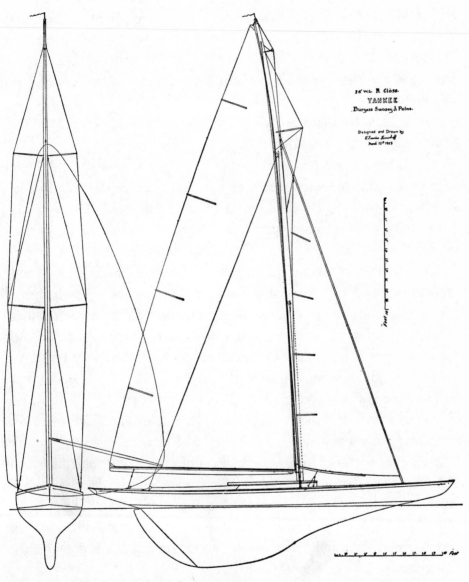

Figure 80. *Sail plan of the R-boat* YANKEE.

ities. The rule requirements make the racer a most expensive yacht to build, which had some influence in developing the numerous one-design classes. While these classes have much in their favor, they have no tendency to improve yacht design. Though some very good yachts have been designed to fit the rule, such as the Cup defense candidate *Yankee*, and the R-class boat of the same name whose plans are reproduced here (Figures 80 and 81), the tendency of the rule to produce a faulty type can be verified by the disturbed wake when driven hard, evident in all boats designed under the rule.

The rather curious tendency of the cruising yachtsmen to follow the features of contemporary racers of the classes under the rule in force is as obvious today as in the time of the "sand-bagger." There has also been a fad for excessive seaworthiness; yachtsmen whose cruises are made in the summer, in comparatively protected waters, insist on cruising yachts suitable for a winter passage in the North Atlantic. These yachts are too often of the "can-buoy" model, slow and exceedingly heavy. The features of the "Universal Rule" racers, their high useless overhangs, very deep draft, heavy ballast, excessively high rigs and a multitude of light sails, complicated gear and high cost; all may be seen in many of the present cruising yachts.

The effects of racing rules on yachts of all types are difficult to foresee when the rules are being made. Often the rule-makers have some particular type of yacht in mind which they wish to encourage, but the rules when put into practice have had the effect of turning out something quite opposite from what was desired. This was the case with the Seawanhaka Rule, which was designed to develop the cutter and "compromise" centerboarders, yet finally produced the scows. Until the desire of owners and designers to outbuild one another no longer exists, it is doubtful that any rule will be wholly satisfactory.

While hull-design has lagged, improvements in rigs have been most rapid during the years following 1920. The old cumbersome fidded topmast and club-topsail has disappeared, to be replaced with the more

354

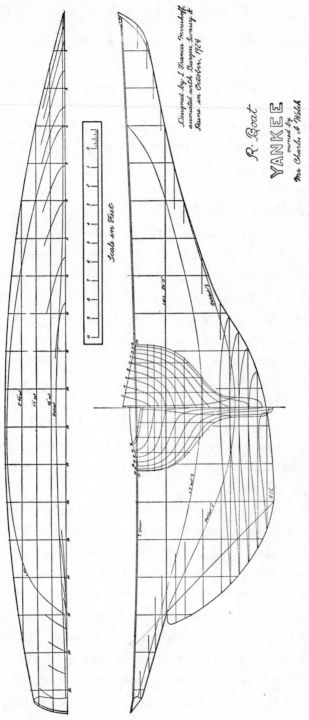

Designed by L Francis Herreshoff,
associated with Burgess, Swasey &
Paine, in October, 1924.

R-Boat

YANKEE

owned by
Mr Charles A Welsh

Scale in Feet

Figure 81. Universal Rule racer, R-class sloop.

355

efficient polemast and leg-of-mutton sail in sloops. The introduction of overlapping headsails and light sails of unorthodox shape has probably been carried to extremes, but much has been learned by these experiments. The schooner rig was revived during the '20's, particularly in medium-sized yachts, and the introduction of the so-called staysail rig gave schooners some advantage under the racing rules. The weakness of the schooner rig is due to some extent to the barring of the overlapping foresail. This offers some idea of the logic of many of the rating rules when the overlaps permitted on staysails and headsails in other rigs are considered. The latest variation of the staysail rig has appeared in ketches, the main-trysail or kitesail rig. This was proposed some years ago by Frederick Fenger, but only recently has come into fashion. The objection to both the staysail schooner and the main-trysail ketch has been the need of much additional sail running before the wind, but Fenger is reported to have overcome this fault to some extent in his version of the main-trysail ketch. The staysail rig was tried in schooners by Robert Bennet Forbes of Boston, as far back as the '50's, but was never adopted by commercial sailing craft because of the objection mentioned. Not only has there been much improvement in the design of rigs, but cutting and manufacture of sails have also improved so that the windward ability of yachts is better than ever before. Except for a natural tendency to go to extremes, particularly in height of rig, the only criticisms that might be levelled at the modern trends in this matter are the increasing complication of gear and over-rigging. In regard to the latter, it is not uncommon to see a 16-foot sloop with shrouds and spreaders that are wholly unrequired. The over-rigging is a prevalent fault in all sizes of yachts, however, brought about by a fetish of reducing the weight of the spars, and so, the strength of the mast to stand unsupported. However, this seems to be a passing objection, for designers are becoming increasingly aware of the effects of the unnecessary windage caused by over-rigging.

The prevalent types of cruising yachts are varied, but the greatest number are of deep draft. There are a very large number of small schooners, somewhat on the lines of the Gloucester Fisherman, as represented by the *Elsie* model, which have been highly developed by John Alden, of Boston. The racing-cruiser type, rigged as orthodox sloops, cutters, yawls, schooners, or ketches, or rigged as staysail schooners or main-trysail ketches, has been developed by W. Starling Burgess, Frank C. Paine, Sparkman and Stephens, Cox and Stevens and Frederick Fenger. *Dorade, Nina, Highland Light, Vamarie* and others of this class of yacht have been very successful in ocean racing. Some of the designers have been exponents of some particular type, as illustrated by the Alden-designed *Malabar*, or fisherman type. Ralph Winslow, who prefers the "Friendship Sloop" model, and Samuel Crocker do work along that line.

From the historical view, the present trend of cruising yacht design shows a reversion to many ideas formerly in practice, but until recently considered obsolete. For example, the loose-footed mainsail of the old "plank-on-edge" cutters and the earlier Baltimore Clipper schooners is again being seen. Many designers have come to the conclusion that the concentrated displacement and useless overhangs of many contemporary yachts are undesirable and are reverting to the hull-forms of the late '80's. The yachtsmen have apparently grown tired of the lack of variety in appearance and rig formerly so marked in the yachting fleet and are building yachts with plumb bows of the old pilot-boats or clipper bows and with great variation in lines, shape of profile and rig. There is also the healthy interest in yachts suitable for given localities, with the result that many old types of local commercial craft are being reproduced in yachts; probably the Chesapeake "Bugeye" is one of the most popular models for yachts of this class at the moment. While there have been numerous attempts to introduce some foreign type, such as the Norwegian fishing and pilot boats, the fads for such craft have been of short duration.

When it is possible for yachtsmen and designers to obtain a more complete knowledge of past experiments in hull-design and rig than is now available, an intelligent and natural development of yacht design, free of fads and the effects of badly constructed measurement rules, seems reasonable to expect. When that time comes, a great amount of "scientific" hocus-pocus will be thrown overboard. Since commercial sailing craft have ceased to play a part in academic naval architecture, the yacht-designer has been handicapped by a lack of the experimental work, and the diffusion of knowledge of the results of such work, that accounts for the rapid development in the design of power craft. How this difficulty is to be overcome is a matter that must be decided before the sailing yacht can make progress commensurate with that of her mechanically powered sister.

APPENDIX

Specifications and Notes

Balsa. References to this type of craft are very difficult to trace. A balsa was captured by Bartolomo Ruiz, pilot of Pizarro, off the coast of Peru, in 1526, according to Prescott, "History of the Conquest of Peru." Charnock could find no earlier reference than 1748; "Relacion Historica del Viage a la America Meridional," necho de Orden de S. Mag & C., Impressa a de Orden de Rey en Madrid, 1748.

French influence. Since the evidence in this matter was assembled in Chapter Two, more letters in regard to French draughts have been found by Mr. M. V. Brewington, Jr. They are as follows:

Franklin and Deane, to Committee of Secret Correspondence. Paris, March 4, 1777. "We send you the draft of a frigate by a very ingenious officer in this service which appears to us peculiarly suitable for our purposes. . . ."

Franklin and Deane, to Committee of Secret Correspondence. Paris, March 12, 1777. "He (the French officer) has built one (frigate) here for the king which we are told exceeds everything in swift sailing. He has furnished us with drafts which we send you."

Franklin and Deane to Committee of Foreign Affairs. Passy, November 30, 1777. "We had engaged an officer . . . to build us a frigate . . . (drafts) of which we sent you."

These letters seem to establish the arrival of French plans in America in the middle of 1777. However, it must be recalled that the American frigates ordered built in December, 1775 were all laid down a year or more previous to March, 1777. Of the frigates built afterwards, the draughts for the *Confederacy* and *Alliance* are known to have been made in this country; leaving only the *Bourbon*, building at Middletown, Connecticut, in 1780–83, unaccounted for. No information regarding her draught has yet been found, but if we accept the possibility that she was built from a French plan, we would not have proof of the French influence, for the *Bourbon* was sold before being ready for sea and there is no mention of her in later accounts. Had she influenced the later frigates, surely there would have been at least one mention of her in the mass of correspondence relating to the frigates of 1794. It seems probable that the Passy letter answers the question raised by these letters. In the first place, it would be very odd if the American agents in

APPENDIX

France were placing a contract for a frigate that was to be built in America; therefore the conclusion must be that the vessel was built in France, from a French plan which was sent to a Congressional committee as evidence of the size and type of ship to be built. If this conclusion is accepted, the origin of the draught used to build the frigate *Deane* at Nantes, France, in 1777 is accounted for. The *Deane*, it will be remembered, was renamed *Hague* in 1782 and finally sold. As far as can be learned, she left no impression on the minds of American shipwrights. It is strange that the later correspondence between Franklin, Jones and Genèt, in 1780, was necessary if the Americans were using a French plan obtained such a short time before, to build frigates in this

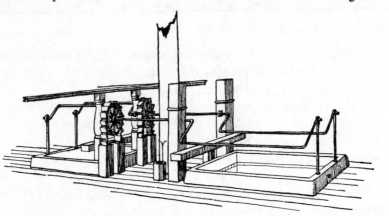

Arrangement of Chain Pumps, during the latter part of the eighteenth century.

country. It seems, therefore, that this whole correspondence refers to the *Deane* and aside from indicating the existence of *one* French plan in America, after all but three of the frigates were either launched, destroyed or captured, gives no support to the theory of French influence.

Centerboards. Patent for a pivoted centerboard was granted Joshua, Henry and Jacocks Swain, April 10, 1811. There are about 120 patents granted for various arrangements and details or design of centerboards. A pivoted board was invented by an Englishman, Shuldham, while a prisoner-of-war at Verdun in 1809; it is probable that many such boards were developed by men in various sections, all working independently.

Guns. The following dimensions were taken from cannon found at Fort Ticonderoga, and give a rough idea of the batteries of ships of the Revolution.

APPENDIX

24-pounder 6" bore—length 11'-7"—diameter breech 23" —diameter bell muzzle 17"
18-pounder 5½" bore—length 11' —diameter breech 17½"—diameter bell muzzle 12"
(Bronze—French, 1780)
12-pounder 4½" bore—length 6'-1"—diameter breech 16" —diameter bell muzzle 11"
9-pounder 4" bore—length 8' —diameter breech 14" —diameter bell muzzle 9½"
(Iron—French, dated 1742. Found at Fort Ticonderoga)
6-pounder 3¾" bore—length 4' —diameter breech 11½"—diameter bell muzzle 9"
3-pounder 2½" bore—length 4'-8"—diameter breech 8" —diameter bell muzzle 6½"
(found at Stillwater, probably British)

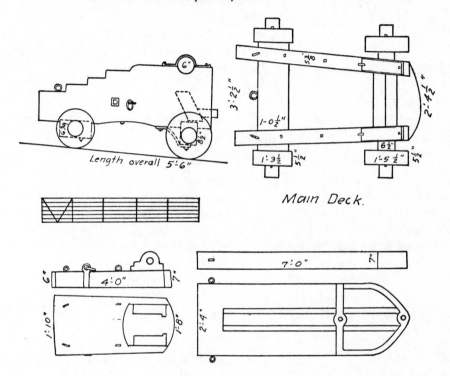

Gun Mountings of United States Frigate PRESIDENT.

Sailing of the President. The following is an extract of a letter from Thomas Holdup (Thomas Holdup Stevens), Midshipman on the *President*, to his father, dated July 19, 1810.

"This ship differs very much from the *Constitution* both in her sailing and rigging, and also her accommodations, for she sails much better and is much lighter rigged. Her berth deck is superior as also her cabin, ward room and steerage, all of which have the convenience of air ports. Her gun deck and

361

fore castle are better but her quarter deck, in my opinion is not as large. Her cockpit and store rooms are far superior to the *Constitution's*. The Master's, Boswain's, Gunner's, and Carpenter's store rooms are forward on the berth deck, her lower topsail, top gallant, and royal yards are much lighter than the *Constitution's;* her standing rigging is smaller but the stuff is much inferior. Her running rigging is in some respects smaller but very disproportioned; and leads very irregular; but I believe the Commodore intends having it altered. The eyes of her standing rigging are very large, and all of the rigging is obliged to be kept very slack for the least alteration in setting it up would eventually destroy her sailing. But upon the whole I am very much pleased with this ship and prefer her to the *Constitution*."

Inventory [1]

Ticonderoga, 2nd Octor. 1776

Recd from James Gardner D. Commiss of Artillery 117

The Following Articles for the Washington Galley

2 18 pound Iron Cannon	80 do . . . . for 2
2 12 ditto do do	80 do . . . . for swivels
2 9 ditto do do	20 Unfill'd Flannell
4 4 ditto do do	Cartridges for . . 12 poundr
20 Round Shott for 18 pounder	Rammers & Spunges
20 ditto do for 12 ditto	2 for 18 pounders
20 ditto do for 9 ditto	2 for 12 pounders
20 ditto do for 4 do	2 for 9 pounders
10 Doubleheaded Shott for 18	4 for 4 pounders
10 ditto ditto for 12	1 for 2 pounders
1 – 2 pound cannon	8 for Swivels
8 Swivels	1 Ladle for 10 pounder
40 Swivels Shott Round	1 do for . . . . 12 do
10 2 pound do do	1 Do for . . . . 9 do
10 Canister Shott for 18	2 do for . . . . 4 do
10 ditto do for 12	1 do for . . . . 2 do
20 ditto do for 9	2 do for Swivels
40 ditto do for 4	1 Worm for 18 pounders
40 paper Cartridges fill'd	1 do . . . . for 12 do
for 18	2 do for 9 do
40 ditto do do for 12	4 do for 4 . . do
50 do . . . . for 9	2 do for 2 . . do
60 do . . . . for 4	2 do for Swivels

[1] In Archives of the War Department, Washington, D.C.

24 Handspikes	4 Quire Cannon Cartridge paper
8 powder Horns	1 Musquet & Bayonet
8 Lintstocks	1 Rifle Gun
10 Priming Wires	2 Priming Wires & Brushes
8 Lead Aprons for Cannons	1 Cartridge to Each Cannon
3 Coils Slow Match	Fill'd with Damaged powder
6 Portfires. .	
12 Tubes	John Thacher Capt.
3200 Musquet Cartridges	
200 Flints.	10 Doubleheaded Shott for 9 ^{dr}
1 Barrel Cont'g 1 hundred W^t powder	Omitted. . . . .

Master-builder's certificate for a privateer, the CHASSEUR [1]

State of Maryland, District and Port of Baltimore. this will certify to All whom it doth or may concern that I master carpenter of Fells Point Baltimore Built the Schooner *Chassuer* for Mr. Wm. Hollins during the year of our lord eighteen hundred and twelve, that she is finished privateer, built with a round tuck and no head, that she is finished in the best workmanlike manner and of the following dimentions to say Eighty five feet eight inches Keel, twenty six foot beam, twelve foot Seven and one half inches hold and that she measures two hundred and ninety five tons and 90/95 of a ton carpenters measurement or thereabouts as Witness Wherof I set my hand this eighth day of Jan. 1813

Thomas Kemp

Sworn before me the day
and year aforesaid

Peter Galt.

Arnold's specifications of a Gondola [2]

Dimensions for two Gondolas to be built at Chamblé

Vizt:
        Length of Keel 45 Feet (48?)
          14 Inches wide, 9 deep
        Breadth of beam 16 Feet
        Depth 3 Feet 6 Inches
        Keelson 12 Inches square
        Floor Timbers 6 Inches square
          12 Inches wood to wood
        Top Timbers in proportion

[1] By courtesy of Mr. S. S. Rabl, Baltimore, Maryland.
[2] Courtesy of Mr. Kenneth Roberts, Kennebunk Beach, Maine.

APPENDIX

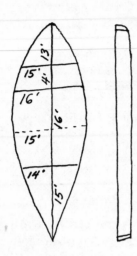

Two Beams amidships, 14 by 4 Inches
Wale Knees 16 Feet asunder
Fore Castle 13 feet long, 4 Inches crowned
Beam ditto 8 by 6 Inches
Carlins 9 Inches square
Stanchions 4 Inches square
Slides
Bottom Plank 3 Inches
Side ditto (illegible, probably 2½ Inches)
Sealing ditto (illegible)
Half Trunnels and half Spikes
Butts bolted
Breast Hook forward and aft
Deadrisings 4 Inches

Chamblé, May 3d 1776
B. Arnold

Model construction. The model-builder usually has his own method, but the planked-model offers many advantages. The easiest way to construct this is by use of moulds, which are cut out of a thin piece of wood, about an eighth of an inch thick, in the shapes taken from the body-plan. These are lifted from the plan only to the level of the underside of the deck, not the rail cap. The top of each mould may thus be cut to the crown of the deck. The frames or moulds are notched to receive the keel, which is cut out of a thin plank of the proper scale in thickness to fit the profile of the model. The stations and rabbet are marked on the keel-piece. Notches are cut in the top of the keel-piece, which may be the underside of deck at the centerline, to receive the moulds, thus locking them into one another. In order to allow for the beveling necessary at bow and stern, the fore-body moulds should be placed so that their after-face is on the station-lines; the after-body moulds should have their forward-face on the station-lines. This makes the actual spacing of the moulds a little greater at the mid-section. By this means, one of the faces of each mould is the true shape; the bevel may be cut from the opposite face. It is best to use square battens, let into the moulds at the top, or underside of deck, to true the sheer, give a foundation for the bulwarks and stiffen the model while it is being planked. The bulwarks are placed after the model is decked and planked, the shape of the stanchions are obtained from the body-plan, of course. It is usually easier to set these by use of templates taken from the same plan if the bulwarks are deep. By reference to these general notes, a little ingenuity and much care an extremely accurate model can be made.

364

APPENDIX

Contract.

PEACOCK, United States Ship.

Articles of Agreement entered into, made & concluded upon this 26th day of July, 1813 between Adam & Noah Brown, of the City of New York, Master Ship builders of the one part, and John Bullus Navy Agent of the United States of America at New York, acting for and on behalf of the said United States of the other part as follows.—

The said Adam & Noah Brown, for themselves, their Heirs, Executors, and Administrators, Covenant, promise and agree to and with the said Navy Agent, and his Successors in office, that they the said Adam & Noah Brown, or their legal representative, shall and will build, or cause and procure to be built, as is herein after set forth, a Sloop of War or Vessel, for the use of the said United States to wit.

The Dimensions, One hundred and Seventeen feet eleven inches upon the Gundeck, Ninety Seven feet Six inches Keel, for tonnage, measuring from one foot before the forward perpendicular and along the base line, to the front of the rabbit of the post, deducting three fifths of the moulded breadth of beam, multiplied into the length of Keel for tonnage, that product multiplied by half the moulded breadth of beam, and that product divided by ninety five, will give Five hundred & nine Tons 21/95 Carpenters measure, by which said Builders are to be paid at Fifty dollars per ton, making the Sum of Twenty five thousand four hundred and Sixty one Dollars and Five Cents, for which sum Said Builders are to build said Ship in a complete and workman like manner, conforming to a draught to be furnished by the Navy Department, and to the directions written and contained on the two Sheets of paper hereunto annexed, the written folios of which are numbered, one to Six—inclusive, and the Signature of the Naval Constructor set at foot thereof, or to such other directions as may at any time hereafter be given by the Naval Constructor, a deviation from any of which is not to be made, in the smallest matter or manner, unless the consent of the Secretary of the Navy shall have been first obtained in writing.

The Vessel is to be afloat, ready for her Armament on or before the twenty fifth day of October next ensuing the date of these presents, and the payments to the Builders are to be made at such periods of progression of the work, so that no more than three fourths of the whole amount shall have been paid, when the Gundeck is planked.

The Vessel is to be built of the best materials cut when the Sap was down, her frame, bottom, planks, wales and thick stuff, the clamps, spirkettings and thick stuff of the deck of White Oak, free from defects, except the Apron, Knight heads, Hawse pieces and main Transom which are to be of Live Oak, the Ceiling deck plank, Beams, Ledges, and plank of the Topside of Yellow pine, free from Sap and all other defects, the top timbers on each side of the ports to be locust, as also the timber heads, all the other top timbers and half top timbers to be of red cedar. The Builders are to include in this Contract to be done by them, the Bowsprit completely fixed, with all its fastenings and appendages complete, comprehending Tops, Caps &c &c as also a complete set of spare Spars for the main mast, including a top mast, yards and Studding Sail yards &c.—To do the Painters work, which includes puttying the nail & Bolt Heads &c both out board and in board, and three good coats of paint. The Carvers Bill, which comprehends the carved work of the Stern if any, of the Badges of the Head &c and fixing the Head and Badges complete. The Plumbers Bill, comprehending a head pump, Hawse and Scupper leads, lead on the taffrell, and knight heads under the Bowsprit, Knees of Cable Bitts, around the inside of the Manger, about the Badges, and all the lead work exclusive of the Ships Chain pumps, Magazine Cisterns, or any that may be appendant to the different Rooms for the accommodation of the Ship, her Officers and Crew. Joiners work comprehending priming out for the Salt below the Wales, the plaining her out board and inboard, her decks plank on both sides, the Carlines, Ledges, Booms, Combings &c &c and all and every part of the Joiner's work excluding the above rooms, for which he is neither to find boards, fastenings or workmanship, nor is he to paint the rooms.—To find all the Blacksmith's Work, comprehending all the Bolts, eye bolts, ring bolts, Spikes, driving & riveting &c. Iron Stauncheons for the ridge rope, all around the Ship, Iron Tiller Spindle, and all the Iron work for the patent Capstern and every article of Iron work that is necessary, as an appendage to the Hull of the Ship, whether it relates to her fastenings, armament or accommodation of rigging &c excluding nothing but such Iron work, as is necessary for the Cabin, and Rooms before mentioned. The Copper Work, including all the fastenings, Spikes Bolts, braces and pintles, dove tails &c as per directions all complete, excepting the Sheet copper, and nails for sheathing, but he is to punch holes in it, and put it on, finding Tar and paper &c at his own expense. In fine to find all materials and workmanship, with the exception only of the rooms before mentioned, for the before mentioned Sum of Twenty five thousand four hundred and Sixty one dollars and five Cents, and the United States are to be at no other expense whatever, the last payment of one fourth of the whole amount, will be reserved until this Contract is fulfilled, when it will be paid immediately. It is understood between the parties, that the Navy Department has the privilege to substitute Mahogany in the place of White Oak for any part of the Ship's construction, the Builders to be charged with the number of feet of Mahogany they receive, at the price of Prime White Oak, of the same Sizes or form, the number of Cubic feet of Mahogany used by the Builders are to be determined by measuring the flitches sawed off in converting the timbers (which must be done wherever practicable) which flitches, the Navy Department will receive, and deduct the number of Cubic feet with which the Builders are to be charged. The Mahogany logs are to be delivered to the Builders in Scows, alongside the wharf, where the vessel is to be built.

The Salt, with which the vessel is to be salted, is to be found and put in by the Navy Department.

All the Materials necessary to build said Ship as aforesaid are to be found by, and at the expense of the Builders and paid for by them, save those which are herein before excepted.

Said Vessel, to be launched and delivered at the port of New York, unto the said Navy Agent, or other authorized officer of the Navy Department for the use of the said United States by and at the expense of the said Adam & Noah Brown, their Executors, administrators and assigns on or before the twenty fifth day of October next ensuing in complete order and condition.

It is declared by the parties to these presents that no member of Congress is to be concerned directly or indirectly, or is to have any interest or emolument whatever, in any part of this contract.

It is further declared by the parties to these presents that the instructions or directions written and contained on the two sheets of paper hereunto annexed, the written folios of which are numbered one to Six inclusive, and the signature of the Naval Constructor set at foot thereof, are as binding on said parties, as were they written in the body of the agreement.

And the said Adam & Noah Brown, do hereby bind themselves, and their heirs, executors and administrators unto the said United States for the due and faithful building, completing and finishing the same ship or vessel in manner before mentioned, and for the delivery thereof, when so completed, at the said Port of New York, to the said Navy Agent, or other authorized officer of the Navy Department within the time, and in the good order and condition before mentioned.

And the said John Bullus, Navy Agent of the United States doth covenant, promise and agree, to and with the said Adam & Noah Brown, their Executors, Administrators and Assigns, well and truly to pay them for the said ship or vessel, the before mentioned Sum of Twenty five thousand four hundred and

APPENDIX

Sixty one Dollars and five Cents, in four equal payments, to be made monthly provided that not more than three fourths of the whole amount shall have been paid, when the gundeck is planked, and provided that the last payment shall be made only when this Contract is fulfilled by the Builders.

> In witness whereof the parties aforesaid have hereunto set their hands & seals the day and year first herein before mentioned.

A & N Brown (seal)

John Bullus (seal)
Navy Agent

Signed, sealed & delivered
in the presence of

W. Howell

George L. Storet.

Specifications, PEACOCK.

General dimensions and Sizes of the Scantling

of a

Sloop of War of 509 21/95 Tons Carpenters measure. . . .

Sizes of Scantling &c

Keel of White Oak in not more than three pieces, sided fourteen inches, and moulded eighteen inches, clear of the Shoe, which will be four inches thick, the Scarphs to be not less than ten feet long, and secured with five copper bolts, to follow an inch auger, well rivetted on substantial copper rings, the ribs to be fastened with two bolts, in each to follow a five eighths auger, the Shoe is not to be nailed, until after the floor and Keelson bolts shall have been rivetted and the under side of the Keel coppered.

Keelson sided thirteen inches and moulded fourteen, taking care that the Scarphs which must be eight feet long do not come over those of the keel.

Stem in two pieces sided fourteen inches, and moulded twelve inches, clear of the rabbit, the Scarphs to be not less than four feet six inches, bolted with three bolts of copper to follow an inch auger, to be well rivetted upon copper rings the nails fastened as those of the Keel.

Apron sided twenty inches to run well over the Scarph of the Stern and moulded eleven inches at head, and thirteen at heel.

Sternpost sided fourteen inches and moulded at head ten inches clear of the rabbit and at heel two feet, bearded on the aft side from its full size at the lower part of the wing transom to seven inches at heel.

Inner post sided at head eighteen inches, to jog in at the chock to fourteen inches, and to be governed down to the heel by the bearding line, moulded eight inches up to the upper side of the chock, and from thence to the under side wing transom to five inches, the seats of the transoms below the wings to be cut square out of it.

Knight heads sided eighteen inches, moulded at head ten inches and at heel twelve, to be bolted into the apron with bolts to follow an inch auger, at about two feet six inches apart.

Hawse Pieces three on each side, sided eighteen inches, and moulded at the head nine inches, at the heel twelve, bolted into the Knight heads, and each other, at two feet six inches apart, taking care not to bolt in the wake of the Hawse holes, the bolts to follow an inch auger.

Hawse holes two on each side to be twelve inches diameter in the clear when finished the leads to be half an inch thick above and one inch thick on the lower part of the circle, graduating fairly all round, and to be nine inches apart.

Scuppers to be hereafter directed.

Wing transom length and mould as per draught, sided Seventeen inches Straight, the second transom sided thirteen inches and all below eleven inch thick except the chock which will be fourteen inches, the wing and Second transom to be bolted with two copper bolts each, to follow an inch and an eighth auger, and all below with one copper bolt after an inch and an eighth auger.

Fashion Pieces one pair sided eight inches, and moulded ten, to be bolted to the wing transom, with two Iron bolts and to the chock with one iron bolt, all to follow an inch auger, the fastenings into the other transoms, will be two locust tree-nails in each end, after an inch and a quarter auger.

Dead Woods fore and aft to be sided the same as the Keel, moulded three and a half inches amid ships, and forward, and abaft according to the draught, the ends that butt against the inner post to be tenoned in it, and the bolts driven through the Stern post so as to secure the ends of the dead wood, upon the top of which there must be a substantial Knee fayed, the arm to notch the chock, and the body at least fifteen feet long, and sided the same as the dead wood, the dead wood forward will run up to, and lap upon the apron, which together with the fore dead wood will be bolted as far as timber D with bolts to follow an inch and an eighth auger, at not more than two feet two inches apart, all below the height of breadth to be copper, the after dead

APPENDIX

wood fastened in the same manner as far forward as timber Sixteen, with copper, the bolts through the Ports and Stem to be rivetted on good rings.

Floors and rising timbers to be of white oak, sided eleven inches, and moulded in throats to fourteen inches, and at Floor ribbon ten inches, both arms to reach the floor ribbon, and if long enough, extend beyond the ribbon to the floor head line, each floor, bolted through the Keel with copper to follow an inch auger, taking care that they are so well on each side of the Keel as at the same time not to interfere with the rabbit, and give room on the opposite side for the Keelson bolts which will follow an inch and an eighth auger. One bolt to be on the larboard in one floor and the next on the Starboard side in the other floor, so that there will be two bolts in each floor, to be rivetted on the under side of the Keel from timber 28 to timber M inclusive.

Lower futtocks to be sided ten inches jog over, and butt on the middle of the Keel off to a point, so as to admit cross cheecks to be well fayed to them and across the Keel, the heels of the Futtocks being snapped well upon each side, to admit the chock to be of same length, the other futtocks and Top timbers sided nine inches, the frame to be moulded from the floor Sirmark, at which it is ten inches by a diminishing line up to the height of breadth which is seven inches, and from thence up to the top height which is five and a half inches, the floor futtocks, and top timbers all to be framed in frames, and bolted with two Iron bolts in each Scarph to follow an inch auger, the facing side of all the timbers must be dubbed fair, and out of winding; there must be chocks fayed at all the heels and heads of all that do not hold the full size, and in every case where a chock is fayed, it must extend along both the head and heel, to secure the timbers the better, and prevent the chock from splitting.

Wales five on each side, five and a half inches thick, by nine inches wide, having above them four Streakes, to be, the first five inches, second, four and a half, third, four inches, and fourth, three and a half inches thick and nine inches wide, and the same number of the same thickness and width, to be below the wales, all to be dubbed off fair with the top side, and bottom plank, which is to be three inches thick, the bottom plank must be drawn well to the timbers, with pure copper spikes, seven and a half inches long (the form to be approved of by the Navy Agent or Superintendent) and fastened off with heart Locust treenails, to follow an inch and a quarter auger, which if not already seasoned must be kiln dried, and to bear a proportion to the Spikes as four is to one, that is, there must be four treenails to one Spike, dipped in tar, driven, the heads to be caulked in a triangular manner, and the points to be wedged with heart pine wedges, these remarks must apply as well to the

APPENDIX

wales and top side, as to the bottom, only that the wales must be fastened with eleven inch iron Spikes, and the treenails of the top side to follow an inch and an eighth auger, the bottom to be butt bolted with copper to follow a Seven eighth auger, there must be two composition dovetails fitted on the scarphs of Keel, Stem and Post, bolted after a Seven eighth auger, and well rivetted, as also four setts of composition braces, and pintles of the size and form to be approved of by the Navy Agent, the Rudder to be round headed.

Inside Work of the Sloop of War
of 20 Guns.

Limbers strakes on each side five inches thick and fourteen inches wide to be nailed within one foot of the Keelson, and the edge next the Keelson to be rabbited on and down two inches, and a ribbon nailed upon the floor along side the Keelson for the limber boards to rest upon, leaving a space below them for the water to have a more free access to the pump well, the rabbit must be so standing that the limber boards can be taken up and put down, without difficulty, the Spikes that fasten the plank whether in or out board, must be of the following lengths for three inch plank, Seven and a half inches, four inch plank, nine inches and five inch plank, ten inches and a half long the form to be approved by the Agent.

BIRTH DECK

Lower or birth deck clamps one Strake on each side fourteen inches wide, and four inches thick, the ceiling to be three inches and have the edges bevelled so as to make the Seams fit as nicely as possible.

Beams to be sided thirteen inches and moulded twelve, of the best heart yellow pine, free from sap or defect, to spring by a mould five inches in thirty two feet.

Lodging knees sided six inches, arm four feet long, and body to reach the next beam, bolted with Six bolts, to follow an inch auger and rivetted upon good rings, they must be kept two inches from the upper side of the beam, and the clamp except at the breech and end of the body of the Knee be trimmed down one inch, so as to give as much air as possible.

Dagger knees sided seven inches, arm to be four feet long and body to run to the opposite side of the next beam, bolted with six bolts to follow an inch auger, and well rivetted as above.

Transom knees sided nine inches, body eight feet long, and arm five feet, bolted with ten bolts after an inch auger.

371

APPENDIX

Carlings or fore and aft Stretchers in two tier, six inches by eight of white oak.

Ledges or thwart ship small beams, sided and moulded five and a half inches, of heart of pine, one between each beam.

Partners of Main & foremasts Seven by twelve inches of white oak kneed with four knees each, mizen partners Six by ten inches secured in the same manner. The partners of the gundeck to be in the same way, only one inch deeper and one inch wider than those below, the knees to be bolted after a Seven eighth auger, the main and fore partners must be apart so as to admit the wedges of the mast to be four inches all round, and the mizen three inches, which are to be heart pine.

Solid water ways to be white oak as long as possible, six inches thick and twelve inches wide, bolted into the side of the Ship, every three feet apart after a Seven eighth auger, to be finished with a feint hollow to the thickness of the deck plank, which must be two and a half inches of heart pine, free from Sap or any defect, and not more than nine inches wide and two Spikes to be driven through every plank, into each beam, and ledge.

Gun deck beams to be moulded thirteen and sided fourteen inches of yellow pine free from Sap and other defects, by the same mould as the lower deck beams to hold their full size at ends.

Lodging knees sided seven inches, the body to reach the next beam and arm to be four feet six inches long, to be bolted with six bolts after an inch auger, they must be kept below the upper side of the beams, as shall be hereafter directed by the Naval Constructor when at the same time, he will give instructions, respecting the air ports &c.

Dagger knees to be sided Seven and a half inches, the arm to be four feet six inches long, the body to reach the opposite side of the next beam, and bolted with seven bolts, after an inch auger, the arms of the Knees of both decks to be hooked and juggled into the beams one inch, leaving a space at the jogs so as to admit a key of two inches being driven to make the work close.

Carlings fixed same as lower deck to be seven by nine inches of White Oak.

Ledges the same, to be six inches square of heart pine.

Solid Water ways Seven inches thick, to be let down with a dove tail upon the ends of the beams one inch, a thick Strake of four inches dove tailed and let down in the same manner, say along side of it, and there must be two bolts driven between every beam, through the thick strake waterways and side, to follow a Seven eight auger, and well rivetted on the inside on rings, the deck plank to be three inches thick of heart yellow pine, not above nine inches

APPENDIX

wide, free from defect, the water way finishes with a feint hollow as on the other deck, and the port cill, which is four inches rests upon it, making the waist from the deck to port cill, Seven inches deep, the bulwork will be

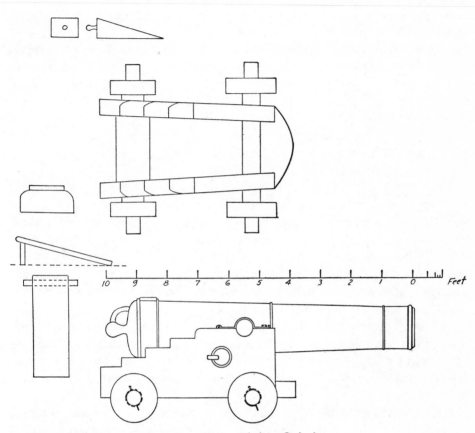

UNITED STATES NAVY 32-POUNDER, 1825–40 (*after Grice*)

planked with two and a half inch heart pine, and finished with a Six inch rail on the top, forming the top of ports, and secured with substantial stay nails &c.

The clamps of gundeck to be in two Strakes on each side, four inches thick and twelve inches wide, as long as possible, the spirkettings of the birth deck to be of the same thickness, in one Strake fourteen inches wide, the filling in plank to be three inches, there must be one opening or list of five inches just below the ends of the Dagger knees of the lower deck and one of the same width between decks, all fore and aft, for the admission of air.

APPENDIX

Fore castle deck beams heart pine moulded eight inches, and sided twelve, secured with dagger knees, sided six inches, arms four feet long and bolted with six bolts, each to follow a Seven eighth auger.

Cable bitts two pair, twelve inches square, to run down and bolt into the lower deck beam tapering to ten inches at lower end, secured with a good standard knee at the foresides of each, sided nine inches, and running over two beams each, and bolting well into them after an inch and an eighth auger.

The patent capstern with all its wrought and cast Iron work, tillers, iron and wooden wheel, hatch, ports, air port, shot lockers, iron Stanchions for the ridge rope and nettings to be subject of future instructions from the Naval Constructor.

All the metal fastenings that go into, or through the bottom below the wales, must be pure copper, and all the iron fastenings must be hammered, wrought iron of the best quality.

The frame of the ship to be the best white oak, except the top timbers, and they are to be of red cedar, as well as the half top timbers, those that form the sides of ports to be of locust, the wales and thick stuff outboard and inboard to be oak, the bottom plank to be oak, and the ceiling and deck heart pine, the plank to be from forty to fifty feet long, except where they must be cut for the purpose of shifting butts, the butts to be six feet apart, on every adjoining Strake, and there must be at least three Streakes between every two Butts, that come upon the same timbers.

In Caulking there must be one good thread driven at least for every inch the plank is in thickness, either on the bottom, sides, or deck, and in building the ship, care ought to be taken to let the Seams be outgaged so that the Caulking may be done more perfectly, the seames of the wales and thick stuff to be horsed in.

If the Department choose to have the decks composition or copper fastened, the builders are to do it, and be paid the difference in price it is above iron.

MEMORANDUM OF THICK STUFF.

Four Bilge Strakes on each side of the Ship at the height of the floor heads, the two middle ones to be four and one half inches thick, and the one above and the one below to be three and a half inches—there must be three strakes of ceiling opposite the Bilge Strakes on each side, the middle one to be four inches thick, and one above and below three and a half inches, to be dubbed off both inboard and outboard, fair with the running plank.

374

APPENDIX

Whereas Adam & Noah Brown have this day entered into an agreement with John Bullus, Navy Agent of the United States at New York, to Build for account and for the use of the United States a Sloop of War or Vessel, agreeably to the annexed Instrument of Writing and Security being demanded from them for the faithful performance of their Contract.

Therefore, Know all men by these presents that we Adam & Noah Brown, of the City of New York Master Ship Builders and Allen Shepherd, Merchant of the City of New York, are held and firmly bound unto John Bullus Navy

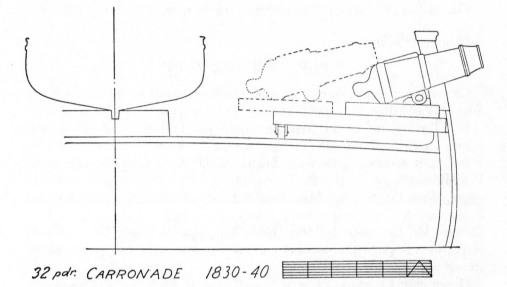

32 pdr. CARRONADE   1830-40

Agent of the United States at New York in the penal Sum of Fifty thousand Dollars, to be paid to the said United States, for the payment of which Sum well and truly to be made, We bind ourselves and each of us, our and each of our Heirs, Executors & Administrators, jointly & severally, firmly by these presents, sealed with our Seals and dated this twenty sixth day of July in the year of our Lord, 1813.

The Conditions of this obligation is such, that if the above bounden Adam & Noah Brown, shall and do, in and by all things, well and truly observe, perform fulfill and accomplish the annexed Contract, by them entered into this day, and shall faithfully in every respect comply with every Covenant therein contained, agreeably to the tenor of the Agreement aforesaid, without any delay or defalcation whatever, then this obligation to excuse, determine and be void, and if otherwise the same shall remain in full force and virtue.

A & N Brown (seal)

Allen Shepherd (seal)

Signed sealed & delivered
in the presence of

W. Howell

George L. Storet.

Copied from CONTRACTS No. 2, Dec. 1810 to June 1818, Navy Dept.

Contract Number 98.

BARKENTINE *JAS. TUFT*

Contract and specifications for building a four masted Barkentine at Puget Sound, Washington, between the following:

Hall Bros. 1/16th; W. H. Marston, 1/16th; Jas. Tuft 1/16th; T. Thompson 1/32nd; Th. Collie 1/16th; Geo. T. Page 1/32nd; E. L. Allen 1/32nd; W. H. Talbot 1/32nd; C. R. Cramer 1/64th; R. B. Hogue 1/32nd; A. C. Cheesebrough 1/16th; Wm. Brooks 1/32nd; W. I. McAllep 1/32nd; H. Piltz 3/32nds; Simpson & Fisher 1/32nd; W. J. Gray 1/32nd; Marschultz & Cantrel 1/16th; I. E. Thayer 1/32nd; Robt. Sudden 1/32nd; Puget Sound Com'l Co. 1/16th; E. G. Ames 1/64th; Port Blakeley Mill Co. 1/16th; I. Burns 1/32nd; Wm. Babcock 1/32nd; W. G. Bluhm 1/32nd; John Poole 1/64th; parties of the first part, and Hall Bros., parties of the second part.

Dimensions: Length in rabbets, 6′ above top of keel, 201′-8″, width 42′, depth 16′-4″.

Timber: Outside of stem, rudder post, bitts (with the exception of pawl and quarter bitts, which shall have "iron bark" corners) cleats, cavels, jaws to gaffs and booms, tressle trees, cross trees and pin rails in rigging, to be hardwood, all other wood not specified, to be yellow fir. Rudder stock oak, 20″.

Keel: To be double 18″ x 30″, with 26″ of keel and shoe below garboards.

Frames: Spaced 34″ from centers, sided 12″ and molded 18½″ at keel, and 8½″ at deck, with stanchions on every frame, sided 12″. The space between the frames on top of keel to be filled in solid.

Keelsons: Main keelson 18″ x 60″—sister keelsons side 18″ and mold 18″; assistant sister keelsons side 18″ and mold 16″, rider sister keelson side 16″ and mold 20″.

Deck Frames: Deck beams side 18″ and mold 16″, to be secured to a clamp

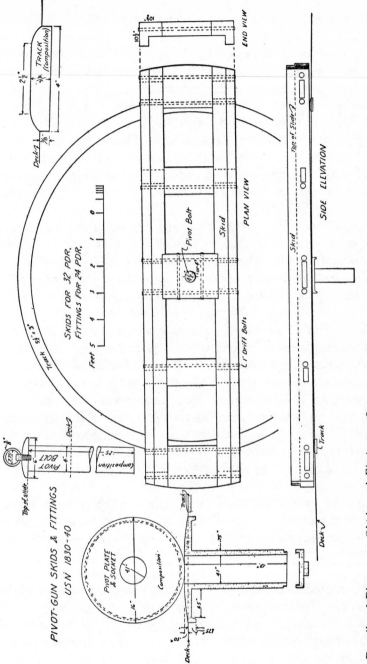

PLAN VIEW

END VIEW

SIDE ELEVATION

SKIDS FOR 32 PDR,
FITTINGS FOR 24 PDR,

Feet 5   4   3   2   1   0

Track 5½" × 3"

TRACK (Composition)

PIVOT-GUN SKIDS & FITTINGS
USN 1830-40

PIVOT PLATE & SOCKET

PIVOT BOLT

Details of Pivot-gun Skids and Fittings, 1830.

377

APPENDIX

14″ in thickness; clamps to be worked onto frames and bolted with four 1⅛″ bolts in each frame, driven from the outside and clinched. Beams to be let into clamp 1″. A chock to be dovetailed between all the beams to come within 3″ of top of beam and flush with clamp and fastened with two bolts in each chock, driven from the outside and clinched.

Hanging Knees: Deck frame to have a hanging knee to each beam, where practicable. Knees to be fastened with 1″ iron; throat bolts 1⅛th″.

Ceiling: Out to turn of bilge 4½″. The two lower strakes of thick ceiling to be 16″ thick, to be followed with three strakes 14″ thick, from thence to clamps 12″ thick; clamps and thick strakes under the clamp 14″ and 13″ in thickness, made flush with thick ceiling. The two upper strakes and clamps scarphed.

Planking: Garboards 8″ in thickness and graduated in three strakes to the thickness of the bottom planks, which is 4½″; wales 6″.

Waterways: Rail, etc.: Three waterways, 13″ x 14″; 12″ x 12″ and 11″ x 12″ lock strakes, worked flush on upper side; bulwarks 3″ thick; rail 5¾″.

Deck: Deck 4″ x 4″. Five strakes each side of hatches 7″ in thickness, to lock over beams 3″; quarter deck 3″ x 13″; housetops 3″ x 4½″.

Fastenings: Keel, keelsons, stem, stern post and deadwood fastened with 1⅜″ iron through bolts in keelson 1½″; sister keelsons and rider fastened with 1¼″; assistant sister keelsons 1⅛″ iron. Three breast hooks and pointers forward and three aft; also breast hooks above and below lumber ports. Pointers fastened with 1⅛″ iron, hooks 1¼″ iron, throat bolts 1⅜″ iron. Thick strakes in bilge and clamps fastened with 1⅛″; thick ceiling fastened with 1″ iron from bilge to clamps, enough driven from the inside to work the plank, balance driven from the outside and clinched. Four bolts to a frame, to every strake of thick ceiling, and all thick ceiling to be edge bolted between each alternate frame.

Outboard Fastenings: Garboards edge bolted to the keel and worked on to the vessel with two galvanized bolts and three locust treenails to each frame; planking to be worked with two galvanized spikes in each frame and square fastened with 1¼″ locust treenails, driven through and wedged on both ends. All planking below the water line to have one additional treenail to each frame. Fastenings for deck, housetops, bulwarks, stern rails, and thick strake under the rail, to be galvanized, all other fastenings used and not specified, to be black-iron. Main deck plank fastened with two 7″ spikes in each strake to every beam. Butt bolts galvanized iron. Composition dovetails at lower part of stern and stern posts; chain plates galvanized.

Caulking: Eight threads of oakum in garboards and hawsed, from thence to planksheer six threads and hawsed. Deck and housetops two threads; seams on bottom painted with copper paint and cemented to the water line, thence to planksheer white leaded; decks pitched.

Forecastle & Cabin: Cabin to be on deck, fitted with water closet and stationary wash stand complete. Forecastle, engine room and galley to be in forward house.

Steering Gear, etc. Vessel to have three composition rudder braces, #9 Robinson's steerer, #7 Hyde's capstan windlass, patent traveler for spanker; spars to be in proportion to the hull, all iron work of the best quality and workmanship.

Rigging, etc.: Forward standing rigging 4½″ wire, main, mizzen and spanker rigging 4¼″ wire, five shrouds each side of foremast, and four shrouds main, mizzen and spanker masts; all stays in proportion to the shrouds; throat and peak halliards 3½″ Manilla; all other rigging in proportion to its use. Standing rigging fitted with turnbuckles throughout.

Blocks and Tackles: Throat, peak and jib halyard blocks 15″ steel rollers; all others in proportion. Three boom tackles, two reef tackles, two watch tackles and three metaline purchase blocks and fall.

Sails. One full suit of sails, made of Woodbury duck, weight in proportion to their size.

Chains, Anchors, Etc. One 3,500 lb. anchor; one 3,000 lb. anchor; one 700 lb. kedge anchor and one 1,000 stream anchor, 75 fathoms, 1¾″ chain, 75 fathoms 1⅝″ chain, 120 fathoms 6″ wharf fast and one coil 4″ running line, chain cat stoppers and shank painters.

Ports, Hatches & Keel. Bow ports 28″ x 30″; Stern ports 26″ x 48″. Ports and hatches tined with iron, keel and shoe metalled to within 9″ of the garboards.

Cabin & Galley Furniture: Carpet, table, chairs, clocks and crockery, cabin and stateroom lamps, lounge, desk and curtains, galley fixtures, galley and forecastle lamps, side lights and anchor lights.

Tanks & Casks: Three iron water tanks, 1,700 gallons in all. Two water casks, 400 gallons in all.

Boats: One 19′ boat and oars, and one 15′ boat and oars, stern davits and falls.

Engine & Pumps: One double 6 x 12 cylinder hoisting engine, connected to windlass, one steam pump and hose, and one deck pump and hose; engineer's tools.

Sundries: Tarpaulins and mast coats, one spirit compass and one brass compass, patent log, sounding lead and line, galvanized chain deck load lashings, sail covers, cargo gaff, ballast tubs, slab saw, lumber rollers, medicine chest,

APPENDIX

bell forward and aft, rigging screws, marline spike and ship's tools. Name in gold leaf on bow and quarters.

Vessel to be built and equipped as specified, and launched on or about December — 1902; always provided that no delay shall be caused the party of the second part, either directly or indirectly, by strikes, lockouts, fires, acts of Providence or other unavoidable causes.

In consideration of the fulfillment of the foregoing contract and specifications, the parties of the first part agree to pay to the parties of the second part the sum of Seventy-four Thousand (74,000) Dollars in U. S. Gold Coin, in the following payments, viz:

$ 5,000 when keel is laid
16,000 when in frame
17,000 when ceiled and deck frame in
17,000 when planked
19,000 when completed.

(Signed) By parties of the first part.

Number 98:

JAS. TUFT

Bowsprit size in knighthead 25″ x 28″; length to first band 20′; diam. 22½″, in band 20½″; length to outer band 15′, diam. 15½″ out, in band 13½″; pole 5′.

Foremast top main rail to cap 52′, diam. in deck 30″, diam. at truss band 5′-3″ below hounds, 28″; mast head 14′, squares 22″ & 20″; necklass 22″ clear; heel band 27″, diam. mainstay band 29½″ scant. Fore topmast, heel to cap 46′, diam. at cap 18″, diam. at spider band 27″ below hounds, 17½″, at hounds 18″; mast head 10′, squares 14¼″ & 13¾″; supporter band for truss 4:-6″ below cap, 18⅛″; fid 5″ x 10″, diam. at fid 20½″. Fore topgallant mast, length 23′-6″, diam. in cap 14¼″, diam. at grommet 13¾″ out, 12¼″ clear, fid 4″ x 7″. Royal mast length 16′, grommet 11″ out, 9½″ clear. Pole 5′, whole length 23′-6″ + 16′ + 13′-6″ + 5′ = 58′.

Yards: Yard arms included in given length.

Foreyard length 82′, diam. 19″, yard arms 18″, bands 11¼″ out, offset 4′-4″.

Lower topsail yard length 75′, diam. 17″, yard arms 18″, band 9½″ out, offset 2′-6″.

Upper topsail yard length 70′-6″, diam. 15″, yard arms 27″, bands 8½″ out.

Topgallant yard length 56′-6″, diam. 11½″, yard arm 18″, band 7″ out.

Royal yard length 47′-6″, diam. 9½″, diam. at eye bolt 15″ from end, 6″.

Skysail yard length 39′, diam. 8″, diam. at eye bolt 12″ from end 5″.

APPENDIX

Main Mast: Diam. in deck 25″, at spider 22½″, heel 22″, mast head 13′, squares 17″ & 14″; wythes 14⅜″ and 15″.

Mizzen Mast: Diam. in deck 24″, at spider 21½″, heel 21″, mast head 13′, squares 16½″ & 13½″, wythes 13⅞″ & 14½″. Length top of main rail to cap 87′-9″. Three masts same length.

Spanker Mast: Diam. in deck 23″, at spider 20½″, heel 20″, mast head and wythes same as mizzen mast.

Main Topmast: Length 61′, diam. in cap 13¾″, at hounds 12½″ and 7½″, grommets 11″ & 6″; pole 13′-6″ + 5′ = 18′-6″.

Mizzen and Spanker Topmasts: Diam. in cap 12¾″, at hounds 11¼″ and 7″. grommets 9¾″ and 5½″; pole 10′ + 5′ = 15′: gaff topsail wythe 5¼″.

Main and Mizzen Booms: Length 39′, diam. 11″, sheet 10¾″, topping lift 10¼″ out, clew 10¾″.

Spanker Boom: Length 58′, diam. sheet 12″, clew 10⅛″, topping lift 8″ out.

Main & Mizzen Gaffs: Length 37′, bands 8¾″, 8″, 7¼″, end 5½″, diam. 9″.

Spanker Gaff: Length 28′, diam. 8½″, bands 8¼″, 8″, 7¼″, end 5½″.

Bobstays: Upper 2¼″ iron rod, lower 2⅛″.

Notes: Offset fore yard from mast to after side yard 4′-4″. Length sling from hounds to center of yards 6′-10″.

Deck Load Lashings:

2 lashings to foremast	25′-2″
2 lashings bet. fore & mainmast	28′-10″
2 lashings " "	30′-1″
2 " to main	45′-4″
4 " bet. main & mizzen	30′-2″
2 " to "	45′-4″
2 lashings bet. mizzen and spanker	30′
2 " to "	29′-8″
2 " to "	44′-10″
2 " aft "	24′
Net tonnage	1,043
Gross	1,274.49

IRON WORK

CHAIN PLATES: FORWARD:

#1	9′-2½″	3 holes 7⅛″ centers.
2	9′-3¼″	" "
3	9′-4¾″	" "

4	9'-7"	"	"
5	9'-7¼	"	"
6	9'-6¾"	topsail halyard, 3 holes.	
7	9'-6¾"	topmast backstays, 3 holes.	
8	9'-7¾"	"	"
9	8'-11⅝"	topgallant backstay, 2 holes.	
10	9'-0⅜"	"	" 2 holes.
11	8'-11⅝"	royal "	2 holes.
12	8'-3¾"	skysail "	1 hole.

MAIN AND MIZZEN PLATES:

9'-3", 4 each side.
Main & Mizzen backstays 8'-7⅞", 2 holes, 1 each side.
Main & mizzen tpgallntbkstys 8'-0⅝", 1 hole.
Spanker plates, 11'-3¾", 3 on each side.
    " backstay plates 10'-8⅝"
    " tpgllnt " 10'-1⅘"
Lengths are given from lower end of turnbuckle to center of lower hole; holes 7⅛" between centers.
Chain bolts, wood and wood, 29".

Contract Number 106.

SCHOONER *CAROLINE*

Contract and specifications for building a four masted schooner
at Puget Sound, Washington, between:
Joseph Knowland; and Hall Bros.

Dimensions: Length in rabbetts, 6' above top of keel, 152', Beam 38', Depth 11'.
Timber: Outside of stem, rudder stock, cleats, cavels, jaws to gaff and booms, tressle trees, cross trees and pin rails in rigging to be of hardwood, all other wood used and not specified to be of yellow fir. Pawl bit to have hard wood corners; quarter bitts, iron. Rudder stock-oak 16" diameter.
Keel: To be 16" x 21". Shoe 4" x 16" with 18" of keel and shoe below garboards. Bilge keels 10" x 14".
Frames: Spaced 33" from centers, sided 12" and moulded 16" at keel and 8" at deck; stanchion on every frame.

APPENDIX

Keelsons: Main keelson 16" x 44"; sister keelson 16" x 32"; assistant sister keelson 12" x 16".

Deck Frame: Beams side 15" and mould 12" at center and 8" at end. Hatch beams 12" x 17"; beams secured to a 12" clamp; clamps worked to frame and bolted with four 1" bolts in each frame, driven from the outside and clinched. Beams to be let into clamp 1". A 5" chock to be dovetailed between all the beams to come within 3" of top of beam and flush with clamp. Chocks fastened with two 7/8" bolts driven from the outside and clinched.

Hanging Knees: Deck frame to have a hanging knee to each beam where practicable, where impracticable, to have a lodging knee. Knees to be fastened with 7/8" iron; throat bolts 1".

Ceiling: Thin ceiling 4", followed with five strakes 12" thick, thence to lower thick strake under clamp 8"; thick strakes 9", 10", and 11", made flush with clamps and 8" ceiling. Three upper strakes scarphed.

Planking: Garboards 7" thick, graduated in three strakes to the thickness of bottom plank 4"; wales 5½".

Waterways, Rails Etc. Two waterways, the inner one forming a lock strake; waterways 12" x 13", lock strake 10" x 14". Rail 6" thick, bulwarks 3", clamps under rail 6", jogged over stanchion 2".

Deck: 4" x 4"; quarter deck 3" x 3"; forward housetop and forecastle deck 3" x 5".

Fastenings: Keel and keelsons fastened with 1¼" and 1⅜" iron, stem, stern post and deadwood fastened with 1¼" and 1⅛" iron. Two breast hooks and pointers forward and two aft; also breast hooks above and below lumber ports. Hooks and pointers fastened with 1⅛" iron, throat bolts 1¼". Clamps in 12" ceiling with 1" iron; 8" ceiling fastened with 7/8" iron, enough to be driven from the inside to work the plank; balance driven from the outside and clinched. Four bolts in each frame in every strake of thick ceiling. All thick ceiling edge bolted between alternate frames.

Outboard Fastenings: Garboards edge bolted to the keel and worked on to vessel with two galvanized bolts and three locust treenails to each frame. Planking to be fastened with two galvanized spikes in each frame to the plank-sheer and square fastened with 1¼" locust treenails, driven through and wedged on both ends. All planking below the water line to have an additional treenail to each frame. Fastenings for deck, housetops, bulwarks, stern, rails and thick strake under rails, to be galvanized. All other fastenings used and not specified to be black iron. Main deck plank fastened with 7" spikes in each strake to every beam. Butt bolts galvanized. Composition dovetails at lower part of stem and stern post. Chain plates galvanized.

APPENDIX

Caulking: Seven threads of oakum in the garboards and hawsed, thence to planksheer five threads and hawsed, deck and housetops two threads, seams on bottom painted with copper paint and cemented to the water line, thence to planksheer white leaded; decks pitched.

Salt & Painting: Vessel to be salted to the lower wale. Bottom two coats of paint; topsides and deck work two coats of paint; spars oiled.

Cabin & Forecastle: Cabin to be on deck; to have water closet and stationary wash stand complete. Forecastle in forward house, with galley and engine room.

Steering Gear Etc.: Vessel to have three composition rudder braces, #6 Robinsons' steerer, #4 Providence pump brake iron windlass, #3 capstan and patent traveler for spanker; spars to be in proportion to the hull; all iron work of the best quality and workmanship.

Rigging: Forward standing rigging 4½″ wire, four shrouds each side. Main, mizzen and spanker rigging 4″ wire, four shrouds each side main and mizzen, and three each side for spanker mast; all standing rigging to be set up with turnbuckles throughout; all stays in proportion to the shrouds. Throat and peak halyards 3¼″ Manila. All other running rigging in proportion to its use.

Sails: Three jibs and jib topsail, foresail, mainsail, mizzen and spanker, and four gaff topsails. Spanker, mizzen, mainsail, foresail and jib to be #1 duck; all other sails to be in proportion to their size and use.

Blocks & Tackles: Throat, peak and jib halyard blocks 14″ steel rollers; all other blocks in proportion. Four boom tackles, two reef tackles, two watch tackles and three metaline purchase blocks and fall.

Chain, Anchors & Lines: One 2,100 lb. Anchor, one 1,600 lb. anchor, one 400 lb. kedge anchor, 120 fthms. 1⅜″ chain, 120 fthms. 7″ hawser, 120 fthms. 6″ hawser, 120 fthms. 5″ hawser, one coil 4″ running line, chain cat stoppers and shank painters.

Ports, Hatches & Keel: Ports and hatches lined with iron, sides of keel, to within 4″ of garboards and bottom between keel and shoe, metalled.

Cabin & Galley Furniture: Carpet, table, chairs, clocks, crockery, cabin and stateroom lamps, lounge, desk, iron bedstead with wire mattress, curtains, cutlery, mirror, linoleum and table linen, galley fixtures, galley and forecastle lamps, side lights and anchor lights.

Tanks & Casks: Three iron water tanks, 1,700 gallons in all. Three water casks, 400 gallons in all.

Boats: One 19′ boat and oars, one 15′ boat and oars, stern davits and falls.

Engine & Pumps: One 5 x 12 double cylinder hoisting engine, connected with windlass, one steam pump and hose, one deck pump and hose; engineer's tools.

Sundries: Tarpaulins and mast coats, two spirit compasses, patent log, sounding lead and line, ⅝" galvanized chain deck load lashings, sail covers, cargo gaff, ballast tubs, lumber rollers, medicine chest, Keane's 12" ventilators, life preservers, buoys, (not under control), lights, fog horn, etc., as required by U.S. Inspection laws, bell forward and aft, rigging screws, marline spikes and ship's tools. Name on Bow and Quarters.

Vessel to be built and equipped as specified, and launched on or about June — 1902, always provided that no delay shall be caused the builders, either directly or indirectly by strikes, fires, acts of Providence, or other unavoidable causes.

In consideration of the fulfillment of the foregoing contract, the party of the first part agrees to pay to the parties of the second part the sum of Thirty-seven thousand, five hundred Dollars ($37,500.00) U.S. Gold Coin, in the following payments, viz;

$ 3,000	On signing the contract.
5,000	When in frame.
8,000	" ceiled and deck frame in.
9,000	" planked up and deck laid.
12,500	" completed.
$37,500.	

(Signed)   Joseph Knowland
"   Hall Bros.

NUMBER 106:

CAROLINE

Bowsprit: Outboard 20', size in knighthead 22" x 26", outer end 15", outer bobstay 15⅜", inner bobstay 18¼" & 17", athwartship, 8½' flat.

Jibboom: Diam. in cap 13½", cap to hounds 13'-6", from hounds to outer band 10', diam. at hounds 13" out, 11½" clear, diam. outer hounds 9" out, 7¾" clear. Pole 4'. Heel band 11" x 9¾".

Foremast: Diam. in deck 24", at spider band 21", hound band 21½" clear. Heel 21". Mast head 11', squares 16" & 13¼". Wytes 13½" & 14".

Mainmast: Diam. in deck 22½", at spider 19½", heel 19½", mast head 11', squares 15¾" & 13", wythes 13¼", & 14".

APPENDIX

Mizzen Mast: Length top of main rail to cap 80′, size same as main mast. All masts same length.

Spanker Mast: Diam. in deck 22″, at spider 19″, at heel 19″, mast head, wythes and cap same as main.

Fore Topmast: Length 51′, diam. in cap 12¾″, hounds 10¾″ out, 9¼″ clear. Upper hounds 7″ out, 5½″ clear; pole 5′ + 8′ = 13′.

Main & Mizzen Topmasts: Length 51′, diam. in cap 11½″, hounds 10″ & 7″, grommets 8½″ & 5½″. Pole 5′ + 8′ = 13′.

Spanker Topmast: Same in all dimensions as main and mizzen.

Booms: Fore, main and mizzen, length 32′, diam. 10¼″, sheet 10″, clew 10″, topping lift 9½″. Spanker boom, length 50′, diam. 11½″, sheet 11½″ clew 9⅛″, topping lift 8″ out.

Gaffs: Fore, main and mizzen length 31′-6″, diam. 8¼″, bands 8⅛″, 7⅞″, 7⅞″, end 5½″. Spanker gaff 26′. Diam. 8¼″, bands 8⅛″, 7⅞″, 7⅞″, end 5½″.

Fore staysail boom, length 26′, clew 7½″, sheet 7½″, topping lift 7″ out, outer end 6½″ out.

INDEX

INDEX

INDEX

Coasters, 258

Collector, revenue cutter, 1803, 184

Colonia, 345

Colonial shipbuilding, 6 ff.

Colonial times, 4 ff.

Colonial vessels, size of, 11; rate of production, 10; relation to English, 16 ff.; review of types, 41 ff.

Columbia, frigate, 1813, 104; 1825 class, dimensions of, 114

Columbia, 1871, 330; 1899, 330, 348

Columbus, ship-of-the-line, 111

Comet, 318, 320

Comet, clipper-ship, 284

Coming, 324

Commodore Hull, revenue cutter, 1812–13, 190, 192

Concord, ship-sloop, 116

Confederacy, 1778, galley-frigate, 58; spars of, 69; dimensions of, 69; description of, 69 f.; mention of, 88

Congress, frigate, 1776, mention of, 57 f.; galley, Lake Champlain, 1776, 71; frigate, 1794, mention of, 87, 127; history of, 92; dimensions of, 92; guns of, 92; frigate, 1839, dimensions of, 117, 120; 128

Connecticutt, gondola, 1776, 72; ship, 94

Conqueror, British ship, 57

Constellation, frigate, mention of, 69, 78, 79, 87, 88; draught of, 89; launch of, 91; rebuilding of, 92; dimensions of, 92; guns of, 92; mention of, 127; yacht, 341

Constitution, frigate, mention of, 78, 79, 88; design of, 86; launch of, 87; comparison of, with *President*, 89, 91; guns of, 92; mention of, 127; Herreshoff yacht, 348

Construction, of ships, excellence, 9 f.; of men-of-war, 45 f.; of *Hudson*, 116; of privateers, strength, 132; of slavers, 158 ff.; of centerboard cases, 167 ff.; materials used in, 246; comparison of in different localities, 276 ff.; of clipper-ships, 286; of down-easters, 287 f.

Consuelo, 348

Coquette, 312

Cormorant, ex-*Rattlesnake*, 134

Cornelia, yacht, 309

Corvettes, description of, 52; *Saratoga*, 1814, 111 f.

Cox and Stevens, 357

Crandall, designer, 264

Crane, C. H., 350

Crawford, ex-*Swiftsure*, 1835, 198, 200; ex-*Jefferson*, 1839, 204, 208; 1848, 212, 214

Crawford, revenue cutter, 198

Crescent, frigate, mention of, 93, 127

Crocker, Samuel, 357

Crocodile, 328

Cross, Stephen & Ralph, shipbuilders, 58, 63

Cross and Merrill, shipbuilders, 105

Crowninshield, B. B., 349 f.

Crowninshields, owner of *Belisarius*, 140

Cruiser, 322

Culley, Lawrence B., shipbuilder, 124

Cumberland, frigate, dimensions of, 114

"Cutter-cranks," 335, 338

Cutter, English, 335, 338 f.

Cutter-galley, mention of, 70; *see also Lee*

Cyane, ship-sloop, dimensions of, 117, 128

Cygnet, yacht, 309

Cynthia, British ship-sloop, 168

Dagger-board, *see* Centerboard

Dale, Captain Richard, 93

Dale, ship-sloop, 118

Dallas, revenue cutter, 1816, 194; ex-*Vigilant* 1824, 198; steamer, 210

Dancing Feather, 334

Daphne, 332

Dare Devil, 321

Dart, British ship-sloop, 169; British privateer, 190

Dauntless, ex-*L'Hirondelle*, 331

David Dows, five-masted schooner, 270

Davis, W. L., 350

Deane, frigate, 60; guns of, 70

Decatur, Commodore Stephen, 89 f.

Decatur, ship-sloop, 118; schooner-privateer, 152

Defender, 348

Delaware, frigate, 1776, 58; ship-of-the-line, 81, 115

Design, of ships, relation of naval to mercantile, 18 f.; men-of-war, 44 ff.; American frigates, 62 ff.; of privateers, 130 ff.; of slavers, 158 ff.; of revenue cutters, 180; of 1815 cutters, 192 ff.; of 1825 cutters, 198 f.; *Morris* class, 203 ff.; *Joe Lane* class, 213 f.; *Salmon P. Chase*, 218; freedom in, 225 ff.; trend of, in schooners, 238; of packet-ships, 278; of *Rainbow*, 282 f.; best, of clipper ships, 283 f.; down-easters, 287 f.

Despatch, British brig, 189

Detector, revenue cutter, 194; 1825, 198

Dexter, revenue cutter, 1832, 204, 208, 209

Dilemma, sloop, 344

Diligence, revenue cutter, 1791, 181; 1798, 182; 1812, 192

Diligente, slaver brig, 163, 245

Disarmament, 1784–94, 77 f.

Dorade, 357

Dobbin, revenue cutter, 1853, 215

Dodo, 318 f.

INDEX

INDEX

INDEX

INDEX

Page and Allen, shipbuilders, 215, 216
Paine, Frank C., designer, 345, 357
Painting, of frigate *Hancock*, 69; of schooners, 246 f.
Pallas, merchant ship, 60
Palmer, 326
Palmer, C. M., designer, 350
Parole, 321
Patapsco, 20-gun ship, 94
Patriot, revenue cutter, 184
Patterson's town, 196
Peacock, ship-sloop, 1813, 105, 108 ff., 110 f., 116, 127, 166, 196
Peake, Sir Henry, designer, 155
Pearl, 312
Peck, John, life of, 134, 138 ff., 141; ships designed by, 138 ff., 141, 142; system of design, 140 f.; William Dandridge, 142
Peerless, 331
Penguin, brig, British, 109
Pennsylvania shipbuilding, colonial period, 8 f.
Pennsylvania, ship-of-the-line, 117, 128
Penquin, 328
Penquin (Herreshoff), 348
Perry, brig, 121, 124, 128, 166, 182
Perry, Commodore, 112
Pet, pilot-boat, 311
Petrel, cutter, 338; revenue cutter, 1866, 216
Phantom, pilot-boat, 249
Phantom, yacht, 330
Philadelphia, gondola, 72; frigate, 93 f.; packet-ship, 280
Philadelphia, Pennsylvania, mention of, 57, 58, 59, 85, 100, 104, 112, 119, 124, 128, 140, 175, 181, 182, 200, 214, 217, 218, 293
Phillip Allen, revenue cutter, 1853, 215, 216
Pickering, revenue cutter, 1791, 1798, 181, 182, 183
Pickle, schooner, British, 172
Pilgrim, cutter, 345
Pilgrim, revenue cutter, 1811, 189 f.
Pilot-boat, construction, mention of, 84; revenue cutters, 182 ff.; *Eclipse*, 216; design of, 227 ff.; *Norfolk*, 227; rig of, 227 f.; *Virginia*, 228; *Swift*, 228 ff.; mention of, 248 f.; *Phantom*, 249; *Adams*, 249; *Hesper*, 254
Pincher, British schooner, 172
Pinckney, brig, 94
Pinks, description of, colonial period, 15
Pinky, mention of, 15; description of, 252 f.
Piracy, in West Indies, 154 f., 239
Piratical schooners, dimensions of, 172
Plans of ships, importance of, 17; early use of, 17 f.; called "draughts," 17; British Admiralty collection, 17 ff.; meaning of lines in, 19 f.; details shown in, 27 f.; completeness of,

28; comparison by means of, 84 f.; *President*, 91; *Constellation*, 89; *Constitution*, 91; Admiralty plans of *Rattlesnake*, 134; slaver-brig, 163; lack of centerboards, 169; 1815 cutters, 192, 194; 1825 cutters, 198; of cutters, 212 ff.; of *Swift*, 1803, 228 ff.
Plover, 332
Pluck and Luck, 318, 321
Plymouth, Massachusetts, mention of, 60 f.
Plymouth, ship-sloop, dimensions of, 120, 129
Pocahontas, 332, 338
Poillon, R. and C., 331
Polhemus, A., 334
Polk, steam cutter, 210
Pomone, British frigate, 90, 189
Pook, Samuel M., designer, 118; ships designed by, 129; Samuel Hartt, 129, 283, 334
Porpoise, schooner, 1821, 114 f., 166; brigantine, 1836; dimensions of, 118, 128, 166, 240
Portsmouth, New Hampshire, 57, 59, 62, 63, 92, 119, 120, 180, 182, 198, 200
Portsmouth, ship, 94, 127; ship-sloop, 118, 119, 129; revenue cutter, 200, 209
Portsmouth, Virginia, 213
Post-ships, description of, 52
Potomac, frigate, dimensions of, 114; revenue cutter, 1809, 184
Poughkeepsie, New York, 57 f.
Preble, Captain, gunboats, 96
Preble, ship-sloop, 118
President, frigate, mention of, 87; history of, 89 ff.; British, 91; guns of Am. frigate, 92; mention of, 102, 108, 114, 127, 280; packet-ship, 280
Price, William, shipbuilder, 98, 101, 183
Prince de Neufchâtel, history of, 146 ff.; owners of, 146, 149 ff.; fight with boats of *Endymion*, 146 ff.; speed of, 149; figurehead, 150; guns of, 150 ff.; comparison with other privateers, 149, 237
Prince de Neufchâtel, English yacht, 150
Prince de Neufchâtel, 295
Priscilla, 338 ff.
Privateers, requirements in design of, 130 ff.; commission of, 130; definition of, 130; fitting of, 131; *American Tartar*, 133 f.; *Rattlesnake*, 134, 142; *Belisarius*, 134, 139 f., 142; schooners, 142 ff.; *Berbice*, 142 f.; *Harlequin*, 144, 146; *Marengo*, 146; *Lottery*, 152; *Decatur*, 152; *Chasseur*, 152; *America*, ship, 152 f.; *Swift*, 152; *Boxer*, 152; *Herald*, 152; *Rambler*, 153; *Anaconda*, 190; *Dart*, 190; *Brava*, 196; *Bolivia*, 200; *Jack's Favorite*, 232 ff.; commission and letter-of-marque, 275
Prospero, schooner, 336
Protector, 26-gun frigate, 61

395

INDEX

Providence, frigate, 1776, 58, 60; gondola, 1776, 72

Providence, Rhode Island, mention, 57, 58

Pulaski, revenue cutter, 198, 200

Puritan, yacht, 340 f.

Queen of France, frigate, 59 f.

Queen of the West, packet-ship, 278 ff.

Question, scow, 349

Quisetta, schooner, 351

Qui Vive, sloop, 348

Racer, revenue cutter, 1866, 217

Radeaux, description of, 54 f.; on Lake Champlain, 70; *Thunderer,* 1776, 72; description of, 76; dimensions of, 76, 167

Radiant, 351

Rainbow, British ship, 64 f.; clipper-ship, 282 ff., 295; design of, 282 ff., 294

Raleigh, frigate, mention of, 57; measurements, 63; mention of, lines of, 67

Randolph, frigate, 1776, mention of, 57; dimensions and description of, 69; mention of, 85

Ranger, ship-sloop, 59

Raritan, frigate, dimensions of, 114

Ratsey, George, 314, 315

Rattlesnake, privateer ship, 134, 142; bonders of, 134; owners of, 134, 275, 282

Raven, clipper-ship, 215

Ray, 309

Razee, *Independence,* dimensions of, 111, 117

Red Rover, opium-clipper, 150

Reliance, revenue cutter, 1866, 217; yacht, 348, 349 f.

Relief, revenue cutter, 1866, 217

Renegade, British schooner, dimensions, 172

Rescue, revenue cutter, 1866, 217

Resolute, revenue cutter, 1866, 217; yacht, 348

Revenge, schooner, Lake Champlain, 72

Revenue cutters, mention of designers, 127, 128; mention of, 154; first ten, estimate for, 179; design of, 180; requirements of, 180; (referenced by name) problems of officers of, 201

Revenue Marine, mention of vessels in, 154; formation of, 176 ff.; reorganization of, 211 f.

Rhode Island shipbuilding, colonial period, 8; frigates, 69

Rhodes, designer, 118

Rhone, packet-ship, 280

Richard Rush, revenue cutter, 1829, 1831–32, 200, 204, 206 f.

Richmond, 332; brig, 94

Richmond, D. O., 332

Rigs, colonial period classification, 10 f.; changes in, 32 f.; of men-of-war, 47 f.; of *Neufchâtel,* 153; of slavers, 159

Roahr, George, 322

Robert McClelland, revenue cutter, 1853, 215, 216

Roebuck, British ship, 58, 61

Roger B. Taney, revenue cutter, 1833, 204, 209

Rogers, Commodore John, 89 f.

Romp, fishing schooner, 253

Roosevelt, Theodore, "Naval War of 1812," 108

Roscius, packet-ship, 280

Roulette, fisherman, 254; fishing schooner, 334

Rowan, Stephen C., 201

Row-boats, description of, 54; on Lake Champlain, 71, 72

Rowland, W. J., 324

Royal Savage, schooner, Lake Champlain, 72, 75

Royal Sovereign, British ship-of-the-line, 117

Rudolph, Captain T. C., U.S.R.M., 205

Sabine, frigate, dimensions of, 114

Sachem, yacht, 341

Sadie, sloop, 348

Sailing craft, mention, Indian, 5; mention, colonial, 5 ff.

Sailing ships, colonial, foundation for evolution, 4 ff.; mention, first American, 6

St. Lawrence, frigate, dimensions of, 114

St. Louis, ship-sloop, 116

St. Mary the First, schooner, 308

St. Marys, ship-sloop, 118, 120; galley, 185

Salisbury, Massachusetts, 59

Sally, revenue cutter, 1819, 198

Salmon P. Chase, revenue barque, 218

Samuel D. Ingham, revenue cutter, 1830, 204, 208; 1848, 212

Samuel Russell, clipper-ship, 282 ff.

Samuel Smith, schooner, 247

Sand-baggers, 318 ff.; dangerous characteristics, 322

Santee, frigate, dimensions of, 114

Santisima-Trinidad, Spanish ship-of-the-line, 117

Sappho, 324, 325, 331 f., 350; speed of, 50 f.

Saratoga, ship-sloop, 59; corvette, dimensions of, 111 f.; ship-sloop, dimensions of (1842), 118, 120, 129

Savannah, frigate, dimensions of, 114; galley, 185

Scammel, 1791, revenue cutter, 180 f.; 1798, 182, 184

Scank, A. A., 334

Schank, Captain, 166 ff.

Schmidt, Jake, 321

396

INDEX

INDEX